BUYING THE WIND

MAINE DOWN-EASTERS

PENNSYLVANIA DUTCHMEN

SOUTHERN MOUNTAINEERS

LOUISIANA CAJUNS

ILLINOIS EGYPTIANS

SOUTHWEST MEXICANS

UTAH MORMONS

REGIONAL FOLKLORE IN THE UNITED STATES

BUYING

THE WIND

By RICHARD M. DORSON

THE UNIVERSITY OF CHICAGO PRESS

CHICAGO AND LONDON

THE UNIVERSITY OF CHICAGO PRESS, CHICAGO 60637
The University of Chicago Press, Ltd., London

© 1964 by The University of Chicago. All rights reserved
Published 1964. Fifth Impression 1972

Printed in the United States of America

International Standard Book Number: 0-226-15861-6 (clothbound)
Library of Congress Catalog Card Number: 64-13010

❧ For ARCHER TAYLOR

ACKNOWLEDGMENTS

THE SKILLED COLLECTORS who are represented in this volume, and their talented informants, have made possible this assembling of oral folk traditions from across the land. My thanks go to the editors of the folklore journals and to the collectors who have not simply given their permissions to reprint but who have uniformly expressed support for and enthusiasm in this undertaking.

Previously unpublished or revised field materials have been especially prepared for this book by Elizabeth Brandon, Calvin Claudel, Thomas E. Cheney, Hector Lee, Harry Oster, Américo Paredes, and John L. Sorenson. My colleague Merle E. Simmons has kindly translated Spanish texts of folktales from New Mexico and Colorado.

Indiana University has generously provided funds for a research assistantship. Valiant assistants who have aided me in assembling this manuscript are Donald M. Winkelman, Barbara Currin Smetzer, Deborah D. Carey, and Barbro Sklute. A grant from the American Philosophical Society helped to defray the expenses of my field trip to the Maine coast in 1956.

CONTENTS

ILLUSTRATIONS

WORDS AND MUSIC

INTRODUCTION:

Collecting Oral Folklore in the United States

THIS IS A VOLUME OF TEXTS. A text, in the parlance of the folklorist, represents the basic source, the pure stream, the inviolable document of oral tradition. It comes from the lips of a speaker or singer and is set down with word for word exactness by a collector, using the method of handwritten dictation or mechanical recording. What the state paper is to the historian and creative work to the literary scholar, the oral traditional text is—or should be—to the student of folklore. He cannot discuss and appraise the aesthetics of oral style if the sources at his disposal mingle the spoken words of an informant with the written intrusions of an editor. Nor can he be sure that the beliefs and values revealed in folklore are accurate testimonials of a given culture if an alien hand from an outside culture has refined and "improved" the raw texts.

Only in the nineteenth and twentieth centuries have collectors deliberately gone forth to record the traditions perpetuated by word of mouth. Even then, the necessity to set down and present these traditions unvarnished and unbowdlerized has but slowly gained acceptance. In the United States, the serious cultural study of folklore has lagged behind Europe, and folklore has served largely as matter for entertainment provided by writers of children's books, assemblers of treasuries, and urban singers of rural songs. Still, serious and dedicated field-workers have steadily accumulated thousands of oral texts, depositing them in archives, or printing them in journals and monographs and scholarly collections. From these materials it is now possible to select a representative sampling of regional folk traditions within the United States.

The oral text differs in important ways from the literary text, which must always be relegated to a secondary position by the professional folklorist. A spoken narrative comes from the speaker's mouth with the freshness and spontaneity—and the garbled syntax and meanderings—of everyday talk. A written retelling is pruned and polished and often enough altered to suit the bias of the author and the expectations of the reader. One line of defense taken by the writer of folktales and collator of folksongs is the contention that the man of letters enjoys the same right to adapt a traditional story or song to his inspired fancy as does any calloused sodbuster of the back country. Under this sheltering thesis have been issued many volumes of literary tales that were never told and composite folksongs that were never sung.

But legends rewritten and ballads spliced together are not folklore, they are literary adaptations of folk materials. Compare the Uncle Remus stories of Joel Chandler Harris with oral texts of Negro tales containing the same plots, and the world of difference between the literary and the folk tale can at once be discerned. Harris provides a setting or framework for his tale, in the characters of the benevolent Negro house servant and the little white boy to whom he relates the cycle of Brer Rabbit. In the story itself, Harris inserts extended conversations between Brer Rabbit and the other creeturs, as well as with Miss Meadows and the gals, who appear to be his own creations. Through the lips of Uncle Remus, he discourses on emotions and moods of the animal characters in the fashion of the novelist; he decks out the story with descriptive details of landscape and hearthside; he injects satirical innuendoes at southern society. A number of Uncle Remus's stories are not known in tradition, and may have been partially or wholly composed by the author. Harris would never have captivated his audience with literal renditions of oral texts, such as Elsie Clews Parsons published, and subsidized, in scholarly monographs in the 1920's. His Uncle Remus fictions stand as a shining example of the inspirational effect folklore themes may exert upon the creative artist.

At the same time it should be observed that the Negro storytellers upon whom he levied too possess talent for artistic narration. This talent lies not in imaginative invention of a new story, but in imaginative presentation of an old one. Southern Negro storytellers, while possessing many individual styles, share a common oral art, for instance in the intonational range which enables them to reproduce vividly the cries of animals and birds, the shouts of preachers, and the sounds of machines, or in the structural knack for recombining small incidents and large episodes into new patterns. To comprehend and appreciate this oral art, as distinct from the literary art of Harris, we must have available the exact texts of folk narrators.

Literary revisions of folklore will always concern the folklorist, both for their revelations of folk influences on the great masters and for their preservation of perishable folkstuff. Lacking field collections before the nineteenth century, the folklorist must turn to a thousand literary sources to capture and to date the traditions of yesteryear. He has recourse to Herodotus and Boccaccio and Chaucer, to medieval romances and jestbooks and saints' legends, to the Thousand and One Nights and the Ocean of Story, to popular songsters and county histories and local newspapers. But his ultimate test to determine the traditional character of a literary text must always be its approximation to a field-collected text. In the hierarchy of folk tradition, Homer ranks below Frank Alley of Jonesport, Maine; for to determine if each has retold the same hoary sailor's yarn, we hold Homer's version up to the one told by the old lobsterman (see p. 39), as he heard it from a fellow who heard it from a fellow—and then surmise that Homer too must have tapped an oral source.

One question continually asked about the relation of written to oral tradition is, Won't the oral folklore die when you write it down and print it in a book? If the folklorist insists on word-of-mouth sources, does he himself not interfere with the folk process when he converts the spoken into the printed word —even granting that he does not tamper with the speech of his informants?

The answer is that the tale-teller and folksinger continue to dispense their traditions whether or not they have ever talked to a collector. On the Maine coast Jim Alley and Curt Morse will spin their anecdotes to their cronies after they are printed in this book, in the same way they did before I ever encountered and recorded them. In each telling they will offer slightly different texts, even of their favorite and oft-repeated prize stories, for their words are fluid and ever changing. Once in writing down the text of a song from old woodsman Pompey Grant, I asked him to repeat a line he had just sung, and he altered a word—"boy" to "lad"—in the ten-second interval between the first and the second utterance. A field-collected text merely freezes one rendering of a continuously varying—and yet remarkably stable—unwritten tradition.

Literary expression does of course affect oral tradition, and the interaction between the two modes calls for the most vigilant detective work by the folklorist in his endeavor to reconstruct the life history of a text. All kinds of printed matter drop into the stream of oral lore: broadside ballads, chapbook and almanac jests, newspaper horror stories, parables in holy scriptures, classical myths, fairy tales, and poems and fictions composed by authors great and obscure. Yet the relationship between the printed and the verbal forms is one of good will rather than hostility; they feed and sustain each other. For an example, learned teachers of the Jewish faith illustrate the lessons of the Old Testament with moralistic tales, which have passed down the centuries side by side with, and dependent upon, the Bible. These folk legends, or Haggadah, have been separately collected and studied by comparative folklore scholars, who recognize their interdependence with secular, Christian, and Moslem folktales. On the other hand, some collections of alleged folk materials, like the Paul Bunyan tales, have enjoyed little or no oral life, and cannot claim a place in the repertoire of traditional texts. The more oral variants we can collect, from carriers indebted to other carriers, the surer we are of the presence of folklore.

. . .

How does a collector snare the elusive oral texts of folklore? Methods will vary according to the project and the kinds of materials sought, whether ballad or legend or proverb or folk-drama, or a general haul. The aims of the field trip should be clearly focused, to avoid a vague and rambling quest. Do railroad workers possess distinctive traditions? Is there a separate folk-culture in this valley or that hill-country area? Has the lore of the Irish survived since their mid-nineteenth-century immigration? Do children's games vary between country and city? Too rarely do creative ideas for collecting open new paths, like John Lomax's song-gathering within Negro penitentiaries, or George Korson's interviewing of coal miners with the assistance of their labor unions. A brilliant hypothesis induced Cecil Sharp to comb the mountains of Virginia, Kentucky, and Tennessee in search of Child ballads. Yet a constricting theory may blind the collector to other riches at his elbow, and Sharp never inquired for olden tales which lay in abundance among his singers.

Having formulated his plan, the prospector equips himself for the trip by canvassing the printed literature on his subject for insights and specific leads. He must gain conversational footholds with his future informants by knowing the terms of their occupation, the place names and landmarks of their localities, the supernatural concepts of their culture. Then he has at his disposal a finding list from which to launch leading questions. In the United States, where at present helpful aids such as collectors' handbooks, field manuals, glossaries, and even representative published collections (save for folksong) are largely lacking, the folklorist must use other resources. He can scour town and country histories, state guidebooks, local color and regional fiction, and studies of immigrant groups for data on folk cultures. Success in the field may to a considerable extent be determined in the library, before the folklorist leaves his home base.

The day comes when the hopeful collector, neophyte or veteran, stands anxiously within the terrain of his choice. What now? Perhaps his doubts have been enlarged by reports, commonly circulated about in-groups, that the people he seeks are clannish and suspicious. He worries that strangers will ridicule his request for old tales or songs. (One experienced collector of Texas folksongs, William A. Owens, departed from the field forever when an old lady snorted at his funny way of making a living.) Possibly he has qualms about disturbing people's privacy, and worming his way into the lives of complete strangers. A more serious problem than any of these, which collectors today must contend with, lies in the pervasive fear of federal agents and investigators.

Nevertheless, our fieldworker possesses several potent assets. Chief of these is time, unlimited time around the clock. He can sleuth for prospects from morning till night, and fit his hours to suit theirs; if the first lead proves faulty, the second or third or fourth may reward. He can find housewives at home in the morning, the breadwinner in the evening, and old folks all day. Again, he may feel sure that most persons relish being interviewed and having their words taken down or recorded verbatim. The stiffest patriarch will unbend when a deferential listener appeals for information about his ethnic or local tradition. Then the mere joy of reciting to an audience keeps a fluent narrator talking long after he has forgotten the scholarly purpose of his visitor.

To build up a list of possible informants in a new community, the collector can call on key individuals whose business demands a breadth of local acquaintance. The Chamber of Commerce secretary, the newspaper editor, the minister and priest, the county agricultural agent, should be able to suggest names. Usually the newspaper office will welcome the chance to print a story about the newcomer and explain his quest in general terms. He should sniff out and hang around gathering places for congenial groups, such as boardinghouse parlors, barber shops, a favorite café. In Newberry, Michigan, I discovered a regular haunt of oldtimers and passers-by in Matt Surrell's auto-parts supply store and garage (converted from a livery stable), and there caught some fine lie-swapping sessions. On a trip to the Negro farming township of Calvin, Michigan, where no village cluster of shops and streets existed, necessity forced me to attend the churches and idle around the tavern, the only two points of congregation. Taverns are not the likely meeting grounds one might think, since the noise and inebriety destroy rather than create rapport; yet Wayland Hand enjoyed success when collecting miners' lore in Butte, Montana, by simply plunking his recording machine down on the bar and setting up drinks in exchange for songs. The old folks' home is often recommended as a calling place, but senile and maundering invalids in these homes make poor informants. In the mission home run by the Reverend Mrs. Toler in Pine Bluff, Arkansas, she proved to be my only good storyteller.

One bridge to the folk group often unexpectedly appears in the person of a volunteer guide, eager to serve as liaison agent and if necessary as interpreter. These valuable aides take an interest in the project through personal curiosity, and become near partners for a while. In Calvin, Michigan, a deacon I met at the Chain Lake Baptist Church, Fred Steele, who had interviewed old residents for a centennial booklet commemorating the church, offered to lead me to likely prospects, scattered through the back roads of the township. Steele savored the genealogical revelations and closet skeletons that emerged from these visits. So did Herschel Cross, who performed the same service for me in Mecosta, Michigan, after the township supervisor introduced him to me as a keen-minded member of a pioneer Negro family. A newspaper reporter in Marquette put me in touch with Aili Kolehmainen Johnson, a second-generation Finn living in intellectual isolation in the village of Gwinn, and there translating the Finnish folk epic, the *Kalevala*; Mrs. Johnson steered me into the heart of the Upper Peninsula Finnish community.

Chance contacts and casual meetings cannot be planned but can be promptly cultivated. In the field, speak freely and in friendly fashion to the hotel clerk, the barfly, and the newsboy, for anyone may prove to be, or lead you to, an informant. Remembering this injunction, I responded to the alcoholic mumbling of the ragged, red-eyed French Canadian who sat next to me at the counter of a café in L'Anse, and eventually Bert Damour spilled forth in a gush his memories of legends and *contes*. Waiting my turn in a barber shop in Negaunee, I heard the old fellow in the chair say something about "fly pie"; asking him further about the matter, I made the acquaintance of a superb swashbuckling raconteur, Swan Olson, who had one time nearly eaten a pie made of basted flies. Sometimes even a point-blank approach will do the trick, if no other means are available and one's nerve is strong. Wandering around the tumbledown Negro settlement of New Bethel in Michigan, without leads or contacts, I saw a fleshy, somber woman standing in the doorway of the last house on the path, and called out, "Do you know any old stories?" Sarah Hall said yes and invited me in. So I met the storytelling mother of three storytelling daughters, who was also the hoodooed ex-wife of still another narrator.

One main rule holds in the field: be yourself. Every collector must win confidences in his own way by projecting his own personality, and sham or hypocrisy or condescension are immediately detected. Quite opposite field methods may thus succeed in different hands. When calling on mountain families in the southern Appalachians, Cecil Sharp simply hallooed lustily on approaching a hillside home in his English knickers and sport cap, and promptly stated his quest for songs. On the same quest in a similar area, Vance Randolph, although himself a resident of the Ozark region and thoroughly familiar with its ways, behaved with excessive caution. He introduced himself by giving the name of a neighbor who had suggested this hillman as a possible singer of old songs, and then explained his desire to publish a singing book of the true old songs. When the hillman promptly declared he had forgotten every song he ever knew, and recommended some other neighbors, Randolph scrupulously wrote down their names, dropped the subject, and talked on neutral matters for a spell. Suddenly he reverted to his original topic, mentioned a song he had recently heard, and began to sing it, deliberately erring. The hillman at once interposed, pointed out the error, sang the piece correctly, and went on to sing his whole repertoire. Both the direct approach of the Englishman and the circuitous technique of the American were successful, for Sharp and Randolph have given us our two major collections of Anglo-American folksongs.

Collecting in big cities poses different problems from fieldwork in rural communities or neighborly towns, and the very idea of the "field" conventionally implies travel to remote and sequestered places. This notion is slowly dying, as we come to recognize that folklore clusters wherever groups of people gather. The Nova Scotian collector, Helen Creighton, found more folksongs in populous Halifax county, within a fifty-mile radius of the city of Halifax, than in all the outlying districts. Southern folksong specialists John Powell and Edwin Kirkland uncovered more singers in the mundane lowlands than in the romantic highlands. A major collecting program in an American city began in Detroit in 1939, under the direction of Emelyn Gardner, and continues today with her successor, Thelma James. Professor James outlines an extensive list of public and private municipal agencies that she has relied on in accumulating lore from fifty of Detroit's sixty-seven nationality groups. They include nationality clubs and societies; ethnic lodges of international organizations (e.g., the Syrian lodge of the Masonic Order) ; settlement houses; city housing, health, and immigration offices (an expressway built through an ethnic settlement caused its dispersal, and only city officials could trace the new addresses) ; recreation centers; labor unions; visiting-nurse centers (one nurse collected three hundred items of birth lore) ; and indeed any agency penetrating into the vast impersonal life of the metropolis. Newspaper notices announce ethnic conventions, festivals, holidays, picnics, weddings, funerals, school programs, and similar occasions where the cultural folklorist may observe and mingle.

Locating informants only begins the battle. Now face to face with a member of the "folk," the collector proceeds to the task of extracting the lore.

"They tell me you know a lot of old tales, the kind people used to tell before radio and television came along. I'm trying to write them down before they get lost, and I wonder if you would help me. I'm a professor from the state college, and I'm interested in any kind of a story that doesn't come from a book."

That may do for an opener. The stranger has explained in a general way his mission, without using the exotic word folklore, identified himself, and asked for assistance. Often the answer comes back, with a laugh, "You wouldn't want the stories I know," and the collector then goes on to focus more sharply his request, perhaps illustrating with a sample text. A good informant catches on right away. The best I ever met, J. D. Suggs of the Negro community in Calvin, Michigan, answered my opening formula by saying with a wide grin, "I know a million stories," and eventually told me nearly two hundred. Of course the circumstances of the encounter, the personalities involved, and the material sought all determine the opening remarks. Helen Creighton customarily begins with some pleasantry. Nothing aids so much as the key terms, local references, and song titles the collector has compiled from his library reading and his previous fieldwork, for these evoke immediate recognition and amusement from the in-group. My very first call in the Upper Peninsula nearly turned out disastrously, for with my foot in the door of Aunt Jane Goudreau's house in St. Ignace, the suspicious old lady of eighty-one denied knowing any tales about Winabijou, the Ojibwa hero, and prepared to shut me out. As a desperate expedient, I asked if she knew about the *loup-garou* (the French term for werewolf). Her mouth opened wide and she stared at me thunderstruck. "How did you hear about the *roup-garou?*" (the local form) Aunt Jane shrilled, and by the time I explained I was well inside the house. It was not the Indian but the French-Canadian tradition to which she belonged—although she possessed Indian blood—and she retained powerful impressions of *roup-garou* shapeshifters from half a century before in St. Ignace. No single word could have more effectively won her confidence.

In this case a personal reference would have helped disarm Aunt Jane. When calling on Suggs, I was able to say that Edith from the tavern had sent me, and later he confided that next day he had checked with Edith on my "credentials." James Carpenter, a Harvard scholar who spent six years collecting in England, saw the door of a Scottish cottage slam in his face; knocking again, he stated that the clan chieftain had sent him there, whereon the peasant woman led him to her hearth and sang over three hundred songs.

Many blind alleys and false scents, wrong steers and frustrations, await the folklore hunter. So-called experts advise him to give up his foolish quest, for all the good storytellers died fifty years ago. After hearing this talk from the local Indianist in Escanaba, who had made a reputation finding arrowheads, I drove out a few miles to the Indian reservation at Hannahville, stopped at the little store where a Potawatomi was buying flour, asked him who could tell me stories, and so learned of his neighbor, Alec Philemon, who dictated tales to me from morning till night. The president of the French-Canadian club in Marquette told me I would have to go to Quebec to find *conteurs,* for all *Canadiens* in Michigan were educated; meanwhile, illiterate old Trefflé Largenesse sat idly on a porch fronting the main street in town, bursting with *contes* and hungry for visitors. While the Indian agent in L'Anse, a college graduate, was explaining how the old Indian traditions had vanished, and reading some to me from an old book, a giant Sioux stuck his head through a window and asked softly, "Is that professor fellow around we were reading about in the paper? We had a social the other night and were telling stories, and wanted him to come down." That is how I met Chief Herbert Welsh, a topnotch narrator.

Again, a seemingly likely informant turns out to be a dud. In the little lumbering town of Nahma, I was directed to one oldtimer who had spent his life in the woods, and presumably bulged with lumberjack lore. The retired jack looked the part all right, battered slouch hat, rolling gait, and woodsy manner, and agreed most genially to talk with me; but to all my queries he replied with monosyllables. "Did you ever have a serious accident in the woods?" I asked him, trying to lead into bad-luck omens and signs. "Yes," he said, "a log once fell on me right here" (pointing to his thigh). And he waited agreeably for the next question. With the master performers, little prodding or prompting is needed; the same question addressed to Charlie Goodman, an old hunter and trapper from Grand Marais, triggered off hours of reminiscences and lore. External appearances, age, sex, situation, education, afford no clue to potential informants. Ten-year-old Effie Dean Hall, thirty-year-old John Blackamore, and sixty-five-year-old Suggs all proved excellent storytellers. Two of my faculty colleagues possessed a fund of Jewish dialect jests from oral tradition. The provost of Harvard University once astonished me by unreeling a string of eccentric-professor anecdotes. Only two generalizations apply, in my experience, to stellar informants: all grasp your mission with a minimum of difficulty, and can produce material immediately, while one can explain all day to a poor informant and get nowhere; and all the master narrators, illiterate or college-bred, possess keen and agile minds.

In the field the greatest disappointments and irritations come after the list of top prospects is compiled. Finding people in, and getting them in the proper mood and environment, demand saintlike patience and tact. As the automobile has accelerated the pace of the collector, so also has it helped disperse the informants. The busy tempo of American life permeates the hinterland as well as the metropolis, and somehow the collector must wrest time from the important pursuits of money-making, hunting and fishing, or attendance at club meetings that occupy his newfound friends. My most arduous chase involved a genial undertaker celebrated as a dialect mimic, who repeatedly promised to meet me and cheerfully broke all our appointments. A secretive woodland Indian often proves much more approachable than the hustling businessman of one's own culture. Several collectors remark on the vexation of pacifying the storyteller's surly spouse. Joe Keast was about to describe an episode where he had gone down into a condemned mine tied to the mining captain, who had just emerged with his hair turned white and his wits gone, when Mrs. Keast rushed into the room and clobbered the daredevil into meek humility—and chased me out. Mrs. Suggs, with whom I had exchanged scarcely a word, once yelled out strangely to me as I was taking her husband into town for a recording session, and Suggs later explained that "the boys" had told her we were actually going off after women.

The most embarrassing interference to my collecting occurred in Sam Colasacco's tavern in Hurley, Wisconsin, the town of a hundred taverns. Sam was revealing to me an extraordinary Italian spell, the *fattura*, whereby a bridegroom could be rendered impotent on his wedding night. A few stools away a sodden, middle-aged peroxide blonde sprawled across the counter, looking up every so often to mumble "Another shot, Sam." Suddenly her bleary eyes turned toward me and she demanded, in an aggressive whiskey voice, "What're *you* doing?" "Collecting folklore," I replied with dignity. "Folklore—whassat?" she blurted, and snatched my notebook from me. I waited in horror while the frump peered over the *fattura* account, thinking she might read aloud some intimate passages, and bring ridicule or wrath upon me in that alien barroom. After a pregnant pause the lady said, "You don't use the Palmer method," and returned my notebook. One drink later she crumpled up, and Sam heaved her across his shoulder and carried her out.

.   .   .

Success or failure in the field may well depend on the casual impression the prospector makes. What does he wear? How should he act? On these questions of field behavior, most experienced collectors agree you should act naturally. Don't dress down or talk down to the folk. "You know," Edith confided to me while I was having supper at her tavern during my first trip to Calvin, "when you first came here we thought you were an FBI agent, but after I saw those patches on your sleeves I said you must be a writing feller, and wore 'em out on a desk." And so, confident in my identity, she directed me to J. D. Suggs, a marvelous raconteur—thanks to the reinforced elbows on an old jacket.

Circumspect deportment goes without saying, for the stranger constantly passes before suspicious eyes. While hanging around Ab and Edith's tavern, I bought rounds for hangers-on but drank only an occasional beer myself. Yet in the Pine Mountain of Kentucky the collector must drink home-brew with the mountaineers to avoid giving grave affront, and he must never address their young women. On revisiting sharp-tongued Carrie Taylor Eaton in Calvin, whom I had first met at an Adventist church service, I was greeted with this abrupt charge: "Is it true you've been molesting our young girls around here?" While I stammered and gulped, the seventy-five-year-old colored woman went on to say that someone with my build had been prowling around, but she had defended me to her kin, saying, "All the time he was with me he behaved like a very moral

man." Politeness must however be balanced with some aggres-
siveness, and the collector must pursue people who deny their
own knowledge and pull books off the shelf, or complain of lack
of time, but in the end thoroughly enjoy narrating.

Even the most willing and co-operative informant cannot
pour forth a stream of lore the way one turns on a spigot or
uncorks a bottle. Items of tradition lie beneath the surface of
the mind, some buried deep in the subconscious, and both narrator and listener must strain to coax them up. "Where do all
those stories come from?" Suggs asked me more than once,
curiously inspecting his anatomy for a possible lodging place.
What the collector can do is help trigger off the tale or song
or riddle with leading questions, or illustrative examples, or if
possible by creating a group situation where rivals match their
stories against each other. We know how conversations among
congenial spirits flow into serial anecdotes and rival wonders
that continue as long as the audience responds with laughter or
awe. But any one member of the party, if approached cold and
asked for jokes, would probably scratch his head blankly. A
delighted audience and two or more talented performers to
sharpen each other's powers provide ideal conditions for the
collector with a recording machine. Once an outstanding informant is unearthed, revisits always yield gold, for his mind
stirs to recollection, and he has learned to dictate or record.

Different kinds of material require different stimuli. Sometimes the personal interview serves best in getting at specific
aspects of folk belief. Confidences that would not be aired publicly are whispered to a sympathetic interrogator. Vance Randolph reports that girls in the Ozarks will sleep with a man
much sooner than disclose to him their credence in witchcraft.
In piecing together a local legend and testing its pervasiveness,
the collector should solicit comments from as many people as
possible in the community and follow the trail much like a
newspaper reporter, asking direct and pointed questions. But
where he casts a broader net, and wishes to discover any bona
fide tradition, he should turn into a sounding board, listen to
whatever his speaker may volunteer, and steer the conversation
only when it is obviously running into arid channels. Melville

Herskovits once recalled ruefully how he checked his Haitian storyteller who had started to talk about Napoleon instead of reciting conventional Anansi tales. During my Upper Peninsula field trip I kept hearing curious jocular narratives in every town, unlike any in printed collections, and so literally had thrust upon me the most conspicuous folktale flowering of the region, the dialect yarn.

Suppose the collector has located and "opened up" a fertile informant, how does he take possession of the folklore? Several possibilities exist. The poorest method consists in noting the motifs and bare outlines of the material, or simply committing them to memory, and filling in the skeleton later on. This procedure conveys the collector's rather than the informant's style, and of course misses the details that enliven a narrative. Every effort should be made to secure the actual words of the speaker, even through slow dictation, at first upsetting to the narrator and finger-wracking to the collector. But the adjustment can soon be made to a snail-paced rhythm, and I have filled many notebooks with dictated tales, all taken in longhand. Do not begin writing until you have established rapport with your informant and know something of his repertoire. In the initial conversation simply jot down a title or a phrase to recall an item you wish to secure verbatim. The advantage in recording lore from dictation lies in the opportunity to ask for repetition of misunderstood words and phrases and obscure meanings, and so to "gloss" the text. The disadvantage comes from the loss of spontaneity and conversational give-and-take characteristic of ordinary speech. An unusual, if not unique, collecting method devised by Austin and Alta Fife overcomes this drawback. While the husband interrogates Mormon farmers, the wife seated unobtrusively in the background notes all comments and traditions in shorthand. However, the most expert stenographer cannot keep pace with a silver-tongued bard. Another couple, the wife a folklore graduate student and her husband a skilled audiovisual technician, have solved this problem. The young lady knocks on the door of a southern home and introduces herself in a soothing North Carolina accent, while her spouse scurries into the background with a portable tape recorder. He turns it on and records the conversation about Doctor Buzzard, legendary healer of Gullah Negroes. So far no one has objected to or been disturbed by this procedure.

Even in the matter of note-taking equipment, methods vary widely. Anthropologist Herskovits never exhibited notebooks in the bush country of Surinam, for fear of arousing the suspicions of the natives. But in cities in Dahomey, West Africa, he set his typewriter on a table and typed the comments of his informants directly from the translations of their interpreters.

Collectors now take for granted an instrument to seize and permanently preserve the living tissues of oral tradition. Following the second World War, electronic recording machines using magnetic tape appeared on the market and became a major accessory to the collector's equipment. Recording apparatus used to secure song texts and tunes of course antedates the invention of magnetic tape. John Lomax and his son Alan built their collection of cowboy and Negro folksongs with disc-cutting machines, and the elder Lomax notes wryly in his *Adventures of a Ballad Hunter* the mechanical griefs that beset him at crucial times when some little doodad misbehaved. The Irish Folklore Commission fieldworkers strapped Ediphone machines to their bikes and registered on cylinders the long, ancient Celtic sagas still known to the shanachies. Today tape recorders are so familiar that, so the story goes, Federal revenue agents in the Kentucky hills carry them to pose as folksong sleuths.

How the great collectors of the nineteenth century would have relished a chance to catch the voices of their star informants! On tape one hears the full-bodied, pristine narrative, replete with inflection and natural idiom; printed words cannot convey this vocal color. What the machine can do that the note-taker cannot is to "encircle" the texts and capture conversational exchange and aside and revelation. I spent one memorable evening in Calvin township shortly after acquiring a portable recorder. When Mr. and Mrs. E. L. Smith and Mary Richardson began conversing about witchcraft, they talked on oblivious of the machine, comparing frights, reproducing the sounds of malevolent beings, and triggering each other into an excited flurry of occult reminiscences. Both Mary Richardson and Mr. Smith disclosed that witches had ridden them breathless; the Smiths confided that witches had plagued their little grandson in that very house; all three fell to discussing means of driving off witches, and Mrs. Smith triumphantly recounted the capture of a witch in the form of a hideous spider, trapped in a sifter full of salt. Without the recorder, this macabre discussion would have reached print, if at all, in fragmentary and truncated form.

Besides the intensive individual field project, other kinds of collecting activity bring to light large bodies of folk material. Co-operative collecting by folklore societies or committees usually aims at limited targets and permits little of the elasticity possible for the opportunist in the field. If the project calls for a county or state inventory of superstitions, place names, or proverbs, questionnaires can be circulated giving sample items and indicating the kind of background information desired. Pleas for such materials in various media, from specialized journals to radio broadcasts, usually bring substantial returns. This kind of endeavor produces an accumulation of small texts for quantitative analysis.

Student collecting may consist of group projects in the lower grades and individual undertakings by college undergraduates, to acquaint them with folklore at first-hand. More than a thousand students in my American Folklore courses mustered collections after I outlined these simple canvassing possibilities.

First, the student can explore himself, since, like every other sentient human being, he has rubbed against folklore at various points in his life—in school, at summer camp, in military service, at factory jobs. What he knows himself, and can now begin to identify as folk tradition, he adds to his sheaf and labels "Myself" as the source, giving the place and time of first acquaintance to the best of his knowledge. A coed once turned in one hundred college folksongs, which she had begun to memorize for her own hobby before taking the course.

An older student of Herbert Halpert was able to set down seven hundred and fifty proverbial expressions she remembered from west Tennessee.

Second, the student's family and relations provide another source, invariably flattered at this show of attention from the younger generation. "This is the course," one folklore professor commences, "where you become acquainted with your own grandparents." European-born relatives should always be interrogated, but old American families too inherit ancestral folk matter. The daughter of a cavalry officer secured from him now-vanished military traditions. Even a young brother or sister can furnish children's lore.

Third, the budding folklorist can pursue his age-group and neighborhood friends and acquaintances with notebook and pencil for their oral gems. Undergraduates move within swirling floods of oral lore: beer-bust songs, dormitory legends, anecdotes of eccentric professors and dumb athletes. In the heterogeneous student body of the modern American university, drawn from all the states and territories of the Union, and from many foreign countries, a collegian finds the folk traditions of scattered regions and lands among his classmates. College life lends itself to "bull sessions," in the dormitory, the grill, the fraternity or sorority, and the enterprising young collector can easily initiate matching contests in exaggerated idioms, logic puzzles, Liberace jokes, and similar current matters.

Fourth, an energetic undergraduate can acquire a taste of fieldwork by developing new contacts through available channels. He can locate ethnic informants by interrogating the International Institute in a big city, or by attending a fair or pageant or celebration bringing together special groups. Seeing a notice in the Lansing newspaper of a local meeting of a Mexican club, a student of mine with some knowledge of Spanish contacted the officers, attended their meeting, made friends, and secured an attractive group of Mexican tales which she published in the folklore section in *Michigan History*.

Institution-sponsored collecting represents still another approach to fieldwork. In Finland, Sweden, Ireland, and Scotland, full-time collectors employed by an archive or museum comb the country for every scrap of folkstuff. Collectors for the Irish Folklore Commission use an exhaustive *Handbook of Irish Folklore* constructed by Sean O'Sullivan (Ó'Súilleabháin), archivist of the commission, which systematically assembles leading questions concerning all aspects of Irish folk life. One interviewer spent two years recording the answers of one informant to the queries in the handbook. In the United States no comparable program exists, although the National Museum of Canada has for a number of years engaged an experienced collector, Helen Creighton, to explore Nova Scotia. The short-lived, depression-born folklore section of the Federal Writers' Project represents the unique instance of government support for nationwide collecting in this country. In spite of its erratic and haphazard administration, the Federal Writers' Project produced several regional folklore volumes of varying merit, as well as folklore sections in most of the state guidebooks. The Folklore Archives of the Library of Congress has co-operated with individual collectors, chiefly through the loan of recording machines, and has accumulated an impressive number of folksong discs.

One American university once sponsored professional folklore collecting as an educational aid. When president of Bucknell University in the 1930's, Homer P. Rainey felt the need for classroom bonds between the student body and their immediate culture, to bridge the chasm created by their forced study of European and classical models. He therefore engaged George Korson to build a file of local folk materials from Pennsylvania, to provide themes and ideas for undergraduates majoring in literature, art, and music. Subsequently, Korson became convinced that coal miners possessed traditional stores of song, legend, and belief, and set out to explore the Pennsylvania anthracite mines, and then the bituminous coal fields of the nation. The United Mine Workers sponsored these enterprises and provided not only financial help but also tactical assistance in gaining admission to the homes and lives of miners.

Just as anthropology stresses the indispensable value of field experience, so should folklore require of all its practitioners the actual taste of collecting at first hand. In most academic circles today, theory enjoys more prestige than ethnographic description, but speculative analysis lives on data from the field. Nor can second-hand acquaintance ever substitute for the personal experience of discovering folklore in its original environment.

. . .

The present volume is intended as a supplement to my *American Folklore,** in particular the third chapter, "Regional Folk Cultures." Four of the five regions discussed there are represented here, by Maine Down-Easters, Pennsylvania Dutchmen, Southwest Mexicans, and Utah Mormons. Three new regions well scoured by collectors are now added, in chapters on Southern Mountaineers, Louisiana Cajuns, and Illinois Egyptians. One region has been omitted, the Ozarks, since its traditions have largely been gathered by a single fieldworker, Vance Randolph, whose books are readily available. Within each regional section the texts are divided according to the genres of folk material—folk narrative, proverbs, riddles, beliefs, folk-drama, and folksongs. Because the faithful collecting of folksongs far outdistances the ingathering of other forms of American folklore, the number of song texts included here has been kept to a minimum and has been selected chiefly to illustrate historical themes. I have added comparative headnotes, citing major reference works and collections, where they have been lacking in the original publications. My footnotes are indicated by symbols, those of the collectors by numerals. The regional grouping of field materials should suggest qualities and characteristics of widely differing folk cultures, even though a given item of tradition may well be found in every region.

* University of Chicago Press, 1959; Phoenix paperback edition, 1960.

I

MAINE DOWN-EASTERS

A VAST AND SPARSELY INHABITED land, Maine still belongs in large measure to the natural order of woods, lakes, mountains, and the sea. Folklore collectors have paid special heed to the lumberjacks who began hewing the white pine in the 1880's and who sang traditional songs at night in the camps or on the spring river drives. An amateurish volume by Roland Gray, *Songs and Ballads of the Maine Lumberjacks* (1924), was soon succeeded by the skilfully presented trove of two intrepid women, Fannie Hardy Eckstorm and Mary Winslow Smyth, whose *Minstrelsy of Maine* (1927) is as notable for its interpretive essays on songmaking in the woods as for its cache of local texts. The most active of New England folksong scholars, Phillips Barry, compiled *The Maine Woods Songster* (1939) from his own field recordings. More recently, Edward D. Ives, in *Larry Gorman, The Man Who Made the Songs* (in press), has pursued the trail of a folk poet whose satirical songs composed half a century ago are still current among woodsmen in Maine and the Maritime Provinces.

Apart from lumberjack balladry, collectors have paid little attention to Maine's store of folk traditions. In *The Folklore of Maine* (1957), Horace P. Beck includes barely a dozen folktale texts. Yet a short field trip "down East" in 1956 acquainted me with a great variety of oral narratives familiar to hardy families living along the coast. These lobster and herring fishermen, whom I have described in *American Folklore,* have lived an insulated and inbred life on the coastal islands and the coastal mainland. A pure Yankee stock, planted on the bays and coves down East in the late eighteenth and early nineteenth centuries, their traditions are shaped in some part by their Anglo-Saxon heritage, in larger part by their livelihoods gained from the fishing waters, and in greatest part by nineteenth-century American village life with its accent on personal idiosyncrasies. Yet many of the seemingly local jokes and anecdotes prove to be European. We may consider each of these elements briefly.

The English influence on the oral lore of these down-Easters appears chiefly in the realm of the supernatural. None of the elaborate wonder tales found among English settlers in the southern mountains, nor the venerated old English ballads plentifully collected throughout New England and the south, emerged during this field excursion. Belief in witchcraft persists, centered around the malevolent figure of Old Mother Hicks, a spiteful sorceress from the previous generation. People still fear mean or "ugly" women with powers to ill-wish, and Frank Alley related to me instances of his own wife who—under quite justifiable circumstances, of course—had laid curses on the hardhearted. Yet on the whole the English contribution seems surprisingly slight. The divinatory practice of "calling the spirits" at a mystic session around the table, so familiar and vital to the islanders, has not been reported elsewhere by folklorists or ethnologists. Clearly a debt exists to the nineteenth-century vogue of spiritualistic seances and to general divination rituals; but the custom of "table-tipping," or invoking departed spirits to gain information for the living, seems a local development.

In the sphere of marine lore, too, the American tradition departs from the English. The most popular legend along the Maine coast deals with an impious wind-buyer who hurls a coin into the sea and raises a storm. Yet for all the instances of wind and storm raisers in folklore and mythology, harking back to the Greek island king Aeolus who controlled the winds, the counterpart of the gale-tossed down-Easter has not yet been sighted. By contrast, Frank Alley's yarn of the sailor who traveled inland until he reached a place where the inhabitants did not recognize the oar on his shoulders matches closely a tale included in the *Odyssey*. In the first case we have a tradition involving an actual belief—the belief in divine retribution meted out to blasphemers—and in the second we have a mariner's floating story.

It is this second kind of short, humorous folk narrative which unexpectedly and repeatedly surfaces on the Maine coast after wandering across Europe. One raconteur in particular, seventy-six-year-old Jim Alley, spewed forth an endless series of comic tales, many of which can be identified as European tale-types, and some of which have not hitherto been found in the United States.

The headnotes to the section "Jocular Tales" document some of these newly reported American examples of international fictions. In one of his rapid-fire jests, Jim Alley tells how an "Irishman Shows Pat a Yankee Trick" to a fellow Hibernian. Talk of Yankees and Yankee tricks pervades the pre-Civil War decades, and the Yankee comes to represent the essence of the homespun American genius. Yet this "Yankee trick" was once played on a stupid peasant by an Hungarian nobleman, according to the lone reference cited under Type 1349D*. Again, the text of Type 1159, *The Ogre Wants to Learn to Play*, which Jim Alley told on the Devil (who having once had his nose caught in a door, is frightened off at the sight of an unclad woman doubled over), is hitherto unreported in the United States, although some two hundred variants are known in the Scandinavian countries. A tale heard among the Accra people in West Africa, and in four east European countries, concerns the foreigner who mistakes the answer "I don't know" in the native language to be a person's name; its first recognition in the United States came in two Negro texts I recorded, involving a colored man and a Mexican, and now Jim Alley produces a version told on "Old Gram Shaw."

Two streams of tradition flow together in the anecdotal lore of down-Easters, the humorous plots of European origin, and the antic experiences credited to local characters in American communities. If a village character attracts sufficient notoriety, a cycle of little tales grows around him which sooner or later includes far-flung and oft-repeated deeds. The character truly exists, and no doubt behaves in an eccentric fashion, but as one local ne'er-do-well is supposed to have said, "There is a great deal stole around here on my credit." Attached to notorious legpullers in Europe and the United States is the answer given by the town Munchausen when his friends ask him to tell one of his famous lies. "Haven't time," he replies. "My uncle just broke his leg falling from a ladder, and I'm on the way to the hospital to see him." And off he rushes. His startled cronies follow belatedly, only to discover that the wag has indeed told a lie. In Jonesport this anecdote was fastened onto Art Church, who perpetrated other deceits. The qualities of low cunning and rustic ignorance distinguish the local eccentric, who thus conforms to the world-wide figure of the trickster and the fool. His eccentric behavior may include, on the positive side, low cunning, effrontery, chicanery, verbal cleverness at making sharp retorts, or special offbeat talents like a genius for gadgetry. On the negative side, local characters display shiftlessness, parsimony, degeneracy, stubbornness, stupidity, and gullibility. Jonesport is typical of communities all over the United States, and even of big city neighborhoods, in which stories, sayings, rhymes, and jingles multiply around colorful characters. The anecdotal legend is the chief narrative form taken by this oral lore.

An anecdote is a brief story told as an actual occurrence connected with a person, living or dead, who is well known to the audience. His fame may be national and international in scope—and personalities in the news frequently attract cycles of anecdotes—or it may be purely local. Many anecdotes turn out to be folktales, fastening onto individuals widely scattered in space and time. Local sayings attributed to the characters become proverbial, or proverbs are put in their mouths, as "There is a great deal stole around here on my credit." Some village bard may rhyme the stories and sayings in folk verses sung along with the time-honored ballads. A vigorous tradition of composing and singing satiric verses flourishes in the Maine-Maritimes area, as Edward D. Ives has demonstrated in his study of Larry Gorman, and in Jonesport the oil tanker crewman Stuart Alley has followed this tradition, contriving songs about the hermit Will Groves, the peddler Eben Stanwood, and a locally celebrated charivari that ended in a lawsuit. In these cases the verses are anecdotes-in-song.

Ordinarily the storyteller and the character are two quite separate personalities in the roster of township celebrities. In 1942, in the inland town of Wilton, Maine, the raconteur "Slick" MacQuoid pointed out to me the Wilton eccentric, Old John Soule, a wizened, dried-up old man, about whom Slick told anecdotes and tall tales. The local character provides one of the subjects for the tales of the local storyteller. Jim Alley continually referred to "old fellows" from the various towns where he had lived, whose peculiarities remained fresh in his mind. With Curt Morse, however, an unusual process was observed, for while he did spin anecdotes about odd people like Captain Horace Smith and the hermit Willie Racker, his favorite subject for personal anecdotes was himself. In daily life Curt played a role as a wag and humorist, and every afternoon he could be seen loitering and gabbing on the main street of Machias, greeting and being greeted with good-natured sallies. In the course of his storytelling, Curt further developed this image of himself, by relating general tall tales as personal experiences—Jim Alley would tell the same tales in the third person—and by expanding real or imagined incidents into personal anecdotes. Usually Curt appeared in his self-portrait as a sorry victim of comical mishaps. His discomfitures while potato farming in Aroostook County illustrate the risks of the native who leaves his regular habitat and occupation to participate in an alien culture. Winning a dead horse in a raffle—a twice-told tale—

her bottom and paint up a little bit, and ground her on a
ed ledge, and she broke in two. And her old frame ribs
ht there now. Sure . . . big four-masted schooner. Old
bs," "Abbie S. Stubbs."

DORSON:

What are some of the superstitions that the seafaring
e believe in?

CECIL KELLEY:

Oh, if you come out on deck and you forget your plug of
cco you never turn around and go back after it. You'd have
all day without a chew. Oh no, never turn around if you
t anything. It's bad luck. Oh, yes, and there's so many
s that's bad luck. Oh, hundreds of 'em.

DORSON:

Oh well, now, what was it they thought was bad luck here?
t the man was drowned?

CECIL KELLEY:

Yes, he lost his man. He had hard luck right on the first
g. He was all done for the season.

DORSON:

Oh, is that so? Does that mean he would have bad luck
rest of the season?

CECIL KELLEY:

Yes, he wouldn't go the rest of the year. He would go
t back to making hay.

DORSON:

Oh, really.

CECIL KELLEY:

Yeah, he was all done with the sea for that year. Oh yes,
ad hard luck the very first day. He was all through.

DORSON:

Were there some other things like that that they believed

CECIL KELLEY:

Oh, yes, oh, yes, lot of 'em. You can't turn a boat around
ainst the sun. No, go right back and put it to the mooring;
uldn't go out for the day. If you started out in the morning,
u had to turn around the first turn you made. If you turn

is a fitting example of Curt's bad luck. Yet Curt is not always the
buffoon, and in one narrative he does hoax the city slickers in a
traditional triumph of the country bumpkin.

As cycles of humorous anecdotes cluster around the local character, so do more serious anecdotes swell the reputation of the local
strong man. New England in particular offers documentary evidence
in numerous town histories and other printed sources of the awe ac-
corded mighty lifters and movers of heavy objects. On Beals Island,
where Barney Beal was born, and along the coast down to Rockland
and Portland, where he traded, families of fisherfolk repeat accounts
of his feats of strength. All members of a family, and not just gifted
raconteurs like Jim Alley and Curt Morse, recite these deeds. In
the more than half a century since Barney's death in 1899, these
oral reports have grown toward legend. In the description, for instance, of the fight between Barney and the Bully of Peak's Island,
who came to fight but hastily departed when he saw Barney lift a
water barrel and drink from the bung, we find a time-honored theme
of heroic combat. Barney is truly a folk-hero, lauded in the living
traditions of a regional community.

. . . .

The texts in this chapter are all from tape recordings I made in
July, 1956, on a field trip to Jonesport and Beals Island in Washington County, Maine. Articles and papers in which I have printed
some of these texts are "Collecting Folklore in Jonesport, Maine,"
Proceedings of the American Philosophical Society, CI (June, 1957),
270–89; "Mishaps of a Maine Lobsterman," *Northeast Folklore,* I
(Spring, 1958), 1–7; "The Legend of Yoho Cove," *Western Folklore,* XVIII (October, 1959), 329–31; "The Folktale Repertoires of
Two Maine Lobstermen," *Internationaler Kongress der Volkserzählungsforscher in Kiel und Kopenhagen,* ed. K. Ranke (Berlin, 1961),
pp. 74–83; "Oral Styles of American Folk Narrators," in *Style in
Language,* ed. T. A. Sebeok (Cambridge, Mass., 1960), pp. 50–51.

A few texts are also printed in my *American Folklore,* pp. 121–
34, in the discussion of "Maine Coast Yankees," but none of these
are reprinted here. Identifications of the chief informants made in
1956 follow.

James Alley, 76, a nephew of Joshua Alley, lives in Alley's Lane
across from Alfred Alley. He knits heads, mends twine, shucks clams,
and delivers papers, but spent much of his life as a lobster fisherman,
and has also worked in the woods. He is in poor circumstances.
Solidly built, with a large face and a raspy voice, Jim speaks

positively, smiles rarely, and lacks any reputation as a storyteller, although I found his repertoire inexhaustible.

Frank Alley, 84, a brother of James, lives alone in a comfortable house in West Jonesport. He is retired from lobster fishing and other work, has to use an ear trumpet, speaks softly and slowly, but in reminiscing can work up a head of steam. His cherubic features suggest Santa Claus, and belie a robust physique. His minister took him for a drive to Yarmouth, Nova Scotia, eighty miles away, earlier in the summer, for the longest auto trip he had ever made.

Maurice Alley, 60, the son of Frank and Emma Alley, inherits the dream power of his mother and the treasure mania of his father. He lives across from Alley's Lane by the beach, and hauls lobster traps in his own boat. He is large of frame, long of face, soft of speech but garrulous and quite without intentional humor.

Curt Morse, 70, lives in the township of Kennebec some five miles out of Machias, on a scenic cove at the end of a road that passes the homes of many of his nephews and nieces, who work in Machias and own restaurants and stores there. Hence he is known throughout the community as Uncle Curt and enjoys considerable reputation as a comical storyteller. After clamming in the morning, he always walks up and down the main street of Machias in the afternoon, gabbing and joking. He has received publicity in the columns of the *Machias Valley News* and from a stint on Gene Hooper's Cowboy Show touring through Maine, but he has never gone outside the state. Curt is weak of sight but refuses to wear glasses; he has square features, a russet complexion, and sandy hair. He used to lobster fish and take out pleasure parties, who relished his humor. He is intensely gregarious.

Cecil Kelley, 54, lives on a main street in Jonesport but spends most of his time in his camp at Head Harbor Island. For years he worked as a lighthouse keeper, but now owns fishing boats and sardine weirs. He is short and stocky, with puffy cheeks and bright eyes, and talks with great flair and gusto. His neighbors regard him as a witty spinner of stout yarns; when recording him I abandoned the attempt to steer the conversation and let him pour his salty talk onto the tape.

Stuart Alley, 58, lives at the end of Alley's Lane. He is a nephew by marriage to Frank and James. Barrel-chested and roundfaced, he speaks rapidly and with continual good humor; his talent proved to be balladry rather than storytelling. He works as an able-bodied seaman on an oil tanker.

1. SEA TR

Bad Luck at Sea

*A number of the maritime beliefs
found in Horace P. Beck,* The Fol
adelphia, 1957). *Fishermen's sup
include leaving the hatch upside
oilskins or black gloves, and cursi
202), and traveling with a blac
68).*

*The following transcripts are take
tape recordings of conversations I h
and Maurice Alley.*

CECIL KELLEY:

I was down here [Jonesport] when we was b
there [Beals Island], father and I, when th
she laid over here. She was going out next spr
was building a new camp down there. We w
another weir. They shipped a crew to come c
watching her—we was down watching her sai
ing her spars come down by the island. All at
right offa there. And when we came up that nig
that they'd lost a man overboard that night, h
never been heard tell of since. And the next fel
other captain—that feller give up, that captai
cause that was hard luck, see, when he first
very superstitious, see, those people. So he g
they sent a new captain. He took her over in t

against the sun, go right back and put her to the mooring. If you went out that day you'd have bad luck all day long. Oh, yes.

DORSON:

Did certain particular ships become bad-luck ships?

CECIL KELLEY:

Well, I don't know as there's anything to that, but there's some things that works kind of funny. Oh, I've had a few new boats built, and I've owned some boats in my life, and I'd never la'nch one dry again. Never la'nch one dry again.

DORSON:

Why is that?

CECIL KELLEY:

You'll have hard luck with her from the day she goes afloat if you la'nch her dry—never do it. La'nch 'em wet, no matter what it costs you, la'nch 'em wet.

DORSON:

What do you mean by that?

CECIL KELLEY:

When you la'nch 'em wet, put on a big party.

DORSON:

I see what you mean.

CECIL KELLEY:

Have everybody drunk that comes to the la'nching.

DORSON:

Well, did you have an experience when you launched her dry?

CECIL KELLEY:

That's right. That's right. I have.

DORSON:

What happened?

CECIL KELLEY:

This last one that Galls built me—of course he belongs to a church over there on the island. They've got one in everybody's dooryard! And I told him, I said, "Now this boat—I've had a lot of boats, and I've la'nched some of 'em wet and some of 'em dry, and I've found out the wet ones pays the most money. Now this one I want to be sure and la'nch her wet. So when she's la'nched, I want to have cake and sandwiches for the ladies, soda pop for the children, and something a little stronger for the gentlemen." And you know, belonging to the church, that damn thing la'nched her two or three days or a week before I even knew she was in the water. And say, I didn't have her a month before she parted her mooring, went ashore and stove her stem in, busted in her garboards. I had to haul her out and have a whole forefoot put in her, all for'ard works.

And about a year after that the boys and I went on a little gunnin' spree in December. I took a party down to the camp, and it come off below zero that night, and I'll be goddamned if she didn't git ashore again, and broke her rudder off, and skeg off, and punch two or three holes in her, and fill her full of water, engine full of water. Cost me six or seven hundred dollars more to repair her again. And I've had hard luck with her. And then I hauled her into the shop and had her rebuilt, and had a new stem put in her, new stern put on her, new shop rudder. When she went afloat that time she was wet, and don't you forget that. And everybody in the crowd was damp. And I hadn't a bit of trouble since, and I could ride her to a pot wap in a hundred-mile gale and she wouldn't part it now. No, sir.

DORSON:

Ride her to a what?

CECIL KELLEY:

Pot wap [warp]. Six thread. And that's a piece of line, piece of rope, not bigger than that cord you've got right there.

DORSON:

A pot wap!

CECIL KELLEY:

Yeah, lobster pot wap. Thick thread. 'Bout a little larger than a lead pencil there. Yeah. The breaking strain is twelve hundred pounds when it's new. And I could ride her to that and wouldn't have to worry a bit, and before she'd take a line too bigger than your neck, four-inch hawser. Yes, sir. Don't never la'nch one dry. No, sir. Now I got a little one down here in the shop we're going to la'nch next week; she don't amount to much. But she'll go aboard wet.

DORSON:

What do you have to drink at these parties, when you launch her?

CECIL KELLEY:

Oh, assortments you know. Assortments, because a man gets drunk quickest on assortments.

. . .

MAURICE ALLEY:

A three-master come in here for a load of coal at Underwoods'. The rats left her. And they said that was bad luck. So when they got the coal out they started down the reach. And before she got out the reach a man fell overboard. He was drowned, and the fishermen went to work, lined trawls across the reach, tried to catch him, but they didn't never caught him. And then she got right off the beacon right down here at Kelley's Point, and both anchors went overboard. And she was held right up there for all day. They got her anchors back and went out on that trip; she upset and was lost.

DORSON:

Why did the rats leave the ship?

MAURICE ALLEY:

I don't know, but they claim if you see rats leaving a ship why you might as well leave yourself, because that's bad luck.

DORSON:

What are some other things that are bad luck on a ship?

MAURICE ALLEY:

Well, a black dress suitcase. Now, Marshall Kelley and I and Jay Slateman and Alfred Alley and Frank Alley was seining. We went all around west'ard and everywhere and couldn't get a herring, and Jay said we wouldn't get one as long as we had a black dress suitcase. Marshall Kelley and I both had black dress suitcases. So we went in Carver's Cove, and coming out of Carver's Cove we throwed our black dress suitcases overboard. Took the stuff out and throwed 'em overboard. That night we went in to Prettymarsh. That afternoon we shut up over a thousand hogsheads' worth of fish.

DORSON:

What else is bad luck on a ship? Something about a hatch?

MAURICE ALLEY:

Yeah. Turn a hatch bottom up that's bad luck, you'll lose the hatch and the hold, bad luck. You go to Boston or anywhere around Rockland. You go aboard one of them fishermen, turn the hatch bottom up, you'll go aboard the wharf in a hurry. Any vessel. They want you awful careful 'bout when they take hatches off you never turn one bottom up.

Buying the Wind

Twelve persons in Jonesport, Beals Island, Columbia Falls, and Machias told me of wicked individuals in the neighborhood who had bought wind and repented when a gale promptly sprang up. Half of these texts center on Paris Kaler, a notorious blasphemer (see the version by Lee Smith in Dorson, American Folklore, *pp. 129–30). Other variants involve George Beal, Captain Belmore, Nick Bryant, Cam Crowley, and Malcolm Lowell, impious men all. Instead of a coin, Lowell threw his jacket overboard to buy a jacket's worth of wind.*

The older compendium by Fletcher S. Bassett, Legends and Superstitions of the Sea and of Sailors, *contains a chapter on "Wind-Makers and Storm-Raisers" (pp. 101–47), but makes no mention of wind-buying. A Hebridean story, "MacVurich Asking for the Wind," lacks the element of purchase (Stories from South Uist, told by Angus MacLellan, pp. 94–95). A Maine coast wind-buyer appears in John Gould,* Farmer Takes a Wife, *pp. 78–79.*

Two texts follow, from Maurice Alley and Donald M. Taverner.

MAURICE ALLEY:

Paris Kaler was the captain of a vessel, and he got out one day and got becalmed. He was going to the west'ard and wasn't no wind. And he wanted some wind, so he throwed a quarter overboard. He wanted to buy a quarter's worth. He said he wished it would blow so hard she wouldn't lug a nail in a paul-post. He said, "I'll stand by with a pin maul to drive it in."

So he said it commenced to blow, it blowed till it blowed the sails off her, and he was three or four days off his course; he was three or four days getting back again. He said if he knew it was as cheap as that he wouldn't have bought half as much.

DORSON:

Well, weren't you on a ship where they bought some wind?

MAURICE ALLEY:

Yeah, we was up buying mussels up to Sheffelin's Point, and the feller was with me he says, "I'm going to buy some wind." I says, "I guess you hadn't better, you'll get more than you bargained for." And he says "I'm going to buy a nickel's worth anyway." So he throwed a nickel overboard, and the time he got in there by Bar Harbor, going up into Sou'west Harbor, we had all the wind we wanted. It breezed up in good shape. We had all we could fly on.

DORSON:

Well is that a bad thing to do, to buy wind?

MAURICE ALLEY:

Yes, never buy wind when you're on a boat. You're daring God Almighty, and he won't stand for that. You'll get all the wind you want.

DORSON:

This Paris Kaler was kind of a bad man?

MAURICE ALLEY:

Yes, he was a wicked man. Paris was swearing, ripping, tearing, a wicked man.

DORSON:

How did he die?

MAURICE ALLEY:

His vessel, the walk caught afire in Boston, and in the excitement of getting it cast off from the wharf he got heart trouble and died.

.   .   .

This text, alone in the present group, was recorded after the Jonesport trip. After giving a talk on folklore at the

University of Maine in August, 1960, I met Donald M. Taverner, secretary of the university's alumni association, who told me this splendid version of the windbuyer, as he had heard it from his wife's father, a retired skipper. Taverner was born in Augusta, Maine, in 1919, and in the course of his talks to alumni groups he often drew on the fund of Maine stories he had absorbed as a boy. At my request, he later recorded half a dozen of these stories and sent me the tape.

The following story was told to me by my father-in-law, Theodore Rowell, of 193 Mariner Street, South Portland, Maine. The story was told to him in about 1890 by one Clyde Wing of Liberty, Maine, who had heard it in the town of Friendship, a coastal village. It concerns the Maine fishing industry at the close of the nineteenth century. At that time Maine fishermen took their two-masted, Gloucester-type fishing schooners off the Grand Banks of Newfoundland. Of course, the objective involved both speed and ice, for the only propulsion was wind, and refrigeration was by natural ice cut from the lakes of the towns bordering the coast which had such inland lakes: towns like Union, Warren, and similar communities. The vessels had their hulls or their holds lined with this ice, and they went off the Grand Banks in an effort to get as large a catch as possible and get back before the ice melted and the fish began to spoil.

On this particular occasion, as told in the story, an old Maine fishing captain, a taciturn and crusty old soul from around St. George, took his two-masted schooner off the Grand Banks and in a very few days had a hull-down catch, and the vessel lay low in the water with many thousands of dollars worth of fish. The old fishing skipper came about and headed back to port, which would have been Rockland, Maine. About a day and a half out of Rockland, the wind "pooched," and the vessel lay still in the water, unable to move. The skipper became concerned about his melting ice and the possible loss of the fish, and the value involved, and the profit, and so forth. Now he was a fine seaman; in fact, the thing in life which he knew best was seamanship; so he brought all his experience and all his

training to bear. He put a longboat overside and attempted
to tow his vessel off a leeward iceberg to catch a breeze, and
that didn't work. So he lined his crew up on the starboard side
of the vessel and ran them to the port side in an effort to heel
the vessel and fill the pip-sail with a little air, and that didn't
work. He tried sculling the vessel with his rudder, and that didn't
work. So finally he turned to the thing which he was second
best at, and that was profanity. He strode back and forth with
a torrent of profanity—everything in the book and a few
things he made up himself.

Now, down below deck was a cook's helper who was a very
pious man, a religious soul who was very much disturbed by
all the profanity drifting through the deckboards to him. He
put dishrags in his ears, he put a pot over his head, he crawled
under the galley; he did everything to drown out the profanity,
but it was no good. He couldn't do it. So finally he mustered
his courage and he went topside. And he faced the skipper on
the quarterdeck and he says:

"Skipper, you're as fine a seaman as ever grew up on the
Maine coast. You know the ways of the sea and the ways of a
vessel. If it was humanly possible for you to move this ship,
we'd be docked at Rockland right now discharging our fish
and gettin' paid off. But it ain't humanly possible, and you
ought to know it. You can't move the ship, and instead of
calling on the only power that can help you, you stand here
and call him bad names. Now you're not going to get any-
wheres that way; you can take my word for that, skipper. The
thing for you to do is call on the Lord, make him a love offering to show your good intent, and ask him to send you a little
wind. Ask him to help you out. Skipper, if you'll do that you'll
get your wind, you'll get your wind, believe me."

Well, the old skipper shifted his cud to the starboard cheek
and spit it up against the mains'l with a great splash. He says,
"By God, I got nothing to lose. I've tried everything else."

And he reached in his pocket, and he got a half-dollar. He
raised his eyes heavenward, held the half-dollar at arm's length,
and said, "Lord, if you're as good as this guy says you are,
ship me a little wind." And he pitched the coin overside.

No sooner had that coin hit the surface of the water than

a 110-mile-an-hour hurricane came up and stripped the vessel clean; the foremast went overside, she lost two boats, two men were washed overside and drowned, and she scudded for shore at seventy-five knots, which is a pretty good speed for a sailing vessel. She piled up on the beach down below South Thomaston, in a tremendous catastrophe of men, fish, rigging, sail, and vessel. And the old skipper came to to find himself below the surface, and about six feet of dead fish covering him. He wormed his way sunward to get the air and found himself looking square in the eye of the old cook's helper, who was just as enthusiastic as he'd been offshore.

"Skipper," said the cook's helper, "Skipper, didn't I tell ye. If ye call on the Lord, ask him to help ye out, make him a love offering to snow your good intent, ask him to slip ye a little wind, that you'll get your wind? You got your wind, Skipper, you got your wind."

So the old skipper, who still had his cud of tobacco aboard, shifted it to the other cheek, looked up and down the beach at the bodies of his men laying in the surf, the fish in the trees, the riggin' up and down the shoreline, timbers all over the place. He said, "Yes," he said, "but by God if I'd known his wind was so damn cheap, I wouldn't a' ordered so much."

The Haunted Ship "Resolution"

The familiar Motif E334.2.1, "Ghost of murdered person haunts burial spot," is present here.

On a trip to Beals Island, I was directed by a young fellow at the pier to Eben Walter Alley, 84, as a teller of old tales. Eben heard the ghostly story that follows from his grandfather John Alley, a pioneer on Wass Island (now joined to Beals by a bridge).

EBEN WALTER ALLEY:

Well, John Alley was in Boston—he was there, I suppose, with a cargo or something. And while he was there this fellow Charles Ayers came around aboard his vessel, that he was acquainted with. And he spent the evening with him. When he went back to his vessel, he went with him so as to give him company back, you know. And when they got round to his vessel, why there was a man on deck. He said he was a large man, and had a piece of rope in his hand. And of course he went right on board, Captain did. Well this fellow took him [Ayers] by the collar, and he started to lick him with this rope. Well of course Grandfather he didn't stop, he went to his vessel. And when he went back to his vessel, why he heard him hollering for help. Well of course he said he didn't dass go back there, because he knowed there was trouble, and he didn't want to get mixed up in it, so he stayed there to his vessel.

Well, then, after that—of course he didn't know what happened—after that he was in Rockport, and he fell in with this vessel. Well he bought her. He thought it was a good buy, and he bought the vessel. And put a couple of men 'board of her and brought her down, and when they took the wind off nor'east they anchored up here in the western bay. And one fellow took the boat and went home and left the other fellow aboard. Well he said he felt kind of lonesome, he went on deck and walked around, and this man started in walking with him. And he walked the deck all night with him. Well in the morning there was a fellow come along with another boat, small boat, and he got in with him and he set him ashore. Well then he told his grandfather where the vessel was, and he went out and got her and took her in to Deep Cove, and then Sunday morning my grandfather, on my mother's side, and some other fellows went down to see the vessel.

DORSON:

What was the name of this other grandfather?

EBEN WALTER ALLEY:

Levi. That was mother's part. And they went down to see the vessel and when they opened the door, the gangway door, there was this big cat down there. He said it was an awful big cat, and her eyes were stuck right out, and he said it scairt him, so they slammed the door to and left. Well, Grandfather went and got the vessel and brought her up here and put her on the beach. Well then after that, mornings he could hear the vessel hail. He could hear this man singing out, " 'Resolution' ahoy."

DORSON:

That was the name of the ship?

EBEN WALTER ALLEY:

That was the name of the vessel, yes. And of course he didn't know what to make of it, but he said he was going to try and find out if he could what it was. And he come over one day and tore the cabin floor off, to see if he could find anything. And that man's bones was under that floor. When he found 'em, he said it come right to him that that was the vessel that that man, John Ayers or Charles Ayers, whichever it 'twas, was licked aboard of. And he took the bones all into a box, and took 'em over there in the lane and buried 'em. And he said he never heard anything more.

But he took the wreckage offa her, he wrecked her for wreckage and put her in the barn. And Grandfather Washington —that was on father's side—he said he used to tend the barn, tend the cattle, and he said when he git through, why that would come to him and would scare him you know, thinking about that man. And he said he would jump just as far as he could jump, and then would go up to the house. And of course the vessel she went to pieces on the beach there, ended up the whole thing.

The Sailor Who Went Inland

A three-thousand-year-old variant of the following tale is lodged in The Odyssey, *a little prettied up by Homer (tr. E. V. Rieu, New York, Penguin Books, 1946, p. 148):*

"You must take a well-cut oar and go on till you reach a people who know nothing of the sea and never use salt with their food, so that our crimson-painted ships and the long oars that serve those ships as wings are quite beyond their ken. And this will be your cue— a very clear one, which you cannot miss. When you fall in with some other traveler who speaks of the "winnowing-fan" you are carrying on your shoulder,

*the time will have come for you to plant your shapely
oar in the earth and offer Lord Poseidon the rich sacri-
fice of a ram, a bull, and a breeding-boar."*

*The currency of this tale among modern Greek sail-
ors, who attach it to St. Nicholas, patron saint of sea-
farers, is reported by Irwin T. Sanders, Rainbow in
the Rock (Cambridge, Mass., 1962), p. 35.*

FRANK ALLEY:

Well there was another one about a young fellow. He started
out, he wanted to get married. And he wanted to marry a girl
that didn't know nothing 'bout salt water or a boat. He wanted
to go back in the country and marry a girl that didn't know
nothing 'bout salt water, nor the boat, nor anything like that.
So he made him a little oar, put it in his pocket, small one you
know. So he traveled along, and he come to an old farmhouse.
He wanted to put up there that night. And a young woman
come to the door, and they guessed they could put him up.
So they put him up, and that evening they got to talking and
he took this oar out to see if she knew what it 'twas. "Well,
now," she says, "that looks like an oar." So he made up his
mind he didn't want nothing to do with that.

So the next morning he started again. He traveled the
night and came to another farmhouse, and they put him up
there. And there was another young girl there about sixteen.
Well he got talking with her and by and by he took this oar
out, asked her what that was. Well she looked it over and she
said it looked just like mother's pudding stick. "Yes sir, there's
the girl I want."

So he stayed there quiet with the farmer and got married.
And first night she started to bed 'head of him. So he got ready,
he went upstairs to bed. When he got up, she was in bed flat
on her back, with all of her clothes stripped off, and her legs
sticking right up in the air. And he says, "What in the world
are you doing there?" "Well," she says, "there's been a squall,
and I've got everything clewed up. Now I'm scudding on the
bare poles."

So I guess he found out she knew something about salt
water.

2. HERO LEGENDS OF BARNEY BEAL

THE SAGA OF BARNEY is sketched in *American Folklore*, 124–28. A broadside ballad about Barney Beal and his feats is reprinted in Dorson, *Jonathan Draws the Long Bow*, 124–25, from the *Lewiston Journal* of November 1, 1938. Other references are given there (p. 125, n. 13) to reports on Barney. The exploits of Barney felling a horse with his fist, and breaking the arm of a Canadian sailor, are mentioned in the Federal Writers' Project, *Maine, A Guide "Down East"* (Boston, 1937), p. 233.

The general motif is F610, "Remarkably strong man," which applies to such stalwarts as Beowulf, Hercules, and Samson.

Barney Kills a Horse with his Fist

> *Motif F628.1, "Strong man kills animals with own hands," applies to the following well-known deed of Barney Beal, of which two texts are given.*

DORSON:

Have you heard stories about Barney Beal? Who was supposed to be the strong man of Beals Island?

CECIL KELLEY:

Oh, yes, sir! Yes, sir! Yes, sir! Know some of Barney's folks.

DORSON:

Uh-huh.

CECIL KELLEY:

I know some tales they told of him; course it's 'fore my

time a bit; they vouch for the truth of them, and maybe they
are so. They claimed he could lug a barrel of flour under each
arm, and small things like that. I guess he was quite a powerful
boy. And I do know that he hit a policeman's horse with his
fist behind the ear and killed him.

DORSON:

My goodness.

CECIL KELLEY:

Broke his neck. Broke the horse's neck because he didn't
like the policeman. He said something to him, and he was in
Portland. And that's when the police were on horses. And he
hauled off and thumped the horse and broke his neck—killed
him right in the street.

. . .

DORSON:

And what was that one about the horse at Rockland?

MAURICE ALLEY:

Yeh, he was up to—well, I couldn't say whether that was
Rockland or Portland, but up that way—that he was goin'
up the road. And he told the boys with him, he says, "If that
hoss un'takes to bite me, I'm going a kill him." And he said,
when he got right long side the horse, he whinnered, and rolled
his ears back, and when he did, he [Barney] hauled off and
hit him, back-handed slap, and the horse dropped right in his
harness, dead. Killed 'em, right there.

Barney Beal Kills Prize Fighter

*Motif F628.2.5, "Strong man kills men with own hands,"
is known in Irish myth.*

DORSON:

And then Barney Beal got in a prize fight at Boston, you were
telling me?

MAURICE ALLEY:

Yeh, he got in a prize fight up there to the west'ard, 'round

Boston there somewhere. And he went in to see the prize fight, but one of the fighters—something happened—didn't show up, so they challenged anybody for three rounds with this prize fighter. So Tall Barney says, "By God, I'll take him on." So he went up there with his leather boots and all, and they hold up a pair of gloves.

And they asked him, they said, "Ain't 'cha goin' put no tights on?" "No," he says, "lick 'im the way I am." So he said he went in the ring, and this prize fighter kinda hauled off to hit Barney in the chin. Barney struck him in the stomach and knocked his stomach right into him. Killed him.

DORSON:

Killed him?

MAURICE ALLEY:

Killed him.

DORSON:

Good Lord.

Barney Beal Lifts Rock out of Dory

> *Motif F624.2, "Strong man lifts large stone," is reported in Irish and Jewish tradition. Frank Alley and his son Maurice give separate accounts of this exploit.*

DORSON:

What do you know about Barney Beal?

FRANK ALLEY:

Barney Beal was a regular giant. He was about six feet and a half tall, great big broad shoulders. He was rawboned, you know. If he'd a been fat, he'd a weighed five hundred. He was great big in his arms. He'd sit in a chair like this and drum a little tune on the floor with his fingers. Just sit in the chair like that—great, long arms. Very good giant.

DORSON:

You saw him?

FRANK ALLEY:

Oh, yes. He'd come down to the house one time, and he'd

been drinking. He'd drink a lot. And his two boys, Charles Henry and little Poley, come down after him in a dory. Well they put a great big rock, all that they could get into the dory. Because they know'd that he was heavy anyway. He weighed about three hundred pounds, you know. An old strappin' giant. And they thought probably he'd been drinking, he'd upset the dory.

So the both of 'em put a big rock in it they supposed that he couldn't get out, see. Well, the bank was steep there. It's worse than that wharf, you know. And he was up to the house there, talking. And they come up after him.

"Well," he says, 'I'll go with you." And he called his hands, "Dewclaws. Dewclaws."

DORSON:

Dewclaws?

FRANK ALLEY:

Great big hands. He called them "Dewclaws." Great big hands of his. Twice as big as mine.

DORSON:

What does that mean, "Dewclaws"?

FRANK ALLEY:

Well, his fists, you know. Hands.

DORSON:

Uh-huh.

FRANK ALLEY:

And, he run down to that steep bank and he run down over that steep bank just the same as a cat. Yes, sir. And down to that dory. And he said, "What in this earth do you have that rock in the dory for?"

He jumped into that dory, picked that rock right up, and hauled it out on the beach. Laid up in the stern of the boat, and they rode him home.

Oh, he was a giant.

.   .   .

DORSON:

Barney Beal did quite a number of remarkable things, didn't he? The time they put the rock in his dory?

MAURICE ALLEY:

Yeh. Will Beal and his brother went down after him. He was down to Hatchet Harbor, down to Uncle Johnny Beal's. And they went down to get him. And they rowed the dory down. And each one of them was around two-hundred-pound men, strong, his brothers. And they turned the dory over on the side, and rolled this big rock in 'er. And then they went down, 'cause they thought Barney was drunk, he'd fall on the side of the dory and upset 'em. So they put that rock in for ballast. And he run down over the hill. When he see that rock, he reached down, he says, "By God, why'd they put that rock in this dory for?" he said. Picked it up, throwed it overboard, set up in the stern, and they rowed him home. Yep, fell up the stairs, set up there, and they rowed him home. Two big men.

Feats of Barney

> *Following are the reminiscences of Barney's son and his great-great-granddaughter.*
>
> *Some motifs already mentioned reappear here, such as F628.2.5, "Strong man kills men with own hands," and F628.1, "Strong man kills animals with own hands." Other motifs are F624.7, "Strong man carries boat," and F631, "Strong man carries giant load."*

DORSON:

This is July 3, 1956, and I am now in the home of Mr. Napoleon Beal, who is one of the only two children living of the famous Barney Beal of Beals Island. Mr. Napoleon Beal is one of twelve children, and only one older brother still survives. Now, how old were you when your father died, Mr. Beal?

NAPOLEON BEAL:

I was around twenty, I think.

DORSON:

Do you remember what he looked like?

NAPOLEON BEAL:

Oh, lord, yes. I used to go around together with him a lot.

DORSON:

What did he look like?

NAPOLEON BEAL:

Oh, he's a nice-looking man.

DORSON:

Uh-huh. How big was he?

NAPOLEON BEAL:

He was six foot six in his stockin' feet.

DORSON:

Uh-huh. And did he have long arms?

NAPOLEON BEAL:

Oh, yes. He could set in a chair and he could touch the floor with his fingers like that, settin' up in the chair.

DORSON:

My goodness. Well, you were telling me that he was in Portland bowling one time and had a little incident.

NAPOLEON BEAL:

Well, I heard it. They told me about it. I never saw it, 'cause I was too young then to be with him.

DORSON:

What happened?

NAPOLEON BEAL:

Well, they got into a little squabble over the bowling, and the old fellow said 'twas his time to bowl, and the other man said 'twas his. So they got into a little squabble, and the old man hit him, and they said it stove his breast in. So afterward, he died.

DORSON:

Oh.

NAPOLEON BEAL:

But he sent down to the vessel—my father's vessel—he sent down for him to come up.

DORSON:

Uh-huh.

NAPOLEON BEAL:

And he [my father] went up and told him that he was all to blame himself and didn't want to have any hard feelings that way.

DORSON:

Uh-huh. Where did your father hit him?

NAPOLEON BEAL:

In the stomach. Right in the breast.

DORSON:

And what happened to him then? What did he do?

NAPOLEON BEAL:

Oh, it just busted his breast in, I suppose.

DORSON:

Uh-huh.

NAPOLEON BEAL:

That's what they said.

DORSON:

And then you were telling me about his lifting an anchor one time. What was that?

NAPOLEON BEAL:

Oh, that was in the Southwest Harbor; they lost an anchor from the vessel, and he went after another one, him'n two of his crew. They—the two—couldn't get it aboard, so they went after someone else. And while they was gone he took it and lugged it down and put it acrost the boat, and he sank right down into the sand so that it was way above his ankles.

DORSON:

You say he used to lug great weights, and you were just telling me some of the things he could carry.

NAPOLEON BEAL:

Oh, yes, he could. When he used to go sailing the vessels taking the clams and stuff to the market, he never used to take a tackle and get it out, he allus handed it right out over the hatchway.

DORSON:

Oh. Well, how heavy would be those barrels?

NAPOLEON BEAL:

Two hundred pounds.

DORSON:

My goodness. And then you were telling how he used to haul the dory.

NAPOLEON BEAL:

Oh, yes, he used to haul the dory up the beach.

DORSON:

Uh-huh.

NAPOLEON BEAL:

A big fifteen-foot dory, and he'd haul it. Hooked his hands, you know, where the breast hooks on the dory and haul her right up on the bank.

DORSON:

And how heavy would that be?

NAPOLEON BEAL:

Oh, land, I don't know. Let's see, that would weigh, I guess, oh seven or eight hundred pounds.

DORSON:

Uh-huh. And then when he was drinking the water from the barrel . . .

NAPOLEON BEAL:

Oh, yes. He would take a water barrel and drink out the bottom hole of the water barrel. Pick it right up in his arms.

DORSON:

How heavy would that be?

NAPOLEON BEAL:

Oh, that would be a hundred fifty, two hundred pounds.

DORSON:

Well, do some of you remember some—have heard some stories about Barney Beal? Can you recall something, Mrs. Napoleon Beal? Anybody here? You must have heard some things about him. Hm? No? There's something else, Mr. Napoleon Beal? About your father? What was the horse story?

NAPOLEON BEAL:

Well, he was in Rockland, I think it was this time, and he was walkin' up the street and a horse was standin'—the man was drivin' the horse on the side of the road. When he went by, the horse nipped at him. And he hauled off and hit him with the back hand—slapped him, and he fell right dead in his tracks.

DORSON:

My goodness.

WOMAN'S VOICE:

Believe it or not.

DORSON:

What was that one you just were telling about?

MRS. ROBERT DAVIS:

Well, you know, when he pulled the dory up by hand, and some boys was having fun with him, and they nailed the dory right down to the slip where he had it there. And he found out what they'd done—they played a trick on him. And he just give one yank on it, and the planks came right off of it. [*Laughter*] Pulled the dory right out.

DORSON:

What's your name, please?

MRS. ROBERT DAVIS:

Mrs. Robert Davis.

DORSON:

I see. You're ——

MRS. ROBERT DAVIS:

Martha Davis.

DORSON:

You're the granddaughter of Mr. ——

MRS. ROBERT DAVIS:

Great-granddaughter.

DORSON:

Great-granddaughter of ——

MRS. ROBERT DAVIS:

And he's a great-great-grandson [*pointing to the baby in her arms*].

DORSON:

Of whom?

MRS. ROBERT DAVIS:

Gregory Beal.

DORSON:

Oh, I see. So he's the great-great-great-grandson of Barney!

MRS. ROBERT DAVIS:

Yes.

DORSON:

Mrs. Davis, you just remembered something else about him. What was that? That fellow came up to fight him.

MRS. ROBERT DAVIS:

Oh, it was a big boxer, wasn't it?

VOICE:
Yeh.

MRS. ROBERT DAVIS:
That come out to the Head [Head Harbor Island] about
him. He'd heard about him. And how strong he was and everything. And he'd come down from Boston to fight with him. When
he saw him down at the wharf, when the man saw granddaddy
coming down the lane with two big barrels, one under each arm,
he turned around and went back to Boston. [*Laughter*]

How Barney Beal Awed the Bully
of Peak's Island

> *The theme of the challenger who flees from the cham-*
> *pion when he sees a demonstration of strength by the*
> *renowned strong man, or one of his relatives, is recur-*
> *rent. Mrs. Robert Davis in the preceding tape told a*
> *variant of the tale here given by Esten Beal. In "The*
> *Mighty Wrestler Usodagawa" (Dorson, Folk Legends*
> *of Japan, pp. 174–76), a challenger departed hastily*
> *when he found he could not move a brazier the cham-*
> *pion's mother held in one hand. Type 1962A, The Great*
> *Wrestlers, involves this kind of intimidation, with ex-*
> *amples reported only from India.*

DORSON:
This is July 17th, 1956, and I am on Beals Island. It is a beauti-
ful day. I'm talking to Mr. Esten L. Beal in his garage. And
Mr. Beal is the grandson of Barney Beal. Who's your father,
Mr. Beal?

ESTEN BEAL:
My father was Charles Henry Beal.

DORSON:
And he was a son of Barney?

ESTEN BEAL:
He was one of the Barney Beal sons. Yes.

DORSON:
Well, you've seen your grandfather then?

ESTEN BEAL:

No. He died before I was old enough to remember him.

DORSON:

Uh-huh. But you've heard your father talk about him?

ESTEN BEAL:

I've heard my father and many other people speak about Grandfather Beal.

DORSON:

What did he look like?

ESTEN BEAL:

Well, he was a tall man. Between six and seven feet tall. I don't know the exact measurements, but he was a big, rawbone man, very powerful. He was considered the most powerful man in this part of the country.

DORSON:

You say that he could lift salt sacks?

ESTEN BEAL:

Yes, he could take a sack o'salt under each arm and walk off with it like I would a loaf of bread under each arm.

DORSON:

How did he meet his death?

ESTEN BEAL:

Well, the way I understand it, he was pulling a fifteen-foot fishing dory up over a sea-wall, and he strained his heart.

DORSON:

Now, you were telling me a very interesting account of the time the bully of Peak's Island challenged him to a fight.

ESTEN BEAL:

Yes, I've heard that story told many a time, that he went into Peak's Island to get water for his fishing vessel. And the bully of Peak's Island met him on the beach and challenged him to a fight. So he told him that as soon as he filled his water barrel why he would accommodate him. So he went and filled his water barrel. And they used to use these large molasses tierces for water barrels. So he brought the water barrel down on the beach, and he said, "Well," he said, "I guess before we start, I'll have a drink of water." So he picked up the water barrel and took a drink out of the bunghole, set it down on the beach, and the bully of Peak's Island walked up, slapped him on the shoulder, and he says, "Mr. Beal, I don't think I'll have anything to do with you whatever."

DORSON:

How heavy would that be?

ESTEN BEAL:

Oh, that would probably weigh five or six hundred pounds, maybe more.

DORSON:

An ordinary man probably couldn't even move it.

ESTEN BEAL:

Oh, an ordinary man couldn't lift it, no.

DORSON:

Where is Peak's Island?

ESTEN BEAL:

Peak's Island is just to the eastward of Portland.

How Barney Beal Got the Bump on his Nose

> *This triumph suggests Motif F614.10, "Strong hero fights whole army alone." Two versions are given of Barney's fight with hostile fishermen or revenue men, by Riley Beal and Jim Alley.*

DORSON:

Today is July 9, 1956, and I am on Beals Island after quite a rough crossing on the ferry. And I am glad to be here in one piece. And I am in the hospitable home of Mr. and Mrs. Riley Beal, who were born right on this island. Is that right, Mr Beal?

RILEY BEAL:

That's right.

DORSON:

What year were you born here?

RILEY BEAL:

1890.

DORSON:

1890. And you're a grandson of the famous Barney Beal?

RILEY BEAL:

That's right.

DORSON:

How old were you when he died?

RILEY BEAL:

I think somewheres right round—between eleven and twelve.

DORSON:

And you saw him pretty often?

RILEY BEAL:

Oh, sure.

DORSON:

You were telling me how he got that bump on his nose. His nose, it was a little broken in this picture.

RILEY BEAL:

That was gotten by a blow from an oar in the hands of an Englishman, from a cutter, down off Grand Manan. They were down there fishing, got inside of the limits, and they were not suppose to be there o'course. So they came after 'em in the cutter. It was a calm day, and they had to come in what they call a longboat, and when they tried to take them in, they wouldn't go—my grandfather and his son, John Beal. They wouldn't go in, and they were bound to take 'em. So they came to blows, and they hit him, my grandfather, across the nose and broke it, broke his nose. So he took the oars and broke them up and threw them overboard. They took a gun to him, and he broke that up, bent it up, and threw it overboard. And the largest man aboard—course he thought he would take 'em —so he took hold his coat to pull 'em in aboard the longboat. So he [Barney] grabbed him by the arm and twisted his arm around till it broke.

DORSON:

Oh, boy!

RILEY BEAL:

That was how it happened, the way he got his nose broken.

. . .

DORSON:

And then there was one time he had a fight with a couple
Gloucester fishermen. You were just telling me about that. He
bent the gun, you remember?

JIM ALLEY:

Oh, that was down back yonder—herrin' in there. Barney
had his herrin' nets out, and he rowed down in the morning, and
there's a couple Gloucester fishermen in a dory, and they was
under his net. And when he rowed by their heads, he could see
them. He was standing up there, shoving that dory with them
oars. Said them oars'd double right up and that dory's bow
would go down every time he'd take a stroke. And see'd them
under his net, and it made him mad.

Well, they see'd him, and they knew it was Barney, and
they knew Barney pretty well, I guess, and they throwed the
net off and beat it and tried to get clear of him. And he pulled
for them, and he found out they's gonna shoot Barney. And
Barney grabbed off the muzzle, and he bent her right up double
and fired her back in the dory, and cuffed their ears in good
shape, and told 'em he wanted 'em to leave his nets alone.

DORSON:

I guess they did.

JIM ALLEY:

Yeah, I guess they did, and that was just as true as I set
here, that was straight.

The Cause of Barney's Death

> Motif F615.0.1, "Death of strong man," is always of
> major importance in heroic legend.

DORSON:

And how did your grandfather meet his death?

RILEY BEAL:

By straining the muscles around his heart by haulin' up a
dory on Pond Island. He done that every day for all summer

and for the fall. He would come in from lobster fishing, get out, put his hand in the back in the stern of the boat in the dory, other hand on the gunn'l [gunwale], and work up, just as easily as any ordinary man could haul up with a small skiff. That was a feat that would take four men to do—four ordinary men.

3. WITCHES AND SPIRITS

TRADITIONS OF NEW ENGLAND witches from printed sources, chiefly town histories, are summarized in Dorson, *Jonathan Draws the Long Bow*, pp. 33–44. Beck discusses witches in Maine in *The Folklore of Maine*, pp. 69–73, suggesting that their origins are imputed to Massachusetts. The story of how Aunt Peggy Beal threw the spell back on Mother Hicks by scorching a bewitched sheep and then refusing to loan an object requested by Mother Hicks is in *Maine, A Guide 'Down East'*, pp. 233–34.

Mother Hicks the Witch

> *Motif G275.3.1, "Witch burned by burning bewitched animal," cites extensive references in George Lyman Kittredge, Witchcraft in Old and New England (Cambridge, Mass., 1929).*
>
> *This recording was made in the house of Margaret Alley, daughter-in-law of the Joshua Alley whom fieldworkers on the* Linguistic Atlas of America *met in 1932, when he was ninety-one, and found to be a remarkable storyteller. The George Lavignys were a younger couple visiting her that evening.*

JAMES ALLEY:

Well, Mother Hicks was a witch. I heard father tell about her. She was a witch. If she wanted anything and you didn't give it, she'd bewitch it, see. And it wouldn't be no good. And they had a cow on Beals Island, and she wanted that cow. And she bewitched the cow. And that cow'd swing around, take jumps, bite herself. Well, they said only thing to do was to kill that cow. That's all there is to it.

So a fellow comes along and say, "Look, do you want to get rid of Mother Hicks?" And they says yes. "You take that cow and kill her and build you up a roaring fire, and fire her innards into that fire, and you'll get rid of Mother Hicks." And they done it. "And it wasn't no time," he says, "they'll be somebody here after something. If they get anything out of your house, she'll get well." And wasn't no time—you've hearn it, Maggie—and wasn't no time before there was two boys come, and they said they had all they could do to keep that innards into that fire, bounds to get out. And he said, "Mother Hicks is burning up, she wants something out of the house." And they wouldn't gin it to her, and that's the end of her. Now I've hearn father tell that. And a lot of people'll tell you that.

GEORGE LAVIGNY:

What happened to Mother Hicks? Did she die, or was she in the fire?

JAMES ALLEY:

No, she wasn't in the fire. When they throwed that innards in, that bewitched her, see, and then she burned up inside.

MAGGIE ALLEY:

She's buried down in Old House Point, this Mrs. Hicks, yes, right down at Old House Point. So it's true.

JAMES ALLEY:

If you could get down to the cape shore and look—I been down there and looked at it—and see a gulch, it's named Mother Hicks's Gulch. And she straddled across that gulch with a apron full of cranberries, and if you could go down you'd see where she straddled; you wouldn't never nobody believe it.

MRS. GEORGE LAVIGNY:

I didn't believe it. I thought Dad was telling fairy tales.

MAGGIE ALLEY:

No, they're true.

JAMES ALLEY:

Well, it's straight in the name of Mother Hicks's Gulch. I been there and looked at it. It's a big long gulch, some wide too, and she straddled across there with a apron full of cranberries.

MAGGIE ALLEY:

If she wanted anything, and you wouldn't give it to her, she'd take and bewitch you. She was just witchcraft.

JAMES ALLEY:

Everybody was scared of her.

Calling Up the Spirits

> *A description of this practice is given in* American Folklore, *pp. 128–29. The use of a witch as medium, in the first transcript that follows, is by no means requisite to calling up the spirits.*

"Uncle Allen Alley Calls Up the Spirit of Mother Hicks"

DORSON:

Well, then, there was one other thing I was going to ask you about. You said that your Uncle Allen used to call up the spirit of Mother Hicks.

JIM ALLEY:

Yeh. That's what he called for.

DORSON:

Well, how would he do it? How did he go about it?

JIM ALLEY:

Oh, he'd just sit there and ask for Mother Hicks. He'd sit there singing a little, "Mother Hicks's spirit, Mother Hicks's spirit." By and by [*knocks*] knocks on the table.

DORSON:

And then would she answer questions?

JIM ALLEY:

Well, you'd ask her questions and she'd [*knocks*] once for "no" and twice for "yes," you know, on the table.

DORSON:

But she was supposed to be a bad spirit, wasn't she?

JIM ALLEY:

Oh, gee, you couldn't believe nothing she told you.

DORSON:

Well, why would he ask for her?

JIM ALLEY:

I don't know. You wouldn't believe—I wouldn't believe nothing. Well, now, I was right there in the house, and Uncle Allen says, "Tip that table over and see how far you can put that table over 'thout that lamp sliding." And the table come right in his lap and the lamp stayed there, right in his lap. And Uncle Allen says, "Now, is there anyone in the house want to pick that lamp up and set it back again, to see if you can make it stay?" I was one of 'em. I picked it up. Two or three of us. You couldn't make that lamp stick on that table to save your life. Flied right off. But it tipped down, the table tipped down when he done it, and the lamp stayed there.

And Harmy Alley come in the door, and there was a pair of scissors on the table, and he says, "Fire them scissors at Harmy." And them scissors and that table tipped quick, and them scissors struck right over his head in the door. I was there, and I seed that when they done that, by gorry. It scairt me. I didn't want to be around when he was following that up. And a lot of people got scared. They wouldn't go there when he called her. If they were there when he called up the spirits, get right out. They'd get right out of the house; they didn't like it.

DORSON:

Well, what would he do? Would he be able to do bad things after he talked with the spirit? Your uncle?

JIM ALLEY:

Why, he'd just ask her questions, that's all.

"The Spirits Reveal Thieves"

FRANK ALLEY:

Father and mother lived over at Warren Kelley's, down there on the island. That was before I was born, you know. And this John Beal lived just acrost the cove, had went down 'round to another cove and had found a log had drifted in there, a good log, and he wanted it, so he went and got a line, a brand new line, and fastened it. And when he went 'round after it, the line was gone. So he didn't know what in the world or who took that line. He wanted to find out, so that night he come over to Uncle Warren's and wanted father and mother to call up the spirits and tell him who got that line. And he didn't know Warren Kelley had got it. He didn't know who got it. Never mistrusted of Warren Kelley.

So they called up the spirits, and they went to guessing, on the island, who got the line. Well, they guessed everybody on the island they could think of but Warren Kelley. Course they didn't want to name him till the last one.

DORSON:

Because they lived in his house?

FRANK ALLEY:

Yes, they lived in his house. And by and by, "Did Warren Kelley get that line?" "Yes." And Warren Kelley was walking the floor. Well, they said, "What did he do with it?" Well, they named everything they could think of. At last they said, "Well, did he make cow-tiles of it?" They said, "Yes, he made cow-tiles of it." And Warren Kelley owned it right up, right there, that he took the lines and made cow-tiles of it.

DORSON:

What's a cow-tile?

FRANK ALLEY:

Well, it's a line you put round their neck and fasten it round the stanchion; you have a stanchion up, see. A cow stands up by the neck against that, and you put a line right around her neck and tie it—it's a cow-tile.

DORSON:

Were there other things which they found that way?

FRANK ALLEY:

Yes. Of course I don't know now. I know I lost lots of lobsters one time in the harbor, and they told me where they went to. The fellow there camped in a boat in the harbor, took an oar and punched the aft end of the car out, and let the lobsters go out.

DORSON:

What's the car?

FRANK ALLEY:

Well, it's a thing that's made, and you put off in the water, 'bout that deep, see, and tain't tight. The boards are about that far apart so the water can go through it, see. Get lobsters in that and keep 'em till the smack comes, and sell 'em.

DORSON:

So they found out that this fellow had done that, to spoil them. Why did he do that?

FRANK ALLEY:

He didn't want me to beat him lobstering. I used to beat him lobstering, and he said, "You've beat me for the last time this fall." And that's just what I done.

DORSON:

Who was that fellow?

FRANK ALLEY:

He was my wife's brother—Austin Kelley.

DORSON:

Did you ever tell him about that?

FRANK ALLEY:

No, I never told him.

DORSON:

But you knew——

FRANK ALLEY:

He showed it right in his face. He never spoke to me for a year afterwards. I knew—I caught some of the lobsters that was plugged in the traps when they was crawling out the harbor.

Curses of Emma Alley

After talking about the witchcraft of Mother Hicks, Frank Alley mentioned some manifestations of occult power displayed by his deceased wife Emma. Frank's brother Jim remarked to me that Emma was the "ugliest" (i.e., meanest) woman he had ever known. Motif G269.10, "Witch punishes person who incurs her ill will," applies here.

FRANK ALLEY:

Well, there was a flying machine come here and landed down here in the cove, and when the tide went down she grounded out on the mud, and we went down there, four or five of us, to look her over, and he wanted to git her off, so he started the machine. And the propeller went so fast that you couldn't see it. And it would almost blow you away from her. It was such a power of a wind. Well Uncle Charles Wood'ard, he got a little too close to the wheel, and he didn't notice it. First thing you know he felt a little sting on his finger and looked, and his finger was gone. Cut it right off. And he was laid up quite awhile with it.

And my wife went around to see if she could collect anything to help him out a little. He didn't have much. So she went round, she went down to Charlie Mansfield, a little short feller, he had a store. And she asked him if he couldn't give her something for Charles Wood'ard. And he was telling her about the weirs they had, and how much fish they were getting every day.

And he said, "I ain't goin' to give you nothin'."

She said, "Look here, Charlie, you won't get another fish out that weir this year."

"Oh," he said, "they're gittin' fish every day, loading boats and lugging up here every day."

"Well," she says, "you won't git another fish this fall." And he never got another fish. That settled it right there.

So she went up to George Harmon's down here, and he kept a drugstore.

DORSON:

Was this on the island?

FRANK ALLEY:

No, this was over here—yes, it was at Jonesport, after we moved over. And she asked George if he couldn't help out a little, and he said, "No, sir. I ain't goin' give him not one thing." She says, "George Harmon, I hope next time I hear from you you'll be dead." And sure enough, when she heard from George Harmon, he was dead.

DORSON:

What did he die of?

FRANK ALLEY:

I don't know what he died with, but he died just the same.

Treasure Guardians

Familiar hidden treasure motifs here are N531, "Treasure discovered through dream"; N556, "Treasure-finders always frightened away"; N576, "Ghosts prevent men from raising treasure."

MAURICE ALLEY:

Momma [Emma Alley], you know she always dreamed of money under the house. And so this day she said she wished there was something under that house would tell her there was money under there. There was something that let go in that house, and she thought the cornerstone fell from right under the house. But there was no stone under it, see, there was just a spiling, and it was lined with dirt, and it had wood around it. And we went under the house, and there wasn't a thing move. And Poppa dug there four or five times, and every time he digged the wind would breeze up and blow the dirt in his face and wheel it right round and round so that he'd have to come up from under the house. And there never have been nobody ever been able to find out if there was any money under there or not.

DORSON:

Well, didn't you go digging for money yourself?

MAURICE ALLEY:

Yeah, and the first time we dug, the hole fill up full of water, and we stopped, and we said we'd go down again. And the next time we went down, the ground was froze so hard that you couldn't even drive a pickax in it. So we never got down again.

DORSON:

How do you explain that?

MAURICE ALLEY:

I couldn't tell you, you just can't dig it. My grandfather, Quaifie Faulkingham, he dug on Mark Island; he said he got money there. And when he was digging there was lizards. He took the lizards up in his hands and rubbed the lizards and took the enchantment off and claimed he got the money off Mark Island. That's Mark Island where they claim pirates has buried money there. There's two people died there, man and a woman. The pirates left them there to guard the money. And it's always a enchanted island. You go down there and you can tell when you go by that island there's a dread there, it looks different. It's kind of a dread. When you go by it, there's some feeling goes over you.

DORSON:

You've been there?

MAURICE ALLEY:

Oh yes. We've been there and you'll never hardly ever land on that island and leave without punching a hole in your boat.

Now, there's a place down to Hatchet Harbor with a blue rock with a white hatchet on it. And a crowd of us went down there to dig, and all we found was lizards. We run, scared us half to death, we didn't know enough to grab a lizard and rub him, take off the enchantment. I been there since, and I've never seen no lizards, but I've never dug for money there again.

Forerunners

> *"Forerunner" is the term used in the Maine-Maritimes coastal area for the general class of omens and harbingers of death. "Token" is an equivalent term in parts of the South. Helen Creighton begins her volume of Nova Scotia ghostlore,* Bluenose Ghosts *(Toronto, 1957), with a chapter on "Forerunners."*

DORSON:

Do you know what a forerunner is?

RILEY BEAL:

Well, I don't really know what it is, but I see one.

DORSON:

You've seen one!

RILEY BEAL:

I certainly did.

DORSON:

What was it?

RILEY BEAL:

It was a forerunner of my cousin down to my camp. I actually see that. I was to work one morning, just after daylight, just before sunrise. I was working on my traps, and I happened to look round, I seed the movement of something, I looked round and there was a woman, a young woman standing there to my doorstep, back to, and she had on just a silk robe. And I could see the muscles of her back as she moved—moving under that robe. And she walked right off the path. I knew that nc one was down there at that time, and of course I thought that it was my son's wife because she was in the hospital, and she was pretty sick at that time. I went in and I told my boy, when he came, what I'd seen. And I thought of course it was my son's wife.

But it wasn't, it was another girl. I didn't dare tell my wife about it, because I was afraid she wouldn't stay there again. But just a short time after this girl died. And that morning that she died—my wife and I was home here at that time, we was in our bedroom asleep and we heard a noise, a rap at the window. My wife got up, raised the curtain, put the light on—raised the curtain, she thought it was the cat coming in—wanted to get in. And when she looked up, she said, "My lord, it isn't the cat." It was a white pillow, silk pillow, laid right against the window. And it passed right off, right away. And about twenty minutes after that, that girl's father came by and said his daughter just died.

That's the same one I see her apparition.

4. ANECDOTES OF
LOCAL CHARACTERS

IN THE TWO CYCLES that follow of stories about Captain Horace Smith and Art Church, each anecdote ends with a quoted saying, in the first group by the discomfited captain, and in the second by a dupe of the wily Church.

Anecdotes of Captain Horace Smith

"Captain Horace's Petty Thefts"

DORSON:

You know one about Captain Horace Smith?

CURT MORSE:

Yeah—he was a real sea captain, a pilot, he was captain of vessels, steamers, and everything. But kinda had hard luck, and he got old, I guess much as eighty-five or ninety years old. He was lame, and he used to stagger round. And he got so, the last of it, he got hard up, so I guess he started stealing, he'd steal everything. So he was hitchhiking along the road, and a fellow hauled up with a pickup, and he said, "Uncle," he says "the seat is full, but if you just as soon ride on the back why all right." So Uncle Horace said, "By Jesus, chum, anywhere that I can get a lift I'll crawl aboard." So he got in the truck. His pants was all torn to pieces, so in the suitcase that was laying in there, there was a blue serge pant's leg sticking out. And he kept working [it] out till he worked the waistbands out, and he said, "By God, chum, them looks to me just like they're just my plumb fit."

So he took his pants off and threwed them away, and worked his pants out. And when he went to put 'em on it was a one-legged man, one leg was gone completely. "Oh," he says, "by Jesus, chum, that's pretty sad, me going around with just one leg and them pants gone."

Yeah, that was a true saying, so they tell me he did.

.　　.　　.

EVA HALL (Curt's daughter):

They used to tell a story about he stole something, put it in a firkin, he thought it was black and it was dark blue.

CURT MORSE:

Well, that was the overcoat he stole down at Sawyer's store in Jonesport. He put it in a firkin to lug it home.

EVA HALL:

One of these big firkins, you know, they used to have, with the cover on.

CURT MORSE:

Well, they had him up to court, and he says, "Why, you're all a goddam pack of liars," he says, "because it was a *dark blue*."

EVA HALL:

"It wasn't black, it was dark blue." He used to come to our house when we were children. Nice old man, but we used to have a lot of fun with the poor old fellow, as children will.

DORSON:

What was that one you just told me about the well and tying up the grass?

CURT MORSE:

Oh, the kids used to have fun, that is fooling, plaguing him a little, but not much because they all liked the old fellow. So it was getting along towards haying time, the herd's grass was awful tall and tough. So he started for the well for a pail of water. Well, the kids, you know, they'd go ahead of him and tie this herd's grass in acrost the path, see, tie the two heads together. When the old fellow come along, he was lame, of course every ten feet he would fall down. And when he come back he said, "By Jesus, chum," he says, "I seen a good many fields of grass, but I never saw a field where the grass all growed in staples."

"Captain Horace's Prayer"

STUART ALLEY:

Captain Horace Smith, yes. Well, he was captain of a big three-topmast schooner. He was out once and caught in a gale. He told the crew, he said, "Boys, I think we're all going to be lost. Now," he says, "all bow your heads while Captain Horace offers prayer." He says [*intoned*]:

"Almighty God, dear kind heavenly Father, we do ask the blessings upon our boys, and on this food and upon top of our boys."

And he spilt the coffee, the ship rolled, and he spilt the coffee on his clothes some, it burned him. He said:

"By the lovely riproaring Carolina Moses Jesus," he said, "we're all going to be scalded to death right here."

"Captain Horace's Christmas Breakfast"

JIM ALLEY:

Captain Horace Smith lived up at Mason's Bay, and his brother lived up here to the beach. So the night before Christmas he thought he'd come down and get something good for Christmas dinner to eat. So Enoch got breakfast ready for him and called him, and he come down and took a look. And he says, "Same old thing, bread and butter."

He didn't think much of that.

Anecdotes of Art Church

"Art Church Tells a Lie"

> *Type 1920B,* The One Says, "I Have Not Time to Lie" and Yet Lies, *is reported nine times in Estonia and eleven times in English-American tradition.*

DORSON:

Now that that whistle has stopped blowing, perhaps you'd tell us one of Art Church's lies.

JIM ALLEY:

Art Church was going down town by Porter Cummings, and Porter hollered, "Art, come in." He says, "I ain't got time." He says, "Come in long enough to tell me a lie." He says, "Well, I'm in a devil of a hurry, I ain't got time." Says, "Your father, I just come down by him and he's cut himself awful, and I'm after a doctor." Well, Porter jumped into his wagon—no automobiles then—and rushed up there, and his father hadn't cut himself at all. And he said, "The devil, he told me a lie right on the road."

DORSON:

Your Uncle Josh Alley one time got fooled by Art Church. You were telling me that this Art Church was quite a fellow. Who was Art Church?

JIM ALLEY:

Oh, a fella lived up Injun River.

DORSON:

What was he known for?

JIM ALLEY:

Well, I don't know.

FRANK ALLEY:

Oh, he was a nice fella, clever.

JIM ALLEY:

Clever.

FRANK ALLEY:

As clever a fella as you ever see. But if he got it in for you, boys, look out. He'd lie to you just as quick as flies.

DORSON:

Didn't he play a trick on your Uncle Josh?

JIM ALLEY:

Yes, he sold Uncle Josh a cord of wood, and he told him the best part of it—he'd find the best part of it was hardwood. And Uncle Josh paid him for it, and when he went out and looked he had just two sticks of hardwood. And Uncle Josh got after him about it, and he said, "I told you the best part—the best of it was hardwood."

"Well," he said, "I only got two sticks of hardwood."

"Art Church Gets Receipt from McFall on Road"

DORSON:

What is that one about the other time he wanted to get a receipt in full?

JIM ALLEY:

He owed McFall a bill, and McFall tried to git it. And he wrote him and wrote him, and Art didn't pay no attention. And at last Art started for Machias, and he got up Mason's Bay, and he met McFall a-comin'! Art says, "I'm just comin' over to pay that bill." "Well," McFall says, "I'm just comin' over at your house after it." McFall's horses headed towards Jonesport, and Art's headed toward Machias.

"Well," says Art, "write me out a receipt, and I'll pay you." He wrote him out a receipt, and Art grabbed it and started his horse, and McFall turned around and tried to get him, but said, "It's no use, he's got the receipt, and that's all there is to it."

Personal Anecdotes of Curt Morse

"Curt Wins a Raffle"

The yarn about a dead horse auctioned off to save the owner its burial price ($2.50 then) can be traced back over a century. See Norris W. Yates, William T. Porter and the "Spirit of the Times" (Baton Rouge, 1957), p. 160, citing the New York Spirit of the Times, XI (1840), 500–501, "A Horse Story," in turn crediting the New Orleans Picayune.

DORSON:

What was the time you won a horse on a raffle?

CURT MORSE:

Oh, an old fella down here had a horse up on tickets, and they wanted me to take a ticket, it was twenty-five cents a ticket, so I took a ticket; number one, I never will forget it. Oh, week or ten days afterward, sent me to come up and get the horse, that I'd won him. So when I got up there the next morning, I had a halter with me and everything to lead him down home, the horse was dead. Damn thing had died that night, and it cost me five dollars to get him hauled off and buried. I have the darndest luck on that stuff.

"Curt Meets His True Love"

A popular divination belief underlies this anecdote. For finding one's future mate with a ball of yarn see Harry M. Hyatt, Folk-Lore from Adams County, Illinois, p. 346, nos. 6992–93; for discovering your sweetheart with a mirror see Ray B. Browne, Popular Beliefs and Practices from Alabama, p. 169, no. 2934.

DORSON:

Now you were telling me when you were a kid you were supposed to be able to find out who you are going to marry with a ball of yarn.

CURT MORSE:

Oh yes, yes, yes. Well, they said that if you wanted to find out who was gonna marry, why you go upstairs and drop a ball of yarn out of the window and wind it up and say, "Whoever I'm to marry," you know, "follow this yarn to me." Something like that. So they'd throw the ball of yarn out of the window, and when she wound it all back again, on the end of it the fellow she was going to marry was supposed to be coming up the stairs holding on the end of the yarn. But that was one of those witch stories there, I don't know.

DORSON:

You tried it one time with a mirror?

CURT MORSE:

Oh, I tried it one time with a mirror, yes. I never was so scared in my life.

CURT MORSE:

DORSON:

What happened?

CURT MORSE:

I sneaked down in the cellar one night twelve o'clock. They'd been talking about it. So I took a little piece of a looking glass, and I went down in the cellar, twelve o'clock alone. It was quiet, dark down there, and I was scared anyhow. And I just said,

"Who are my true love's-to-be,
Look over my shoulder in this mirror to me."

Well, before I got "me," the tomcat jumped on the potato bin, and I darn near fainted away. I don't know how much proof that was. [A comic reference to his wife, whom Curt speaks of goodnaturedly as always badgering him; he calls her "Dynamite because she blows up so much."]

"Curt Plays Croquet"

DORSON:

Now what was that one time you were in the croquet game, you were telling me about?

CURT MORSE:

Oh, that's the time that the Kennebec boys here played Roche Bluff. Of course we were all poor, and we didn't have any bats, or balls, or gloves, or anything like that, so we made our bats out of yellow birch—you know, we got 'em green, to make them heavier and tougher. So we knocked all the old yarn balls to pieces we had around there.

So Roche Bluff wanted to play us a game one afternoon, and we didn't have no balls that we could play with, so I said I'd fix it. So I went down to an old lady called Aunt Nettie Bryant, and I stole a couple of her croquet balls. And, boy, would they smart when they hit your hand! Well, I never could see very good, see anything coming at me. So this Maury Watts, a big two-hundred-and-forty pounder, picked that ball off the end that yellow birch stake bat, and I didn't see it coming, never landed, or never struck a thing till it hit me right on my Adam's apple here. I passed out, and I don't know how the game came out. Because according to experienced fact I been scared of a ball game ever since.

DORSON:

You've never played croquet since?

CURT MORSE:

No, I don't want to talk about it.

"Curt Digs Potatoes in Aroostook County"

DORSON:

Then there was a funny experience you were telling, Curt, about the time you went to Aroostook County to get some potatoes—big potatoes.

CURT MORSE:

Well, it was kind of slack time in the lobster fishing. There wasn't many lobsters anyhow. Fellow lived just a little ways from me had an old Model T Ford. He wanted me to go up to Aroostook County with him and pick up potatoes. Well, I didn't think much of it, but after a while he talked so much I told him we'd start. So in the morning, the next morning, he come down and got me aboard. We started off.

She was running pretty good, one of those old-fashioned Model T's. We got over to Princeton, there was something in the starter knocking. I thought there might be a fella under the hood working or something, some mechanic. So we took it in the garage there, and we didn't have much money, and the fella I was with had twelve cents; two of them was those big penny tokens. So we went down to the restaurant while the fella was going to work on the car, he showed us where the little restaurant was. Went down and the fellow ordered up fried chicken and a full-course dinner. Anyhow, it sounded like a big dinner on twelve cents. Well, we got dinner, and when we got back to the garage the fella had the little motor out on chain fold. I told him we didn't have much money, and we's going up picking the potatoes, and I wished he do it as cheap as he could.

So I guess he let us off. That night when he got her back in was seven, six or seven dollars. Well, we got her up to Danforth the first night. We stayed there and had it put in the garage over-night so the boys wouldn't steal her.

And the next day we started along, and I didn't know much about a car. I thought somebody fired at a partridge or some-thing alongside of the road, and then we had a flat tire. So I asked Marston Fenoury, the fella I was with, I said, "How do we fix it?" And he said, "Well, I'll show you." So he got out, and then under the back cushion he had a piece of a cedar pole of, oh, about fifteen inches long or more. So I lifted up the wheel, and he put that in under the axle. We got her patched up with some old rubbers, his wife's rubbers, shoe rubbers.

We got up to a place called Fresh Air, Free Air. I didn't know much about this Free Air at that time, I was never much around cars nor garages. So I told the fella, I say, "Is it all right to use this thing?" And he said, "Yes," and he showed me how to stick it on the nipple there. So I piled it right to her. Well, we got up a little ways further, and the whole four tires blowed out. Seems as though I'd put too much air in them.

Well, we got up a little ways further, and the whole four flat tires blowed open. Anyhow, we walked her up. I had to buy an inner tube, one tire and four inner tubes I guess I bought. They was all split to pieces. So the next time I asked him how much we'd better put in, and he said after he got hold of her and was pumping her up there by hand, he says, "I don't know, but we'll put aplenty." And I pumped till I played myself out, and he pulled a dingus out of his pocket and stuck it on there. sssssssss, eighteen pounds, and there I was sweating and played out. So we walked her up there after a while.

But that night where we stayed in a bunkhouse of a fella that we worked for, there was a little French fella there, kinda of a thick-faced fella, and he got to bragging on what he could do. I never had seen a potato patch outside of a few bushels a-planting. I told him, I says, "I betcha five dollars that I can pick more potatoes tomorrow than you can." He says, "You're wrong." So the next day, just as day was breaking, we started in. That night I had eighty-seven barrels, and he had a hundred and four. He took my four dollars, and that next night we laid in the field bed, and in the morning I put my stockings on somebody else's feet—I was stone dead. I even tried short-waisted corsets, and it was no good. I never got nothing after that. Fact, I ain't eaten fifteen pounds of potatoes since, about twenty-five or thirty years.

DORSON:

I guess the moral of that story is, a lobster fisherman should never go picking potatoes.

CURT MORSE:

Oh no, no, never never leave your job and start something new.

EVA HALL:

Don't forget to mention about the sore finger that he got.

CURT MORSE:

Oh, yes, well the fun of it was, that while we's up there, this fella was—I think he was marked to be a billy goat because he was covered with reddish hair: fingers, arms, head, neck, and all, and the potato mud had cracked his fingers. So there was an old lady up there, and she said if he had put a piece of yarn in each joint of his fingers and tie a bow knot on the back of 'em, heal 'em right up. So—it did look kinda funny, so when we was eating supper, and I told Maury, the fellow I was with, I said, "You know, where I come from, everybody when they sit down to eat usually takes their mitten off." The old fella of the place there, the old farmer, got an awful kick out of it anyhow.

"Curt Plants Bulls"

This anecdote falls under Motif X1420, "Lies About Vegetables."

CURT MORSE:

A professor had this stuff that he was experimenting on, at some big institution. I was fishing traps, and I had a big stand of squash and punkins, and he asked me if it would be all right if he injected some of that serum, to see if he could put a meat flavor through 'em. So I told him I didn't care if he was darn fool enough to do it. He said if he damaged it in any way, shape, or form, his institution would pay for it. So I never thought anything more about it, and I went to hauling traps. And about two weeks later I thought I'd go down and take a look at 'em. I had a few minutes to spare. And that is when I got the surprise of my life. When I got down on the field there wasn't any punkins or squashes. All I found is a whole stand of little white-faced bulls and heifers, standing there hung to each vine.

"Curt Goes Deer Hunting"

> *This is a Münchausen tale, Type 1889A, Shooting off the Leader's Tail, keyed to Motif X1124.1. Baughman cites three examples from West Virginia and Texas, all told on hogs. A newspaper text of 1857 is abstracted in Dorson, American Folklore, pp. 52–53, also involving hogs. An oral text collected in Michigan but set in Maine, with a moose as target, is in Dorson, Bloodstoppers and Bearwalkers, p. 261.*

DORSON:

What was that one you just mentioned about cutting off the deer's tail?

CURT MORSE:

Oh, that puts me in mind, you know I used to go up river with the boys, on a boat—take a month every year. They come from everywhere, and I used to go up there on the camps. So, I didn't know that somebody with fine shot had put this big buck's eyes out. And I want to tell you how that Nature, I don't know, everything looks after one another. So, I was setting there on an old log and I had a nice new pump gun, fulla buckshot, about fifty yards from where I'se settin', and out walked this doe. Well, at that time of year, I said, there must be a buck right behind her. When her hindquarters come out by the jack-fir, I noticed this big buck had her tail in his mouth.

And when she'd stop, he'd feed, and when she'd start along he take hold of her tail and she'd lead him everywhere.

So I said, "Well, I didn't know he's blind." So I took dead aim at the side of his head, and I shot a little too far to the left, and I shot her tail right off, and I left him standing there with that tail in his mouth. And I walked up and took hold of that tail and kind of jerked a little on it and led him right home. That's the biggest buck I ever got.

"Curt Fools the City Fellows"

DORSON:

Then you had another experience, Curt, when you made those city fellows believe you were hauling an anchor.

CURT MORSE:

Oh, yeah. Well, there wasn't much to that, but it was a big anchor, at least it looked like a big anchor. Anyhow, I was hauling traps, and I got it caught on one of my traps, and I hauled it up and so I couldn't hold it and get it aboard too, so I had to get another fellow to help me. I took it ashore, and it had corroded over with rust and stuff from the ocean bed so it looked like about a ten-ton anchor. It was perfect anyhow, rust color.

So I had it down on the shore by my camp, and there was a couple of guys come down from New York, and they had some lobsters and had 'em cooled and was looking at that anchor. Well, when we got ready for the house—actually the anchor itself didn't weigh over seventy-five pounds—when we got ready for the house, I thought I'd take it along with me up to the house. So I put it on my shoulder, and these guys kept looking at me and looking at me—got to arguing about the heft. One fella said—at least, he'd bet a dollar it would weigh eight ton. We got up the house, and I laid it down, and the fella says, "Well, just why'd you bring that anchor up the house with that much heft, mister?" Well, I says, "The heft don't 'mount to much." I said, "When I see a heavy storm coming up, I always take my boat under the other arm."

Well, when I dried off and knocked the stuff off it, it didn't weigh over seventy-five pounds. It was just the corroding on it, don't you know, that it looked like a big anchor. It was a big anchor by the looks of it. Well, I got a kick out of it, and I guess they did, and they went off arguing about the anchor. They was going to have it put in a New York paper: "A Man Lugging Ten-Ton Anchor Up Across Field."

DORSON:

Didn't one of them say if the sand was soft you couldn't——

CURT MORSE:

Oh, yes, the fella says to the other fella, "If that land hadn't been dry and hard, he'd never got up there because he'd sunk in to his knees with that much heft on his back."

5. JOCULAR TALES

Stories about Couples

"The Devil Caught"

This is Type 1159, The Ogre Wants to Learn to Play, *Grimm No. 8, Motifs K1111.0.1, "Ogre's beard caught fast," and K1755, "Ogre terrified by woman's legs." The opening Motif E282, "Ghosts haunt castle," usually initiates Type 1160,* The Ogre in the Haunted Castle.

This tale is widely known all over Europe, 104 versions having been collected in Finland and 86 in Sweden. No texts are reported from the United States.

JIM ALLEY:

There was a house haunted, and nobody could live in it. And they'd give it to anybody'd live in it. So a fella said he'd live in it, so he took his wife, went over there, lived in that house. Along come the devil in, and he come in there, and so he going to have a game of cards with the fella. So they played a game of cards, if the devil beat him, he'd kill him. And so the devil beat him.

Well, the fella says, "I'd like to have one more—offer you one more thing before you kill me." And he said, "What is it?" "I'll bet my nose"—and the devil had a long nose—said "I'll bet my nose is longer than yourn." He says, "No, t'aint." There's a crack in the door, and he got the devil to shove his nose through the door and when he did, he shoved a knife right through and pinned him right there, fastened him.

"Well," he said, "you let me go, I'll never bother you again.

You can have anything there is here. All but that tree outside, don't take them apples off that tree. If you do, I shall appear to you. You can have anything and live here, and I'll never bother you." So he said, "All right."

So they was living in peace. By and by, the woman wanted an apple off that tree. And he said, "Don't touch it, if you do the devil'll come." By jeem, she picked one of them apples, and she looked and the devil was coming. "Just one thing to get ready now or he'll kill us." She said, "What is that?" "You haul your pants right down, and bend over and stick your ass right up to him, and that'll stop him." She didn't hurry, and he said, "You do what I tell you, and that'll save you."

So she done it, and he got eye on her, and he said, "Oh no, you'll never get my nose in another crack."

DORSON:

That stopped the devil?

JIM ALLEY:

Yes, you see he had his nose in that crack, in that door, and he pinned him that night, and he let him go, and he said, "You'll never get my nose in another crack." He let him go.

"Father and Mother Both 'Fast'"

Two variant texts are in the Indiana University Folk-lore Archives in the folder "Hillbilly Jokes," collected in Michigan in 1954 by Alysanne Dove and Stuart Small. The theme of the cuckolded husband appears in Type 1425B, Why Seventh has Red Hair (French-Canadian).

DORSON:

There's another cute one about the fella going with the girl, and his father told 'em——

JIM ALLEY:

Oh, yes. Well, a fella stayed with a girl, and by and by he went to his father and he said, "Father, I'm going to marry that girl." He says, "John, let me tell you—I'se fast when I was young, and that girl's your sister."

Well, he felt bad and he left her. By and by, he picked up another one, and he stayed with her for a while, and he went to his father and he said, "Father, I'm going to marry that girl." He said, "Johnny, I was fast when I was young—that girl's your sister."

Felt awful bad, and so one day he's setting up by the stove with his head hung down, and his mother said, "What's the trouble, John?" "No nothing." She says, "There's something, and I want to know what it is. Why did you leave that girl, the first one you stayed with, and you left your second one?" "Well," he said, "Father told me he was fast when he was young, and they's both my sisters." Says, "Johnny, I want to tell you something, I was fast when I'se young, and your father ain't your father at all."

"The Beans in the Quart Jar"

DORSON:

Well, there's another one that fits in there, about the beans in the quart jar.

JIM ALLEY:

The old man had taken sick and thought he's gonna die anyway, so he called his wife in and confessed, he said, "I been stepping out, and I want to be honest with you, and I want to ask your forgiveness before I go." And she said, "All right," she said, "I'll forgive you." She forgive him.

By and by, she was taken sick and she called him in and she said, "Now, look, I stepped out quite a lot, and I want to ask forgiveness." He said, "Yes, I'll forgive ye." She said, "Every time I stepped out I put a bean in a quart jar. And you'll find they're all there on that mantlepiece, except that quart I cooked the other Saturday."

"Now's Your Chance"

> *Paul Green, the distinguished dramatist, author, and storyteller, related a variant of this story to me in Chapel Hill, North Carolina, in August, 1954.*

DORSON:

Then there was another cute one you were telling me about this traveling man who asked for a bed from the farmer.

JIM ALLEY:

You want that on there?

DORSON:

Oh, sure, that's a cute one.

JIM ALLEY:

Well, there's a farmer. This fella was traveling along, he traveled all day long, come night he tired. Young fella, nice-looking fella. Knocked at a farmhouse. A man come to the door, wondered what he wanted. And he says, "I'd like you to put me up tonight." "Can't do it." Says, "I can give you some supper, but I can't put you up, I've only got one bed." So the old lady kinda took a liking to him and says, "Husband, we can put him up tonight." "Well," he says, "how, we only got one bed?" Says, "I'll sleep on the far side and you in the middle and he on the back side." "Why," he said, "I didn't think of that."

So he had his supper, and he liked cheese pretty well, and he commenced to eat, and about all he'd eat was cheese. So the farmer said, "Look, leave a little bit of that cheese for me, I want some for breakfast." Well, the fella kinda got infronted, and he pulled away from the table.

They got to bed, and in the middle of the night the farmer heard a racket in the barn. Went out there to see what's going on, and the old lady says, "Now's your chance." And he got out of bed and et the rest of the cheese.

"The Looking Glass"

> *Type 1336A, Man Does Not Recognize His Own Reflection in the Water (Mirror), is known in Europe, Asia, and the United States. Under Motif J1795.2 *, Baughman gives three references, from Westmorland, Missouri, and New Mexico.*

DORSON:

Then, what was that one about the fellow looking in the mirror?

JIM ALLEY:

Well, this fellow, his wife was jealous as the devil. "Chasing another woman," she said. So he come home, and [she] give him an awful calling down, and he wouldn't pay no attention to her, and he went over and looked in the looking glass. By and by, she said, "What are you looking in that looking glass for?" "Oh," says, "nothing." She went along and took a look in the looking glass and said, "That's the bitch you're chasing, ain't it?"

"Looking for a Man Boss"

> Type 1366A *, Search for Husband in Command, perfectly matches the present text. It is reported only from Finland. My colleague, Robert E. Quirk, told me a version (1961) in Jewish dialect he remembered hearing on the radio in Camp Bowie, near Brownwood, Texas, during World War II.

DORSON:

Here it is in the evening, and we're still in Kilton's Store. The pro and con club is in full blast, and Jim Alley's got a couple more to tell. What's that one, Jim, about the hen and the horse?

JIM ALLEY:

Well, a fellow workin' for a man, and his boss went out and hitched up two horses: black one and a white one. And he put twenty-five hens in the box. Now he said, "Wherever you find—you go out with them horses, and whenever you find a woman boss, give 'em a hen, and wherever you find a man boss, give him a horse." He said, "All right."

And he give away twenty-four hens. He had one hen left. He said, "I guess I ain't gonna give a horse away." He said he'd come to a house and a feller out the door—big feller, choppin' wood. Every time he strike he said, "That ax go clear into that wood." He said, "If he chops this far, I'm going to give him a horse. Give one of my horses away." Had one more hen left.

He said, "Who's boss here?"

He said, "I'll give you to understand I am."

He said, "All right. I'll give you a horse. Go take one, any one you want."

He said, "What do you mean?"

"Why," he said, "I'm giving a horse away where there's a man boss."

"Well," he said, "all right."

So he said, "I'll take the white one." And he started to take him out to the fields, and a little frail woman come to him. "What are you doin'? Is this man giving you a horse? Well," she says, "if he gives you a horse, take the black one."

He says, "No, I'm going to take the white one."

She says, "You heard what I told you."

He looked again, and he said, "I guess I'll take that black horse."

He [the fellow] said, "No you don't—your wife gets a hen."

"Old Couple's Three Wishes"

> *Motif J2075, "The transferred wish," can appear independently, as in this text, or as an element in Type 750A, The Wishes, which is Grimm No. 87, widely diffused in Europe.*

DORSON:

Then there's another one about three wishes.

JIM ALLEY:

An old man and old woman going to have their wishes, so, whatever they wished, they could have. So, the old man wanted to wish, and the old woman says, "No, let me wish." He says, "All right." So she says—they just had a baby—says, "I wish I had a barrel of rags." Made the old man mad, and he said, "I wish they were up your ass." Well, then he had to take another wish and wish them out, and got nothin'.

"The Old Woman Who Was Always Saying 'Scissors' "

> *Type 1365B,* **Cutting with the Knife or the Scissors,** *very popular throughout Europe, is reported eleven times for North America and England by Baughman. A journalistic text from the* **Boston Yankee Blade,** *XIII (Dec. 17, 1853) is printed in Dorson,* **Jonathan Draws the Long Bow,** *p. 230.*

DORSON:

Then there was the old woman who was always saying scissors.

CURT MORSE:

Oh, yes, that old woman was always saying scissors. Her husband got so disgusted and worn out every time he'd speak to her, she'd say "Scissors." He says, "Look, if you ever say scissors again, I'll drown you." She says, "Oh, scissors." And she as a woman always got the last word, guess they're about all the same in that respect, but anyhow, he held her under, he held her head under water. She couldn't say scissors, but she was making her fingers go like a pair of scissors.

"The Drunk and the Devil"

> *Analogous jests appear under Motifs J1250–1499, "Clever verbal retorts (repartee)." Thus when nuns tell a man they are daughters of God, he replies, "Come and marry me; I should like such a rich father-in-law" (J1261.1.1).*

JIM ALLEY:

There was a fellow—he drinked all the time, he'd get drunk, and his wife tried to break it. She couldn't break him drinking. So she thought up a scheme. So she'd see a fellow, fixed it up with him—rigged up the devil and get in the cemetery. And he'd come through the cemetery. And he'd come through the cemetery to cut off about a half a mile when he come from downtown. And get him rigged up with a red suit on—rigged up [like] the devil and hide there behind them gravestones. And when her husband come along he'd jump at him. So he got all rigged up and went in there and by 'n by her husband come, staggering along.

He jumped right up in front of him, and he said, "Old man." He said, "Who are you?" He said, "I'm the devil." "Well," he said, "let's you and I shake hands, I married your sister."

Stories about a Man

"The Traveler and the Baby"

> Cf. "The Farmer's Daughter" in Ralph S. Boggs, "North Carolina White Folktales and Riddles," Journal of American Folklore, XLVII (1934), 310–11. Boggs comments on his three texts: "I have found no parallels for this type. Is it uniquely American?"

FRANK ALLEY:

You know, there was a fellow one time. He was a-going along the road, and it come night, and he wanted a place to put up. So, he come to a farmhouse, an old farmhouse, and he went there, and he wanted to know if they could put him up. And the old man says, "We've only got one bed." He says, "You can stay if you sleep with the baby." Well, he didn't like the idea of sleeping with the baby, so he says, "Can't I sleep in the barn?" He said "Yes! you can sleep in the barn, if you'd like, in the hayloft."

He went out to the haybarn and slept that night. And in the morning, just after daylight, he heard the barn door open. And then he looked out, you know, and there was a pretty girl about sixteen. He said, "Who are you?" She said, "I'm the baby." She says, "Who are you?" He says, "I'm a damned fool."

"The Old Man Crying"

> *Type 726,* The Oldest on the Farm, *Motif F571.2.*
> *From Ireland alone 161 texts have been collected. See*
> *Dorson,* Negro Folktales in Michigan, *pp. 181–82, "The*
> *Old Man," and note 145, p. 229, which abstracts a tennis*
> *version told by champion Vic Seixas.*

DORSON:

Now you're going to tell about how the old people——

CURT MORSE:

Yeah, how the old people marched along the line. One day I started for town, and there was an old fellow up in our district settin' alongside the road with long thick whiskers, and he's crying. I says, "What are you crying about, Uncle?"

"Well," he says, "my father just gave me a awful basting."

I says, "What in the devil the old man lick you for?"

He says, "Cause I was throwing some potatoes at grandpaw."

DORSON:

And then, what was that other one about the old man?

JIM ALLEY:

Well, a fella went into a house, and a fella settin' there on the doorstep alone, he was an awful old man. He says, "Can I go in the house?"

And he says, "Yes, my son's in there."

And he went in, and he says, "That your father out there?"

And he said, "Yes."

"Well, what are you crying for?"

And he says, "Why he give me a lickin'."

He said, "What for?"

He said, "Sassin' my grandfather."

So he went out, and he looked. "Your son said you give him a lickin' for sassin' his grandfather."

He says, "I did."

And he says, "Where is your grandfather?"

And he says, "In the next house."

And he said, "I went over, and he was so old, he had four inches of moss right on his back."

His boy was over a hundred.

"The Man Who Had a Calf"

> *Type 1281A,* Getting Rid of the Man-eating Calf, *is reported from northern and eastern Europe, with one Spanish-American example. A French-Canadian text I collected in northern Michigan combines this tale with Type 1739,* The Parson and the Calf, *in which a man thinks he is going to have a calf when a cow's urine specimen is substituted for his own. See Dorson, "Aunt Jane Goudreau, Roup-Garou Storyteller," Western Folklore, VI, (1947), 27, "The Man Who Had a Calf." This episode is simply hinted at in the opening sentences below.*

DORSON:

Then there was the story told about the man who thought he had a calf. Remember that?

JIM ALLEY:

Well, they claimed there was a fella was going to have a baby. So he didn't want to disgrace the town so he left it. It was late in the fall. It was cold, and he traveled all day, coming through the woods, and he picked up a pair of boots. A bear had et the man up. Just the legs in the top of the rubber boots, leather boots, froze in there. So he said, "Them's new boots, I'll take them along with me." So he got to a house and knocked there at the farmhouse. Farmer come to the door, and he wanted to know if he could put him up there for the night.

"Why," he said, "I haven't got any bed." He says, "I'll lay behind the stove anyway." So the farmer didn't notice the boots he had when he left 'em outdoor. And when the farmer went to bed, he went and got the boots and put them behind the stove, to thaw out the legs out of them, the man's legs out.

So, in the night the farmer's cow had a calf, and it was cold so he thought he'd bring the calf in alongside the stove.

So the fella was asleep, and he woke up and seed that calf and said, "It ain't a baby, it's a calf." And he forgot his boots, and went, run and got out the house, and away he went. And the farmer got up in the morning, and the boots was there with a man's legs in 'em. And he said, "I ain't going to keep no calf'll eat a man." So he killed the calf.

"Paying for Beer with Peanuts"

> *Type 1555A, Paying for Bread with Beer, Motif K233.4, is known in the United States and French Canada, and in one Walloon instance. See Dorson, Jonathan Draws the Long Bow, p. 21, for examples from the Boston Yankee Blade, XI (May 8, 1852), and oral tradition in Vermont (1939).*

DORSON:

What was that one about the fellow who bought the peanuts and the beer?

JAMES ALLEY:

Yeh. Fellow went into a store, and he says, "I guess I'll have a pint of peanuts." So he got the peanuts. After got 'em —he hadn't et none of them—he says, "I—I dunno. How much is your beer?" Told him. He says, "Well, I guess I'll have a bottle of beer." So he gives the storekeeper the peanuts back and started——

The storekeeper said, "Look, you didn't pay for the beer."

"No, I give you the peanuts for the beer."

"Well," he said, "you didn't pay for the peanuts."

He said, "Well, I ain't got 'em. You have."

DORSON:

Pretty good. You better watch out for that, Charles, in case that fellow comes in here.

"The Indian's Three Wishes"

> *Type 1173A, The Devil is to Fulfil Three Wishes of the peasant, who asks for all the tobacco and brandy*

*in the world, and then some more brandy. Keyed to
Motif K175. Reported only from Sweden.*

JIM ALLEY:

Why, the Indian wished a first wish, he wished all the Bay of
Fundy was rum. "Well," they said, "what's your next?" He
said, "Mount Desert Hills was a lump of sugar." "Well," he
said, "what's your next?" He says, "A little more rum."

Stories about a Woman

"The Minister and the Woman in the Woods"

*Type 1833E, God Died for You, is known in Germany,
Finland, Switzerland, and France. Under Motif J1738.6,
"Letting in the light," Baughman gives references
from Texas, New York, New Jersey, Georgia, and
Arkansas.*

DORSON:

What was that one you were just telling about the minister in
the woods?

CURT MORSE:

Well, he was travelin' through the woods and he come to
this little tarred-paper shack, and this woman was standin' in
the door, and he says to her, and he says, "Evening, mam," he
says, "any prostitutes live down here?"

She says, "Christ, Mr. Jones killed somethin' yesterday,
and he got its hide down on the barn," she says, "you can go
look."

He says, "My poor sister." He says, "Haven't you seen
Jesus?"

She says, "They ain't been a Christ that's sold down here
for three or four months."

He says, "Why you poor, dear, weak sister."

She says, "If you'd eat as many blueberries as I have and
had the cholera as long as I have, by God, you'd be weak."

And he says, "You're all living in the darkness."
She says, "I wouldn't if that damn fool I married would
put a window on the end of that shed."
That's all.

"Old Gram Shaw"

> *Type 1700, "I Don't Know," is known in eastern Eu-*
> *rope, West Africa, and among United States Negroes.*
> *See Dorson, Negro Folktales in Michigan, "Colored*
> *Man and the Mexican," p. 79, and note 47, p. 216.*

DORSON:

And then—what was that one about old Gram Shaw?

JIM ALLEY:

Yeah. That's a fellow was in a place where he couldn't
understand what they said or nothing. So he got hungry, and
he went to a house and knocked on the door. Says, "Can I get
some dinner here?" He'd say—— All they'd say, "Old Gram
Shaw." Well, he'd leave. And then he'd go to another house and
ask them. It was "Old Gram Shaw," and he was about starved
to death. At last he walked and fell into a funeral procession.
Somebody was dead. And he said "Who's dead?" They said,
"Old Gram Shaw." He said, "I darned glad of it, I'll get some
dinner now."

"The Old Lady with Poor Eyesight"

> *Type 1456, The Blind Fiancée, Motif K1984.5. United*
> *States Negro texts I collected are in* Negro Folktales
> in Michigan, *pp. 192–93;* Negro Tales from Pine Bluff,
> Arkansas, and Calvin, Michigan, *pp. 99–101 (2);*
> Southern Folklore Quarterly, *XIX (1955), 113.*

JIM ALLEY:

Well, there was an old lady and she wanted to get married, and
so they said, "You're too old. You can't get married, you're
losing your eyesight." No, she wasn't. So they went and stuck

a needle up in the barn and told her, "We've stuck a needle up in the barn and wanted to see if you could see it."

And she got out and looked, and said, "Dear me, I see the needle but where is the barn?"

Wanted to get married awful bad.

Stories about Irishmen

"Three Irishmen Have a Dream Contest"

> *Type 1626, Dream Bread, is found in Europe, Asia, and North and South America. Another variant was given me in Columbia Falls by Luther Sawyer, told on Uncle Elrie Sawyer, with a pie as the prize.*

DORSON:

Then, what about the Irishmen and the loaf of bread?

JIM ALLEY:

Well, there's three Irishmen, and they only had one loaf of bread between them, so they said, "Now, I'll tell you what we'll do. We'll all go to bed and in the morning wake up and the one tells the biggest dream has the bread." So they say, "All right." So in the morning they got up, and one fellow told his dream, and the other fellow—his turn, so he told his dream, and he looked at the third one, and he said, "What was your dream?" And he said, "I dreamed I was hungry last night, and I got up and ate the loaf."

"Irishman Saves Himself First"

> *This joke gives a twist to Type 1882, where a man buried in the earth or caught in a log goes home to get a shovel or an ax to free himself. This European tall tale has become established in English-American tradition.*

DORSON:

What's that one about the Irishman who fell into the sea?

JIM ALLEY:

Oh. They were out in the lake. There was a big crowd on the shore, and the boat capsized. The other fellow in the boat with him couldn't swim. And the Irishman swum for the shore. And they kept hollering for him to "Save that man, he can't swim." The Irishman never said nothing. By and by he landed, and he said, "Bejethers, I had to save myself first, now I'll go back and get him."

"Pat's in the Mire"

Cf. the variant in Italian dialect in Dorson, American Folklore, pp. 141–42, reprinted from Dorson, "Dialect Stories of the Upper Peninsula," Journal of American Folklore, LXI (1945), 146, No. 62, "Stuck in the Mud."

DORSON:

Then there was the other Irishman got stuck in the mire. What was that?

JIM ALLEY:

Well, he called for help. They said, "What's the trouble?" He said, "Pat's in the mire." And they said, "How far is he in?" And he says, "Shoe tops." Well he said, "Can't you get out?" He said, "No, bejethers, he's head first."

"Irishman Bets with Bartender"

Type 1551, The Wager that Sheep are Hogs, Motif K451.2. A world-famous tale, found in the Ocean of Story, the Gesta Romanorum, and the Shakespeare Jestbooks, and in the New World in Brazil, the Spanish Southwest, and among the French in Missouri. The present text reverses the standard plot by having the confederate Irishman reveal the ruse.

DORSON:

What was the one about the three Irishmen who'd nothing to drink?

JIM ALLEY:

They wanted something to drink, and they didn't have the money to buy it with, and so they picked up a squirrel. So now they says, "What are you going to do with him?" He says, "We're gonna get something to drink. I'm gonna send you in. Now, you go in and tell the bartender and bet him that squirrel is a toad. You say—tell him that's a toad. And if he wants to get the proof, you leave it to the next man to come in, and," he says, "I'll run right in and tell him that's the truth, that's a toad."

So he went in and said, "Look! you know what that is?" And he says, "Why," he says, "it's a squirrel." He says, "It tain't, and I can prove it by the next man come in." And he said, "All right."

So the feller run in, and he says, "That's right, that's a toad." Well, they got their drink.

And then they went to the next barroom and wanted another drink. And so sent the other feller in. And he said, "What's that?" He says, "That's a, that's a toad." And he said, "No, it ain't." He said, "I'll bet you the drink this toad's a squirrel." [*Laughter*] He give himself away, see; he didn't get no drink.

"Irishman Shows Pat a Yankee Trick"

Type 1349D *, What is the Joke? is reported only from Hungary, as told on a nobleman and a stupid peasant.

DORSON:

Well, the pro and con club is once more in session. Jim Alley's going to tell about the Irishman who showed a Yankee trick. How's that go?

JIM ALLEY:

Well, there's a—let's see, get that right now. Oh, yes, an Irishman met a Yankee, and the Yankee says, "Look, you want to see a Yankee trick?"

He said, "Why, yes." The Irishman said, "Sure."

So the Yankee put his hand on a rock, and the Irishman said, "Hit at that."

The Irishman hauled off and hit it; he [the Yankee] took his hand off it. Well he says, "I'm gonna have that on Pat."

So he fell in with Pat, and he said, "Pat, I want to show you a Yankee trick." And he says, "What is it?" "Well," he said, "I'll show you." And he looked around, and he couldn't find no rock to put his hand on, and he put his hand up here and said, "Hit at that."

And Pat hauled off and hit it, and he hauled his hand away and Pat knocked the Irishman down.

That's a Yankee trick he had.

6. LOCAL BALLADS

"The Serenade"

A notorious incident and a long-standing custom account for this ballad composed by Stuart Alley. The folk custom widely known as the shivaree or charivari —called a serenade in Jonesport—is thus described by Maurice Alley.

"When two people got married, why, if they didn't treat with candy, cigars, and things, we used to ser'nade 'em. Take guns and washtubs and wash-boilers and everything that would make a noise, and then we'd go over and pound the windows and almost tear the house down, and they had to treat, or they'd keep right at 'em till they did treat, or they'd tear the house down on the island."

. . .

On one occasion a jolly group did go down to serenade Millard Urquhart (who still lived in Jonesport in 1956), after his wedding to one of the Alley girls. In this instance the bridegroom bombarded the serenading party with missiles, and then hauled them into court at Machias for invading his house and land. The cause célèbre is here recalled by Merton Hall, a garage owner in Jonesport, who participated in the doings.

"Well, I don't remember too much about it, it was quite awhile ago. I know we went down in all good faith to have some fun, and it didn't end up so good. We had kind of a rough time. We were marching round the house playing our horns, my brother and I, beating on drums and one thing and another. First thing we know we got a pan of ammonia—one fellow got a pan right in the face. It stood him on his head out in the grass. The next fellow, there was a chamber mug come out the window, and I mean come out the window. And that did a good job too. Next thing we know we got a charge of shot. One woman got hit in the belly with the salt, another one got an eye put out. We had quite a time. It cost my father fifteen dollars apiece, for my brother and I, in Machias court.

"And there was another fellow there that he joined the crowd to go to Columbia Falls to take the train. He didn't know he was in the outfit, but he wasn't in a way. But he got over to the courthouse, and I told the deputy sheriff, I said, 'Howard Kelley, I think, was in this crowd.' And he put his name right down, and it cost his father fifteen dollars too."

This event inspired Stuart Alley to write and sing "The Serenade."

Come all you people of Jonesport
That want to have some fun,
We'll go down to serenade Millard,
Yes, come on every one.

They started down to Sawyer's Cove,
Millard, he lived down there.
If there are any fun going on,
We're going to have our share.

When they got down to Millard's
It must have been nine o'clock.
When their noise it had begun,
Ed Alley went out and told them to stop.

"Now," says Millard, "I'll show that crowd
Who will have the most fun."

So with rock salt and ammonia
He loaded up his gun.

As soon as the gun was loaded
For the chamber he did go.
Millard says, "I will give that crowd
A big surprise I know."

When Millard pulled the trigger
How the salt did fly.
Hattie Jake and Lowell Sawyer
Nearly lost their eyes.

Now when Hattie did go home
And the story was told to Jake,
He didn't stop for a minute,
Was up for a law scrape.

They first went to Machias,
And tried the law scrape there,
Appealed it through to Calais,
And the serenade ended there.

"The Injun Devil"

> *This song, by Stuart Alley, commemorates a notorious
> local character, Will Groves, nicknamed the "Injun
> devil." Charles Kilton, owner of a little grocery store
> in Jonesport which also served as a meeting place, thus
> described him: "Will Groves went into a life of a hermit
> in an old boat, and stayed in the harbor near Jones-
> port for several years. He didn't take too much pride
> in himself. In fact, he grew a beard so long that it
> reached nearly down to his feet. That is the truth."*

There's an image in the thoroughfare
Of an Injun devil I declare,
Digging clams he gets a share,

He neither shaves or cuts his hair.
    Fall a little all a liger oh.

Aboard the boats he sits and sings
From morning until evening,
Never goes home from fall till spring,
And never washes, the dirty thing.
    Fall a little all a liger oh.

Ashore to the Injun's beach he rows,
He digs clams till he robs the crows,
And how much longer no one knows,
The Injun devil, old Will Groves.
    Fall a little all a liger oh.

He lives and sleeps in a leaky old boat,
And he'll stay aboard as long as she'll float.
He sleeps on the floor with naked feet,
When the water gets to them it's an eight-hour leak.
    Fall a little all a liger oh.

Now I'll end what I've composed,
This is the story of old Will Groves,
And where he comes from
No one knows.
    Fall a little all a liger oh.

"Eben Stanwood the Peddler"

*Another character put into song by Stuart Alley was a
local peddler, Eben Stanwood. Speaking of him, Jim
Alley recalled how he would use a breadbox for a sleigh
on the icy hills. Once, "the sled swung off and went
into a hen pen one side and out the other, and he said
the hens were all over him." Charles Kilton commented,
"He was a small guy that done business in a big way.
He figured that if he lost a cent or two on an article,
if he sold in large quantities, why, he was really doing*

*business. The more he sold, even though he lost, the
more money he was making."*
Corris and Mell was the name of a local store.

There's a man at West Jonesport, Eben Stanwood by
      name,
And from what nation we know not where he came.
It's up at West Jonesport, you may ask me no more,
There Eben set up a small store.
From West Jonesport to Sawyer's Cove he goes jogging
      along,
He's either whistling or singing a song.
When you go to West Jonesport call in to his store
And he will treat you quite well I am sure.
For every can of milk you buy of Eben, you see,
He'll reach in the showcase, and a corncake goes free.
How he sells things so cheap it is hard to tell
He is third part cheaper than Corris and Mell.

"The Champion of Moose Hill"

> *G. Malcolm Laws includes this song in* Native American
> Ballads, *Appendix II, "Native Ballads of Doubtful
> Currency in Tradition," p. 260. His single reference
> is to Fanny Hardy Eckstorm and Mary W. Smyth,*
> Minstrelsy of Maine *(Boston and New York, 1927),
> pp. 126–28, which has an eight-stanza manuscript text
> very close to the present one. This is a composition of
> the well-known lumberjack folk poet Larry Gorman,
> whose biographer, Edward D. Ives, prints twenty-six
> of his texts in* Larry Gorman, The Man who Made
> the Songs *(in press).*

DORSON:
This is July the twelfth, 1956, and I am in Columbia Falls, in
the home of Mr. Lorey Grant who was born here eighty-two
years ago and has spent his life in the woods as a lumberjack
and as a hunter and knows lots of hunting stories and old

songs. And you were just telling me about a song made up about Emery Mace. Who was Emery Mace, Mr. Grant?

POMPEY GRANT:

Emery Mace was a man born right up there in where that tannery was. He lived right there.

DORSON:

Oh. What tannery was that?

POMPEY GRANT:

That was the Amherst Tannery, that wasn't Beddington's Tannery.

DORSON:

Oh.

POMPEY GRANT:

There was two tanneries right near together. The Amherst Tannery and Beddington Tannery's right near together.

DORSON:

How far away was that from here?

POMPEY GRANT:

Well, it's about, oh—let's see—Amherst is about seventy-five miles from here.

DORSON:

And who made up the song? About Emery Mace? It's a man in the tannery?

POMPEY GRANT:

Yes, it was a man worked right in the tannery, worked there for years.

DORSON:

Oh.

POMPEY GRANT:

I used to know 'im just as well as I know you. But, y'know, I forget names.

DORSON:

Yes, well, how does that song go?

POMPEY GRANT:

Well.

You people all, both great and small,
I pray you lend an ear.

My name and occupation
    You presently will hear.
My name it is bold Emery Mace,
    I practice the fistic skill,
That fatal night when I got tight
    Got knocked out on Moose Hill.

That fatal day I chanced to stay
    To Moose Hill for a spree.
It was the plan of every man
    To prove my destiny.
I saw it in the faces,
    And I read it on the bill.
That if I was tight I'd have to fight
    That night upon Moose Hill.

I let them run and have their fun,
    I hoed right in with them.
Now was Mrs. Giles she was all smiles
    I saw her wink at Nahum,
Why, Nahum he jumped and grabbed me
    And tried to hold me still.
While Mrs. Giles a club she piles
    Upon me at Moose Hill

The first blow that she struck me
    Fell fair upon my head.
For twenty minutes I laid there
    An' thought that I was dead.
The ladies to revive me,
    They did try all their skill,
But they thought that I must surely die
    That night upon Moose Hill.

I did not die, I'll tell you why,
    My skull was only cracked.
It's little you know, the awful blow
    That lady gave poor Mac.

It would have killed a tiger,
 Or slain the wild gorill'
But you know that Mac had better luck
 Than to get murdered on Moose Hill.

My brother Fred stood at my head
 So mournful he did cry.
Poor little lad, he felt so bad,
 He thought that I would die.
For he knew that he alone would be,
 To pay the funeral bill.
For he knew that Mac had had hard luck
 And was penniless on Moose Hill.

I did not die, I'll tell you why . . . (*No* . . .)

I've fought them all, both great and small
 For the best I did not care.
I never fought them with a club,
 I always fought them fair.
I beat the Amherst Champion,
 Fred Titus I nearly killed.
But I lost the belt by a single welt
 From a lady on Moose Hill.

It's now I'm done, my race is run,
 My fighting days are o'er,
I must confess my mind's oppress,
 I'll mount the stage no more.
It's from the ring I'll gently spring,
 But it's sad against my will
That Helen bold the belt shall hold
 As Champion of Moose Hill.

"The Jam on Gurry's Rock"

The most celebrated Maine lumberjack ballad, and one of the best known of all American folksongs. See G. Malcolm Laws C1, p. 143. An intriguing exploration of its possible origins is in Eckstorm and Smyth, Minstrelsy of Maine, "The Pursuit of a Ballad Myth," pp. 176–98. The usual spelling is Gerry.

DORSON:

Now, you know another song about Gurry's Rock. How does that go, Mr. Grant?

POMPEY GRANT:

Gurry's Rock?

DORSON:

Yes. The one you were just singing to me. Starts off, *It being on a Sabbath morning.*

POMPEY GRANT:

It being on Sabbath morning——

DORSON:

Yes.

POMPEY GRANT:

As you shall understand——

DORSON:

You want to sing that?

POMPEY GRANT:

[*Laughter*] I will if I can get the tune.

DORSON:

Yes, sure.

POMPEY GRANT:

It being on Sunday morning, as you shall understand. I don't know as I can sing it.

> Six young Canadians shanty boys did volunteer and go
> To break the jam on Gurry's Rock
>   With the foreman John Monroe.
> They had not rolled off many logs

When the boss to them did say,
"I'll have you lads be on your guard
For the jam will soon give way."
He had not more than spoke these words
When the jam did haul and go.
And carried away the six French lads
And the foreman John Monroe.

Will that record the tune?

DORSON:

Yes; it's recording it. Um-hmm. Okay, go on.

POMPEY GRANT:

What was it starts next, I forgot that song.

DORSON:

To search for their dead bodies——

POMPEY GRANT:

To search for their dead bod—— No, there's some words, comes in there or oughta come in there to make that song come right.

DORSON:

Oh, *He had not more than spoke these words*—— Was that it?

POMPEY GRANT:

No.

He had not more than spoke these words
When the jam did haul and go.
And carried away those six French lads
And the foreman John Monroe.
When the sad news at the camp
His comrades came to hear
To search for their dead bodies
To the river did prepare.
To search for their dead bodies
Through sorrow, grief, and woe,
There bruised and mangled on the beach
Was the head of John Monroe.

Now what we got?

DORSON:

There was one fair form——
POMPEY GRANT:

There was one fair form among them
    A girl from Saginaw town
Whose screams and cries did rend the skies,
    For her own true love was drowned.

DORSON:
There was more to it?
POMPEY GRANT:
Oh, I think there was more words to it, but that's all I
can seem to get.
DORSON:
Where did that actually happen?
POMPEY GRANT:
Why, it happened here on the Penobscot or Androscoggin
River.
DORSON:
Hmm.
POMPEY GRANT:
Yeah, they used to drive, you know, there, on them big
rivers.
DORSON:
Yes.
POMPEY GRANT:
Them big rivers in the northern part of the State of Maine.
DORSON:
Yes, and what was the actual rock where the jam took
place?
POMPEY GRANT:
Well, it's in there somewhere, I was never on that river.
Up there, but it's in 'round Grand Stone, what they call, used
to call Grand Stone, that's an awful piece of falls, rough water
on the river there. But it was right in that vicinity somewhere
where that happened.

II

PENNSYLVANIA
DUTCHMEN

THE "PENNSYLVANIA DUTCH" COUNTRY of rolling farmlands in the fertile Susquehanna Valley presents a fully rounded folk culture, possessing both the oral traditions and the manual arts. A European impress remains strongly evident, not merely in the cycles about prankish Tyl Eulenspiegel of the Harz Mountains and the knuckleheaded Swabians, or beliefs in wizards or *brauchers,* "who can do more than eat bread," but in the very speech that transmits tradition, the Pennsylvania dialect enduring since the late seventeenth century. The dialect is a folk speech; it deviates from standard German and even from the Old Country Germanic dialects, it is spoken by the farmerfolk of eastern Pennsylvania, and it is replete with proverbial expressions and idioms. More accurately than geographical or ethnic factors the dialect defines the folk community, for Pennsylvania Dutchmen have moved to midwestern states, and various German and Swiss stocks and even their Irish and Italian neighbors in America share the dialect.

Still, this folk culture contains many American as well as European elements, in spite of its seemingly alien speech and customs. There is the customary process of local coloring, which results in stories of Eulenspiegel—now become Eilischpijjel—hiring out to a farmer in the Poconos, and of a Swabian who asks that an American wedge be substituted for the carpenter's "Swabian wedge" (a technical term); or again in a folksong caricaturing the highly individual personalities in the Merztown cornet band. Beyond the mere intrusion of American names and places, a less apparent Americanizing influence can be seen in the nature of the folk materials. Here is no transplantation of the Grimm household fairy tales and legends, but rather a display of magical belief tales and anecdotes of foolish characters. Perhaps if tale collecting had been undertaken in Pennsylvania in the 1850's (the substantial compendium of Thomas R. Brendle and William S. Troxell appeared in 1944) when other aspects of the folk culture, like the folk crafts of tinware, pottery, and furniture design, were blooming, then a full repertoire of Märchen might have been recovered. Local characters abound but tend to become proverbial rather than anecdotal in the Keystone state, in contrast to the state of Maine. An eccentric personality and his humorous experiences is suggested in the saying "Like Joe Schneck, he dragged his wife by the hair for love," but with this and numerous other reported proverbs the story has disappeared. Rather the anecdotes cluster around imported stock characters, the Swabians and Eulenspiegel.

Of all American regions, German Pennsylvania is the most fully collected. The conception of folklore held by Pennsylvania Dutch ministers, doctors, professors, and businessmen helps explain why they have collected and published so extensively and exclusively in their own area. A clear statement is provided in a paper on "Pennsylvania German Folklore: An Interpretation," by John Joseph Stoudt, read at the 1952 annual meeting of the Pennsylvania German Folklore Society and printed in Volume XVI (p. 161) of its publications:

> Objectively viewed, then, Pennsylvania German folklore is simply history controlled by the central dominating idea of the Pennsylvania German, or the Pennsylvania Dutch if you prefer, an idea which gives past events significance, meaning and life. This view, embodied in the work of our Society, is the recording and interpretation of past events under the controlling idea which gives them meaning for us. This history is smaller than provincial history in scope, larger than regional history, and it includes all meaningful events and material controlled by the dominant conception, Pennsylvania German.

Stoudt then credits the Romantic revival and the German philosophical idealism of Schelling and Hegel with enlarging the conception of historical truth. In his sense, "Pennsylvania German folklore is the history of the Pennsylvania Germans." Folklore thus embraces written and oral literature, folk piety, arts and crafts, the "shared world of social amusement and community living," and "man's place in nature and the world in general."

This concept is evident in manifold publications. Even in the first volume of the *Journal of American Folklore* (1888), Dr. W. J. Hoffman discoursed for ten pages on "Folk-Lore of the Pennsylvania Germans," rambling over farming superstitions, courting customs, house types, and witchcraft beliefs. Three substantial series currently devote their contents to cultural and folk materials of this people. Since 1890 the Pennsylvania German Society, with headquarters in Norristown, has issued a yearly work which has provided such important contributions to folklore as Edwin M. Fogel's *Proverbs of the Pennsylvania Germans* in 1929, *Folk Medicine of the Pennsylvania Germans: The Non-Occult Cures* by Thomas R. Brendle and Claude W. Unger, in 1935, and for its fiftieth volume in 1944, the assembling of *Pennsylvania German Folk Tales* by Brendle and Troxell. Yet another series of handsomely bound and illustrated books, sponsored by the Pennsylvania German Folklore Society, Allentown, commenced publication in 1936. This series, in spite of its title, ranges over the whole extent of Pennsylvania Dutch culture. Individual numbers deal with Pennsylvania German wills, barns, tombstones, and *Fraktur*-writing. A comprehensive illustrated report by Elmer L. Smith depicts *The Amish Today* (Vol. XXIV, 1960). One monograph inquires into *Mysticism in the Devotional Literature of Colonial Pennsylvania* (Vol. XIV, 1949). Even fictional works are included; *Marriage by Lot* is a "Novel based on Moravian History" (Vol. XXII, 1958), and "En Quart Millich un En Halb Beint Raahm" (Vol. IV, 1939) is a copyrighted German comedy.

The third and most animated organization is the present Pennsylvania Folklife Society, formerly the Pennsylvania Dutch Folklore Center, in Lancaster. Its prime mover is Alfred L. Shoemaker, whose thesis is simple: the Pennsylvania Dutch (*not* German, an ethnic term) folk culture of southeastern Pennsylvania is the fountainhead of American civilization. From it have come such major contributions as the Easter bunny. Even the term "Dutch" is now dropped from the masthead, and "Pennsylvania" alone sufficiently indicates the domain of the Dutchmen, whose influence permeates their cultureless—or colorless—neighbors of British ancestry. "Folklore" yields to the incantatory term "Folklife," which embraces every artifact of daily living, from cookie-cutters to decorated privies. So *The Pennsylvania Dutchman,* commencing as a weekly tabloid in 1949, and changing to a monthly magazine in

1954, is rebaptized *Pennsylvania Folklife* in 1957. The contents and format however remain the same, folksy journalism on homey topics liberally adorned with photographs and illuminated covers and salted with regional promotion, a formula also followed in the pamphlets and gay books issued by the Society on such topics as Christmas, Easter, and barns in Pennsylvania. Since 1953 the Center has sponsored a week-long summer fair at Kutztown netting $90,000 from over 100,000 visitors, who can learn how to water witch, powwow, and cook mush. A Pennsylvania Folklore Museum was established in 1961 on a forty-five-acre estate outside Lancaster, and an eleven-day "Pennsylvania Dutch Harvest Frolic" was held there that fall.

The Pennsylvania Dutch Folklore Center did not neglect oral literature. Two fresh folksong collections are *Songs Along the Mahantongo* by Walter E. Boyer, Albert F. Buffington, and Don Yoder (1951), giving rhymed translations for English singers, and *Pennsylvania Spirituals,* including 150 song texts collected in Pennsylvania Dutch by Don Yoder (1961). Yoder has also tape-recorded witch tales, including one of a bewitched automobile.*

Few outsiders have entered the field of Pennsylvania Dutch folklore. One notable exception is George Korson, the collector of coal miners' traditions, who in 1961 published *Black Rock: Mining Folklore of the Pennsylvania Dutch.* But by and large the Pennsylvania Dutch intellectuals and scholars have remained a group apart. Their introspection is attributable to the same motives that have inspired folklore collecting in small, proud nations like Ireland and Finland.

* "Witch Tales from Adams County," *Pennsylvania Folklife,* XII (1962), 29–37, gives 19 texts in English from a single informant. Yoder's well documented article in the same magazine on "The Folklife Studies Movement" (XIII, 1963, pp. 43–56) gives the history and viewpoint of the Shoemaker school. Yoder discussed "Spirituals from the Pennsylvania Dutch Country" in the *Pennsylvania Dutchman,* VIII (1956–57), 22–33.

1. BRAUCHE AND HEXE

The Sixth and Seventh Books of Moses

Motif D1678, "Magic book, once used, compels person to do evil," occurs in the next three selections. The Sixth and Seventh Books of Moses are constantly alluded to in European popular tradition as diabolical writings. Other relevant motifs are G303.17.2.7, "Devil disappears amid terrible rattle"; G303.16, "How the devil's power may be escaped or avoided"; and G265.8.1.1, "Gun bewitched so that it will not hit target."

Texts from Thomas R. Brendle and William S. Troxell, Pennsylvania German Folk Tales, Legends, Once-upon-a-Time Stories, Maxims and Sayings (Norristown, Pa.: Pennsylvania German Folklore Society, Vol. L, 1944), pp. 150–51, 71–72.

"A brauch book is no evil book," said old Mr. N——. "There is nothing in such a book but prayers and there are some persons who call it a prayer book. *The Sixth and Seventh Book of Moses*, however, is an evil book. With that book one can do all kinds of evil, if one renounces God and swears allegiance to the devil.

"They say that book is printed in black and red, black pages with white letters and white pages with red letters. I never saw a copy. The D—— family of the D—— valley got possession of such a book and swore allegiance to the devil. An old dragon—a dragon is a devil with a big fiery head and a long tail—lived in the Blue Mountain not far from the D—— home.

"One night the dragon came down from his den and passed close by the D— home. The D—s ran out and yelled, 'Dragon, dragon, we need money. Give us money. We need money.'

"The dragon turned around and, rumbling and hissing, came upon them. They fled indoors and had barely time to close and bar the door against him. Thereafter, whenever they went out of doors at night, something unseen would lay hold of them and cast them to the ground.

"I would not like to touch the *Sixth and Seventh Book of Moses.* There was a maid who read in her master's copy in his absence. She read until the devil appeared and took her into his power, and made her do his will; she took the chaff out of the chaff bags and burned it; she pulled up the newly planted onions and reset them with their heads up and stalks down; and then the devil took a crock, knocked out the bottom and directed her to pump it full of water; and this she was doing when her master came home and released her by reading backwards.

"There was a famous hunter who had such a book which he used in hunting. He told his boys that they could never shoot a deer.

"The boys went out hunting and came upon a giant buck deer. They shot at him, and missed; they shot again, and missed. Despite all the shooting the buck stood still and looked at them. Then one of the boys cried, 'By Judas, that must be our father.' I don't know but that he was right."

.　.　.

Old A— could do more than eat bread.[1] One day in the absence of A— the boys of his place and neighbors' boys played hide-and-seek at his home which was a log house. One of the boys hid behind the chimney under the roof, and there he found a book which he opened and tried to read, and immediately A— stood before him and struck him a harsh blow.

[1] *"Hot meh du kenne wie Brod esse."* A cryptic expression which implies that A— was engaged in sorcery. This legend is frequently heard in the Lehigh Valley.

"What are you doing?" he demanded. "Get off as fast as you can."

Now A—— had been away from home, but as soon as the boy opened the book, he was there.

One day A—— talked in a strange and mysterious way, and that night there was a rumbling around his house and a noise as of a chain dragged over the roof. In the morning A—— had disappeared, and was nevermore seen.

Victor Baer, Schnecksville, Pa.

. . .

A man, A—— by name, was spoken of as having dealings with the devil. He was known to possess a book by which he was able to do all kinds of evil. One night as A—— lay in bed there was a noise as of a chain being dragged across the roof.

A—— arose and said, "I must go outside."

His wife begged him, "Don't go! Oh, don't go!"

However, he went out of the house, and that was the last time he was ever seen.

The son found his father's book and read in it. He read so much that he came under the power of the devil. He lost his peace of mind; he could not eat by day, nor sleep at night. Finally he took sick with a high fever; and at night his room was all fiery.

Then a man came along and read him free [2] from the devil. The book which had caused all the trouble was taken and put in a log in the pig stable.

[2] *"Ihn frei gelese."* By reading an "evil book" one can summon the devil voluntarily or involuntarily. Suppose one should come across an "evil book," as the *Seventh Book of Moses* and, merely out of curiosity, start to read in it. Were one to read on and on, one would finally come to a point beyond which one could not continue; one would "lose himself" among the words and become confused and puzzled like a fly entangled in a spider's web. This is spoken of as reading "until one is fast, *sich fascht lese."*

Then, if still able, one should retrace his steps by reading backwards, and in this way retreat out of the maze over the same road by which one entered. If this is not done, the devil will appear, and seek to lay hold of the reader.

The only way to escape from the devil is to have someone read a formula which will compel the devil to relinquish his hold. This is "reading one free," and can be done by a *braucher.*

Detecting the Witch

> *The Motif G271.2.5, "Bible used in exorcism of witch,"*
> *is combined here with Motif H251.3.2, "Thief detected*
> *by psalter and key," which cites references in Kittredge,*
> Witchcraft in Old and New England. *Other motifs*
> *are D1810.0.2, "Magic knowledge of magician," and*
> *G265.4, "Witches cause disease or death of animals."*
> *Text from Brendle and Troxell, pp. 140–41.*

The L— family had been unfortunate. Their poultry was dying off; a cow had died and another cow was giving bloody milk. The father said, "Something is wrong here," and summoned a *braucher*.

The *braucher* came to the house, heard the story, and then asked for a New Testament. It was brought to him. Then he arose and locked all the doors of the house, and also the doors of the room in which the family was sitting.

He took the big Dutch door key and tied the Testament to the key, and told the father to help hold up the Testament by the key with his thumb and forefinger. Together they held up the book.

The father was then directed to think of the person or persons who might have bewitched the cattle. The father thought of one, then of another. As often as he thought of one certain woman the Testament turned; otherwise it was at rest.

When the father was satisfied that he had the right person, the *braucher* said, "Now I shall mark that person."

Then they went out into the yard to a large cherry tree. There a hole was bored, and a plug was made of the same wood and fitted into the hole. The *braucher* took a mallet and lightly struck the peg three times, each blow in one of the highest names.

"Why not knock the plug all the way in, and do the thing rightly?" asked the father.

"Shu-sh! Had you said this to me while we were in the house, it could have been done; but out in the free air, she has heard all," answered the *braucher*. Having done this he went home.

Meanwhile the family waited for developments. A few days later a woman went about in our neighborhood loudly complaining that she was being accused of being a witch, and not a word had been spoken by the family about her. She complained of pain at her kidneys. The cattle all became well.

Told by one in Northampton County who believed the story.

Stilling the Blood

> *Charms for stopping the blood are given in Randolph, Ozark Superstitions, pp. 121–61; and see Dorson, Bloodstoppers and Bearwalkers, pp. 150–65 for examples and pp. 291–93 for references.*
> *Text from Brendle and Troxell, p. 108.*

Old Mr. N. was a *braucher*. He could still the blood for any person whose full name was known to him no matter how far away.

One could telephone to him and ask for his immediate services and he would respond by stilling the blood.

He would say:

> "Three roses stood on the Lord Jesus' grave,
> The one was named humility,
> The other was named gentleness,
> And the third was named God's will.
> So shall the blood for N. N. be still."

Lehigh County.

The Golden Ring

> *Motif D1417.1, "Magic circle prevents escape."*
> *Text from Brendle and Troxell, p. 100.*

"My uncle's horse ran away, and went out to the S—— place. I ran after, and caught him in the barnyard. But when I tried to lead him home, I lost the way out, and kept on going around and around in the barnyard. I walked around and around in a circle. Then came S——. "What's the matter?" he asked.

"I can't find the place to get out," said I.

"Right in front of you is the place," said S——. And so it was.

"S——, every evening, took holy water, and squirted a ring around his buildings. This he called his golden ring,[3] and whoever trod into that ring was bound and could not leave without his permission.

"I was not the only one who got into that ring. Two men drove on the road past the S—— place one night, and came upon a blown down willow tree that blocked the way. They decided to drive through the S—— barnyard, and then back to the road. They drove into the barnyard, and there they were held immovable all through the night. When daylight appeared in the east, S—— raised the window of his bedroom, and called down, 'Now, you can go.' "

As told by a resident of Egypt.

The Bewitched Automobile

> *The collector cites Motifs G265.8.3.2, "Witch bewitches wagon," and G271.6, "Exorcism of witch by countercharm."*
>
> *Text from Don Yoder, "Witch Tales from Adams County," p. 34. Recorded in English from Frank Eckert, then 87, on June 7, 1958, in Aspers township in south-central Pennsylvania.*

Well, now, I'll tell you a story what happened to an old lady and her husband down close Hanover. They decided they'd buy themselves a new car—so they did. Well, when Saturday evening come, why, the old gentleman said to his wife, "Now, let's take a ride in the new car, this evening." "All right." They started off and they got in as fer as Hanover. And right at the square in Hanover the car stopped. Nobody could start it. They done everything they knowed, got garage fellows there to look at it, nobody could find anything wrong. Car wouldn't move. Somebody said, "Well, you go out to Mrs. K. and tell her about this."

Went out to Mrs. K. and told her, and Mrs. K. said, "Well, I'll write you on a piece of paper here and you don't—you're not to read it. You take it back to the car and put it on the starter and put your foot on this paper, on the starter, and," she said, "your car will go." And so they did. Went back, a whole crowd around the car. They put this piece of paper on the starter and he put his foot on it, and the car started right off, and away they went. Didn't have no more trouble that evening with the car.

So the next morning some time, why, they got someone come and said, "Well, the neighbor woman over here is *awful* sick." "Well," they said, "what's wrong with her?" Said, "She's in bed, she's jist that sick she can't be up." And this was the woman that put the spell on the automobile. And Mrs. K. fixed *her* business fer her that she didn't bother nobody around there fer awhile.

2. FARM FOLK BELIEFS

FROM EDWIN MILLER FOGEL, *Beliefs and Superstitions of the Pennsylvania Germans* (Philadelphia: American Germanica Press, 1915). In his introduction Fogel states: "In the present study only the more distinctive Pennsylvania German counties were taken into consideration, viz: Berks, Bucks, Carbon, Dauphin, Lebanon, Lehigh, Lancaster, Monroe, Montgomery, Northampton, Northumberland, Schuylkill, Snyder and York. They cover an area of more than 8,000 square miles and have a population of more than one and one-quarter millions." He collected the 2,085 beliefs in the volume himself by word of mouth.

In printing his texts Fogel gives the German dialect original, the English translation, the counties in which the belief is known, and some comparative references and German texts. His bibliographical references are given following the belief texts, pp. 124–25.

Stockraising and the Barnyard

745. 'S ērscht kalb fume rind zīkt mer net uf, mer ferkåfts. (Af)

> *The first calf dropped by a cow should not be raised, it should be sold.*

> *Das erst geborene kalb einer jungen kuh (färsenkalb) darf nicht gezüchtet werden, weil jede erstgeburt zur zucht untauglich ist.* BS 33 p. 127.

758. Wammer fī schlacht, darf mers net dauere oder 's gēt lang net dōd. (Af)

*You must not pity an animal which is being slaughtered,
or else it will die hard.*

*Wenn man ein vieh, das geschlachtet wird, beklaget, so
kann as nicht ersterben.* GR 561.

761. *Wammern scheierschwalm dōtmącht gebe di kī blūtiche
milich.* (Be, Bu, D, Lb, Lh, Lnc, Na, Nu, Sn, Y)

Kill a barn swallow and the cows will give bloody milk.

*Wenn man eine schwalbe tötet oder forttreibt, geben die
kühe rote milch und man hat unglück mit dem vieh.*
Z 744.

772. *Wann en kū der wi'derferkau ferlīrt, hot si hōle haerner
un der wolf im schwanz. Nō bōrt mern loch in jēder
haern un schtritzt fun īre ēğne mi'lich nei˜. Wanns
horn net blūt is si schlimm grąnk. Nō mącht mern
balle fun holler rinn un schībts re der hąls nunner.* (Af)

*When a cow has indigestion it has "hollow horns" and
"wolf in the tail." Bore a hole into each horn and
inject some of the cow's milk into it. If there is no
bleeding, the cow is seriously sick. Make a ball from
the bark of the elder bush and push it down her throat.*

*Bohre ein loch in das horn, das hohl ist, und melke von
der nämlichen kuh milch und spritze sie in das horn.
Dies ist die allerbeste kur für hohle kuhhörner.* Hoh
p. 36.

788. *Wąnn en lōs schpīlich waert, schitt re 's sēfewąsser fum
bąlbire un di hōr ąs mer sich im bąlbire ąbschneit ei˜,
oder mer gebts re im saufe.* (Af)

*When a sow comes in oestrum give it the soapy water and
the lather after shaving, either directly or in its food.*

799. *Wąnn en gaul gfaun'dert is, nemm en frischer mensche-
drek, wikel en in en willner lumbe un dūn um gaul
sei˜ gebi'ss.* (Af)

To cure founder (laminitis) *wrap human feces in a woolen rag and tie it to the horse's bit.*

Wider die rehe, nimm dem pferd seinen zaum und ziehe das gebiss durch menschenkot, zaume das pferd damit auf und hebe ihm die nasenlöcher zu bis er niesen muss. Ho p. 85; cf. Alem 20.282.

816. *'S kalb muss mer hin'nerschich di dir naus dū~ un in ēm o'chtem, nō blaerrt di kū net.* (Af)

If you back the calf out of the stable while holding your breath, the cow will not low for its calf.

Die kuh wird schweigend und mit zurückgehaltenem atem in den stall geführt, so schreit sie dann nicht. Wu 439.

849. *Wammer am butter drēe is un er will net zamme gē~, soll merrsåğe:* Butter, butter, butter, *dich, 'S is ken aer'ğeri hex wi ich.* (Bu, D, Lb, Lh, Lnc, Mt, Na, Nu, Sc)

If butter is slow in coming, say: Butter, butter, come, there's no greater witch than I. Come, butter, come. Come, butter, come. Peter's waiting at the gate. Waiting for a buttered cake. Come, butter, come. H 67.

859. *En kū wū blūt'ichi mil'ich gebt is ferhext.* (Af)

Bloody milk indicates a bewitched cow.

Rote milch einer behexten kuh muss kochend mit ruten gepeitscht werden. G 3. 540.

861. *Wann di mil'ich ferhext is soll mern glidich eise nei~ dū~.* (Be, C, D, Lb, Lh, Lnc, Na, Sc)

Thrust red-hot iron into bewitched milk.

Wenn beim buttermachen die milch lange nicht bricht, nehme man einen küchelspiess, mache ihn glühend und stosse ihn in den butterkübel. Geschieht das, wird die hexe damit gebrannt und die milch bricht. Z 544.

At the present day the good housewife puts a hot iron into the cream during the process of churning to expel the witch from the churn. D Y 170.

862. *Mit Kaerfreidåks oier kammer gūt brauche.* (Be, C, Lb, Lh, Mr, Nu, Sc, Y)

Eggs laid on Good Friday are useful in powwowing.

Eier, welche von schwarzen hennen am Karfreitag gelegt werden, behält man fleissig auf; denn sie sollen in verschiedenen dingen wunderbare wirkung haben. V A S 2. 78; Wu 71.

An egg laid on Good Friday is preserved as a charm. V S L 2.1.224.

876. *En ungliksoi schmeisst mer hin'nerschich i'bern dạch, nō gēts unglik mit faert.* (Af)

Throw a dwarf egg backwards over the roof and the bad luck will accompany the egg.

Auffallend kleine hühnereier, sogennannte unglückseier, müssen "hinterschtöwerscht" d. h. nach hinten übers dach geworfen werden. Alem 20.284.

889. *Wammern bri hinkel setzt, muss en weibsmensch di oier im schaerz naus dråǧe fer setze.* (Af)

Eggs will hatch better if carried to the stable by a woman in her apron.

To secure hen birds the woman who sets the hen should carry her eggs in her chemise to the hatching nest. G Scot 141.

897. *Wann di hinkel net lēǧe wolle takscht en sein im hinkel-schtạll uf "oier zēe sents dutzend," nō lēǧe si giwiss.* (Bu)

When hens don't lay tack up a sign "Eggs, 10 cts. a dozen," and they will certainly begin to lay.

Planting, Sowing, and Reaping

943. *Di būne blanzt mer im iberschtēede.* (Af; Heidelberg)

Plant beans when the horns of the moon point upward.

955. *Iberm reddich sēe muss mer såğe: so lang ạs mei͠ årm, so dik as mei͠ årsch.* (Be, Lb)

When sowing radish seed say: as long as my arm and as big as my ass.

969. *Mer muss ken pēterli ins haus blạnze oders schtaerbt ēns aus em haus.* (Af)

A member of the family will die if you transplant parsley into pots.

Ausgegrabene petersilienwurzeln darf man nicht wieder pflanzen, sonst pflanzt man seinen besten freund oder den gatten in die erde, bringt ihm den tod. Wu 425.

It is unlucky to transplant parsley. V S L 2.168.

973. *Im unnerschtēende mūnd soll nix geblạnzt waerre ạs ạn de schteke nuf soll, wi zum beischpil būne un aerbse.* (Af; Heidelberg)

Climbing plants, e.g., beans and peas should not be planted in the decrease of the moon (or when the horns of the moon are turned downward).

Plant peas and potatoes in the increase of the moon. C S A 1120.

1009. *Wạmmer blạnze, oder sō ebbes grikt daerf mer sich net bedanke oders si wạxe net.* (Af)

Never thank anyone for plants for the garden; they will not grow if you do.

Für geliehenen samen darf man nicht danken, sonst gedeiht er nicht. Wu 405.

1039. *Schnē unnerblūğe is juscht sō gūt fern feld ạs mischt un kạ'lik.* (Af)

Turning down snow with a plow is as good for a field as manure and lime.

April schnee düngt. . . . Z 1305.

1041. *Wammer di grumbire uf der Sēnt Patricksdåk blạnzt gebts grōsse un si gebe gūt aus.* (C, Lnc, Mt, Nu, Sn, Y)

If you plant potatoes on St. Patrick's day potatoes will be large and the crop big.

1055. *Bēm wū wider ausschlạğe solle misse im zu'nemmede ạb'kạkt waerre.* (Af)

If trees are to sprout again they should be felled in the increase of the moon.

Bäume, welche wieder aus der wurzel ausschlagen sollen, müssen im zunehmenden mond gefällt werden. B S 33. 128.

It is lucky to fell trees at the wane of the moon. H 51.

1066. *Wạnns gschwi'schich Grischdåk un Neijōr windich is, schpile di ebbelbēm, nō gebts fil ōbscht.* (Be, D, Lb, Lh, Lnc, Mr, Na, Sc, Y)

If there are high winds between Christmas and New Year, the trees copulate and there will be much fruit.

Ist es zum Neujahr windig, so gibt es viel obst. Wu 197.

1082. Wann en bâm net drăǧe will lâd mern mit eise un schtē͂.
(Af)

If a tree will not bear fruit load it with iron and stones.

Packt man im Brandenburgischen schwere steine zwischen die zweige, so werden sie schwer tragen. M D V 207.

BIBLIOGRAPHY AND ABBREVIATIONS

Af   All of the fourteen Pennsylvania German counties of Pennsylvania.

Alem   *Alemannia. Zeitschrift für Alemannische und Fränkische Geschichte, Volkskunde, usw.* Freiburg, 1873.

Be   Berks County.

B S   *Baltische Studien.* Vol. 33. Stettin, 1883.

Bu   Bucks County.

C   Carbon County.

C S A   Fanny D. Bergen. *Current Superstitions collected from the oral Tradition of English speaking Folk.* Boston, 1896.

D   Dauphin County.

G   Jakob Grimm. *Deutsche Mythologie.* Vierte Ausgabe, besorgt von E. H. Meyer. Berlin, 3 vols., 1875–78.

G R   *Die gestriegelte Rockenphilosophie, oder aufrichtige Untersuchung derer von vielen superklugen Weibern hochgehaltenen Aberglauben.* Chemnitz, 1759. von E. H. Meyer.

G Scot   Walter Gregor. *Notes on the Folk-Lore of the Northeast of Scotland.* London, 1881.

H   Sarah Hewett. *Nummits and Crummits. Devonshire Customs, Characteristics and Folk-Lore.* London, 1900.

Hlbg   Heidelberg.

Ho   *Die Land- und Haus-Apotheke, oder getreuer und gründlicher Unterricht für den Bauer und Stadtmann, enthaltend die allerbesten Mittel, sowohl für die Menschen als für das Vieh besonders für die Pferde. Nebst einem grossen Anhang von der Aechten Färberey, um Türkisch-Roth, Blau, Satin-Roth, Patent-Grün und viele andere Farben mehr zu Färben.* Erste Amerikanische Auflage. Herausgegeben von Johannes Georg Homan, in Elsasz Taunschip, Berks Caunty, Pennsylvanien. Reading: Gedruckt bey Carl A. Bruckmann, 1818.

Hoh	*Der lange Verborgene Freund, oder: Getreuer und christlicher Unterricht für jedermann, enthaltend wunderbare und probmäszige Mittel und Künste, sowohl für die Menschen als das Vieh. Mit vielen Zeugen bewiesen in diesem Buch und wovon das mehrste noch wenig bekannt ist, und zum allerersten Mal in Amerika im Druck erscheint.* Herausgegeben von Johann Georg Hohmann, Nahe bey Reading, in Elsasz Taunschip, Berks Caunty, Pennsylvanien. Reading: Gedruckt für den Verfass, 1820.
L	Felix Liebrecht. *Zur Volkskunde. Alte und neue Aufsätze.* Heilbronn, 1870.
Lb	Lebanon County.
Lh	Lehigh County.
Lnc	Lancaster County.
MDV	Elard Hugo Meyer. *Deutsche Volkskunde.* Strasburg, 1898.
Mr	Monroe County.
Mt	Montgomery County.
Na	Northampton County.
Nu	Northumberland County.
Sc	Schuylkill County.
Sn	Snyder County.
VAS	Anton Birlinger. *Volkstümliches aus Schwaben.* 2 vols. Freiburg, 1862.
VSL	Vincent Stuckey Lean. *Lean's Collectanea. Collections of Proverbs, Folk-Lore and Superstitions, also Compilations towards Dictionaries of Proverbial Phrases and Words Old and Disused.* 4 vols. Bristol, 1902–1904.
Wu	Carl Friedrich Adolf Wuttke. *Der deutsche Volksaberglaube der Gegenwart.* Dritte Bearbeitung von Elard Hugo Meyer. Berlin, 1900.
Y	York County.
Z	Ignaz V. Zingerle. *Sitten, Bräuche und Meinungen des tiroler Volkes.* Zweite vermehrte Auflage. Innsbruck, 1891.

3. BELIEF TALES

Christmas Eve in the Stable

This episode combines Motif B251.1.2.3, "Cows kneel in stable at midnight of Eve of Old Christmas," with a legend involving Motif M341.1, "Prophecy: death at certain time." The same combination is found in Helen Creighton, Folklore of Lunenburg County, Nova Scotia *(Ottawa, 1950), No. 46, "Oxen," p. 18. Separately the belief and the legend turn up in Dorson,* Negro Folktales in Michigan, *"Twelve Days after Christmas," pp. 151–52, and note 106, pp. 224–25, and "Charlie and Pat," pp. 72–73, and note 41, pp. 214–15.*

Text from Brendle and Troxell, pp. 79–80.

The month of December, called in the dialect, *Grischdmunet*, is the month of spirits. Then, as at no other time, the spirits are abroad, and he who has been born in this month can see, hear, and speak with them. The activity of the spirits reaches its height on Christmas Eve, at midnight, when all living nature is moved and becomes articulate; * bees in their hives buzz a language which then and only then can be understood by the hearers. They may even leave the hive, fly around, and speak; horses and cattle speak, and tell of things that shall come to pass.

There was a farmer of rough speech, and of harsh ways toward his horses. He had heard of the mysterious happenings at midnight on Christmas Eve, but would not believe that they were true, and persisted in this attitude despite the asseverations

* In the dialect, *alles bewegt sich.*

of his friends that they themselves had heard horses and cattle speak at that hour. He would "see for himself" and only after he had seen with his own eyes and heard with his own ears would he believe.

So, one Christmas Eve, several hours before midnight, he stole into the horse stable and hid in a pile of straw that was used for bedding for the horses. At midnight he heard one horse say to the other, "We have a very cruel master, and this night we shall kick him to death."

The farmer rose up from the pile of straw, and in groping his way to the stable door was kicked to death by the horses.

Lebanon County.

Sewing on Ascension Day

> *Motif C631.2, "Tabu: spinning on holy days," is closest to the present tradition.*
>
> *Text from Brendle and Troxell, pp. 83–84. From Montgomery County.*

Old Mrs. N., who lived in the hills south of Pennburg with her son's household, wore a nightcap that had been made for her on Ascension Day.

One day a storm came on, with fearful flashes of lightning and peals of thunder. Unlike other storms, it didn't move on but stood over the house with the clouds almost touching the treetops.

The family became frightened, and luckily one of them remembered the old belief that nothing was to be sewn on Ascension Day, and also recalled that the grandmother's nightcap had been sewn on that day.

Quickly the son took the nightcap and hung it on the clothesline out in the yard. He had scarcely re-entered the house before there was a terrific clap of thunder, and when they looked out into the yard they saw that the cap was torn into pieces.

So the story goes, with each community having its own version.

Taking Off of the Moon

*From Don Yoder, "Witch Tales from Adams County,"
p. 36. The informant, Frank Eckert, 87, was a butcher
by trade. Recorded in English, June 7, 1958, in Aspers,
in southern Pennsylvania.*

And I wouldn't butcher in the takin' off of the moon.[1] I always
butchered in the growin' of the moon, killin' a beef or killin'
my own hogs. I said, other people, I'd butcher anytime they'd
want done, but not for myself. And I said that I wouldn't
butcher in the takin' off of the moon, because that meat, them
hams and shoulders, that you'd cure fer your own use, would
all shrink up in a certain amount that they'd lose, it seems. The
meat would dry up. And the same way with beef—beef will do
the same thing. You take a piece of beef that was killed in the
takin' off of the moon and cook it, and you'd weigh that piece
of meat before you'd put it on the stove to roast it or cook it.
You seen what it looked like when you put it on, and when it
was cooked or fried, whatever you done with it, it was shrunk
up, pretty near one third it looks you'd lose.

And I said it was *proven*, that I *done* it, and *seen* it done.
I say anybody that wants to try it can try it and find out for
their own satisfaction.

[1] The expression "takin' off" of the moon is a Dutchism for decrease or
waning of the moon, from the Dutch dialect *op-nemma* (*abnehmen*), *to*
decrease.

4. NOODLE TALES

Eileschpijjel

Eileschpijjel is a beloved character throughout the Pennsylvania Dutch region. He is known as "Eileschpijjel," "Eideschpiggel," "Till Eileschpickel," "Eire Schpickel," "Eilenshpiggel," and even as "Eirisch Bickel." A large number of stories have collected around his name. Most of them present him as a more or less lovable character, and without the brutality and maliciousness which appear in the European stories of him. He is regarded by some of our people as a real person who lived in the not far distant past. "My father knew Eileschpijjel well," said one man.

"Eileschpijjel often came to my grandfather's house," said another.

"Eileschpijjel was still living when my father was a little boy," said a third.

However, one said, "The old people thought that Eileschpijjel was the devil."

Of a person who persists in doing things in his own peculiar way, it is said, "He is a real Eileschpijjel,"[1] or "He has the ways of Eileschpijjel."[2]

When a person succeeds in performing a difficult task in the presence of others, not infrequently the remark is made, "Eileschpijjel is the master of the devil"; if he fails, "The devil is the master of Eileschpijjel."[3]

---

[1] *"Er is en rechder Eileschpijjel."*
[2] *"Des sin so Eileschpijjel Schtreech."*
[3] *"Dar Eileschpijjel is iwwer dar Deiwel." "Der Deiwell is iwwer dar Eileschpijjel."*

From Brendle and Troxell, pp. 153–54. For European stories of Till Eulenspiegel see Das Volksbuch von Tyl Eulenspiegel, edition Eugen Diederichs. The following four Eileschpijjel tales are from Brendle and Troxell, pp. 161–65.

In the Windy Poconos

Eileschpijjel was servant to a farmer up in the Poconos. One day he was sent out into a very stony field to pick stones and haul them to a stone fence with a two-horse team.

Eileschpijjel drove into the field which was literally covered with stones. When he saw the endlessness of his task, he quit and drove home.

"What's wrong?" asked the farmer.

"It is so windy out in the field that whenever I throw stones on the wagon from one side the wind blows them down on the other side. Such work I do not like and I am leaving for another job until the stones have been plowed under and the field is fit to work in," [4] said Eileschpijjel.

Thomas Snyder, Allentown, Pa.

Eileschpijjel the Plowman

Eileschpijjel was hired by a farmer to plow. The farmer went with him into the field where he was to plow.

"How shall I plow?" asked Eileschpijjel.

There was a hog at the other end of the field, and the farmer, pointing to it, said, "Plow all the way to the hog, and back." [5]

In the evening when Eileschpijjel brought the horses in to the barn the farmer asked, "Is there still much to be plowed?"

"It all depends on how far the hog will go," [6] answered Eileschpijjel.

[4] ". . . bis di Schtee unnergeblugt sin un mar kann verschtennich drin schaffe."
[5] ". . . uff seli Sau zu."
[6] "Es kummt druff a wie weit ass di Sau noch lauft."

The Wagon Load

> *Type 1242,* Loading the Wood, *is reported only for northern Europe.* Brendle and Troxell *comment, "This is one of the most commonly heard Eileschpijjel stories."*

Eileschpijjel went with a two-horse team for wood. As he threw piece after piece on the wagon, he said, "If the horses can pull this piece, they can pull the next one."

Reasoning thus, he kept on loading until the wagon was completely filled. Then he found that the horses were unable to pull the load.

He proceeded to unload, saying as he threw off piece after piece, "If they can't pull this piece, they can't pull the next one."

Reasoning thus, he kept on unloading until the wagon was empty.

Then he drove home with an empty wagon.

> *Robert Ohlinger, Wescosville, Rte. 1, Pa.*

Eileschpijjel's Smoke Pipe

> *Type 1157,* The Gun as Tobacco Pipe, *is known in northern and eastern Europe. A Finnish-American text appears in* Dorson, Bloodstoppers and Bearwalkers, *pp. 143–44, and an 1844 journalistic version is cited in* Dorson, Jonathan Draws the Long Bow, *p. 55.*

Eileschpijjel was out hunting with an old musket. The devil came along and seeing the musket asked, "What is that?"

Eileschpijjel answered, "A smoke pipe," [7] and turning the end of the barrel to the devil, said, "Take a puff."

[7] Eileschpijjel calls the barrel of the musket a smoke pipe. The devil understands him to mean a pipe for smoking tobacco which in the dialect is called *Schmokpeif.*

The devil took the end of the barrel into his mouth and began to suck. Thereupon Eileschpijjel pulled the trigger, and the bullet and the smoke flew into the devil's mouth.

The devil, coughing and gasping for breath, spat out the bullet and said, "You—you surely use strong tobacco."

Anson Sittler, Egypt, Pa., and many others.

The Great Need

> *A combination of Type 1541,* For the Long Winter,
> *Type 1540,* The Student from Paradise (Paris), *and*
> *Type 1384,* The Husband Hunts Three Persons as
> Stupid as his Wife. *Summarized in Dorson,* American
> Folklore, *pp. 82–83.*
>
> *Text from Brendle and Troxell, pp. 31–33.*

Years ago there lived out in the back country a couple that was very saving. The man would often say to his wife, "We must save for the time when the great need comes." [8]

One day the man went to work and his wife was left alone. There was a knock at the door. She opened the door, and, not knowing the one who knocked, asked, "Who are you?"

"I am Mr. Need," came the answer.

"Are you he whom the people call the 'Great Need?'" asked the woman.

"Yes, I am he," was the answer.

"Oh! My husband has been waiting a long time for you, and now I shall give you all the money that we have saved for you," said the woman.

She got all the money that they had saved and gave it to him. When her husband came home, she said, "Mr. Great Need was here, and I gave him all that we had saved for him."

After the husband had recovered from his surprise he said, "You are so stupid that I do not care to live with you. I am going away, and I shall never come back unless I find a person more stupid than you."

---

[8] *"Die gross Nod."* An old dialectal expression for famine. The woman took it to be the name of a person.

So he went away and traveled on until he came to a big barn where some men were busily at work.

"What are you doing?" he inquired.

"We are putting the white horse up on the hayloft for a nest egg," [9] they replied.

"They are very stupid but not as stupid as my wife," said the man as he continued on his way.

He came to a high hill, and went down into the valley. There a little hut stood, with its windows open, and a little old woman sitting inside. He entered the hut.

When the woman saw him she said, "From where do you come?"

"Down from above," [10] he answered.

"I am glad to see you. Tell me, how is my son Michael getting along up there?" she said.

"Not so well," answered the man. "He is very poor. He has no money, no clothes, and no food."

"Oh," said the woman as she rose from her chair, "I am so happy that somebody has come with whom I can send things to my Michael."

She gathered food and clothes and all the money she had and told him to take them along for her Michael.

The man concluded that he had now met someone who was more stupid than his wife, and he went home and lived with his wife happily ever after.

Hattie Lerch, Allentown, Pa.

Counting Noses

Type 1287, Numskulls Unable to Count Their Own Number, *includes Motif J2031.1, "Numskulls count selves by sticking their noses in the sand," which is reported as a Hodja Nasreddin story. See* The Khoja:

[9] *"En Neschtoi."* When eggs were lifted out of a nest, one was always left in the nest as a nest egg. This was supposed to induce the hen to keep on laying. The white horse was intended to induce a mare to lay a colt.

[10] *"Vun owwe runner."* This expression means "to come down from a hill into a valley," "to come down from the uplands," and also "to come down from Heaven." The woman took the last meaning.

> Tales of Nasr-ed-din, *tr. Henry D. Barnham (New York, 1924), pp. 59–63. In the dialect the stupid Swabians are known as "di dumme Schwowe."*
>
> *Text from Brendle and Troxell, p. 110.*

Do you know why the Swabians before they decide a matter say, "Let us count noses?" It was this way.

Thirteen Swabians were traveling through the country, in a group. One day they got the notion that one of their number was missing. To find out whether all were there they took to counting. The first one counting three," [11] and so on until the last who was twelve.

"There are only twelve of us," said the one who counted.

"You are wrong," said another. "Let me count."

So he counted: "I am I; you are one; you are two"; and so on to the last who was twelve.

A third counted, with the same results.

They could not agree whether one was missing or not; but to settle the matter they decided to stick their noses in the mud, and then count the marks. This they did, and found that all thirteen were present.

Commented one, "I sort of thought that all were here." [12]

The Swabian Wedge

> *Motif J1805.1, "Similar sounding words mistaken for each other" is the closest motif.*
>
> *Text from Brendle and Troxell, p. 119.*

A Swabian who had newly come to America found work in a cooper shop. One day he found that the staves of a barrel that he was setting up didn't fit together tightly and that a small fissure remained. "What now?" he asked a fellow-worker.

The man answered, "That's easy. We'll pound a stupid Swabian into it." [13] Meaning thereby a wedge which was em-

---

[11] *"Ich bin ich; du bust ains, du bist zwa."*
[12] *"Ich han so halner geglaubt as fehlt keiner."*
[13] *"Do schlajje mar en Schwob nei."*

ployed for such contingencies and which was called "a Swabian." The Swabian did not understand the reference and, because he was the only Swabian in the shop, became alarmed for his own safety and in a trembling tone asked, "Would not a stupid American do as well?"

Lehigh County.

5. PROVERBS

THE FOLLOWING PROVERBIAL expressions are selected from Edwin Miller Fogel, *Proverbs of the Pennsylvania Germans* (Pennsylvania German Society, 1929). Fogel opens his volume with the statement, "The proverb plays a surprisingly prominent role in the speech of the Pennsylvania Germans; it is the very bone and sinew of the dialect. . . ."

On the question of English versus German origin of these proverbs, Fogel found that one half seemed to be of German origin, one tenth British, one tenth both German and British, while for the remainder he could locate no parallels.

The Pennsylvania Dutch dialect text is first given, followed by an English translation and, if they exist, parallel sayings in English and high German. Two English and four German collections are cited, and the bibliography follows the texts.

Farm Sayings

22. *'R macht åge wī'n gschtoche kalb.*

   He makes eyes like a slaughtered calf.

   Er glotzte mich an wie ein gestochen kalb. Wi 90.2.

31. *Å~ gebōre wī'm* kalb's *schtubbe.*

   It is as natural to him as butting is to a calf.

38. *D'r hammer wērt aus faerm* ambōs.

   The anvil outlasts the hammer.

97. *'R bat sō fīl as's finft råt im wage.*

He does as much good as the fifth wheel in a wagon.

Der ist so nutz als das fünft rad am wagen. Wiii 1083.31.

166. *De elter d'r* bok, *de schteif'r seī̃ haern.*

The older the billygoat, the harder the horn.

Je älter der bock, je härter das horn. B 467.

167. *Schtōsweis, wī'm* bok *di milich.*

It comes in fits and starts, like milk from a buck.

200. *Jēder mutter lōbt ir* butter *wanner å schtinkt as sī'n net fresse kann.*

Every woman praises her butter, even though it is so rancid that she can't eat it.

Jede frau lobt ihre butter. Wi 1127.480

211. *'R* danzt *wī en alti kū.*

He dances like an old cow.

Er tanzt wie eine kuh auf dem seil. Wiv 1032.98.

216. *'S flīge em ken gebrōtne* daube *ins maul.*

Roasted pigeons will not fly in one's mouth.

Die gebratenen tauben fliegen keinem ins maul. B 3643.

227. *'S waert enihau* dåk *wann å ken håne grēt.*

Day will dawn anyhow, even though no cock crow.

Es wird doch tag, wenn auch der hahn nicht kräht. Wiv 1003.257.

243. *Sō* daer *as'n holzbok.*

As lean as a sawhorse.

254. *Du machscht aerger wīd'r* deibel *an de rībe. D'r deibel grikt di rībe un dū's graut.*

You perform worse than the devil in the turnip field.
The devil gets the turnips and you the tops.
Er nimmts überhaupt wie der teufel die bauern. B 3654.

335. *Sō* dot *as'n makrel.*

As dead as a mackerel.
As dead as a herring. H 61.

351. *Jēders muss sibe pund* drek *un en wik'l waerik ime jōr fresse.*

Each one must eat seven pounds of dirt and a hank of tow per year.

392. *Sō* dumm *as seibūne schtrō.*

As "dumb" as firewood; as thick as a stick.

399. *Sō* dumm *as seibūneschtrō.*

As stupid as horse-bean-straw.
Er ist dümmer als saubohnenstroh. Wv 1201.110.

458. *D'r* esel *hots aus d'r wand gschlage.*

A mule kicked it out of the wall (a bastard).

561. *En grōssi* frå *un en grōssi scheier sin kem mann ken schåde.*

A big wife and a big barn will never do a man any harm.

679. So *bēs as en* gluk *mit ēm junge.*

As cross as a hen with one chick.

684. De nēcherm gnoche *de sīssr's flēsch.*

The nearer the bone, the sweeter is the flesh. H 380.

Je näher am bein, je süszer das fleisch. B 1009.

801. Jēder håne *fecht's bescht uf seim ēgne mischthōf.*

Every cock fights best on his own dunghill.

A cock fights well on his own dunghill. Liii 380.

Der hahn ist keck auf seinem mist. B 1655.

807. Dēl leit hen ken haern. *Wammer ne pår droppe oxe blūt uf di schtaern dropse dēt, grēchte si haerner.*

Some people have no brains. If you dropped some ox-blood on their foreheads, they'd get horns.

821. Daert hokt d'r hås *im peffer.*

There the rabbit squats in the pepper; that's the crux of the situation; ay, there's the rub.

Da liegt der hase im pfeffer. B 1692.

829. Jeders muss sei ēgni haut *zum gaerber dråge.*

Every one must carry his own hide to the tanner.

Every man must skin his own skunk, i.e., bear his own burthen. Liii 458.

Jeder kann seine haut gerben lassen, wo er will. Wii 440.59.

851. Sō hendich *as en schupkaerich in d'r kich.*

As handy as a wheelbarrow in the kitchen.

866. En gscheit hinkel *lēkt å alsemol nēbichs nescht.*

Even a clever hen will lay outside the nest; mistakes are made even by the best of men.

967. *D'r bauer het sei* kalb *net schike breiche,* a͞er *hets selber sȧge kenne.*

The farmer need not have sent his calf, he could have told it himself.

1205. *Di alt* lōs *hot di weis gfresse.*

The old sow ate the tune. (*A remark made when music is out of tune, time, or pitch.*)

1223. *Wi d'r* mann, *sō sei fī.*

As the man, so his cattle.

1232. *D'r* Maerz *sȧkt zum Horning, wann ich* wa͞er *wi dū, dēts kalb f'rfrīre in d'r kū.*

March says to February: If I were like you, the calf would freeze unborn.

1259. *'N armi* maus *as juscht* ē~ *loch hot.*

A poor mouse that has only one hole; a prudent man has more than one string to his bow.

Eine arme maus die nur ein einzig loch hat. B 2484.

1284. Wa͞ers ērscht in di mīl *kummt grikt's* ērscht gimȧle.

He that cometh first to the mill, grindeth first. Liii 488.

Coal pit law: First come, first served. Liii 441.

Wer zuerst kommt, der mahlet zuerst. B 4209.

1286. *D'r* miller *is 's* ērscht *as rumgukt wann ebber dib greischt.*

The miller is the first to look back when you cry "thief."

Teach a miller to be a thief. Liv 107.

Thieves are always the first to cry out at being suspected. Liv 157.

*Nichts kecker als des müllers hemd weil's täglich einen
dieb am kragen nimmt.* B 2561.

1289. *Bleib uf deim ēgne* mischthaufe.

Stay on your own dunghill.

1386. *Aus gebakne* oier *gebts ken hinkel.*

*You can't hatch chickens from fried eggs; you can't eat
your cake and have it.*

Aus gebackenen eiern schlupfen keine hühnchen. B 774.

1397. *D'r* ox *schtēt am baerik.*

The ox stands before the hill; a person is in a quandary.

Da stehen die ochsen am berge. Wiii 1107.342.

1473. *En blindi* sau *finnt å alsemōl en ēchel.*

Even a blind pig will sometimes find an acorn.

Eine blinde sau findet manchmal auch eine eichel. Wiv
10.96.

1476. *Wann di* sau *satt is schmeisst si d'r drōk um.*

When a pig has enough it upsets the trough.

Wenn die sau genug hat, stosst sie den kübel um. B 3162.

1520. *Sī hot ibers* schilscheit *gikikt.*

*She kicked over the swingle tree; she strayed beyond the
paths of virtue; she has lost her virginity.*

1549. *'S nemmt en schlecht* schōf *as sei ēgni woll net dråge kann.*

It's a poor sheep that can't carry its own wool.

A lazy sheep thinks its wool heavy. H 21.

Das ist ein faul schaf, kann man sagen, das seine wolle nicht gern tut tragen. H 21.

1550. *Allemōl as'n* schōf *blaert f'rlīrts'n maulfol.*

Every time the sheep bleats it loses a mouthful.

Asses that bray most eat least. H 77.

1578. *Mit* schpek *fangt m'r di meis.*

Mice are caught with bacon. Use proper bait if you want to make a catch; good bait catches fine fish.

Mit speck fängt man die mäuse. MS.

1617. *Ich schmeiss d'r å mol en* schtē *in d'r gårte.*

I'll throw a stone into your garden some time; I'll do you a favor some time; one good turn deserves another.

1705. *Wū hemmer als minanner* sei *g'hit?*

Where did we herd swine together?

Wo haben wir miteinander säue gehütet? B 3174.

1707. *'S schtēt uf* sei fedre.

It stands on hog feathers; the thing looks dubious.

Die sache steht auf saufedern. B 3122.

1715. *'R is in re* sēkmīl *gebōre.*

He was born in a sawmill; he never closes any doors.

1809. *Wamm'r mit de* welf *gēt muss m'r mit ne heile.*

If you travel with wolves, you've got to howl with them; when in Rome do as the Romans do; if you travel in fast company, you've got to keep step or drop out; do as the rest do.

Wer unter den wölfen ist, muss mit heulen. B 4114.

1822. *'R hot å pår in d'r wēt.*

He is also pasturing a few; he has several bastards.

1824. *Lēre wēzeēre schtēne gråd in di hē, folle henke d'r kopp.*

Empty ears of wheat stand upright, full ones droop; the shallow brained carry their heads high.

Leere körnchen stehen hoch, die vollen neigen sich. Wii *1547.2.*

1825. *Gūt* giwetzt *is halber gimēt.*

A sharp scythe makes mowing easy; well begun is half done.

1827. *Sō* wilkume *as en sau ime rībeschtik.*

As welcome as a pig in a turnip patch.

1868. *Sō zē wi'n seirīsel.*

As tough as the snout of a pig.

1935. *'N gelådner* wage *grext, 'n lērer rappelt.*

The loaded wagon creaks, the empty one rattles.

Personal and Local Proverbs

82. Like Drumbore's bake oven, well planned but a failure.

133. Minding his own business made Girard rich.

179. Holds out like Butz bread, all eaten two weeks before the cheese.

576. He'll eat along like Knappenberger's colts. (One more or less won't make any appreciable difference.)

634. Good night, Matilda, you'll find the money on the window sill.

637. Money rules the world and ignorance the people of Frush Valley.

699. Straight through, like Herman's bull—from the loft to the cow stable.

874. Old Hammel said he always was a back number; when he was young the old folks knew it all, and now the young know it all.

1106. You almost feel you had to cross the Lehigh to get water. (Isn't that enough to drive you crazy?)

1110. Like Dietz's funeral—went to nothing.

1172. Like Joe Schneck, who dragged his wife by the hair for love.

1285. Ran like Hain's mill—it didn't.

1704. When Gackenbach's pigs have enough to drink they do not need any feed.

Wellerisms

A Wellerism is a form of proverb that contains a quoted saying. It is named after Sam Weller, who uttered such proverbs in Charles Dickens' Pickwick Papers.

361. "All depends on the drop," said Hans, when the woman with a drop hanging on her nose invited him to take potluck.

457. "One must remember where it comes from," said the farmer when the mule kicked him.

"Rough as it runs," as the boy said when his ass kicked him.

620. "Great cry and little wool," quoth Eulenspiegel, when he shore the sow.

641. No learned man ever dropped from heaven. "Nor any ox," said old Haas.

1172. "For my own pleasure," as the man said when he struck his wife.

1547. "Thanks, I am not hungry, I have 'schnitz' in my pocket," said old man Moser when invited to take potluck.

1843. "Just as you please," said Peter to the bull as it shook its head.

BIBLIOGRAPHY AND ABBREVIATIONS

B Wilhelm Binder. *Sprichwörterschatz der Deutschen Nation.* Stuttgart, 1873.

H William Carew Hazlitt. *English Proverbs and Proverbial Phrases.* London, 1889.

L Vincent Stuckey Lean. *Lean's Collectanea.* 4 vols. Bristol, 1902–04.

MS Eduard Muret-Sanders. *Enzyclopädisches Wörterbuch.* 4 vols. Berlin, 1905.

WdVs Edmund Hoefer. *Wie das Volk spricht.* Stuttgart, 1886.

W Karl Friedrich Wilhelm Wander. *Deutsches Sprichwörter-Lexikon. Ein Hausschatz für das deutsche Volk.* 5 vols. Leipzig, 1865–70.

6. PROVERBIAL TALES

Think Thrice Before You Speak

Type 1562, Think Thrice Before You Speak, has been collected in Europe, chiefly in Finland and Sweden, but is not reported for the New World.
Text from Brendle and Troxell, p. 87.

A common variation of this proverb is, "Think thrice before you speak; but not in case of fire."

A boy had been told by his father that he should always think three times before he spoke. One day, as they were sitting near the hearth, the boy saw that the pocket of his father's coat was burning.

"I think"—a pause—"I think"—a pause—"I think. Father, your coat pocket is burning," said the boy.

After the father had put out the fire, he angrily said to his son, "Why didn't you tell me sooner?"

The boy answered, "You said I was to think three times before I spoke, and that is what I did."

"But not in case of fire," said the father.

Julius Lentz, Laurys, Pa.

The Best of Three (1)

Type 1452, Bride Test: Thrifty Cutting of Cheese, is No. 155 of the Grimm Household Tales, "Brides on Their Trail." Baughman reports it twice in the

*United States, under Motif H381.2.2, "Bride test:
thrifty scraping of bread tray," from North Carolina
and Missouri.*

*Brendle and Troxell explain that this and the follow-
ing story are based on the proverb "Mittelmâs, di
beschde Schtrâs," "Between the extremes lies the best
course." Texts from Brendle and Troxell, pp. 94–95.*

A young man told his mother that he would like to marry but
feared that he might not choose a good wife, and he would like
to have his mother's counsel.

His mother said to him, "Saddle your horse and ride to the
home of the girl that you have in mind. When close to her home,
dismount and tie your horse to a tree. Then, go towards the
house, and when the girl appears, as she will, say to her, 'My
horse has been suddenly taken with colic. Would you kindly give
me a handful of the scrapings of the kneading trough for him.' "

The son did as directed. He rode until he came close to the
home of a girl whom he knew fairly well. Then he dismounted,
tied his horse to a tree, and walked towards the house. The girl
came out on the porch, and he asked her for a handful of scrapings of the kneading trough.

She answered, "That I shall gladly give you."

She went into the house, and came back with two heaping
handfuls saying, "If this isn't enough, I can get more."

The young man thanked her and left. He returned to his
mother and recounted to her his experience. She shook her
head, and said, "Try again."

On the following day, the son rode forth again. To his request, the second girl replied, "When we are through baking, we
clean our kneading trough, and there are no scrapings to be
gotten."

When his mother heard his account, she shook her head,
and said, "Try again."

He rode forth the third day, and went towards the home of
a girl of whom he had heard but whom he had never met. To his
request, she answered that she didn't know whether she could
get any scrapings for him but she would try.

After a while she came out with a small handful and said, almost apologetically, as she gave them to him, "This is all I could get out of the corners of the trough. I am sorry that I cannot give you more."

He thanked her and rode back to his mother, who smiled when she heard his story. "That," she said, "is the one for you. Seek no further."

Lebanon County.

The Best of Three (2)

> *As a schoolboy in New York City in the 1920's I heard and believed the story of a job interview test: a book is left lying on the office floor; if the applicant leaves it there or asks if he should pick it up, he fails to get the job, but if he picks it up immediately he is hired. Text from Brendle and Troxell, p. 96.*

A farmer went out seeking a servant. He came to one likely young man and after speaking about a number of inconsequential matters, asked, "How long can you plow with a stone in your shoe?"

The young man answered, "All day long."

The farmer went on. He asked the same question of a second man. "How long can you plow with a stone in your shoe?"

This young man answered, "Oh, a half day or so."

The farmer went on. He came to a third man. Again he asked, "How long can you plow with a stone in your shoe?"

"Not a minute," answered the man. "If a stone gets into my shoe I take it out immediately."

The farmer was satisfied with this reply and hired the man.

Carbon County.

7. RIDDLES

The Riddle of Ilo

Comparable riddle legends can be found under Motif H790, "Riddles based on unusual circumstances." The "neck" riddle below is excluded by Archer Taylor from his English Riddles from Oral Tradition (Berkeley and Los Angeles, 1951), but he comments on its popularity throughout Europe. Neck-riddle is the term for an event known only to the riddle-maker, and so insoluble; it saves his neck when his life is at stake. In German it is Halslöserätsel. Another neck-riddle is given in Dorson, American Folklore, pp. 96–97. From John Baer Stoudt, The Folklore of the Pennsylvania-German (The Pennsylvania-German Society, Vol. XXIII, 1910), pp. 61–63. Chapter IX is devoted to "Riddles and Catches."

The giving and guessing of riddles often afforded delightful entertainment at many a gathering on a cold winter's night, or on a Sunday afternoon, at the stately farmhouses of Pennsylvania Germans. On these occasions none were more popular than the Legend Riddles, especially those in which a humble peasant outwits the king and his court. The circumstances usually are that a young man, or sometimes a young lady, guilty of some capital offence, is promised his or her freedom upon the condition of inventing a riddle, which neither the king nor his court can answer. The most popular of this class is the

Ilo riddle which is common, in some form or other, to all Saxon people. In England it takes the uncanny form of:

> I sat wi' my love,
> And I drank wi' my love,
> And my love she gave me light;
> I'll give any man a pint o' wine,
> That'll read my riddle aright.

The reading is: "I sat in a chair made of my mistress's bones, drank out of her skull, and was lighted by a candle made of the substance of her body."

In the Rhine provinces this riddle takes the following form:

> *Auf Ilo geh ich,*
> *Auf Ilo steh ich,*
> *Auf Ilo bin ich hübsch und frei,*
> *Rat't meine Herren was soll das sein.*

The explanation is rather pleasing. A nobleman had a dog, Ilo by name, of which he was quite fond, and upon the death of this household pet the master had a very fine pair of shoes made from its hide.

Among our Pennsylvania German folk this riddle has expanded itself into a quite delightful legend.

A young man guilty of some capital offence was brought before the king one morning, who being in a kindly mood, promised the young man his freedom upon the condition that he would invent a riddle that neither he nor his court could solve. The young man went to his home, put on a different pair of shoes, quickly returned, and expounded the following riddle:

> *In Inia gehn ich,*
> *In Inia stehn ich,*
> *In Inia bin ich hübsch un frei;*
> *War kan roda was des mag sei.*

> In Inia I walk,
> In Inia I stand,
> In Inia I am happy and free,
> Who can guess this riddle for me.

The king and his court were puzzled. He was asked to explain. Whereupon the young man said: "I had a dog [named Inia] of which I was very fond. Upon its death I flayed him, tanned the hide, and made this fine pair of shoes out of the leather thus obtained, hence the riddle." The king was pleased and sent the young man upon his way home rejoicing.

Riddles of the Farm

> *From Stoudt,* The Folklore of the Pennsylvania-German, *pp. 71–83.*

Was geht un geht,
Un steht un steht?

(En Mühl.)

What goes and goes,
And yet stands and stands?

(A Mill.)

En Feld foll braune Schoff,
Un der Hiltze Jergel schiest danoch.

(En Bockoffa foll Brod.)

A field full of brown sheep,
And wooden Jergel shoots at them.

(A bake oven filled with baked bread.)

Vier rolle Ronse,
Vier Kappe danze,
En Knick-knock,
Un en Brod-sock.

(En man, wage und vier gäul.)

Four round bellies,
Four caps a dancing,
A knick knack,
And a bread sack.

(A man, wagon, and four horses.)

En Muhl hot sieve Ecke,
Im jedem Eck stehne sieve Säck,
Uf jederm Sack hocke sieve Katze,
Un jeder Katz hot sieve Junge,
Dann komme der Müller un sei
Frau noch in die Mühl nei,
Wie viel Füss sin noh drin?

(Vier Füss, es anner sin Dobe.)

There is a mill with seven corners,
In each corner stand seven bags,
Upon each bag sit seven cats,
Each cat has seven kittens.
Then the miller and his wife come in the mill.
How many feet are now in the mill?

(Four feet. The cats have paws.)

Was is das fern armer Drop,
Muss die Steg uf un abgeh uf em Kop?

(Shuhnagel.)

What poor fellow passes up and down the steps on his
head?

(Shoe-nail.)

Fleesh hinne, Fleesh forne,
Eise und Holtz in der mitt.

(Der Bauer am bluga.)

Flesh at both ends, iron and wood in the middle.

(A farmer plowing.)

Was steht uf em Fuss un hots Herz im Kop?

(Kraut Kop.)

What stands on its foot and has its heart in its head?

(Cabbage-head.)

Was wachst uf seim Schwantz?

(Rüb.)

What grows on its own tail?

> (*Turnip.*)

Wie is der Buchwetze iver der See komme?

> (*Drei-eckig.*)

How did buckwheat come across the ocean?

> (*Three-cornered.*)

Was hots Hertz im ganze Leib?

> (*En Baum.*)

What has its heart in its whole body?

> (*A tree.*)

Was guckt em halve Hinkel gleich?

> (*Die anner helft.*)

What resembles half a chicken?

> (*The other half.*)

Was hots grösst Schnubduch in der Weld?

> (*En Hinkel.*)

What uses the largest handkerchief in the world?
   (*A hen; for it wipes its nose anywhere on the earth.*)

Fer was geht der Bauer in die Mühl?

> (*Weil die Mühl net zum Bauer kummt.*)

Why does the farmer go to the mill?
   (*Because the mill will not come to the farmer.*)

Fer was hen die Müller weisse hüt?

> (*Fer ufzuduh.*)

Why do millers have white hats?

> (*To wear.*)

Fer was schmokt der Schornstee?
                              (*Veil er net jawe kann.*)
Why does the chimney smoke?
                              (*Because it cannot chew.*)

Was kauft mer bei der Yord un weart es aus beim Fuss?
                                    (*Karabet.*)
What is bought by the yard and worn by the foot?
                                    (*Carpet.*)

*Was geht im Haus rum un legt deller, un was geht ums
Haus rum un legt deller?*
                              (*En Frau un en Kuh.*)
*What goes about in the house and places plates, and
what goes around the house and makes platters?*
                              (*A wife and a cow.*)

*Was geht ums Haus rum un legt weisse Schnupdücher uf
die Fenstere?*
                                    (*Der Reife.*)
*What goes around the house and places white handker-
chiefs upon the windows?*
                                    (*Jack Frost.*)

*Welle lichter brenne länger, die von Inschlich oder die von
Wachs?*
                              (*Sie brenne kärtzer net länger.*)
*Which candles burn longer, those of tallow or those of
wax?*
                              (*They burn shorter, not longer.*)

*Wann neun Vogel uf em Baum hocke un du scheisht drei
defon runner, wie viel hocke noch druf?*
                                    (*Keene.*)

*If nine birds sit on a tree and you shoot three down, how
    many remain sitting?*

(*None.*)

Was geht noch der Krick un last sei Bauch daheem?
(*En feather bet.*)
What goes to the creek and leaves its belly at home?
(*A feather cover.*)

Mit was ver Auge kann mer net sehen?
(*Gra-Auge.*)
What eyes have no sight?
(*Gray eyes, corns.*)

*Was is der unnerschied zwischig e'm wagen-rad und
    'm lawyer?*
(*'N wage-rad schmeirt mer bis es nimmie greist, un en*
    lawyer *mus mer schmeirer bis er greist.*)
*What is the difference between a wagon wheel and a
    lawyer?*
(*One must grease a wagon wheel until it does not
    squeak, and a lawyer one must grease* [pay] *until
    he squeaks* [yells enough].)

8. SONGS

THE THREE SONG TEXTS that follow are reprinted from the chapter on "Pennsylvania German Songs," by Thomas R. Brendle and William S. Troxell, in *Pennsylvania Songs and Legends,* edited by George Korson (Philadelphia, University of Pennsylvania Press, 1949; reprinted Baltimore, Johns Hopkins University Press, 1960), pp. 62–128. The authors tell how they undertook song-collecting in the 1930's and recorded over two hundred imported, indigenous and borrowed folksongs, the one major genre not previously represented in Pennsylvania German lore. They printed their texts in German dialect and English translation, with melodic transcriptions.

We Journey to America
(Wir reisen noch Amerikâ)

> *"The wide currency in the Pennsylvania Dutch region of this 'beloved song of the emigrants' is indicated by the different variants we heard in Lehigh, Northampton, Berks, and Northumberland counties. The song must have reached Pennsylvania soon after publication in Samuel Friedrich Sautter's* Collected Poems of a Poor Schoolmaster *(Karlsruhe, Germany: 1845).*
>
> *"Sung by Mrs. Jane Masonheimer at Egypt, Lehigh County, 1936." Thomas R. Brendle and William S. Troxell, in* Pennsylvania Songs and Legends, *pp. 66–68.*

1.   The day and hour are here
      When we journey to America.

The wagon stands ready at the door;
We go with wife and children.

2.   The horses are already hitched to the wagon,
Now, kindred and friends—
The horses are already hitched to the wagon—
Clasp our hands in a last farewell.

3.   Ah, friends, restrain your tears,
Though we shall never see each other again;
Ah, friends, restrain your tears,
Though we shall never see each other again.

4.   As the ship moves out of the harbor,
Voices are raised in song;
As the ship moves out of the harbor,
Voices are raised in song.

5.   We fear no disaster at sea,
For God is everywhere;
We fear no disaster at sea,
For God is everywhere.

6.   And when we get to Baltimore
We'll stretch out our hands,
And cry, "Victory,
Now we are in America!"

When I Came to This Country
(*Wann ich vun dem Land rei kumm*)

> "*This cumulative ballad was probably brought into Pennsylvania by the early immigrants. We heard different versions in Lehigh, Berks, Snyder, and Northumberland counties.*
>
> "*Sung by Marvin Wetzel at Crackersport, Lehigh County, 1939.*" *Brendle and Troxell in* Pennsylvania Songs and Legends, *pp. 68–71.*

1. When I came to this country
   I was a poor man;
   Then I bought a chicken
   And began housekeeping.
   Should the people ask
   The name of my chicken,
   Gickerigie is the name of my little chicken.

2. Then I bought a duck
   And began housekeeping.
   Should the people ask
   The name of my little duck,
   End-of-the String is the name of my little duck,
   Gickerigie is the name of my little chicken.

3. Then I bought a cow

   . . . .

   Open-and-Shut is the name of my cow.
   End-of-the-String is the name of my little duck, etc.

4. Then I bought a little goose

   . . . .

   Bobtail is the name of my little goose,
   Open-and-Shut is the name of my cow, etc.

5. Then I bought a horse

   . . . .

   Oats-Mouth is the name of my horse.
   Bobtail is the name of my little goose, etc.

6. Then I bought a dog

   . . . .

   Always-Well is the name of my dog.
   Oats-Mouth is the name of my horse, etc.

7.   Then I bought a house

.   .   .   .

In-and-Out is the name of my house,
Always-Well is the name of my dog, etc.

8.   Then I got a wife
And began housekeeping.
Should the people ask
The name of my little wife,
Hell-Devil is the name of my wife,
In-and-Out is the name of my house,
Always-Well is the name of my dog,
Oats-Mouth is the name of my horse,
Bobtail is the name of my little goose,
Open-and-Shut is the name of my cow,
End-of-the-String is the name of my little duck,
Gickerigie is the name of my little chicken.

The Merztown Cornet Band
(*Di Matztown Cornet Band*)

> *Referred to in Dorson,* American Folklore, *p. 87.*
>
> *"This is another indigenous ballad, still commonly heard
> in Berks and Lehigh counties. It was improvised a cen-
> tury or more ago in honor of a cornet band in Merztown,
> a village in the northeastern section of Berks County.
> The ballad mentions various members of the band and
> satirizes their playing. Other bands took up the ballad
> and adapted it to their own purposes, substituting their
> own names, places, and allusions for those in the original
> version. Thus, in one form or another, the ballad attained
> widespread circulation. It was in the repertoire of many
> ballad singers. Note its use of Anglicisms and American-
> isms.*
>
> *"Sung by Samuel Haas at Chapmans, Lehigh County,
> 1937." Brendle and Troxell in* Pennsylvania Songs and
> Legends, *pp. 114–17.*

1.
A cornet band meets in Merztown
And pays no rent;
For the schoolhouse is given for their use
At a dollar for a whole year.

2.
There are twenty-four men
Including Big John Poe;
Some are big and some are fat,
Some are Democrats and some are Whigs.

3.
Kuder teaches with ability,
He has a black beard;
He teaches the band this evening
For a dollar and thirty cents.

4.
Billy Walbert blows bass
And say that it's a serious matter;
He blows bass and looks as cross
As a cat at a big piece of cheese.

5.
Allen Trexler, without joking,
Blows the second bass;
He lost his notebook
While going up the Noodletown hill.

6.
Milton Schubert, the squire,
He plays the baritone;
He plays his horn in good style
Though he still lacks hair on his chin.

7.
Milton Warmkessel, my dear people,
Sleeps already with a wife;
He plays the B trombone
With a face like a raccoon.

8.
Denny Webb also belongs to the group,
Now, boys, play, "Red, White and Blue."

He plays tenor, oh, so softly;
He likes cakes and wine.

9.   Oliver Schubert, think of this,
He also has a wife;
He plays his horn up and down
And says it is a deuced job.

10.   Isaac Warmkessel, O my dear,
Says the band members like beer;
He plays alto for the band,
"Yankee Doodle," "Dixie Land."

11.   Then, too, is Frantz Keiser,
The greatest laugher in the band;
He sticks to his D-flat cornet
Like a rooster to his nest.

12.   Johnny Barley, not a dope,
He plays the little drum;
He is young and small
But already tickles the girls.

13.   Peter Walbert, well learned,
Takes his club in hand;
And beats the large drum—
Peter Walbert is not dumb.

14.   Last of all is Big John,
Who is always present;
He keeps the band house in repair;
He was along to the Kutztown Fair.

15.   He is the man with the big hat,
The ladies say that he looks good;
He leads the parade through mud and mire,
And keeps the children out of the way.

III

SOUTHERN
MOUNTAINEERS

✣ OF ALL THE DISTINCTIVE regions in the United
States, the one most customarily linked with folklore is
the southern Appalachians. Here is seen folklore's natural habitat, in
the popular image shaped by *Esquire* drawings of hillbillies, Al
Capp's cartoon strip of Lil Abner in Dogpatch, and newspaper features about the feud of the Hatfields and the McCoys. This image
conjures up a longhaired, skinny mountaineer in threadbare overalls
and a slouch hat upending a jug of corn whiskey as he sits in the
squalor of a mountainside shack surrounded by dirt-eating infants
and scrawny swine. Here a city observer can find the muse of old
folksong and the well of primitive superstition in their pure state,
protected by layers of folkways in which laziness, filth, incest, and
violence breed unchecked. Sophisticated urbanites regard these submarginal folk living in mountain hollers since late colonial times with
amusement and even a certain fondness, for they are safely tucked
away behind the Appalachian wall, while their quaint folk products
served up by beatnik performers titillate audiences in city cabarets.

How much truth is there in this conceit of the southern mountain poor white as the innocent repository of the nation's richest
store of folklore? On the side of accuracy can be granted the view
that a uniform culture does prevail in the region, a point stressed by
an early collector, E. C. Perrow, in a pioneering article on "Songs
and Rhymes from the South":

> The region of the southern Appalachian Mountains, em-
> bracing the southwestern portion of Virginia, eastern Kentucky,

western North Carolina, East Tennessee, and the northern portions of Georgia and Alabama, constitutes a country which, though divided among several States, is indeed a unit with regard both to the country and to the character of its people.*

In this mountainous terrain the folklore collectors have enjoyed a field day, reaping harvest after harvest. Following Perrow's first forays, which placed on record in the *Journal of American Folklore* a considerable sheaf of short folksongs and popular rhymes and jingles, the Englishman Cecil Sharp made his celebrated excursion deep into the North Carolina hills in 1916 and 1917. Ever since the publication of his massive collection, *English Folk Songs from the Southern Appalachians* (two volumes, 1917, reprinted 1932, 1960, with Maud Karpeles as co-author), old English ballads and the southern mountains have been linked. Sharp did indeed uncover and make known to the world the retention in the United States of a large number of the prized English and Scottish traditional ballads which Francis James Child had canonized in his classic edition from 1882 to 1888. Other collections followed through the 1920's, rising to a flood in the 1930's. During this decade such titles appeared as Célestin P. Cambiaire's *East Tennessee and Western Virginia Mountain Ballads* (1934), Harvey H. Fuson's *Ballads of the Kentucky Highlands* (1931), George Pullen Jackson's *White Spirituals in the Southern Uplands* (1933), John Jacob Niles's *Songs of the Hill-Folk* (1934), Mellinger Henry's *Folk-Songs from the Southern Highlands* (1938), Dorothy Scarborough's *A Songcatcher in Southern Mountains* (1937), and Mary Wheeler's *Kentucky Mountain Folk-Songs* (1937). The year 1939 saw the publication of Josiah H. Combs's *Folk-Songs from the Kentucky Highlands,* John H. Cox's *Traditional Ballads Mainly from West Virginia,* and Jean Thomas' *Ballad Makin' in the Mountains of Kentucky.* While collections were being made for other parts of the country, no section came close to rivaling the southern mountains (uplands, highlands) in volume and quality of traditional song.

Then a new surprise added to the luster of the region, with the report of an elaborate folktale tradition. When the sociologist Isabel Gordon Carter published a sheaf of "Tales from the Southern Blue Ridge" in the *Journal of American Folklore* in 1925, folklorists were startled to recognize the style and matter of European wonder and magic tales flourishing among a people of English stock. The revelation of Child balladry in the mountains was less astonishing, since

* *Journal of American Folklore,* xxv (1912), 137.

these ballads did thrive in old England, as Märchen did not. Iron-ically, the chief teller of these narratives, a "little old bent-over lady," Mrs. Jane Gentry of Hot Springs, North Carolina, had previ-ously sung sixty-four ballads for Cecil Sharp, but could not under-stand why anyone would bother with these stories. "Old Jack, Will and Tom Tales they are called. They're the oldest stories that have ever been in existence, I reckon. Old Grandpop aluz told us—we'd hire him to tell us. Law, he could tell 'em."

Now that collectors knew the tales existed, they could inquire for them, and books of mountain stories began to appear. In 1936 Richard Chase, a Virginia schoolteacher, met a young man named Marshall Ward who told him of the talefests led by his "Uncle Mon-roe" at Beech Creek in Watauga County, western North Carolina. Later, Uncle Monroe set down a statement on his sources:

> I did learn the most of these tales from Council Harmon, my mother's Daddy, in the year of 1886 and '87 and '88. He was about 80 or 85 years old when I learned these tales from him. He told me he learned the tales from his grandfather and he said the tales was learned from the early settlers of the United States.*

Subsequently Chase learned that Council Harmon was also the grandfather of Jane Gentry. Hence the Beech Mountain tradition of Jack tales has proliferated through one family tree. From this reper-toire Chase published in 1934 *The Jack Tales,* told in "The South-ern Mountains," a cycle of the Jack, Will, and Tom yarns, and followed this with two other collections, *Grandfather Tales* (1948) and *American Folk Tales and Songs and other examples of English-American Tradition as preserved in the Appalachian Moun-tains and elsewhere in the United States* (1956). These volumes did not meet the full standards of the professional folklorist, as they made use of composite texts.

About the same time, in the Pine Mountain region of eastern Kentucky, another schoolteacher, Leonard Roberts, discovered won-der tales among his students, and traveled up creek bottoms in Leslie and Perry counties to their homes to record their parents and grand-parents. His publication of *South from Hell-fer-Sartin, Kentucky Mountain Folk Tales* (1955) brought to light an unsuspected number of European tale types. From the same general area came another

---

* Richard Chase, "The Origin of the Jack Tales," *Southern Folklore Quar-terly,* III (1939), 188.

major collection by Marie Campbell, also a schoolteacher, who returned to earn a doctor's degree in Folklore at Indiana University. Her *Tales from the Cloud Walking Country* (1958) grouped the stories around individual raconteurs she met while teaching in mountain settlements like Caney Creek, Knott County, in eastern Kentucky. There she also found recollections of the English mummers' play among the old mountaineers, the only instance reported in the United States.

One feature to emerge from this notable spate of collections was the prominent part played by clannish families in the transmission of folklore. Besides the Gentry-Harmon-Ward clan, the Ritchies of Viper in Perry County in the Cumberland Mountains of Kentucky have become known as the *Singing Family of the Cumberlands* (1955), the title of an autobiographical account by folksinger Jean Ritchie. In *Up Cutshin and Down Greasy, Folkways of a Kentucky Mountain Family* (1959), Leonard Roberts concentrated on the Crouch family of tale-tellers, belief-carriers, and ballad-singers.

This impressive evidence of southern Appalachian folklore riches seems to support the stereotype of the hillbilly as the prime bearer of tradition and superstition. Further support comes from the extensive collections of all genres of folklore in the Ozarks published by Vance Randolph. The Ozark hillman closely resembles the southern mountaineer, and in fact the Arkansas uplands were largely settled in the early decades of the nineteenth century by migrant Appalachian folk.

Still, the stereotype is grossly misleading. Folklore thrives in the cities as well as in the mountains, in the lowlands as well as in the uplands, among the literate as well as amid the unlettered. One collector in Knoxville, Edwin C. Kirkland, has related how he uncovered more Tennessee folksongs in the nearby low country than he did on tedious treks to the hills. Egypt in southern Illinois, a region set in the midwest prairie, has yielded large caches of tradition. The most telling argument to be made against the association of ignorance and sloth with folklore abundance is the plain fact that mental gifts —an alert mind, a retentive memory, a fluent tongue—are needed to transmit the texts of tradition. The senile and the witless lack these gifts. True, the lower economic groups and social classes of the backcountry possess their share of articulate and silver-tongued tradition carriers. Yet traditions function within a culture or a subculture, and to extrapolate them from the culture is to distort the picture and make it appear that mountain folk talk only in proverbs and always carol before breakfast. If collectors had concentrated on, say, children's games in the big city in the 1920's and '30's, they could have produced an impressive array of books with titles such as *London Bridge in New York, Hopscotch in Hoboken,* or *A Gamecatcher in Northern Metropolises.*

But in the twentieth century, urban readers relish songs and tales from the remote and faraway hill country.

1. JACK TALES

Jack the Giant Killer

*This lengthy narrative joins together several episodes
in the tale cycle of Types 1060–1114, "Contest between
Man and Ogre," including Type 1060, Squeezing the
(Supposed) Stone, Type 1088, Eating Contest, and
Type 1063B, Throwing Contest. The series concludes
with Type 1121, Ogre's Wife Burned in His Own Oven.
These combats between Jack and the stupid giant have
been reported in Indian, Negro, and English traditions
in North America. French-American and Greek-
American texts I collected in Michigan are printed in
Bloodstoppers and Bearwalkers, "Roclor and the
Giant," pp. 95–99, and in Fabula, I (1957), "Tales of
a Greek-American Family on Tape," pp. 132–33.*

*In the summer of 1923 Isabel Gordon Carter obtained
fifteen long narratives from Mrs. Jane Gentry of Hot
Springs, North Carolina, whose grandfather had heard
them from his mother. Mrs. Carter wrote down the tales
exactly as she heard them, keeping the inconsistencies
of Blue Ridge speech, such as "clomb" for "climb" and
"uz" for "was," which were often used indifferently in
the same sentence.*

*Text from Isabel Gordon Carter, "Mountain White
Folk-Lore: Tales from the Southern Blue Ridge," Journal of American Folklore, XXXVIII (1925), 351–54.*

One time they was a fine wealthy man lived way out in the forest.
But he couldn't have nothing, hogs and sheep and cows and sech

like because the giants killed 'em. So he went out and put him up an ad-ver-tise-ment (put up a board or hew out the side of a tree and write what he want to). So he put up one for some one to clear land. Little old boy Jack saw hit and he tramped and tramped until he got away out in the forest and he called, "Hello." Old man hollered, "What'll ye have?" Jack says, "I've come to clear yer land." "All right," says the man. It was Sunday evenin' un they uz havin' supper. The old lady says, "What'll ye have for supper, Jack?" He said mush and milk. While they was makin' the supper a preacher come in an' they sit the mush away and they fried him a chicken and fixed some coffee and fixed a good supper. After supper Jack tol 'em he wanted a piece of leather so he made him a pouch, a sort of haversack thing to tie around his waist. Next morning they got up, asked Jack what he'd have for breakfast. Said, "Jest give me that cold mush and milk." He'd take a spoonful and then poke one in a hole in his pouch. So he got it full. Then he said he was ready to go to work.

So man says, now he says, "Jack, I don't want you to back out, but I'm no a wantin' any land cleared. I want to kill them giants over there and I'll give a thousand dollars a head for them—some of 'em has two heads, and I'll give you five hundred dollars down, and five hundred dollars when you come back."

Jack says, "Give me a tomihawk." (That's a thing like a hatchet 'cept it has two heads to hit. They used hit in olden times. Indians use to use hit to scalp with.) "And I may be in for dinner, and hit may be night when I get in." So they give him a tomihawk and he went over in the forest and climb a great long pine.

Along about one o'clock he looked way down in the holler and saw a great old giant a comin' up with two heads. So he says to himself, "Land I'm gone." So the old giant come up, and he says, "What are you doin' up there?" Jack says, "I'm a clearin' timber." Giant says, "Come down from there, you ain't got sense enough to clear timber, you have to have an ax and chop down timber." So Jack come down a little way. "Have ye had yer dinner?" says the giant. Jack says, "I've had my dinner." Giant says, "I'm sorry, I jest come to ask you to

come down and take dinner with me. Come down, let's wrestle
and play a while." Jack says, "All right, bedads, I'll be down."
So Jack come down and down, till he got right on a limb a top
the giant. He had no idea of comin' down when he started, jest
tryin' to bluff the giant.

Jack says to the giant, "I can do somethin' you can't do."
Giant says, "What is hit?" Jack says, "I can squeeze milk out
of a flint rock." Giant says, "Oh ye can't do hit?" Jack says,
"Yes I can, you hand me up one and I'll show you." So giant
handed him up one, and Jack gits hit right close to his little
old pouch and squeezes milk out on the rock and drapped the
milk on the giant. Giant says, "Hand me down that rock; if
you can squeeze milk out of hit, I can." Jack handed it down
to the giant. The giant was so stout that when he put his hands
to hit, he just crushed it into powder.

Jack says, "I told you you couldn't squeeze milk out of
hit. I can do something else you can't do." "What's that?"
"I kin take a knife and cut my belly open and sew hit up again."
Giant says, "Oh you can't neither." "Yes, I can," says Jack.
"I'll show you, hand me your knife." So the giant hands him
up his knife and Jack cut that pouch open and sewed hit up
again. "Now didn't I tell you I could?" Giant says, "Hand me
down that knife," and he just rip his belly open and fell over
dead. So Jack crawled back down and tuk his tomihawk and
cut off his head. And that evening late he come waggin' him
in a giant's head. That jest tickled the forest man and he paid
Jack a heap of money and says, "Now Jack, if you kin jest
get the rest of 'em; they's a whole family of 'em."

So next morning Jack took his tomihawk (or Tommy
hatchet) and went over and climb the big old pine agin. So
long about noon he looked down the holler and he saw two giants
a comin' each with two heads on. So they begin to get closter
and closter. Jack climb down and tuk out down the holler and
as he went he filled his shirt tail with rocks. After a while he
come to a big old holler log and he climb in hit with his shirt
tail plumb full of rocks. So the giants went up and mourned
over their brother. And they went down past Jack sayin',
"Poor brother, if we jest knew who it was a murdered him,

we'd shore fix him." Jack was a layin' in there with his heart jest a beatin'. They passed the log and said, "Let's pick up this log and carry hit down to poor old mother for some kindlin'." So they each tuk an end and carried hit a little ways.

Jack thought he'd try his rocks on 'em. So he crawled up pretty close to the end and throwed a rock and hit one of the giants. Giant says to the other one, "What you hit me for?" Giant says, "I didn't hit you." "Yes, you did too." Then Jack crawled back and throwed a rock at the other giant. "What you hit me for? I never hit you." "I didn't hit you." "Yes you did too." So they fit and they fit and fit and directly they killed each other; one fell one side of the log dead and the other on the other side. So Jack crawled out and cut their heads off and went on back home.

So he was gettin' him a pretty good load of money and was gettin' awfully tickled. The forest man were plumb tickled too and said: "Jack, if you jest can get the rest. But watch out they don't get you." "Bedads they won't git me," says Jack. So next morning he says, "Give me my tomihawk," and he went on out. So along in the evenin' he looked down the holler and saw a little old giant comin' up about his size. "Well," says Jack, "I've about got 'em from the looks of this one." This little giant come up a talkin' to hisself. Looked up in the tree and saw Jack sittin' there. "Stranger, can you tell me who has killed my poor old brothers?" "Yes, I killed your brothers and bedad, I'll come down and kill you if you fool with me." "Oh please, Jack, please Jack, I'm all the child my mother's got left, and you kill me there won't be nobody to get her wood this winter and she'll freeze to death. If you'll come down I'll take you home with me and we'll have the best dinner." So Jack went on down.

Giant went to his mother and says, "Jack come home with me, and he says he's the one who killed brothers but he's not much." So Giant's mother says, "Well, come on in Jack, you'uns go out and play pitch crowbar awhile." Jack couldn't lift it. Little old giant pick hit up and throwed hit about one hundred yards. Jack went over and picked up one end and begin to holler: "Hey, uncle. Hey, uncle." Giant says, "Hey, Jack, what you hollerin' about?" "I've got an uncle in the Illinois who is a blacksmith and I thought I'd jest pitch hit to him." "Oh don't do that Jack, hit's all we have." "Well if I can't pitch hit to Illinois, I won't pitch hit at all."

Little old giant slipped back to the house, "Mother, I don't believe Jack is much stout." "Well, we'll see," says the mother. "Here boys, take these pails down to the river." Little old giant tuk the buckets and when he got to the river he stove in his bucket and put hit up full and then he stove Jack's in and put hit up full. Jack begun to roll up his sleeves. Little old giant says, "What you goin' to do, Jack?" "Oh thought I'd carry up the river." "Oh don't Jack, mother might walk in her sleep and fall in." "All right," says Jack, "but I wouldn't be ketched a carryin' that little old bucket."

So they went on back. The mother had a big hot oven sittin' in front of the fire with a plank across hit. "Get on this plank, Jack, and I'll ride ye," says she. So Jack got up un she shuck him and shuck him trying to shake him into the oven but he fell off on the wrong side. "Let me show you," says old mother giant, and she got on and Jack give her a shake and popped her in the oven, and he had him a baked giant in a minute. Little old giant came in, says, "Mother, mother, I smell Jack." Jack says, "No you don't, that's your mother ye smell." When little old giant sees Jack, he begin to holler, "Oh! Jack, I'll give ye anything if you won't kill me." "All right, give me a suit of invisible clothes."

So he give him invisible suit and Jack just went over the house and tuk what he wanted, all that was any account, because the giant couldn't see him. And Jack tuk a sword and walked up to the little old giant and stuck hit in him and went and got him some silver and when I left there, Jack was plumb rich.

Quare Jack

Recorded in 1955 by Leonard Roberts, who writes: "This is the most unusual medley of stories and anecdotes that I have ever collected in the mountains. It has

Jack said, "That's a purty hard thing to do but I'll try."
So that evening Quare Jack got ready to steal the horse.
vent to town and got him a quart of liquor and put some
ing draught in it and went along down to the barn where
oldiers was watching. They didn't know him and didn't
he was sharp enough to try stealing the horse. They
"Well, we're glad you come, Quare Jack." Said, "A feller
ming tonight to steal this horse and we're going to get

Jack said, "I'll help you and we'll shore get him." So he
in and was setting around like he was waiting to help 'em
he kept taking a little drink out of the bottle and they
ed it passed around. Time it was all gone they was napping
round the barn. Soon as they got asleep old Quare Jack
n the man's horse and rode it off. Next morning Jack come
the road riding the man's horse and he said, "Jack, you
my horse last night." Jack told him he shore did and got
hundred dollars.

Well, the old man told 'em to come back next day and he'd
'em one more time. They went down there and the man
"Now boys, I want you fellers to come back tonight and
the sheet out from under my wife and the ring offen her
r and I'll give you a hundred dollars."

The older boys said, "We are all out of money; we hain't
othing left but our horses." He said he'd take their horses
e bet.

So that night they went down there and they worked every
they knowed how to get the old man out of the house,
they couldn't get him out a-tall. They went back home
told Quare Jack what the trick was. Wanted him to lose
of his money.

So Quare Jack told 'em he would go down and try to get
things from the old woman. He knowed they was a man
been buried in the graveyard that favored him a little
so he goes and digs this old dead man up and takes him
to the front of the man's house and stands him up again'
st. He ties a rope to the dead man and eases around into
rner of the house right side the door. He makes a noise

*at least four story types all of which are somewhat rare
in English-American tradition: Type 853, Catching the
Princess with Her Own Words; Type 1525, The Master
Thief; Type 1653, The Robbers under the Tree; and
Type 1525R, The Robber Brothers."*

*Of these, Type 853 is known in the French and Spanish
traditions in North America, Type 1525 to Spanish,
French, Polish, and Negro storytellers in the United
States, and Type 1653 among French, English, Spanish, and Negro groups in North America. Type 1525R,
a Scandinavian story, has not been reported for the New
World.*

*"Quare Jack" was printed in the Kentucky Folklore
Record, IV (Jan.–March, 1958), 1–9. The collector
adds: "I recorded this important tale from Cornelius
Allen, age about 50, Sizerock, Leslie County [Ken-
tucky], in 1955. He had heard it about 1910 from a
man in Magoffin County, where Mr. Allen once lived."*

One time there was a farmer who had a lot of real estate and
some money and he had three sons named Tom, Bill, and Jack.
So he decided to divide up some of his property and give it to
his two eldest sons. But the one called Jack was a little foolish
and uncertain and they allas called him quare.

So this farmer set aside about six hundred dollars and
some horses and other stock and he give Tom and Bill three
hundred dollars apiece and a big fine horse, bridle and saddle,
but he didn't give the least un anything, just called him little
Quare Jack.

So Bill and Tom started out one day, said they was going
out to trade and increase their money and stock. They started
out down the road and little old Jack said, "I'll go too."

They said, "Ah, you needn't to go," said, "You're walking and we'll be riding. You can't keep up."

Jack said, "Ah, I'll go along anyway."

So as they went on down the road, Quare Jack had a little
old knife in his pocket and he got it out and picked him up a
little stick and went whittling along the road. Directly he
said, "Well, I'll just put the rest of my stick in my pocket—

might need it some time." The older boys went riding on, watching Jack and laughing at him. Went on a little piece farther and Jack found an agg, looked like a duck agg. He picked it up, said, "I'll put you in my pocket—might need you atter while."

The boys went on down the road riding and got ahead of Quare Jack. They come to a man's house and he had a sign by the road, said, "Anybody that can go in and get a joke on my gal I'll give him a hundred dollars. If you don't you give me a hundred."

The boys stopped and thought it was a good way to increase their money. So old Tom got down and went in but he couldn't get no joke on the gal. Bill said, "Let me try it." So he went in and he couldn't get no joke on her. They lost a hundred apiece and was feeling bad about it.

Old Quare Jack come along about that time, said, "What's up, boys?"

"Well," they says, "nothing you can do. This man wants somebody to get a joke on his gal." Jack says he'll go in. They said, "Ah, you old fool, you needn't got in there, you can't do nothing."

Quare Jack said he's go in anyhow and he went in and saw the gal setting in the middle of the floor in a chear and he spoke, "Howdy-do, ma'am."

"Howdy-do," she says and then she said, "Fire in my tail!"

And he says, "Hot enough to toast a agg?"

And she says, "Yes, have you got ary agg?"

"Shore," he says and pulled that duck agg out of his pocket.

And she says, "We'll have to have a stick to stir it with."

He says, "I've got your stick," and he pulled his stick out of his pocket. The gal was beat and couldn't say another thing and so the old man paid him off and Jack made a hundred dollars right there.

This old man was a kindy rich old feller and he told 'em to come back the next day and he's give 'em some more tricks. The boys started out riding and Quare Jack walking. They tried to keep him from going but Jack told 'em he'd go anyhow. They beat him there and the old man says, "Well, boys, I'll

give any man a hundred dollars to take th[...] river and dip it full of water and bring it u[...] "I need some water."

Well, Tom put up his money and took[...] to the river. He'd dip up the water and[...] run back out. Dip it up and it'd run rig[...] back up and handed the sifter to Bill and[...] done the same thing. Couldn't get no wat[...] other hundred apiece. Old Quare Jack co[...] time and asked them, "What's the matter,[...]

They said, "Hain't nothing you can[...] hundred apiece trying to do it."

Jack said he'd go in and see what i[...] the old man said, "Take this sifter down t[...] it back full of water."

Jack said, "That's a purty hard thin[...] it."

He took the sifter down there at the[...] it up full of water and it'd run out, dip [...] A little bird flew up over him in a bush and [...] it with mud, daub it with mud." So Jack[...] sifter with mud and filled it up full of wat[...] to the old man. The man says, "Jack, looks[...] you another hundred dollars." So Jack n[...] and his brothers just a hundred apiece.

The old man told 'em to come back n[...] what they could do. The boys rode down[...] The old man come out and says, "Boys, if[...] my horse out of my barn at nine o'clock [...] another hundred dollars." They just had a[...] they decided to try and maybe get their mor[...] they tried and tried but the soldiers was w[...] couldn't get noways near the barn. Next [...] come down and asked 'em what was up a[...] go in and find out. We just lost all our mo[...]

Jack went in and the old man said,[...] steal my horse out of my barn at nine o'cl[...] you another hundred."

and rackets around the house and the old man looks out and
sees what looks like Jack standing out there. He says to his
wife, "That's old Quare Jack out there trying to get me up.
Just pay no attention." Jack rackets around for an hour or
two, keeps 'em awake, and the old man says, "That Jack is disturbing my peace. He's already got a lot of my money." Says,
"I believe I'll slip out and kill him and get all my money back."

So he slips over to the winder and he saw that shadder out
there and he pulled down and shot right into that dead man.
Jack pulled the rope about that time and made the dead man
fall over. He said, "I got him, old woman. Be back directly."
He went out there to get the money offen Jack, and while he
was out of the house old Quare Jack run in the house and called
in the bedroom, "Old woman, give me the sheet offen the bed
and the ring offen your finger," said, "I've killed Jack and I
have to leave. His brothers will come back on me for this."

So he got the ring and the sheet and got out of the house
before the old man got back. The next morning he walked in
with the sheet and the ring off the wife's finger. So the old man
had to give him another hundred dollars. He went on back
home with all that money jangling in his pockets. But Tom
and Bill had lost their money and their horses and they didn't
have nothing. They was plumb out. Their father wouldn't give
'em any more and had left the country, and they couldn't do
nothing but just stay there and try to keep house.

They didn't have much to keep house on, so Tom and Bill
said, "Well, tomor'r night we're going to get us a sheep. We
got to have something to eat." Old Jack wanted to go with
them but they said, "No, you got money and won't spend it,
and so we won't let you go."

He said, "I want to go anyway," but no, they wouldn't let
him go. They left him in the bed and took off, but Quare Jack
knowed about where they was going and he took a nigh cut
through the fields and come to the pen of the sheep and had
him a hammer along and went in and hid. They come up and
said, "Well, here they are." One of them said, "You catch one
and I'll hold the door and let you out." So he stuck his head in
and begin to crawl up toward a big white sheep. About that

time Jack up with his hammer and give him a crack in the head with that hammer. And he jumps back and says, "Gosh, that un butts—they must be a buck in there!"

The other one says, "Let me in there and I'll get one." He sticks his head in and moves around trying to feel for a sheep. Old Jack was ready and give him a good sized beck with that hammer. He jumped back out and said, "We can't get nary sheep—that old buck'll kill us." Said, "Le's go back and come tomor'r and get us a chicken."

So they started back around the road home and old Quare Jack cut back through the nigh way and beat them back home. He jumped in the bed and covered up and when they come he acted like he was sound asleep. They made a little noise and he raised up and said, "Boys, did you get ary un?"

"Nope, didn't get nary un. They butt. We might get some chickens tomor'r night."

"Well, can I go with you?"

"No, you won't go."

The next night they got ready and started, and nope, they wouldn't let Quare Jack go no matter how much he begged 'em. Jack let 'em get a good start and he got up and found him a pair of pincers and took the nigh way and beat 'em there. He found the chicken house and got inside and pulled the door to. They come up and said, "Here they are. You get in and get a big fat one while I watch and hold the door."

One of them slipped in the door and begin to feel around on the chicken roost for a big fat un and old Jack reached out with his pincers and give his finger a good pinch. He scooted back out of there, said, "Them hens pecks awful hard." The other un said, "Le' me get in there and try one." Soon as he got in and feeling around, old Jack just like to pinched his finger off. And he back out, said, "Lord have mercy, how them pecks. We can't get nary one."

They took off back home empty-handed and old Quare Jack took the nigh cut and beat 'em back. Got in bed. They come in says, "Well, boys, we can't get nothing to eat."

Jack raised up, "What's the matter? Didn't you get none?"

"Nope."

"What's the matter you can't?"

"They peck too hard."

Jack said, "If you fellers would let me go with you I would get something to eat."

They said, "Oh, you would, would you? You're so foolish they hain't no use in you going."

The next night come and they wanted to go steal a middling of meat at a man's house. Jack wanted to go and finally they let him go if he would promise to be quiet and not to tell nothing on 'em. So they went to this man's meathouse and Tom and Bill slipped in first and got 'em a middling apiece. Come out and they whispered to Jack, says, "When you get yourn you bring the door to." Jack thought they meant for him to bring the door along on his back. He got his middling of meat out and laid it down and started tearing the door off and that door was banging and whanging. The boys got scared, afraid all that noise would wake ever'body in the house up and they throwed down their meat and took off. Jack finally got the door off the hinges and put it on his back and throwed his middling up there and took out after them.

They was to meet again under a big tree along the road, and so old Jack took the door and meat on and took another nigh cut and beat 'em there. He didn't want to wait there in the road and so he decided to climb the tree with his door and meat. Up the tree he went and waited for them. Purty soon they come up to the tree, so tired they just set down. One of 'em said, "Well, now what'll we do?"

The other un said, "I don't know 'less we get down here and pray for the Lord to send us something to eat." One of 'em wanted the other to pray. Finally one of 'em got down and said, "Well, good Lord, we've had bad luck." Said, "We're hungry; send us some meat."

So old Jack he was up in the tree with his meat and he just turned that middling loose and it come tumbling through the branches and fell right in front of them boys. Well, that made the other un anxious to pray too. And he said, "I'll pray this time." The other un said, "Go ahead." So he said, "Good Lord, send us down a table to eat the meat on."

Here come the old door down through the tree just lambanging and they jumped and grabbed it and set it up. Laid their meat on it, but the meat was kindy dirty where it had hit the ground. One of them said, "This meat is kindy dirty; we need something to wash it off with." So he said, "Good Lord, send us down some water to wash this meat with."

So Quare Jack was ready for 'em and he just turned some water loose all over them. One of 'em jumped back, said, "Whew, this smells bad; we can't wash our meat with this." Old Jack come down out of the tree laughing fit to die and they knowed that he was not so quare after all. They went on home and old Jack kept 'em all up awhile till the two older boys could get on their feet. And they settled down and lived purty good after that.

2. JOCULAR TALES

The King and Old George Buchanan

"There are a great many similar saws current which are generally fathered on George Buchanan, the tutor of James VI," wrote the Scottish collector, J. F. Campbell, in a note to a Highland text (Popular Tales of the West Highlands, 4 vols. [2d ed., London, 1890–93, II, 406]). *These pranks and witticisms found their way into chapbook literature, e.g.,* The Witty and Entertaining Exploits of George Buchanan, Commonly Called the King's Fool.

As commonly happens with notorious figures, they become magnets for floating jests and sayings. Actually this is Type 921, The King and the Clever Peasant's Son, an extensively studied tale, with 228 Irish, 177 Finnish, 56 German, 50 Swedish, and 16 French texts known. However, only one is reported for England, and only the present example in English-American tradition. Pertinent motifs are H561.4, "King and clever youth"; H583.3, "King: What is your brother doing . . ."; H583.5, "King: What is your sister doing . . ."; H587, "King gives enigmatic order to minister"; J1161.3, "Trespasser's defense: standing on his own land"; J1189, "Clever means of avoiding legal punishment."

Text, and Campbell reference, from Isabel G. Carter, "Mountain White Folklore: Tales from the Southern Blue Ridge," Journal of American Folklore, XXXVIII (1925), 370–71. *Informant Susie Wilkenson was born in Sevier County, Tennessee, in "the year of the rebellion."*

In olden times they was a king (jest a king of the United States, I reckon—that's jest the way they told hit) and they was old George Buchanan, he was called the king's fool, and he didn't like the way the king made the rules. The king made a law that anyone come in and asked him to pardon 'em he'd pardon 'em and not law 'em. George Buchanan didn't like this law, so he kept a doin' things and then askin' the king to pardon him. Finally at last he come in and told the king to pardon him fer knockin' a man's hat off the bridge and the king did and then George said, "His head was in hit." But the king had done pardoned him and couldn't do nothing.

The king told him he'd behead him if he didn't come to the king's house tomorrow at noon, "Clothed and onclothed, riding and walking." So George tore one breech leg, one shoe and one sock, one half his shirt. He bridled his old ram sheep and put a saddle on hit and throwed one leg over hit and time of day come he went hoppin' up to the king's door. So the king says, "I thought I told you to come clothed and onclothed and a ridin' and a walkin' both." "I did, sir," says George. "Part of me's clothed, part of me's onclothed, one of my legs rode and one walked."

So the king tuk him to be his fool but before he tuk him he went to George's house; wasn't anyone there but George's sister who was in the back room. King says, "Where's your mammy?" and George says, "She tuk some honey to go to town to buy some sweetenin'." (Tuk some honey and went to git some sugar.) He headed the king that way. "Where's your poppy?" "He's gone to the woods. What he kills he'll throw away and what he don't kill he'll bring back." (He uz picking off lice.) "What's your sister doin'?" "She's in the back room mournin' fer what she did last year." (She uz having a baby.) You see George headed the king every time.

So George, he was called the king's fool. So he tried to do one thing and another to make the king make good laws. The king had a law that a man could burn his own house down anytime he had a mind to. So George built a house next to the king's and filled hit with shavin's. King says, "George, what er you doin'?" George says, "I'm fixin' to burn my house."

King says, "George, you can't do that, hit'll ketch my house."
George says, "Hit's the law." So king says, "If you won't burn
hit I'll pay you a good price." George says, "All right, if you
make a law that you can't burn a house without you tear hit
down and pile hit up. That's the law now.

The king keep a-pardonin' George fer things he'd do, and
atter awhile he told him that whatever George wished he could
have. So George wished to be the king and the king his fool.
So the king says, "George, you headed me all the time, now
you got my seat." So George sat up there awhile and then give
hit back to the king if the king ud promise not to grant nothing
until he seed what he was a grantin'. So the king told him,
"Now, George, you leave here and don't you show yourself on
Scotland land any more." So George he left and put England
dirt in the bottom of his shoes and got England dirt and put
in his hat and he come where they was havin' court, and the
king said, "Fetch him here; I told him I'd behead him if he
ever stood on Scotland land any more." And they went and
fetched him and he says, "I'm standing on England land and
livin' under England land." So he headed the king again. And
the king never could head George and George never would let
the king make no bad laws.

Jest come to where they was a-holdin' court to law people,
you know.

Kentucky Highland Jests

*The four jests that follow were written down from
memories of his youth in Hindman, Knott County,
eastern Kentucky, by Josiah H. Combs (1886–1961),
the pioneer collector and author of* Folk-Songs du Midi
des États-Unis *(Paris, 1925). A memorial number of
the* Kentucky Folklore Record *devoted to Combs gives
useful information about his career (III [1957], 67–
69). The tales were published as "Some Kentucky Highland Stories," with an introduction and notes by Herbert
Halpert (Kentucky Folklore Record, IV [1958], 51–
53). In a foreword Combs wrote: "I was born, 'bred-*

and-buttered' deep in the heart of the Kentucky mountains, in the 'pure feud belt.' "

"The Cuspidor"

See the Arkansas text in Randolph, The Devil's Pretty
Daughter, pp. 136–37, with comparative notes by Randolph and Herbert Halpert, pp. 217–18. A Kentuckian
figures in a version in Anecdotes for the Steamboat and
Railroad, by an Old Traveller (Philadelphia, 1854,
p. 18, reprinted in B. A. Botkin, A Treasury of American Anecdotes [New York, 1957], p. 31).

Discussed with reference to Davy Crockett in Dorson,
American Folklore, p. 62.

Green Dyer, of Knott County, found himself sitting in a big
plush chair in the spacious lobby of the old Capitol hotel, in
Frankfort. With a quid of "long-green" in his mouth, he was
letting out from time to time a sluice of "ambeer" (tobacco
spittle), which spattered the tile floor. Noticing this, the desk
clerk sent a boy around to place a nicely burnished cuspidor
in front of the mountaineer. To keep from hitting it, Green
squirmed and spat in another direction. The boy again placed
the cuspidor in front of him. This was repeated a number of
times. Finally tired of craning his neck to spit, Green looked
up and said to him: "Say, son, if you don't take that damned
thing away from here, I'll spit right in the middle of it d'reckly."

"The Poor Provider"

Josiah Combs first published this jest in a privately
printed pamphlet, The Kentucky Highlander (1913),
p. 25. A Texas text is in Straight Texas, Publications
of the Texas Folklore Society, XIII (1937), 90–91, and
an Idaho text in Idaho Lore, p. 119 [H. Halpert].

A mountaineer weighed down with a "turn" of corn on his back
was trudging along a footpath on the mountainside, on his

way to the gristmill. An idler in the shade down on the main street of the village on the other side of the stream saw him, and quipped: "Jist look at that feller over there with that sack o'corn on his back an' a-goin' to mill. I'll bet right now he ain't got a pint o'liquor in his house."

"Healthy Hogs"

> *A variant from the Upper Peninsula of Michigan is in a privately printed pamphlet by Arthur Quirt,* Tales of the Woods and Mines *(n.p., n.d.).*

The county health officer was making the rounds. At one mountain cabin he could see that several hogs slept under the floor of the cabin. He said to the mountaineer:

"Don't you think that is unhealthy?"

"They ain't a one of them hogs died yet," replied the mountaineer.

"The Revenue Man"

> *See the Arkansas text in Randolph,* The Talking Turtle, *pp. 125–26, and the notes by Randolph and Halpert, p. 209.*

The revenue men were looking for a moonshine still. They stopped at the mouth of a creek, where a little boy was shooting marbles in the road, near the cabin. Then, "truth or consequences," with the following dialogue:

DEPUTY COLLECTOR:

Sonny, does your daddy have a moonshine still?

BOY:

Yeah, he does.

D. C.:

Will you show me where it is?

BOY:

No I won't.

D. C.:

You'll show it to us now, won't you? (He dangles a gold watch before the boy's eyes, just as the officer did in Merimée's "Matio Falcone.")

BOY:

Yeah, I will, fer that.

D. C.:

Come on, then, let's go. (He starts up the creek.)

BOY:

Wait a minute, y'ain't gimme the watch.

D. C.:

Oh, we'll give it to you when we get back.

BOY:

No, ye won't; y'ain't a-comin' back.

North Carolina Mountain Jests

> *The next four humorous tales were collected by the American folklorist and folklore bibliographer Ralph Steele Boggs on a field trip "through the extreme southwestern section of North Carolina, which is inhabited chiefly by White settlers of English, Scotch, Irish, and German extraction, who work by themselves their tiny farms between the mountains." He published the results in "North Carolina White Folktales and Riddles," Journal of American Folklore, XLVII (1934), 289–328. The following texts are from pp. 306–8, 317, 320.*

"The Laughing Horse (Ox)"

> *Under Motif J1169.5, "The laughing ass," one European text is cited. An extended Connecticut version (hog laughs at sheep) by Seba Smith from the New York Spirit of the Times, XVII (March 20, 1847) is reprinted in Dorson, Jonathan Draws the Long Bow, pp. 91–93, and references are given to 1848 and 1895 literary texts from New England.*
>
> *Informants T. J. Barnett, 59, Cherokee County, and W. L. Pierce, 45, Edgecombe County.*

Version A

Two boys went on horseback to call on two sisters. They tied their horses outside an' went in. One slipped out an' cut off the tail of the other boy's horse, an' came back in the house, an' told him someone had cut off his horse's tail. The other boy went out, an' knew that the first must have done it, so he cut the first boy's horse's mouth from ear to ear, an' went back in the house an' told the first boy his horse was laughing to see a tailless horse.

Version B

Once there was a poor boy an' a rich boy, and they were both in love with the same girl. The poor boy cut off the rich boy's horse's tail. When the rich boy found it out, he went out an' cut the poor boy's ox's mouth from ear to ear. Then he called the poor boy, an' showed him the ox an' said, "See, your ox is laughing at my horse."

"Old Whiskers"

Informant B. L. Lunsford, 49, Buncombe County.

One Saturday a farmer went to town an' his friends talked him into gettin' his whiskers all shaved off, an' gettin' his hair clipped close. That night he went home late, an' his wife was already in bed. He slipped in easy, undressed quietly, an' got into bed softly with his wife. She ran her hand over his smooth face an' said, "Young man, if you're goin' to do anything, you'd better be agittin' at it, 'cause Ole Whiskers'll be here pretty soon."

"The Tricky Yankee"

For ante-bellum newspaper examples of Yankee tricks see Dorson, Jonathan Draws the Long Bow, pp. 78–94.

> *In Type 1530,* Holding up the Rock, *reported in east European and Spanish-American tradition, a trickster similarly dupes and robs a man by having him support a heavy rock.*
>
> *Informant B. Lunsford, 52, Buncombe County.*

A Yankee stopped at a southern hotel. The hotelkeeper had heard that Yankees were tricky, so he asked the Yankee to show him a trick. The Yankee promised to show him one before he left. After a few days the Yankee said he was going to leave, so he'd show him that trick. He asked the hotelkeeper for a brace and bit. Then he asked him to show him his best barrel of wine in the cellar. The Yankee bored a hole in one side of the barrel, an' asked the hotelkeeper to plug it up with his right thumb. Then he bored a hole in the other side, an' asked him to plug it up with his left thumb. Then he laid the brace and bit up on the shelf an' walked off without payin' his board bill. The hotelkeeper was afraid to take out his thumbs an' run after the Yankee, because it would mean the loss of his best wine.

"The Witchball"

> *Under Motif G269.21.1, "Witch causes person to break wind in presence of others," Baughman gives a Florida Negro reference along with the present example.*
>
> *Informant V. Ledford, 76, Clay County.*

Once there was a poor boy who wanted to marry a girl, but her folks didn't want him. His grandma was a witch, an' she said she'd fix it up. She made a horsehair witchball, an' put it under the girl's doorstep. The girl come outside, passin' over the witchball, an' went back in the house. She started to say somethin' to her mother, an' ripped out [*crepitus ventris*], an' every time she spoke a word, she'd rip out. Her mother told her to stop that or she'd lick her. Then the mother went out for somethin', an' when she came back in, she broke wind, too, every time she spoke. The father come in an' he did the same thing.

He thought somethin' was the matter, so he called the doctor, an' when the doctor come in over the doorstep, he started to poop with every word he said, and they were all atalkin' an' apoopin' when the ole witch come in, an' told 'em God had probably sent that on them as a curse because they wouldn' allow their daughter to marry the poor boy. They told her to run an' git the boy, 'cause he could marry their girl right away, if God would only take that curse offa them. The ole witch went an' got the boy, an' on her way out, she slipped the witchball out from under the doorstep. The boy an' girl got married an' lived happy ever after.

3. MURDER LEGENDS AND BALLADS

The Crying Stair Well

This account, told with complete conviction, is filled with folk attitudes and ideas. Recognizable motifs are E334.2.1, "Ghost of murdered person haunts burial spot," and E402.1.1.3, "Ghost cries and screams," both familiar in Great Britain and the United States. A similar legend of the Crying Bog in Narragansett, Rhode Island, involves the murder of her two children by an Indian squaw (Dorson, Jonathan Draws the Long Bow, pp. 170–71).

Recorded in November, 1958, in Bloomington, Indiana by Mary Felder, a graduate student in Folklore at Indiana University, from Zelphia Harding ("Minnie") Simmons, 38, a hotel cook, born in Flatrock, Kentucky.

Now, I don't want to cast a hazard on the Catholic belief, but one time my stepmother and her parents—she was a young girl about seventeen—they moved in an old-fashioned log cabin. She said she had the funniest feelin' when they moved in this house, they got moved in just about sunset one night. They was in this ole log house, and she did have the funniest feelin', she said, "Mom, I don't think I want to go to bed tonight." They had moved out on Cumberland Ridge in Kentucky, oh forty years ago—fifty years ago, I guess it was. And she said to Ella she heard the awfulest creaking about sunset on the porch, and they had an ole-fashioned "antell" woodbox at the foot of the stairs; it was a three-story house and always in those three-story log-cabins is an antell. Great big long wooden box, just about that long and looks like a casket; it sets there in all stair wells—it's a case for wood.

She said just about sunset they heerd the awfulest squeakin', and she said, "I got shivers up and down my spine," and they'd heard some tales bein' told about this place, see. They rented it for seventeen dollars for six months; I think it was they leased it. It was back in the ole days, you know, and she said she had the awfulest feelin', and that stair well kept botherin' her, and she said about eight o'clock the awfulest wailin' they ever heard started cryin' out—she said they heard babies a-cryin' all over the house seven o'clock in the night. And this supposed to really happened, and they moved right out of that house.

And she said, "Mom, I'm not a-goin' to sleep." And she set up night and she watch that stair well, and that box, and she said, "I couldn't get my mind off that." And so, about nine o'clock, she fell asleep and she said, "I had the awfulest dream." She said, "Somethin' told me to go to the rear of the house— I mean it dark, and no matches, nothin'—and look in the rain barrel and my answers would come clear." You see, she's got seventh sense, Cory has, 'cause she can't read or write.

And she said, "I went out there an' looked, and the awfulest feelin' come to me. Somethin' told me to go in and look in the stair well box, and my answers would be cleared—set a spirit free." So she went back and set in the chair and never remembered doin' it. And the next mornin' she said, "Momma"— they was a lock on that stair well and they didn't understand why—so she said, "Momma, let's break that lock on that stair well, I'm nervous about it." Her mom said, "Aw, sis, that ain't for you to look at, leave that alone."

So Cory went on for about a week, a-havin' nightmares every night, and they'd still hear the cryin' every night. And their mom said, "Aw, that's just boards a-creakin', that ain't no baby cryin', you just think it is." Cory said, "Yes, I know it is." So one night she and Caroline had been sleepin' upstairs and the noise got so loud they couldn't take it, and [this] one night they was layin' downstairs on a pallet. And she said, "Boy, about nine o'clock the awfulest wailin' come out," and she said that stair well just echoed. And in the mornin' she said, "I'm doin' somethin' about this." So her mom got her real busy so she couldn't get her mind on the stair well, the next day, washing you know, like a mother will when they got a family.

She said, "Mom kept me away from that stair well just a week too long, some time today I'm goin' to open that; I'm goin' get the ax and knock it off." So sure enough, about five o'clock that evenin', she caught her mom busy in the kitchen, she said, "Sally, will you and Caroline help me bust that lock?" And they said, "Yup."

So she took the old ax and busted it open and raised the lid, and you know what they found in there? The skeletons of five little babies, in that stair well. And they found out, two [or] three days later, the neighbors tole them, that the woman that lived in that house—a young girl—killed herself, and the parents moved away; and later, the father hung hisself. See what I mean, that wasn't superstition, that really happened.

[The informant obviously at this point expected me to get the implications which I had missed; the following comments were in response to my questions.]

The five babies were the young girl's—she drowned them in the rain barrel, that was the interpretation. She had drowned them in the rain barrel, and put them in the stair well and locked them up. Year by year. Her parents never questioned why the stair well kept locked 'cause they thought it was her hope chest—hope chest of the Devil. So the babies that she borned and lived, she drowned them in the rain barrel, that's true. She drowned them 'cause she wasn't married; you don't know what traditions is in Kentucky, they pretty near hang 'em for havin' a baby and not bein' married down there. Don't you know that?

Old Foster

This is a form of Type 955, The Robber Bridegroom, with Motif H57.2.1, "Severed finger as sign of crime,"

*and Motif R135.0.5, "Trail of thread." The tale is
Grimm No. 40, "The Robber Bridegroom," widely reported in Europe (60 texts from Lithuania, 93 from
Denmark, 73 from Germany). Baughman cites two
eastern Appalachian texts from New York and Kentucky.*

*Collected by Isabel Gordon Carter from Jane Gentry in
1923 in Hot Springs, North Carolina. Text from Journal of American Folklore, XXXVIII (1925), 360–61.
This text has taken the form of a believed tradition, or
legend.*

They use to be an old man, he lived way over in the forest by
hisself, and all he lived on was he caught women and boiled 'em
in front of the fire and eat 'em. Now the way my mother told
me, he'd go into the villages and tell 'em this and that and get
'em to come out and catch 'em and jest boil they breasts. That's
what she told me, and then I've heard hit that he jest eat 'em.
Well, they was a beautiful stout woman, he liked 'em the best
(he'd a been right atter me un your mother) so every day he'd
come over to this woman's house and he'd tell her to please
come over to see his house. "Why, Mr. Foster, I can't find the
way." "Yes, you can. I'll take a spool of red silk thread out
of my pocket and I'll start windin' hit on the bushes and it'll
carry ye straight to my house." So she promised him one day
she'd come. So she got her dinner over one day and she started.
So she follered the red silk thread and went on over to his
house . When she got there, there was a poor little old boy sittin'
over the fire a boilin' meat. And he says, "Laws, Aunt"—she
uz his aunt—"what er you doin' here? Foster kills every woman
uz comes here. You leave here jest as quick as you can."

    She started to jump out the door and she saw Foster a
comin' with two young women, one under each arm. So she run
back and says, "Jack, honey, what'll I do, I see him a comin'?"
"Jump in that old closet under the stair and I'll lock you in,"
says Jack.

    So she jumped in and Jack locked her in. So Foster come
in and he was jest talkin' and a laughin' with those two girls
and tellin' the most tales, and he was goin' to taken 'em over

to a corn shuckin' next day. Foster says, "Come on in and have supper with me." So Jack put up some boiled meat and water. That's all they had. As soon as the girls stepped in and seed the circumstance and seed their time had come their countenance fell. Foster says, "You better come in and eat, maybe the last chanct you'll ever have." Girls both jumped up and started to run. Foster jumps up and ketched 'em, and gets his tomihawk and starts upstairs with 'em. Stairs was shackly and rattly, and as they went up one of the girls retched her hand back and caught hold of a step and Foster jest tuck his tomihawk and hacked her hand off. It drapped into whar she was. She laid on in there until next day atter Foster went, then Jack let her out.

She jest bird worked over to where the corn shuckin' was. When she got there Foster was there. She didn't know how to git Foster destroyed. The people thought these people got out in the forest and the wild animals ud ketch 'em. So she says, "I dreamt an awful dream last night. I dreamed I lived close to Foster's house and he was always a-wantin' me to come to his house."

Foster says, "Well, that ain't so, and it shan't be so, and God forbid it ever should be so."

She went right on, "And I dreamt he put out a red thread and I follered hit to his house and there uz Jack broilin' women's breasts in front of the fire."

Foster says, "Well, that ain't so, and it shan't be so, and God forbid it ever should be so."

She went right on, "And he says, 'What er you doin' here? Foster kills every woman uz comes here.' "

Foster says, "Well, that ain't so, and it shan't be so, and God forbid it ever should be so."

She went right on, "And I seed Foster a-comin' with two girls. And when they git thar the girls their hearts failed 'em and Foster ketched 'em and gets his tomihawk and starts upstairs with 'em."

Foster says, "Well, that ain't so, and it shan't be so, and God forbid it ever should be so."

She went right on, "The stairs was shackly and rattly and

as they went up, one of the girls retched her hand back and caught hold of a step and Foster jest tuk his tomihawk and hacked her hand off."

Foster says, "Well, that ain't so, and it shan't be so, and God forbid it ever should be so."

She says, "Hit is so, and it shall be so and here I've got the hand to show."

And they knowed the two girls was missin' and they knowed it was so, so they lynched Foster and then they went and got Jack and bound him out.

"Lula Voyers"

This is an exclusively Kentucky ballad. Laws under F10, "Lula Viers," cites only one field text in print, from Jean Thomas, Ballad Makin' in the Mountains of Kentucky (New York, 1939), pp. 144–46, and two Library of Congress recorded texts, all from Kentucky. In his fifth chapter, "The American Ballad as a Record of Fact," Laws reprints Thomas' text (pp. 67–69) and confirms its accuracy. In 1948 Laws wrote the clerk of the Floyd County Court in Prestonburg, Kentucky, who supplied details of the 1917 murder at Elkhorn City in the Cumberland Mountains close to the West Virginia line, corroborating the ballad account. Missing in the ballad is the fact that Lula Viers had a child out of wedlock by her murderous lover.

The text below was printed in the Kentucky Folklore Record, *II (1956), 60–62, in a collection of "Floyd County Folklore," edited by Leonard W. Roberts, who comments that he had heard the story and ballad of Lula Viers in both Floyd and Pike counties. Sung by B. E. D., who heard it from Ted L. Akers of Allen, Kentucky, who had it from Lorene Newsome of Big Mud Creek, Kentucky.*

1. Come all you young people from all over this wide world
   And listen to a story about a poor little girl.

Her name was Lula Voyers, in Auxier she did dwell.
A place in Old Kentucky, a town we all know well.

2. She loved John Coyer, engaged to be his wife.
He ruined her reputation and stole this sweet young life.
They went to Elkhorn City, sixty-six miles away.
They put up at the hotel until the close of day.

3. When darkness fell upon them, they walked out for a
stroll.
It was in cold December and the wind was blowing cold.
They walked down by the river, cold water was running
deep,
When Johnny said to Lula, "In the bottom you must
sleep."

4. "O! Do you mean it Johnny? It surely cannot be.
How could you bear to murder a helpless girl like me!"
She threw her arms around him, saying, "Please spare my
life.
Send me home to Mother if I cannot be your wife."

5. She threw her arms around him and down before him
kneeled.
Around her neck he tied a piece of railroad steel.
He threw her in the river, the bubbles rolled around
And burst upon the water with a sad and mournful sound.

6. He hastened to the depot to board a train for home.
He still was believing his crime would never be known.
John Coyer joined the army, many months had come and
passed
When in the Ohio River this body was found at last.

7. They sent for a reporter, his name was R. O. Bent.
He printed it in the paper and around the world it went.
Lula's mother read the news while sitting in her home.
She quickly left her chair to reach a telephone.

8. She sent a message to Ironton, saying, "I will go and see
   If the body is my daughter. It surely cannot be."
   She boarded a train for Ironton and arrived right at the
      place.
   It was in a morgue so drear she looked on her child's face.

9. John Coyer was arrested and confined to Floyd County
      jail,
   And guarded as a wilful murder, no one to go his bail.
   Soon an army officer came and took him off to France.
   John Coyer never went to trial nor sought to clear his
      name.

"The Murder of Lottie Yates"

> *The following account written by Virgil L. Sturgill of
> Washington, D. C., originally appeared in the* Kentucky
> Folklore Record, *V (1959), 61–64, and* North Carolina
> Folklore, *VI (1958), 26–28. Another, longer text of
> "Lottie Yates," running to thirty stanzas, was printed
> in the same issue of* Kentucky Folklore Record, *pp.
> 65–69. This variant was collected by Cratis D. Williams
> from Mrs. M. E. Ekers, who took it down from the sing-
> ing of her brother, Lindsey Adams, on Daniels Creek,
> Lawrence County, Kentucky. Williams included it in his
> University of Kentucky M.A. thesis of 1937 on "Ballads
> and Songs."*

The incidents related in this tragedy are entered in the court
records of Carter County in eastern Kentucky, where I was
born and where I spent the first fifteen years of my life. For
the text and music, we are indebted to Mrs. Julia B. Kiser of
Gregoryville in Carter County, who permitted me to record
her singing of this ballad on tape, May 29, 1957. Mrs. Kiser
was a girl in her teens when the tragedy occurred. She remembered clearly all pertinent detail of the tragedy and sang it
with vigor that belies her eighty years.

"The Murder of Lottie Yates" is one of two surviving ballads that come from the pen of Elija ("Lige") Adams, a gifted folk-poet and singer of that period. Of the background and training of this itinerant minstrel, poet, and folk-historian, little is known, but he was a real person and very much alive and active near the turn of this century. This is attested to not only by Mrs. Kiser, but by my eighty-four-year-old father and relatives on my mother's side of the family. The skill with which he treats his material, the style and phraseology which he employs reveal innate talent and an understanding of forms employed in older English and early American ballads. This song, like his better-known "Ashland Tragedy," was probably issued originally as a broadside, but so far as known, no copy of it survives today.

1.   Come listen, friends, while I relate
    Of a crime committed in Kentucky state.
    It was the murder of poor Lottie Yates,
    I hope she's passed through Heaven's gates.

2.   It was one night in the month of May
    While she in bed with her baby lay,
    The dirk was hurled with a wicked dart
    That caused poor Lottie and her babe to part.

3.   He raised the window with full intent,
    To talk to her he was deeply bent,
    And as he talked his heart grew cold.
    O such a crime, it would damn one's soul!

4.   "He's killed me now," she faintly cried.
    Her father soon was by her side.
    Do all he could, it was in vain.
    He could not bring her back again.

5.   Her life blood rushed from its fountain head
    While she lay gasping on her bed.
    Her mother shrieked with grief so wild,
    And the father sank by his dying child.

6.   With throbbing heart he dashed away.
       The broken knife at the gateway lay.
       It done its work when Lottie fell.
       Of such a crime it is hard to tell.

7.   Go look on the grave where Lottie sleeps.
       Though tears may flow and hearts may weep,
       Her loss to you might be her gain.
       Though Lottie's dead, she will live again.

8.   He's done the crime and fled away.
       God's vengeance followed him day by day.
       He was taken at last and placed in jail,
       No mercy lent nor gave him bail.

9.   "I did the crime," he did confess,
       "The cause of it was jealousness.
       May God forgive us both I pray,
       And save us both on Judgment Day."

10.   The night before the trial came
       A crowd did take the Willard train
       And made a rush for the prison cell.
       Who were these men? I cannot tell.

11.   They marched through town with a steady pace.
       To the jailor's house they went in haste.
       They made him give those iron keys
       That unlocked the prisoner's cell with ease.

12.   The key was turned; the door did creak;
       The prisoner screamed and loud did shriek.
       He knew his time was short to be,
       From iron bars he would be set free.

13.   They placed the culprit on the verge,
       No funeral song nor lonesome dirge,
       With none to sing but the nightingale
       To mourn his loss or sad bewail.

14.   The time has come; he must make the leap
        While frantic shadows o'er him creep.
        He's gone; he's swung beneath the sky.
        For a cruel murder he had to die.

15.   This ends these lines of which we read
        Of a crime so black with its bloody deed.
        May all mankind who marry a wife
        Live true and faithful all their life.

This ballad contains the incidents of Lottie's murder at the hands of her estranged husband, Oscar (or "Os") Porter. At the time of the incident, she was living with their infant son at her father's home in the Willard community in Carter County. As told in the song and stated by Mrs. Kiser, "Porter came to the Yates home one night, raised the window, and stabbed her to death while she lay in bed. This was in the year 1895. He dropped the murderous knife near the yard gate as he fled. Later he was arrested, confessed the crime, and was confined in the county jail at Grayson. Emotions ran high in the community, and a mob took the law into its own hands. They stormed the jail and took the prisoner to nearby E. K. Junction (now Hitchins) in the same county and hanged him from the nearby railroad trestle." My father also confirms these facts as follows: ". . . the murder of Lottie Yates was in 1895, and Porter was hanged on the E. K. [Eastern Kentucky] Railroad bridge crossing the Little Sandy River between Grayson and E. K. Junction. A piece of rope left tied to the bridge remained there for some time after the hanging, and I saw it while walking over the bridge."

"Zeb Tourney's Gal"

> *From Kelly Combs, a Kentucky mountaineer living on Bull Creek in Gander, schoolteacher Marie Campbell garnered some of the fine points of mountain feuds. "A feud comes of siding in of blood kin with one another and believing all the bad things air spoke or even hinted*

*at about t'other side. The kin on both sides gits their
old guns cleaned up and packs 'em. 'Taint only gitting
even makes 'em do hit but being suspicious and not
wanting to be unpertected. Plenty times they don't put
no trust in the law and the officers."*

*Combs knew and sang half a dozen feuding ballads, but
the following song was sung to Miss Campbell by Mace
Whitaker of Rock House Creek, who had whittled out
his own wooden leg.*

*Text from Marie Campbell, "Feuding Ballads from the
Kentucky Mountains,"* Southern Folklore Quarterly,
*III (1939), 171–72. Laws E18 also cites an Alabama
text and a Library of Congress recording from Virginia.
Laws thinks the piece too cleverly melodramatic for a
local composition.*

Down in the Tennessee mountains,
Away from the sins of this world,
Dan Kelly's son, there he leaned on his gun
A-thinking of Zeb Tourney's girl.
Dan was a hot-blooded youngster,
His pap raised him sturdy and right,
And he had been sworn, from the day he was born,
To shoot every Tourney on sight.

"Powder and shot for the Tourneys
Don't save a hair on their heads,"
Dan Kelly cried as he laid down and died,
With young Danny there by his bed.
Dan took the oath with his pappy,
And swore he would kill every one,
With his heart in a whirl
With his love for the girl
He loaded his double-barreled gun.

Moon shining down on the mountain,
Moon shining down on the hill,
Young Dan took the tip,

Swung the gun to his hip,
And started out to slaughter and kill.
Over the mountains he wandered,
This son of a Tennessee man,
With fire in his eye,
And his gun at his thigh,
A-looking for Zeb Tourney's clan.

Shots ring out on the mountain,
Shots ringing out in the breeze,
Dan Kelly's son there
With smoke in his gun,
The Tourneys all down on their knees.
The story of the Kellys and Tourneys
Rang far and wide out o'er the world,
How Dan killed a clan,
Shot 'em down to a man,
And brought back old Zeb Tourney's girl.

4. CANTE FABLES

The Cante Fable in Eastern Kentucky
By LEONARD ROBERTS

Adapted from Midwest Folklore, *VI* (1956), 69–88.

The *cante fable* is a form of folktale that is told in prose interspersed with song. But since the tunes have been most difficult to execute by those not skilled with an accompanying instrument and most easily left out of printed texts, we count those stories *cante fables* having lines or stanzas of verse that are usually recited more dramatically than the prose. Examples of this form of folktale are found in virtually all of the older collections of folk-literature, such as those from India, Arabia, Persia, and medieval France.

The status of the *cante fable* in recent folk literature has not been given any definitive treatment that I am aware of, but those few folktale students who have had occasion to comment upon the form have thought it to be in a state of obsolescence and decay. One of these commentators was Joseph Jacobs, the editor of four volumes of English and Celtic tales. In connection with "Childe Rowland," a well preserved *cante fable* in his *English Fairy Tales*, he reviews the form in ancient collections, finds about 36 per cent of the first fifty tales in the Grimm collection to be *cante fables*, and, after discounting from his volume the ballads and setting aside the drolls which have a different origin, he finds that almost all of the remaining ordinary tales have vestiges of the *cante fable* form.

In my own collecting I have found unmistakable examples of the *cante fable*, in three types of folklore: songs, riddles, and folktales. I say "unmistakable" because I have come to the conclusion that the performer himself knows the form and likes to use it. The performers that I have heard take some pride in saying rapidly and dramatically an oft-repeated line or a stanza of verse in their stories. They are proudest, of course, if they can show their skill in a complicated run in formula tales, or a tongue-twister in songs and riddles. I have learned to recognize these exhibitions of my performers as *cante fables*.

I have fewer examples of the form in songs than in the other categories, but I have heard many more such songs than I have been able to record. Most folksingers with any sized repertory have one or two which, in part or entirely, they "talk off." Two examples are these:

The Arkansas Traveler

"Can you tell me where this road goes to, mister?"
"I've lived here all my life and it hain't gone nowhere yit!" And then he strikes up his banjo and sings——

But I've been a-gettin there, gettin there gettin there,
I've been a-gettin there just the same. Etc.

Fox Hunting

In this example the performer uses a banjo and twangs a string or hits dissonant chords or swings into jig time to imitate dog calls, dog yelps, cold trails, and hot scents. In the meantime the performer tells in prose the narrative of a good fox hunt, all the way from the dooryard to a rock cliff on top of a hill where old Bugle, old Blazer, old Spot, and the two pups have holed a fine red fox.

Almost all riddles require some prose interpretation, even if just a word or phrase. And it is to be expected that in the long passage of time some of their answers will be lost. But of the few hundred riddles that I have collected among the eastern Kentucky folk not one is without an answer. This applies also to those that have a narrative to explain their meaning. Some of these, permitting a criminal to go free if he can make up an unriddlable riddle, have been classified as "neck riddles" by Archer Taylor, in his Introduction to *English Riddles from Oral Tradition*, p. 1.

The King's Servant

> For discussion of this riddle see Dorson, American Folklore, *pp. 96–97*.

This is the story of a king. He told his servant that if he would make a riddle that he couldn't onriddle why he would free him. He was under bondage. He said:

> Good morning, good morning, your ceremony, king,
> I drunk a drink out of your morning spring;
> Through the gold the stream did run,
> In your garden that was done;
> If you can onriddle that I'll be hung.

He got the queen to help him and they met out in the garden and he nursed her breast through one of her gold rings. The king didn't onriddle it and he went free.

Love I Set

> Love I set, love I stand.
> Love I hold in my right hand,
> Love I see in yonders tree,
> If you can onriddle that
> You can hang me.

Woman had to make a riddle to free her lover who was about to be hung. So she took her dog named Love and killed it and put pieces around, one under her chair, one in her right hand, and one in a tree. They couldn't onriddle it and he was free.

The Slave's Riddle

Back in the time when kings had slaves he'd tell 'em if they
could make a riddle up that he couldn't onriddle, he'd free 'em.
He sent a slave out to see about his old sow, and he found she
had one pig and it dead. He come back and said:

> She had a red pig,
> And a dead pig,
> A boar pig,
> And a pore pig,
> How many pigs is that?

The king guessed four but they was just one. The slave went
free.

The Gold in the Chimley

> *Out of four versions of this old, well-known story, Type
> 480, The Spinning Women by the Spring, two of them
> are told almost entirely in verse. I give the shorter
> cante fable in full.*
>
> *A detailed monograph of Type 480 based on over nine
> hundred variants has been published by Warren E.
> Roberts, The Tale of the Kind and the Unkind Girls,
> (Berlin, 1958).*

Once upon a time there was two girls. They were sisters, and
one went to a witch's house to get a place to stay. Well, the witch
said, "All right, you can stay." Said, "I'm goin to the store and
don't you look up the chimley while I'm gone."

While she was gone she looked up the chimley. There hung
a bag of gold. She got this gold and started, and come to a cow.
The cow says, "Please milk me, little girl, I hain't been milked
in several long years."

She says, "I hain't got time."

She went to a sheep and the sheep said, "Please shear me,
little girl, I hain't been sheared in several long years."

She says, "I hain't got time."

She went on to a horse, and the horse said, "Please ride me, little girl, I hain't been rode in several long years."

She said, "I hain't got time."

She went on and come to a mill. The mill said, "Please turn me, little girl, I hain't been turned in several long years."

The little girl said, "I hain't got time." She went over and laid down behind the door and went to sleep.

Well, the old witch come back, and her gold was gone. She started out and come to the cow and said,

> Cowel o mine, cowel o mine,
> Have you ever seen a maid o mine,
> With a wig and a wag and a long leather bag,
> Who stold all the money I ever had?

She said, "Yeau, she just passed."
Went on to the sheep, said,

> Sheep o mine, sheep o mine,
> Have you ever seen a maid o mine,
> With a wig and a wag and a long leather bag,
> Who stold all the money I ever had?

She said, "Yeau, she just passed."
She went on to the horse and said,

> Horse o mine, horse o mine,
> Have you ever seen a maid o mine,
> With a wig and a wag and a long leather bag,
> Who stold all the money I ever had?

The horse said, "Yeau, she just passed."
She went on to the mill and said,

> Mill o mine, mill o mine,
> Have you ever seen a maid o mine,
> With a wig and a wag and a long leather bag,
> Who stold all the money I ever had?

It said, "She's layin over there behind the door."

She went over there and turned her into a stone. She got her gold and went on back home.

Well, the next girl come along and said, "Can I get to stay here?"

She said, "Yeau, but I'm going to the store," and said, "don't look up the chimley while I'm gone."

When she got gone she looked up the chimley. There hung this bag of gold. She got it and started. Come to this cow, and the cow said, "Please milk me, little girl, I hain't been milked in several long years."

She milked the cow. Went on to the sheep. The sheep said, "Please shear me, little girl, I hain't been sheared in several long years."

She sheared the sheep. Went on to the horse. The horse said, "Please ride me, little girl, I hain't been rode in several long years."

So she rode the horse. Come to the mill. The mill says, "Please turn me, little girl, I hain't been turned in several long years."

She turned the mill.

Well, the old witch come back, and her gold was gone. She started. She come to the cow and said,

> Cowel o mine, cowel o mine
> Have you ever seen a maid o mine,
> With a wig and a wag and a long leather bag,
> Who stold all the money I ever had?

She said, "No."
She went to the sheep——

> Sheep o mine, sheep o mine,
> Have you ever seen a maid o mine,
> With a wig and a wag and a long leather bag,
> Who stold all the money I ever had?

Said, "No, I hain't never seen her."
Went on to the horse and said,

> Horse o mine, horse o mine,
> Have you ever seen a maid o mine,
> With a wig and a wag and a long leather bag,
> Who stold all the money I ever had?

Said, "No, I hain't never seen her."
She went on to the mill and said,

> Mill o mine, mill o mine,
> Have you ever seen a maid o mine,
> With a wig and a wag and a long leather bag,
> Who stold all the money I ever had?

It said, "Get up in my hopper, I can't hear good."
She got up in the hopper and said,

> MILL O MINE, MILL O MINE,
> HAVE YOU EVER SEEN A MAID O MINE
> WITH A WIG AND A WAG AND A LONG LEATHER BAG,
> WHO STOLD ALL THE MONEY I EVER HAD?

The mill started grinding and ground her up.
The little girl she got up, turned the stone back into her
sister and they lived happy ever after.

A Cante Fable in North Carolina

The Untrue Wife's Song (1)

*An abbreviated form of Type 1360C, Old Hildebrand,
a widely disseminated European anticlerical cante
fable. An extensive note to a New Jersey text by Herbert Halpert, Journal of American Folklore, LV
(1942), 134, emphasizes the North Carolina focus of
English-American examples.*

*Collected by Ralph S. Boggs from B. L. Lunsford, 49,
Buncombe County, N. C., and printed in the Journal of
American Folklore, XLVII (1934), 305. Boggs also
obtained another, more conventional text.*

Once a man an' his wife were ridin' on a ship. One day the man
was talkin' to the captain, an' they got to talkin' about women.
The captain said he'd never seen a virtuous woman. The man
said his wife was virtuous, and the captain bet the ship's cargo

against the man's fiddle that he could seduce the man's wife
within three hours. The man sent his wife up to the captain's
cabin. After waiting for two hours the man became a little on-
easy, so he walked by the captain's cabin, an' played on his fiddle an' sang:

> For two long hours
> You've resisted the captain's powers.
> The cargo will soon be ours.

His wife heard him, an' from within she sang back:

> Too late, too late, my dear,
> He has me around the middle;
> Too late, too late, my dear,
> You've lost your damned old fiddle.

The Untrue Wife's Song (2)

> *Here is a more complete text of "Old Hildebrand" which
> follows more closely the plot of Type 1360C. The title
> character in Carter's text, "Little Dicky Wigbun," is
> close to Halpert's "Dicky Wigdon," as printed by him
> in "The Cante-Fable in New Jersey," Journal of Amer-
> ican Folklore, LV (1942), 134–35.*
>
> *Text collected by Isabel G. Carter from Jane Gentry,
> Journal of American Folklore, XXXVIII (1925), 366–
> 68. The priest of European versions gives way to a cap-
> tain in the preceding example and to a vague "passen-
> ger" here.*

He was a little bit of a man and his wife didn't like him nary a
bit. She loved the old passenger. I don't know what the old
passenger was. They uz men use to travel about and they called
'em the old passenger. So she was all the time playin' off like she
was sick and sending little Dicky Wigbun to the Clear Apsul
Springs to get Clear Apsul Rum fer her. (I don't know what
Clear Apsul Rum were, it's just in the story; they didn't really
have anything like hit.) She was hopin' the wild varmints ud get

him and eat him up and she cud have the old passenger. So one day he uz going down to the spring and he met the peddler.

Peddler says, "Dicky, where you started?" "I've started down to Clear Apsul Springs to git my wife some Clear Apsul Rum."

Peddler says, "Dicky, I'm jest as sorry fer you uz I can be. Your wife don't care nothing fer you." "You think she don't?" "No, she's jest sendin' you off down here to see if you won't get killed by the wild animals. You jest get in this knapsack of mine and let me carry you back to your house and let you see what's going on." "Well, I believe I will," says Dicky. So Dicky got in the haversack.

Got to Dicky's house and the peddler says, "Kin I stay all night?" "Yes, I guess ye can, but my husband's not here." So he went in and says, "Mrs. Wigbun, kin I bring my haversack in? I dropped hit in a mud hole down the road a piece and I'm feared I'll get my rations wet." "Yes, I guess ye kin." So the peddler went out and cut a couple of holes so's Jack cud see out and just picked him up and carried him into the house.

So the peddler says, "Let's all sing some little ditties." "All right," the passenger says. "Well now, Mrs. Wigbun," says the peddler, "you sing the first one, then Mr. Passenger, you sing the next one and then I'll sing one."

So Mrs. Wigbun sings:

"Oh, Little Dicky Wigbun
To London he's gone
To buy me a bottle of Clear Apful Rum,
God send him a long journey never to return
Through the green wood and below."

"Well now, Mrs. Wigbun, that's a pretty song, sing hit agin."

"Oh, Little Dicky Wigbun
To London he's gone
To buy me a bottle of Clear Apful Rum,
God send him a long journey never to return
Through the green wood and below."

"Well now, Mr. Passenger, you sing yourn."

"Oh, little Dicky Wigbun thinks
Who eats of his sweets and drinks of his drinks,
And if God spares my life
I will sleep with his wife
Through the green wood and below."

"That's pretty, sing hit agin."

"Oh, little Dicky Wigbun thinks
Who eats of his sweets and drinks of his drinks,
And if God spares my life
I will sleep with his wife
Through the green wood and below."

"Now, Mr. Peddler, you sing yourn," says Mis' Wigbun.

"Oh little Dicky Wigbun, he's not very fur,
And out of my knapsack I'll have him to appear
And if friends he don't like, I stand to his back
Through the green fields and below."

"So they hung the old passenger all right away
And they burnt Dicky's wife the very next day
Through the green fields and below."

5. RIDDLES

THESE RIDDLES, collected in the North Carolina mountains, belong to
a familiar pattern, the seemingly obscene question with an innocuous
reply. See Taylor, *English Riddles from Oral Tradition*, Nos. 1739–
1749, pp. 687–88, "Erotic Scenes," for examples of this pattern,
mainly from southern Negro tradition.

Texts from Ralph S. Boggs, "North Carolina White Folktales and
Riddles," *Journal of American Folklore*, XLVII (1934), 320–21.

The ole man shook it an' shook it;
The ole woman pulled up her dress an' took it.
> *A man shook apples out of a tree, and his wife
> caught them in her dress.*

The ole lady pitted it an' patted it;
The ole man down with his breeches an' at it.
> *She made up the bed, and he undressed and got
> into bed.*

When it goes in, it's stiff an' stout;
When it comes out, it's flopping about.
> *Cooking a cabbage.*

Big at the bottom, an' little at the top,
An' a little thing in the middle that goes pippity pop.
> *A churn.*

Little Jessie Ruddle,
Asettin' in a puddle,

Green garters an' yaller toes;
Tell me that riddle or I'll smash yer nose!
          A duck in a puddle of water.

About six inches long, an' a might pretty size;
Not a lady in the country but what will take it between
     her thighs.
          The lefthand horn on a lady's side saddle.

6. FOLK DRAMA

MARIE CAMPBELL, noted collector of Kentucky mountain folklore, published the following discussion and text of an English mummers' play in *Journal of American Folklore*, LI (1938), 10–24.

With the references she gives to Edmund K. Chambers, *The English Folk-Play* (Oxford, 1933) and Reginald J. E. Tiddy, *The Mummers' Play* (Oxford, 1923) should be added Violet Alford, *Sword Dance and Drama* (London, 1962), the most recent investigation of the mummers' traditional ritual play.

Survivals of Old Folk Drama
in the Kentucky Mountains
By MARIE CAMPBELL

The first hint that there were any survivals of old folk drama in the Kentucky mountains came from Aunt Susan on Caney Creek. One day in the summer of 1925, when I went to her house to buy eggs, she complained that I had not been there for more than a week. My excuse that I had been busy making costumes for a play during the hours I was not teaching reminded her of her pap's talk about play acting which his pap had told him about. Aunt Susan said her grandpap always acted out "The Turkish Knight," and that her pap had learned the speech and, when she was a child, had taught it to her. She said the play had not been given within her or her pap's lifetime, and so she knew nothing of the play except grandpap's part. She said she had never known of any "old time play acting being done whiles I recollect." Some time later Aunt Susan let me copy her grandpap's speech.

I thought no more of old-time play-acting in the mountain country till on Christmas Eve in 1930 some of the men and boys at Gander presented for me an old mummers' play. Later two of the men gave me a fairly complete text for the play.

Since that time an old couple have given me a text for an old Plough Monday Play which their memory had kept alive, although they had never heard that it was ever really acted out.

The three contributions just mentioned and one scrap of song drama are the only survivals of folk drama contained in this collection, and I am fairly sure that there are no more such survivals to be found in this area. All of the contributors were old people, and the play presented at Christmas time in 1930 was almost as new for the young people who belonged to the community as it was for me. Thirty or more years had passed since its last performance, and the play will not be presented again by this community because the two men who knew the text are both dead. So are Aunt Lizbeth Fields and Aunt Susan, the two old women who contributed the two fragments of old plays. And the last time I heard from Aunt Mary and Uncle Joe they were "all broke down and a sight how puny."

The mummers' play given in this collection, though not identical with any of the texts given in Chambers' *The English Folk-Play* or Tiddy's *The Mummers' Play*, does contain the essential core of the mummers' play: the presentation, the combat, the lament, the cure, and the quete. The presence of this essential core of action establishes the identity of the play as an authentic survival of an old mummers' play, however corrupted the text may be.

Though it is certain that the text of the Plough Monday Play is incomplete and is further corrupted by the interpolation of part of an Elizabethan jig, yet it does have certain conventional characters of the traditional Plough Monday Play as discussed by Chambers and Tiddy. Aunty Mary and Uncle Joe's Plough Monday Play has the plough boys, Old Jane and Tom, the rustic fool, conventional characters of the Plough Monday Play. As in the mummers' play there is a combat and a cure.

The two additional fragments of old drama testify to the truth of Aunt Lizbeth Fields' statement that "the old-time play-acting has nigh about faded out in the mountain country."

The Christmas Play

THE PRESENTER—not in costume.

FATHER CHRISTMAS—Santa Claus suit borrowed from the school. Holly in his beard. Carried a frying pan and a dead rabbit.

DAME DOROTHY—A man dressed in bright colored woman's clothes. Veil made of an old window curtain served as a mask. Red paper pinned inside the front of her dress was displayed later as blood.

OLD BET—A man dressed as an old woman. Apron, bonnet and shawl. Mistletoe on bonnet.

THE BESSIE—A man dressed as a woman with a cow's tail fastened on. Grotesque mask of brown paper with horns sticking up. Holly on the horns. Carried two cow bells strung across his hips.

LITTLE DEVIL DOUBT—A boy with his face blacked. A hump on his back. Gay red paper streamers tied around his arms and neck. Holly on his hat.

PICKLE HERRING—A man wearing a woman's "bedgown" under a man's overcoat. Carried an inflated pig's bladder colored like a balloon. A dunce cap with gay streamers served as a mask. Many floating red paper streamers.

DOCTOR GOOD—A man wearing a long-tailed coat, spectacles, and a very high top hat. Face painted very red. No other mask. Holly on his hat. Carried a doctor's bag.

CHORUS—Eight high school boys wearing the white smocks of the home economics class. Paper bags over their heads as masks. Holly wreaths around their necks.

According to Tom and George Fields the following parts of the costuming were "fixed by the way the old time folks decked out to go mumming":

The red paper or cloth pinned inside Dame Dorothy's dress and used to represent blood.

The woman's clothing on **Old Bet.**

The cow's tail, the woman's clothing, and the cow bells on **The Bessie.**

The "bedgown," the dunce cap, and the inflated bladder for the **Pickle Herring.**

The professional garb and red mask on **Doctor Good.**

The white smocks on the chorus.

Holly, masks, and gay streamers on the cast. Other items of costuming were merely rustic attempts at disguise.

(*After a huge bonfire has been made to give heat and light.*)

PRESENTER:

We air now aiming to give a dumb show for to pleasure the Little Teacher for not going off to the level country to keep Christmas with her kin. Hit ain't noways perfect the way we act out this here dumb show, but hit ain't been acted out amongst our settlement for uppards of twenty or thirty year, maybe more. I reckon folks all knows hit air bad luck to talk with the dumb show folks or guess who they air. Now then we aim to start.

(*The Presenter goes into the cabin and comes out walking backward with a broom.*)

PRESENTER:

    Out comes I hind part before,
    With my big broom to sweep up the floor.

(*He sweeps a wide circle, all the time muttering over and over.*)

    Room, room, gallons of room.

(*When a circle of sufficient size has been swept, he stops muttering and begins the presentation of characters. When each character's name is called, the character struts around the outside of the circle and steps out of the circle until his part in the action of the play.*)

PRESENTER:

1.   In comes old Father Christmas,
        Welcome or not, welcome or not,

I hope old Father Christmas
Never is forgot, never is forgot.

2.   In comes old Dame Dorothy,
Drinking liquor's all her folly,
Wearing silks and being bawdy.

3.   Old Bet comes in once a year
To get her kissed and bring good cheer.

4.   Oh the next that now comes in
Is the Bessie as you see,
He's a woman or a man
With a cow's tail, can you see?

5.   In steps black faced
Little Devil Doubt,
Humped over bad
Toting his burdens about.

6.   Pickle Herring he comes in
To join the dance,
Wearing a bedgown
Instead of his pants.

7.   Here's the doctor pure and good
With his pills he stops the blood.

(*The Presenter steps back among the spectators and
Father Christmas and Dame Dorothy enter the circle. Old Bet
and The Bessie tease the audience, she pretending to kiss the
men, he the women.*)

FATHER CHRISTMAS:
Here come I, old Father Christmas, welcome or not;
I hope old Father Christmas will never be forgot.
We are come to laugh and cheer,
And if our pudding it be done,

We'll fry this hare and have some fun.

DAME DOROTHY:

I'll beat it and bale it
And cut it in slices,
And take an old pot,
And boil it with spices.

FATHER CHRISTMAS:

You'll fry this hare and yet no word be said,
For if you dare to boil the hare,
With my pan I'll crack your head.

DAME DOROTHY:

How can you crack my head?
My head is made of steel.

(*The Bessie and Old Bet join the chorus and they repeat
all conversation up to the time of the arrival of the doctor.*)

DAME DOROTHY:

I'll cut you into button holes,
And make your buttons fly.

FATHER CHRISTMAS:

I'll fill your body full of bullets,
And make your blood fly.

DAME DOROTHY:

I'll cut your coat all full of holes,
And make the rags fly.

FATHER CHRISTMAS:

I'll cut you down the middle,
And make your blood to fly.

DAME DOROTHY:

I'll cut you small as flies,
And use you up to cook mince pies.

FATHER CHRISTMAS:

If your blood is hot,
I'll make it cold,
As cold as muddy clay.
I'll take your life and blood,
And throw the hare away.

(*They fight. The Bessie and Old Bet join them. Dame Dorothy is helped by The Bessie, Father Christmas by Old Bet.*)

DAME DOROTHY (*showing the red paper on her breast*):
Old Father Christmas,
See what you've done!
You've bloody killed
Your own loved one! (*Falls dead.*)
(*The Bessie and Old Bet run away.*)
FATHER CHRISTMAS:
Horrible, terrible,
See what I've done!
I cut her down
Like the evening sun! (*Chorus repeats.*)
Is there a doctor to be found
To cure her of this deep and deadly wound? (*Chorus.*)
Oh is there a doctor near at hand
To heal her wound and make her stand?

(*The chorus, which has been repeating all conversations up until now, repeats the last of Father Christmas' speech and is silent until the end of the play.*)

DOCTOR GOOD (*enters with Pickle Herring, who weeps over
        Dame Dorothy*):
Yes, there is a doctor near at hand
To heal her wound and make her stand.
FATHER CHRISTMAS:
What can you cure?
DOCTOR GOOD:
I can cure the itch, the spots, and gout,
If there's nine devils in, I take six out.
FATHER CHRISTMAS:
What's your fee, Doctor?
DOCTOR GOOD:
Fifteen pounds, it is my fee.
FATHER CHRISTMAS:
Work your cure and let me see.

DOCTOR GOOD:
I will. Where's Pickle Herring?
PICKLE HERRING:
Oh here's Pickle Herring.
DOCTOR GOOD:
Hold up her head.
PICKLE HERRING:
Will she bite?
DOCTOR GOOD:
Yes.
PICKLE HERRING:
Hold her yourself, then.
DOCTOR GOOD:
What's that, you rascal?
PICKLE HERRING:
Oh I hold her, sir.

(*He raises Dame Dorothy's head. Doctor Good gives her a pill. She jumps up.*)

DAME DOROTHY:
Once I was dead and now I'm alive.
Blessed be the man that made me revive.
DEVIL DOUBT (*entering*):
In comes I, Little Devil Doubt,
With all my family on my back.
Christmas comes but once a year,
And when it comes it brings good cheer.

(*Devil Doubt takes Father Christmas' pan and collects gifts of people and lays them on the Little Teacher's hearth each time he gets a panful. The chorus sings "Jingle Bells" and "Come All Ye Faithful" while he is making the collection. When Devil Doubt returns the pan, Father Christmas sweeps everybody out of the circle and then sweeps the hearth in the teacher's cabin, explaining that it is bad luck to carry out ashes on Christmas Day.*)

FATHER CHRISTMAS:
Our show is done, we stay no longer here.
God bless the mistress of this house,
And when she wakes up Christmas Day,
Lord Jesus, bring her cheer.

(*The mummers depart singing the "Mummers' Carol."*)

The Turkish Knight

Aunt Susan of Caney Creek gave this fragment of "old time play acting" in 1925. She said this was the speech her pap's pap used to say in a "piece of play acting." She said she learned it from her pap and she had no idea what the rest of the play was, for it had not been "acted out since my grandpap's time." This speech of Aunt Susan's pap's pap is similar to the speech of the Turkish Knight in a play from Weston Sub-Edge, Gloucestershire (J. E. Tiddy, The Mummers' Play, Oxford, 1923, p. 167).

In comes I the Turkish man,
And in my hand a frying pan.
I thinks myself a jolly old man.

I went up a straight crooked lane. I met a bark and it dogged at me. I went to the stick and cut a hedge and killed a little red dog on tother side of a ten-foot wall. Nine days after tomorrow I picks up the little dead red dog and rams my arm down his throat and turns him inside outards and follows after him.

Last Christmas night I turned to spit,
Burned my finger and made it itch.
The sparks flew out of the cradle,
And the pot lid jumped offen the table,
And swore he'd fight the frying pan.

As I was going along standing still, I come to King Charles up an iron pear tree. He asked me the way to get down. I said, "Pitch thee poll first into a pit."

I went on a bit further and I met two old women working butter, and they did mum and mutter. They asked me if I could eat a cup of cider, and drink a bread and cheese. And I said, "No, ma'm, thank you ma'm, if you please."

And I went on a bit further and I come to the land of plenty with stones of plum puddings, houses thatched with pancakes, and pigs running about saying, "Who will eat me, please?"

And now if this frying pan had a tongue,
It would go on with the story and tell you no wrong.

7. CAROLS

Mummers' Carol

Tom and George Fields did not give a copy of the "Mummers' Carol" with the text for their mummers' play. But at Christmas time in 1935 Susan Fields, Tom's wife, sent the version given below. It came with Susan's explanation that Tom used to sing the tune to the clacking of his old water mill, but now that he had a gasoline engine he was "like to fergit hit." So she had one of her children copy it for me (Marie Campbell, Journal of American Folklore, LI [1938], 14–15).

There is six days all in a week,
All for a laboring man,
But Christmas Day is the day of our Lord,
Both Father and Son.

Our Christmas celebrate, my man,
Down your knees do fall,
And then do pray the Lord Jesus Christ
To bless and save you all.

The Cherry Tree Carol

Marie Campbell also collected three texts of a Christmas carol, the famous "Cherry Tree Carol" (Child 54), which was sung before the acting out of the mummers' play. A discussion is in Coffin, The British Traditional Ballad in North America, *pp. 65–67. Coffin notes that the first American text was printed in 1915, and that there are five American story types. The present text belongs to Type A, with Christ in the womb asking the cherry tree to bow down, when Joseph refuses to pick cherries. The text also contains the feature of January 6 being mentioned as the date of Old Christmas, reminiscent of the dropping of eleven days from the calendar in 1751.*

Oh Joseph was an old man,
An old man was he,
And he courted Virgin Mary,
A maid of Galilee.

And Joseph and Mary
Were a-walking one fine day,
"Here are apples and cherries
Pretty to behold."

Then Mary said to Joseph
So meek and so mild,
"Joseph, pick me cherries,
For I am with child."

When Joseph he got angry,
In anger all he flew,
"Let the father of your baby
Pick cherries for you."

Then the babe it spoke a few words,
A few words to the tree,
"Let my mother have some cherries,
Bow down, you cherry tree."

The cherry tree bowed low down,
Bowed down to the ground,

And Mary she ate cherries,
While Joseph stood around.

Then Joseph took Mary
On his knee,
"Oh tell of your baby,
When will his birthday be?"

"On the sixth of January,"
The babe said softly,
"On the sixth of January
My birthday will be."

IV

LOUISIANA CAJUNS

✿ HISTORY AND GEOGRAPHY have joined to create the regional folk culture of southern Louisiana. This is bayou country, a waterland, sprinkled with swamps and marshes, overhung with the branches of great oaks, festooned with trailing moss. The Mississippi River, pouring its thousands of tons of muddy water each year into the Gulf of Mexico, inundates the delta with torpid streams which the French settlers called "bayous," from the Choctaw "bayuk." Along these sluggish river roads the inhabitants travel by pirogue and skiff and lugger and barge; they pole their eggshell pirogues—hollowed from cypress logs—through narrow inlets, then switch to outboard motors and cabin craft as the waters widen.

People who live in the bayou country that stretches west from Baton Rouge and New Orleans on the lower Mississippi toward the Texas border are popularly called Cajuns. Historically, Cajun is a corruption of Acadian, and dates from the sad influx of French settlers dispossessed from Acadia in Nova Scotia. They had colonized there in 1604 and been exiled by an English decree in 1755, after France had lost most of her New World holdings to England. A year later the first Acadian contingent reached the Louisiana colony, originally claimed for France by La Salle in 1682, and were hospitably welcomed by the governor, Baron de Kerlerec. Louisiana remained French until 1762, when it was ceded to Spain by the Treaty of Fontainebleau, and then retroceded in 1800 by the secret Treaty of San Ildefonso. This development moved President Jefferson to initiate the diplomatic events climaxed in 1803 by the celebrated Louisiana Purchase. With so strongly rooted a French ancestry, Louisiana has retained such institutions as the parish instead of the county system of local government, the Code Napoleon in place of Anglo-American common law, and a French patois that has fended off spoken English. North of New Orleans and the bayou region a different culture prevails, the general southern culture of cotton and sugar planters, Negro sharecroppers, and red-necked white farmers from the hills.

In French-speaking Louisiana, the Creoles are the aristocrats and the Cajuns the peasant folk. The names have come to designate social classes rather than the conjectured strains of racial descent— pure French as opposed to halfbreeds—which they originally indicated. Now the elegant families of New Orleans with Parisian tastes call themselves Creole, and refer to the shrimp fishermen, the muskrat trappers, the moss pickers, the oystermen as Cajuns all. In her exploring trip to the Louisiana backwaters, described in *Cajuns on the Bayous* (1957), Carolyn Ramsey encountered numerous communities of a "general mixtry," in which the Acadians and French mingled their blood with Indians and Negroes, Spaniards and Italians, Chinese and Manilamen, Germans and Slavs. If these peoples spoke a patois, they were known as Cajuns.

Unlike the German-speaking farmers of Pennsylvania, who organized three societies to study and publish reports on their own folk culture, the French of Louisiana have until recently shown little interest in such self-scrutiny. One reason was the Creole-Cajun division which hindered a sense of cultural homogeneity. Cultural groups, whether on a national scale like the Finns and Japanese, or within regional enclaves, like the Pennsylvania Dutch and Canadian French, develop a concern with their own submerged traditions when they have attained some measure of affluence and position. Then the intellectuals pry into their folk backgrounds.

One scholar of French descent, Alcée Fortier (1865–1914) single-handedly called attention in the 1890's to the French folklore of Louisiana. Fortier, who became a professor of Romance languages and dean of the graduate school at Tulane University, was born in St. James Parish, Louisiana, of Breton stock. He read a paper on "Bits of Louisiana Folklore" before the Modern Language Association in 1888, and published a tale collection from Negroes speaking the Creole dialect, *Louisiana Folk-Tales,* with the original French texts and English translations, in 1895 as the second memoir of the American Folklore Society. In 1892 he founded and served as the first president of the New Orleans (later Louisiana) Folk-Lore Association, and the American Folklore Society elected him president in 1894. As much the philologist as the folklorist, Fortier sought Negro tales in lower Louisiana from his interest in the truncated dialect developed by French-speaking slaves. His brief introductory comment to the forty-one Louisiana tales reveals the patronizing attitude of nineteenth-century intellectuals toward these products of a "childlike people."

The Negro storytellers in Fortier's early sampler present much the same tradition reported by recent collectors of Cajun narratives, for instance in offering the well-known cycles of Foolish John or Jean Sot, and Bouki and Lapin. Tar-Baby and other tales of the rabbit so popular among American Negroes appear both in Fortier and in recent Cajun collections, although they are not found in American white tradition. The plots of these animal tales are for the most part derived from European sources, and the inference follows that African slaves in the United States learned tales from their white masters and mistresses. The Canadian French tradition contains Jean Sot and abundant *Märchen,* but not the Bouki-Lapin cycle. Presumably the Cajun repertoire is indebted to the southern Negro repertoire as well as to its own French heritage.

Further evidence of Cajun borrowing from Negro sources can be seen in the descriptions that follow of conjure, hoodoo, and *gris-gris,* as secured by Elizabeth Brandon from Cajun informants. These terms are all designations for occult practices among southern Negroes, and their practitioners are indeed specifically referred to in these interviews as Negroes.

In her account of the *traiteurs* of southwest Louisiana, Elizabeth Brandon has documented the practice of occult healing by Cajun folk doctors. This case too indicates a mixture of traditions; the hoodoo-men with their malevolent magic descend from the vodun cults in west Africa which reached the United States, and especially New Orleans, via the West Indies; the faith healers belong to a general European species which in the United States takes such specialized forms as bloodstoppers, burn healers, and wart charmers.

Distinctively French elements are not as conspicuous as might be expected in the Cajun folklore. The demonology of *loup-garou* (the werewolf) and *lutin* (the elfin horseman), common enough among the *habitants* of French Canada and northern Michigan, is not in evidence. From France the festal custom of Mardi Gras carries over as the carnival day of Shrove Tuesday, and has acquired local features of the bayou country, particularly the steaming gumbo dinner that ends the wild parade, and the begging song chanted by the riders. The parlor games and dances described by Calvin Claudel from his own family tradition echo pastimes of Old France, though with diminishing vigor.

The decade of the 1940's has seen a renewed and broadened interest in the French Cajun lore which Fortier had tentatively explored half a century before. In 1939 there appeared a collection of *Louisiana French Folk Songs* by Irène Thérèse Whitfield, complete with phonetic as well as French texts, musical transcriptions, names and descriptions of informants, and bibliographical references. Whitfield made a threefold division of Louisiana French, Cajun, and Creole folksongs, based on dialect differences. Thus the Cajun patois employs *"quoi sta fait"* for *"qu'est-ce que tu as fait"* and *"je vas"* for *"je vais."* Whitfield writes (p. 68):

> The modern Cajun-French folk songs are probably indigenous to Louisiana. They seem endless in length, because they are played over and over again until they run on and on and on like the flat country of the southern part of the state which developed them. They fit the "pulling and pushing" of the accordion, having been made so to speak "of the accordion," "by the accordion," and "for the accordion." No other instrument seems to have quite the quality that makes the Cajun tune so appealing.

Commendably, Whitfield analyzes the emotional qualities and character traits contained in her stock of forty-five Cajun songs. The generic type she sees revealed in this body of lyric songs is an amorous, carefree, ardent, jealous lover, delighting in his *belle,* but also in cards, drink, and dances. This gay Cajun cavalier shows little spirit of reverence, mentioning the Lord only once. In the lack of spirituals, shouts, and other religious songs the Cajun tradition breaks sharply from the Negro. Also absent are any elements of the supernatural, a lack illustrated in the disappearance of the ghost-wife from *"Eyouss Que T'es Parti"* (see Oster, *post,* p. 284, and Whitfield, pp. 119–21).

A number of these Cajun songs are local compositions, based on trivial but engaging incidents. *"Madame Baptiste, Tirez-Moi Pas"* is said to have originated in Duson, in ridicule of chicken thieves raiding the yard of Mrs. Baptiste Lagneaux; according to one singer, when the little son of the thief told his mother that his father had been shot at, she grumbled, "I told papa not to go tonight; we still had some left." A poignant lament which a heartbroken lover sang at the *bal de noce* (wedding dance) of his lost sweetheart, bears the Anglo-French title *"Bye-bye Fédora."* It is credited to an accordion player of Rayne, and the names of the three protagonists are known. As the bereaved Cajun sings his plaint of grief and his request to Fédora that she not forget him, the bride is supposed to lower her veil to hide her tears. The departure of a young Cajun swain against his mother's wishes to join his sweetheart in Texas is memorialized in *"Quand je suis parti pour le Texas."* Texas held out opportunity and adventure to the Cajun, and jobs in the oil fields around Port Arthur.

Other little songs deal with comical matters. One tells of a trip to Saint Martin by the numerous Voorhies family—a song composed by Judge Voorhies himself, father of fourteen; another of the length of the beard of a dance hall proprietor in Lafayette Parish, Toto Simoneaux, who parted his beard in two and tied it at the back of his neck. In the dialogue verses between wife and husband in *"Et Où c'est que Tu es Parti?"* he expresses his wish for *"Un gallon de couche-couche et une douzaine d'oeufs."* *Couche-couche* is a Cajun delicacy of fried cornmeal, with which he would gladly glut himself even if it killed him, since he has to die anyway. The body of Cajun songs disclose the emotions, attitudes, and humor of a folk group with a clarity seldom on view in American regional folksongs.

Other collectors have placed on record valuable materials from Louisiana French tradition. During the 1940's Calvin Claudel, himself the son of Cajun parents in Avoyelles Parish, began printing folktale texts of Foolish John, Bouki and Lapin, and Snow Bella, chiefly in the *Southern Folklore Quarterly.* Two holders of the doctor's degree in folklore from Laval University, Corinne Saucier and Elizabeth Brandon, prepared their dissertations on the folk customs of Avoyelles and Vermilion parishes in southern Louisiana, applying the methods they had learned from Luc Lacourcière, director of Laval's splendid archives of the French folklore of North America. Following European models, their field reports emphasize calendar festivals, traditional occupations, *rites de passage,* sample games, proverbs, riddles, tales, and songs. Saucier published *Traditions de la Paroisse des Avoyelles en Louisiane* in 1956 as Memoir 47 of the American Folklore Society, and in 1962 *Folk Tales from French Louisiana,* a small volume giving English translations only of thirty-three *Märchen,* noodle stories, and animal tales. Brandon printed *"La Paroisse de Vermillon* [sic]: *Moeurs, Dictons, Contes et Légendes"* serially in the journal *Bayou* (1955–57, Nos. 64–69).

On joining the English faculty at Louisiana State University in Baton Rouge, Harry Oster helped reorganize the Louisiana Folklore Society in 1956. The society began issuing a publication, *Louisiana Folklore Miscellany,* and sponsoring record albums of regional folksongs. In his collecting trips around the state Oster recorded singers in all five Louisiana song traditions—Old French, Cajun, Negro, Negro-French, and Anglo-Saxon. Long-playing records with accompanying booklets prepared by Oster and issued by the society between 1957 and 1959 are titled "A Sampler of Louisiana Folksongs," "Folksongs of the Louisiana Acadians Recorded in Grand Mamou," and "Angola Prisoners' Blues." Between 1957 and 1962 Oster edited some twenty-seven folkmusic albums from his own field collections in Louisiana. "Cajun Folksongs" was issued in 1962 (Prestige International, Bergenfield, N. J.) and "Southern Prison Blues" the same year (J. S. Dansk Grammofonpladeforlag, Copenhagen, Denmark).

As a result of these activities, we can obtain a generous sampling of the lore possessed by Cajuns living in the bayou country.

1. FOLKWAYS

Folkways of Avoyelles Parish

By CALVIN CLAUDEL

The French folklore of Louisiana is found in the central and southern parishes of the state. To these French traditions has been added the enrichment of Indian, Negro, and Spanish folklore elements.

The French-speaking inhabitants with their stock of folklore stem from two groups of settlers, those who came directly from France throughout the eighteenth century and those who came from Acadia late in that century. Although the Acadians were latecomers in colonial Louisiana, they really harked back to an earlier tradition since they had settled Acadia early in the seventeenth century. These Acadian settlers, whose language and customs were rather archaic and therefore considered provincial, gradually mingled with the other peoples in Louisiana throughout the nineteenth century. The language of these various French-speaking inhabitants, which for convenience can be called Louisiana French, became more or less homogeneous, varying from the literary French of the cultured Creole to that of the unlettered Acadian folk.

The early settlers dispersed along rivers and bayous from New Orleans to outlying rural areas, taking with them their seafaring ways and traditional lore from France, and established settlements on the banks of such streams as Bayou Lafourche, Bayou Teche, and Red River. Communities were knit together by their system of waterways, and the giant artery of the Mississippi linked them with the other French trading posts and settlements throughout the Louisiana Territory. A boat was called a *voiture*, or carriage, and the bayous and rivers served as highways of transportation and communication. With the invention of the steamboat, trading prospered, and along waterways the boat landings became focal points where boats unloaded bales of goods from foreign lands and reloaded cargoes of cotton and syrup in return. Stories, songs, and customs were spread by persons voyaging along these routes.

Because of this seafaring tradition, possibly reminiscent of the wanderings of the Acadians, there are a number of nautical terms in the French-Acadian language. For instance, the word *amarrer*, meaning "to make fast a boat," is used instead of the standard French *lier* or *ficeler*, "to tie." Thus one says, "*J'amarre mon cordon de soulier*"—"I make fast my shoestring." The verb *démarrer*, "to untie or unfasten," is similarly used. The verb *gréer*, "to rig," means "supply" or "stock." The noun *baille*, "tub," is also originally nautical.

A typical community of French-speaking inhabitants may be found in the centrally located parish of Avoyelles. Its capital is Marksville, with under four thousand people, and its chief waterway is the Red River, dotted with boat landings. Folktales and customs of this region represent the folklore of Louisiana as a whole and show a close relationship with such faraway places as Missouri, whose traditions are similar. (See Joseph M. Carrière, *Tales from the French Folk-Lore of Missouri*, Evanston, 1937.)

While a few of these French settlers were wealthy slave-owners, a large number did not possess slaves or means, and these especially preserved and fostered oral traditions in their close-knit community life. Their French dialect retained a freshness and vitality not found in the educated speech of Creoles. They might work with their own hands at a trade, till their own small plot of ground as *habitants* or farmers, or work for a planter as *mains*, or hands.

Houses were built of cypress, weatherboarded on the outside and often plastered on the inside with a combination of clay and moss, which was also sometimes used for making chimneys in the poorer homes. A front porch, or *grande galérie*, ran the width of the house. A hallway through the center separated the rooms on both sides. In the more opulent homes there was a *grenier*, or garret, ventilated by dormer windows. The huge front room, or *chambre devant*, was heated by a big fireplace around which the family life centered in winter. Houses were covered with cypress shingles, or *mérains*, which required a special traditional skill to make as they were cut with one stroke of the shingle ax from a *bille*, or section of a log. These shingles were also used to cover an added roof projecting fanlike from the front of the house, and called a *fausse galérie*, or false gallery. In the uplands, the houses were supplied by artesian water from wells, while in the bottomlands cypress cisterns caught rain water for drinking, since the well water there was only used for livestock because of its insipid taste, described as *fade*, or flat. Every home had a backyard, or *cour derrière*, and a front yard, or *cour devant*. Flanking the house was the *corrail*, corral or livestock lot, in which was found the *hangar*, or barn. Next to this was the *parc*, a small pasture or pen. The *arpents*, or acres behind the house, comprised the *clos*, or field, in back of which were woods or thickets. This original architecture is still traditional.

French-Acadian family life continues to be integrated by a strong feeling of neighborliness. This was even truer in the old days, because of the lack of public entertainment. Families would often visit for *la veille*, a night gathering for chatting and exchanging folktales. They came together for a *battage de riz*, or rice threshing, during which they sang folksongs and perhaps joined afterwards in a chicken gumbo and rice supper. Fiddlers played while couples danced, changing partners and swinging them right and left. Neighbors would often help each other to build a house or other structure. Such help was called giving a *coup de main*, or helping hand.

Among the Louisiana French folk there used to be a custom of community butchering, or the *boucherie de campagne*, for which a number of families would pool together. One month a certain member would butcher a beef and they would all share it, and the next month another member would do the same. The cow or ox was maced over the head with an ax, immediately slit under the throat, strung to a sturdy limb of a tree by the hind legs, and deftly skinned. The animal was then quartered and cut into pieces. Choice bits of fresh meat were called *grillades*, which were immediately cooked and eaten with rice and gravy.

Hog butchering time comes in late fall when cold weather is in the air. The fat pig is slit under the throat with a sharp butcher knife, the gushing blood being caught in a pan. A huge black washpot of iron, which is also used for boiling clothes out in the back yard, is full of boiling water, under which a fire is roaring. The hog is seized by the ears and dipped around in the scalding water and afterwards scraped white. Then there is fresh meat in abundance, and a good neighbor will always send some to a relative or friends close by.

The blood is cooked and seasoned and stuffed into the entrails by blowing into a bamboo tube placed through one end of the open gut. This sausage is called *boudin*, or blood sausage. The washpot or *grande chaudière* is used again for making cracklings or *gratons*. Fat slices of meat are put into the pot with a little water, allowed to boil and boil until the grease runs out and the slices turn into brown, twisted crisps, which are eaten with syrup during the wintry months. Some of the entrails are hung to dry and become chitterlings, or *andouilles*, to make gumbo. Hams and slabs of pork may be salted or hung in the smokehouse where they are allowed to remain while a slow fire, made of sassafras, smolders. One of the following folktales deals with the robbing of a *boucanière*, or smokehouse, by Bouki and Lapin, the Brer Rabbit characters of Louisiana French folklore.

Christmas and New Year represent an important season. Long beforehand cakes are baked, geese and pigs fattened. At Christmas, children receive presents in their stockings or shoes and join in the wine drinking at the sumptuous noon feast, whose choice dish may be a roast suckling pig, or *cochon de lait*. New Year's Day is celebrated with rounds of feasting and cheek-kissing among relatives, all wishing each other happiness and prosperity. The practice of kissing relatives and members of the family upon every occasion of arrival and departure

shows the close feeling of family ties. The sixth of January is
the Day of Kings, or *Fête des Rois*, which is closely tied in with
the *Noël* celebration, and often referred to as Little Christmas.
It is the church day of Epiphany and serves to commemorate
the folk tradition of the arrival of the Magi with presents for
the Christ child. Persistent Catholic religious folk custom in
Louisiana is that of praying and making votive offering to saints.
Grateful recipients of presumed favors received from this or
that saint will run an advertisement in the Personal column of
the daily newspaper in somewhat this matter: "Thanks to Saint
So-and-So for favor granted." Though quite sincere, these
thanks may sometimes seem comical as the time when a deceased local politician was once thanked among the saints. Saint
Roch cemetery in New Orleans has a shrine for its patron saint.
Here the crippled come to be healed on Good Friday. Discarded
crutches and the like are to be found around this shrine.

Among the most popular forms of family recreation were
many children's games, which are fast disappearing today. My
father remembered a game he played as a child, which was called
"La Boutique"—"The Shop." It was a sort of counting out
game of hide-and-seek, that went this way in French:

> Pin-pi-pot, Laurent,
> Tu iras à la boutique
> Acheter avec le marchand.
> Va faire bouillir ton pot!

> Pin-pi-pot, Laurent,
> You'll go to the shop
> And buy from the merchant.
> Go and boil your pot!

The one who was "It" was sent to the "shop" back of the
house, to remain there until he was called to hunt for the others.
The last line of the rhyme was the signal for the hunt to begin.

For other age levels there were appropriate games. As already seen, religious festivals and holidays afforded occasions
for folk entertainments and customs, in which the whole family
might take part. When boys and girls were approaching mar-

riageable age, they participated in games and contests that led into parties, dances, and balls.

There was a game called *tirer le pategaud*, shooting the popinjay. (The word is pronounced "potgo," and derives from French *papegai*.) A group of enterprising persons made a bird of wood decorated with plumes and ribbons, and placed on a pole. Everyone shot at this bird. If someone shot off the head or demolished a considerable portion of it, he was then declared king and had to give a dance or party. Variation of these is the three-day tournament contest, still found in Ville Platte of Evangeline Parish. Called *le tournoi* in French Louisiana, this tournament theme is found in the folktale "Golden Hair," heard in Marksville. In this tale a young lad named Golden Hair, who is disguised as a cabbage wormer at the king's castle, participates with his talking mare in a three-day tourney to win the princess's hand. The tournament is reminiscent of medieval games.

Another rather cruel sport, which has disappeared today, was "Pulling the Goose's Neck." A goose was tied to a tree or post, and riders would rush by on horseback trying to pull off the creature's neck. This ceremony too seems to have been associated with the *pategaud* party, because one would pull off the goose's neck, win the queen, and become king at the party that followed.

Young unmarried groups of boys and girls liked to play forfeit games. One game, which Mrs. Marie Louise Couvillon of Avoyelles Parish played at Moreauville, was "*La Bague de la belle Bergère*"—"The Ring of the Beautiful Shepherdess." A leader holding a ring passed it around to each member of the group, secretly leaving it with one person. Then the leader would ask one of them by name, "Who has the ring, my fair shepherd Calvin?" Calvin would reply, "It is my fair shepherdess, Mary." If his guess was wrong, the leader would say, "You are mistaken, my fair shepherd, Calvin! You must give a forfeit." Then Calvin had to pay a forfeit by way of putting an object of some kind into a hat. If he guessed right, the shepherdess might be asked to bow to her lover. After the hat contained a number of objects, the leader would pick a boy's object or a girl's object from the hat, hold it over someone's head and ask, "What hangs over your head? Is it a man or a woman?" If it was a boy who missed, he had to crow like a rooster or do a similar absurd antic which would evoke gales of laughter from the unsophisticated audience.

This shepherd and shepherdess game is interesting historically. It is no doubt a survival of seventeenth and eighteenth-century French *précieux* parlor games. In any case, it was the type of game played in polite society.

Another game Mrs. Couvillon mentioned as very popular was *"Tourner l'Assiette,"* or "Spinning the Plate." A person would spin a plate and afterwards called another person by name to catch it before it stopped turning. If he failed to catch it, he paid the usual forfeit.

The writer's parents often played forfeit games as a boy and girl. The game they played was less formal. They played it in French as well as in English since there was a growing tendency for English to supplant French. The leader would say, "I pass and hold all that I give you. Who has the ring?" The leader might act like a sleight-of-handster and recite a little rhyme, *"Cache, cache, Nicolas; je te passe la bague, tu l'auras; tu l'auras pas"*—"Hide it, hide it, Nick. You'll have it; you'll have it not." Sometimes this game was played with a thimble, which was called *"Jouer au dé."*

Another game the writer's parents enjoyed playing was *"Sur la Sellette,"* "On the Culprit's Seat." Having someone in mind, a leader sent around inquiring in whispers from everyone as to what or whom this person resembled. When the leader received a particularly amusing or apt description of the person, he would address him or her, saying, for instance, "You look like a jar of vinegar making a face." Then the accused would guess who said this, and if he did, the person he found guilty had to come take his turn on the Culprit's Seat. Occasionally girls were said to resemble nicer things, such as, "You look like a pretty flower," or, "You resemble the most beautiful flower." Here were some of the resemblances:

You look like a rose.
You look too much in love.
You look like a skinny cow.

> You look like an old, wet hen.
> You look like cornbread with too much soda.
> You look like a dirty rag.
> You look like an old broken wheel.
> You look like a cat that lost her kittens.

These are but a few of the many folk similes and expressions used in daily life. To describe a sickly complexion, one would say, "He is as yellow as a pumpkin." To describe a dishonest person, one would say, "He is as crooked as a barrel of snakes." "Your eyes are bigger than your stomach" was a current proverb to describe a greedy person. An expressive folk proverb was the saying, *"Quand un chien a la gale, il faut que la peau tombe"*—"When a dog has mange, his hide must fall off."

Saturdays were known as "sweet Saturdays," because the balls or dances were given on that night. One had to be invited to attend. Crowds would come from distances in wagons and buggies. They would bring lamps since lighting was scarce. These were of brass and without globes. Some balls had as many as twenty-five lamps. Music was furnished by a string band, which was composed of such instruments as the violin, guitar, mandolin, cornet, and bass fiddle. The fiddler was the most important performer, and for smaller dances was often the only musician available. While pausing occasionally to take *filet*, *coup*, or a shot of liquor from a nearby jug, the fiddler would tap his foot, moving his body up and down as he pulled his bow rapidly across his screeching fiddle. He would also whine a plaintive or gay song in a high-pitched, nasal voice, according to the occasion, while people danced, swinging their partners right and left.

In the singing of the musicians, and often in that of the dancers, dances were associated with folksongs and games. Boys and girls danced and sang the *danse ronde*. My parents remembered the English words to this dance song:

> Go in and out the window,
> Go in and out the window.
> Stand forth and face your lover,
> Stand forth and face your lover.

You kneel down to your lover,
You kneel down to your lover.

For this dance a circle was formed; sometimes the girls were inside and sometimes the boys, alternately weaving in and out. The *danse ronde* was also called "Marching Around the Levee" and "Marching Around your Lover." Another couplet might appear in the song, such as "Stand forth and choose your lover. . . ." Occasionally the lovers might kiss, but only if in the last stages of courtship. It was a big thing to kiss a girl or see her ankle, because nine yards of cloth were used to make a dress. Another variant couplet to this dancing game was "Stand forth to your lover and measure your love. . . ." Lovers would then show the extent of their love with an arm, finger, or fingernail.

Besides the different variations of the *danse ronde*, couples danced quadrilles, waltzes, glides, polkas, and the like. The dances Mrs. Couvillon attended were somewhat more fashionable. Negroes played music, kept time, and were well groomed in black suits, bow ties, and split-tail coats. Their favorite dances were the cotillon, quadrille, lancers, varieties, polka, and square dance.

Weddings were often the occasion for folk games and singing, which dealt with the theme of courtship and marriage. Mrs. Couvillon said that when her youngest brother married, she and a young man sang *Le Papier d'Épingles* in a sort of little play. This was a well-known French folksong in Louisiana, and quite similar to the English, "I give to you a paper of pins and that is where my love begins. . . ."

The *charivari*, or shivaree, is a noisy celebration given an old widower who marries a pretty young girl. A crowd, loaded down with horns, bells, pots and pans, will gather in front of the couple's home and din away until the husband invites them all in for a drink. If he does not respond, the noise is kept up all night. So the person who remarries lays in a stock of liquor for such an occasion.

Folksinging and dancing in Louisiana is not as prevalent as it used to be. A number of older inhabitants still remember folksongs which are of French European origin and which have undergone relatively few changes in comparison to the folktale. For instance Mrs. Couvillon sang a complete version of *"Malbrough s'en va-t-en guerre"* that varies only slightly from the French version. She also sang a *"Cantique de Noël"* and several other songs with her daughter. A number of songs of English-speaking Americans also took root in Avoyelles Parish, such as the ballad of "Charles Guiteau," "The Boston Burglar Boy," and "The Lightning Express."

The folktale is a well-developed side of folklore among the inhabitants with French traditions in the southern half of Louisiana. Among the folk in such a parish as Avoyelles, evenings used to be spent frequently in telling and listening to folktales. In summer this was done on the front gallery, and in winter in the big front room around the fireplace. Oftentimes neighbors from nearby or across the bayou would come to visit for *la veille* (*la veillée* in standard French), or an evening together. These occasions for hospitality and exchanging stories were a deep-rooted custom. The narrator usually drew from a repertory of traditional tales, handed down from generation to generation. All listened eagerly, and no one tired of listening to the same tale.

Among the characters of Louisiana folktales, the most interesting perhaps is the numskull type, called Jean Sot, or Foolish John. Jean Sot is a stupid errand boy who never does a single thing right, despite his mother's patient prompting and exasperated scolding. This literal-minded boob never learns from his mistakes, but repeats them over and over, to the merriment and laughter of the folk audience. Jean Sot is an ancient type in folklore, and is directly related in role and in name to the *Zanni* of the *Commedia dell'arte* and the zany of modern times seen in movies and on television. Some of the tales centering around Jean Sot are highly salacious and earthy.

Another series of stories centers around the two humorous animals Bouki and Lapin, the stupid and clever rabbit, who are found in the medieval stories of the *Roman de Renart*. They talk and behave like human beings. These characters are great favorites with the Creole Negroes of Pointe Coupee Parish. Lapin the rabbit is usually the clever one and may be associated with other stupid animals. The stories always follow the pattern of the trickster and the dupe.

The following tales,* as well as the preceding songs and poems, were recorded on phonograph records, transcribed from the Louisiana French, and translated into English by the writer.

* Save for two collected by Elizabeth Brandon.

2. CONTES POPULAIRES

Bouki and Lapin in the Smokehouse

> *A variation on Type 41,* The Wolf Overeats in the Cellar, *Motif K1022.1. This is Grimm No. 73, "The Wolf and the Fox." Six texts are reported in French-American tradition, and it is known in Puerto Rico and among West Indies Negroes.*
>
> *Recorded by Calvin Claudel from his mother Mrs. Leota Edwards Claudel. Born in Marksville, Avoyelles Parish, in 1883, of Scotch-French descent on her mother's side and English on her father's, Mrs. Claudel was orphaned at three and brought up in a French-speaking family. She learned her large repertory of tales from her foster-father, "Fey" (Ferrier) Goudeau, of Goudeau, a village in Avoyelles Parish.*
>
> *Claudel writes, "Bouqui [sic] and Lapin stories seem to have taken stronger root in Louisiana than anywhere else, although they are found in Haiti, Santo Domingo, the Bahamas and Missouri" ("Louisiana Tales of Jean Sot and Bouqui and Lapin,"* Southern Folklore Quarterly, *VIII [1944], 287).*

Once there were two fellows who were very fond of each other. They were good friends. One was called Bouki and the other Lapin. Bouki was poor and always hungry. At home he never had anything to eat. Thus he would go to Lapin's to eat.

One day Bouki went to spend the day at Lapin's house. He said to Lapin, "Where do you get all this good meat? As for me, I never have anything."

"Why, that's a secret," replied Lapin.

"Tell me."

"Oh, I can't tell you that!"

"Ah, yes! You must tell me," insisted Bouki.

"Well, I get it out of the smokehouse of the Frenchman living nearby. Come here tonight at midnight. You must not come before the roosters crow for midnight, when all the lights are out, because we will get caught."

"That's fine," agreed Bouki.

Bouki went home. What did he do that night but put a blanket under his arm and leave. On his way he took a cane and fixed it into a sort of stick. He continued on his way with this.

Now when he reached Lapin's, it was dark. He went into the henhouse. He was anxious, in a hurry to leave. He seized his stick and began to poke the rooster to make him crow. "Crow!" cried Bouki. "Crow for midnight!"

Yet the rooster would not crow, but only went, "Kood koo dook! Kood koo dook!"

"Crow, I tell you!"

"Kood koo dook, kood koo dook!"

Lapin came outside, wondering to himself, "What can be after my chickens?"

Well, the noise stopped. Lapin went back to bed. A little while afterward, the rooster started again. Bouki cried, "Crow, rooster! Crow for midnight!"

"Kood koo dook!"

Lapin came outside. "Why, what is after those chickens? Is it you, Bouki? Go back to bed! It's too early. We will get caught. Those Frenchmen will catch us. We will get nothing. Go to bed!"

So Bouki went, hid himself behind the henhouse in the weeds. He stayed hidden there until midnight. Then the roosters crowed, and Lapin got up. They got ready and left. Bouki took his blanket along, putting it under his arm. Now he thought to himself, very anxious, "I will fill my blanket up full of meat. As for me, I will carry out enough."

So when they got there, they went into the Frenchmen's smokehouse. Bouki spread his blanket upon the ground. He began piling up meat, sausage, in fact all sorts of good things to eat that were in there. Lapin himself cut off a piece of meat and then went out, leaving through the hole by which he had entered.

Lapin left, but Bouki stayed. The latter took the four corners of his blanket, tied them together, took hold of the bundle, and tried to leave by the hole he had entered, but the pack of meat would not go through. He tried, pulled, pulled, it would not pass. Eh! He was tugging! Broad daylight came, and Bouki was still pulling. The sun rose. Bouki was still tugging.

The Frenchmen opened their door, came outside, and saw in the corner of the smokehouse something tugging at a bundle. "What can that be?" they wondered. They advanced, saw what it was. Bouki told them he was very hungry. They seized him and got out a big rawhide whip. They gave him a big beating. Then they gave him a large piece of meat, saying to him, "Go home and eat now!"

So this gave away Lapin's secret. He was never able to return to the Frenchmen's smokehouse to get meat. Bouki had spoiled the sauce, and they had nothing after that.

Bouki and the Rabbit and the Well

> *Type 175,* The Tarbaby and the Rabbit. *A famous international tale, known throughout Europe, and popular in Africa and India. It is widely reported in the Spanish-American and New World Negro traditions but not from French-Americans.*
>
> *Collected by Elizabeth Brandon from Mrs. Nicholas Benoit, Gueydan, Louisiana, 1952.*

Bouki wanted to dig a well so as to have water because water wasn't plentiful. He said to the Rabbit, "Help me, we are going to dig a well to have water. I'm tired of drinking dew-water." But Rabbit says, "Not I, I don't want to be bothered. I prefer drinking dew-water."

Bouki dug the water well alone. But he couldn't have any water. Every morning he was going with his bucket, the well was dry. He says, "There is someone who takes my water. Something must have happened because the well has no water. I'm going to make a little Negress of tar and I'm going to put her on the edge of my well and I'm going to see who it is who is taking my water."

In the evening Bouki went to sleep. Rabbit came to take Bouki's water. When he arrived, the Negress was on the edge of the well. She had her tar. He says, "Little Negress, step back from there," he says "I want water." The little Negress didn't move back. He says, "I'll punch you," he says, "if you don't get away from the well." He gave her a punch with the fist and got stuck.

He says, "Little Negress, get away from there," he says, "I have another fist, and I'm going to give you another punch." He gave her another punch and got stuck. "Little Negress, I'm going to poke you with my foot." The little Negress didn't budge. He gave her a poke with the foot (which got stuck). "Little Negress, move away from there. I still have another foot and I'm going to kick you with the other foot." He gave her a kick with the other foot and he remained stuck. "Little Negress, get away from there, I'm going to butt you with my head." The little Negress didn't go away. He hit her with the head. He remained stuck. He says, "Little Negress, if you don't go away from there," he says, "I'm going to give you a blow of the stomach." He hit her with the stomach and remained stuck.

In the morning Bouki arrives. Rabbit was really glued to the little Negress. He says, "Ah, now I know who it is that was taking my water, it was you," he says, "now I know! Now," he says, "I'm going to fix you." He makes a big fire and puts on a pot of water to heat. He says, "What'd you like better for me to do?" "Oh," Rabbit says, "no matter what, just so you don't throw me into the briar patch," he says. "Throw me into the fire or in the water," he says, "I'd prefer that." So Bouki threw him in the briar patch. He made his escape. "Ah, he says, "I'm where I came from, now I'm where I came from."

Foolish John and the Errands

Several numskull tale types are here represented: Type 1271C*, Cloak Given to Stone to Keep It Warm, known in Norway and Japan; Type 1291B, Filling Cracks with Butter, a story attached to the Balkan character Hodja Nasreddin, and known in Hungary and in Missouri French tradition; Type 1642, The Good Bargain, episode I, "Numskull throws money to frogs so that they can count it" (Motif J185.1.1), which appears in Grimm No. 7 "The Good Bargain"; and a tale-incident based on Motif J2461.1, "Literal following of instructions about actions."

Variants on this cycle from Louisiana French tradition appear in Marie Thériot and Marie Lahay, "The Legend of Foolish John," Southern Folklore Quarterly, VIII (1943), 154–56; and Corinne L. Saucier, Folk Tales from French Louisiana, pp. 69–70, with a parallel Canadian French text, pp. 71–74.

Collected by Calvin Claudel from Mrs. Leota Claudel of Avoyelles Parish. Printed in his "Foolish John Tales from the French Folklore of Louisiana," Southern Folklore, Quarterly, XII (1948), 157–59, where it appears with three other texts and a discussion of the boob character in popular literature.

Once there was a woman who had a boy whom she named Foolish John [Jean Sot]. He was very backward and stupid.

One day his mother called him, "Foolish John, come here. Go buy me some cotton cloth and thread at the store." He came, she gave him the money, and he left to go buy the cloth and thread.

On his return, he saw a little gum tree shaking in the wind. It was cold that day. Eh! the wind was blowing at the tree. It was cold. Foolish John stopped to look at the little gum tree.

"Poor little gum tree!" he exclaimed, "I'm sure you are cold. Wait, I'll fix you so you won't be cold!"

He took the cloth, wrapping all the tree with it. He then took the thread, winding it all around so the cloth would not untwist. Then he left for home. When he reached the house, his mother asked, "Where is my cotton cloth?"

"Well, Mama," he explained, "I met a poor little gum tree. Indeed it made me feel sorry. It trembled, had a chill, and was cold."

"Oh, my! Foolish John, a tree does not get cold! You're a big boob! You should have brought my cotton and thread to make your shirt."

"Well," said he, "I bundled up the little gum tree with it. It was chilly because it was shaking."

The next day she sent him to the store to buy some lard, and he left to get it. On his way back he passed alongside a little pond that had dried up. It was very flat, and where the water was withdrawn, it was all cracked up.

Now Foolish John saw this, took the lard, and began to grease the cracks by smearing the lard over them with a little stick. "Poor little pond!" said he, "I'm sure it is aching. It is chapped up. Let me grease it well." He greased the little pond well, filling all the cracks with the lard.

He returned home. "Where is my lard?" asked his mother.

"Why," explained he, "I met a little pond, Mama. It was all chapped, and I greased it with the lard. I am sure it ached."

Well, the next day it was something else. "You will go buy me some needles," said his mother. "I want number seven."

"All right," he replied.

Foolish John left and got the needles when he reached the store. He started back. On his return, he passed alongside a ditch where there were frogs croaking, "Eight, eight, eight, eight!"

"You are lying, it's not eight!" shouted Foolish John. "I tell you it's seven!"

"Eight, eight, eight, eight," croaked the frogs.

"You lie, it's seven! Here, count! Look and you will see for yourself!" he said, throwing the needles into the ditch.

Foolish John stood waiting and finally said, "Throw me back my needles." He waited and waited. "Throw me back my needles," he cried, "Mama will be angry."

The frogs did not return the needles. He kept standing, waiting. Finally he returned home. "Where are my needles?" asked his mother.

"Well," explained he, "a frog persisted in telling me the needles were size eight. I threw them into the ditch for her to see for herself. The nasty thing never returned them to me!"

"Why, you are a boob!" she screamed. "Frogs croak at night. It's nighttime now. You should have brought my needles to do some sewing."

So never, never was the mother able to get any good results out of Foolish John or get him to do anything straight. He was a real Foolish John for good.

Now she told Foolish John, "You will go milk the cow this evening."

The mother went into the kitchen to get the milk pail ready. She washed it to give it to Foolish John to milk the cow.

Suddenly she heard the shot of a gun outside—bang! She looked outside, saw the cow limp about, fall over, and kick around. Now since *tirer*, the Louisiana French word for *milk*, also means *shoot*, Foolish John had shot the cow instead of milking her.

"Foolish John," she yelled, "You shot the cow!" Meanwhile Foolish John had the gun in his hands. "Why surely, you told me to shoot her for supper, so I shot her."

"Oh my! You've killed the cow! We'll have no more milk now. How will we do now without milk? Ah, it is a misfortune indeed to have around the place someone so stupid!"

Foolish John and Parsley

Motif J2462.1, "The dog Parsley in the soup," is an episode in the popular European tale of The Foolish Bridegroom, *Grimm No. 32,* "Clever Hans." *Nine texts*

*are reported in French-American tradition, six from
Canada and three from Louisiana.*

*Collected by Calvin Claudel from Mrs. Oneida Bou-
dreaux Vives of Orleans Parish, Louisiana.*

One day Foolish John's mother had to leave the house. Before
leaving, she said to him:

"Foolish John, I am going to leave the house to do some
business. You are too foolish; I can't depend on you, so I'll
have to go myself. Now while I am away, watch the soup on the
stove. Don't forget to put parsley in the soup."

After saying this, his mother left, leaving Foolish John
alone. Now it happened that there was a dog in the household
who was called *Percy*. In French *Percy* is pronounced like the
word *persil* which means *parsley*. What did Foolish John do but
go and catch the poor animal by the tail and put him into the
pot of boiling-hot soup! Percy kicked and howled. His front
feet, sticking out of the pot, contracted, and his face was fixed
in a grin.

When Foolish John's mother got home she asked him,
"Foolish John, did you put parsley into the soup as I asked
you?"

"Yes, mother," he answered, "come see. Percy is smiling
from happiness."

Roclore

*Several well-known European tale types are combined
here: Type 1641, Doctor Know-All, the world-wide
episodes I, "The Sham-Doctor," and II, "Betrayal of
the Theft"; Type 1590, The Trespasser's Defense,
which appeared ante pp. 181–83 as an incident in the
southern Appalachian legend of "The King and Old
George Buchanan"; and Type 1737, The Parson in the
Sack to Heaven, found all over the world. Two texts of
"Roclore" are in C. L. Saucier, Folk Tales from French
Louisiana, Nos. 14–15, pp. 50–54, both containing Type
1525, The Master Thief.*

Collected by Elizabeth Brandon from Edgar Boudreaux, Abbeville, in 1953.

Once Roclore, the clever fellow, was living with the king and the king took a cricket and put him under a glass. And when Roclore returned from work he said to Roclore, "Well," he says, "Roclore, you have to guess what is under this glass." "Well," Roclore thought that he was caught and he says, "Caught like a cricket." So the king says, "Ha, ha," he says, "you are safe," he says, "I won't be able to destroy you."

So it was like that. The next day while Roclore was returning from work, the servants steal from the king a ring that had a diamond in it. So when Roclore returned from work, "Well," the king says, "Roclore, I'm going ￫ put you in a room until tomorrow and," he says, "tomorrow if you have not guessed where my ring is," he says, "I'm going to destroy you." Hm, Roclore didn't know what to do. He was put in a room, he was locked in a room. In the evening, when the servant came to give him his meal, Roclore wanted to say that he had taken one meal before getting killed, so he says, "Well," he says, "one taken." Oh, it was they, the servants who had stolen the ring. So the servant girl goes there and tells the other one, "Believe it or not," she says, "one taken," she says, "he's going to turn us in." "Oh," the other one says, "never!"

So when it was the next morning, she brings his breakfast. And when he finished eating his breakfast, "Well," he says, "another one taken." She goes away, she runs to the kitchen, she says to the other servants, she says "We are caught," she says. "He says, 'Another one is taken.'" "Oh," the third says, "at noon I'm going to take him his dinner to see."

So she goes to take him his dinner. Roclore eats, he heaves a heavy sigh. "Well," he says, "three taken anyhow." So she says, "Mr. Roclore," she says, "if you won't turn us in, we are the ones that have the ring. But," she says, "how will we tell the king that you found the ring?" "Well," he says, "catch the biggest turkey in the yard and then," he says, "I'm going to tell him: You have to catch the biggest turkey in the yard and he has the ring in his crop or in his gizzard."

Well, they were very glad because it was they who stole the ring. So they went to the kitchen and talked the matter over. And then they went out and when the last turkey came and went by they made him swallow the ring. So the next morning when the king wanted to do away with Roclore, he comes to the room with a dagger to kill him.

"Well," he says, "this morning your life is going to be ended because," he says, "you'll have to answer the riddles I told you about, you have to find where the ring is."

"Well," he says, "Sir," he says, "if you catch the biggest turkey in the yard, if you have it killed and look," he says, "the ring is either in his crop or his gizzard. The servants swept it outside and then," he says, "the turkey swallowed it." "Ho boy," he says to the servants, he says, "kill the turkey immediately and look for it." So they caught the turkey, they were sure glad, they went, they killed the turkey and then they opened it and in the crop there was the ring. "Well, I'll have to release him. But," he says (to Roclore), "you'll have to get out of here, out of the country, I don't want you here at all any longer." "Well," Roclore says, "all right, I'm going to go away."

He left the room, he went away and he went to Spain. He stayed in Spain for about a year. There there was a good ball game that was coming up over here so he says, "Well," he says, "I'm going to the ball game." But his wife says to him, she says, "Roclore, the king is going to kill you, he forbade you to put your foot on the soil of Louisiana." He says, "I'm going anyway." He took his buggy, then he filled his buggy with dirt of Spain, then he put his feet on it. He went to the ball game. The king found him there. He sees his buggy. He says, "Didn't I tell you that I was forbidding you to put your feet on the soil of Louisiana?" He says, "Thank you, sir," he says, "my feet are not on the Louisiana soil," he says, "I'm on Spanish soil, I put my feet in my buggy." But he had to leave anyway. The king says, "Get out of here." So he left.

Then, about five or six months later, Roclore comes back to Louisiana. The king meets him. "Now," he says, "my chap, I got you." He puts him in a bag to go drown him. They leave in a kind of a cart, he was going to drown him, and then the king, he stops on the road to chat with some friends of his and Roclore was in this bag. So he speaks with his friend a while. A horseman was coming "prta-ta, prta-ta, prta-ta." Roclore noticed that it was a horseman who was coming. He starts crying in the bag, "Oh, oh, oh," he says, "I would not like to marry the king's daughter, not I." The guy stops, he says, "What is it that you're saying?" He answers, "The king wants me to marry his daughter," he says, "and I wouldn't like to marry the daughter of the king"; and all along the king was going to drown him. So the horseman says, "Well," he says, "let me get into the bag." he says, "I'll marry her." "Oh," Roclore says, "here!" He puts him in the bag, he gets out of there, then he leaves and then he gets on the horse and goes away. The king didn't look at the bag, he went, he took the poor guy, he drowned him! In this way Roclore escaped. He took the horse and then went to other places.

Then, a few months later, Roclore comes back to sell some mules in Louisiana. He comes with some big Kentucky mules, a big herd of mules. The king meets him. "But," he says, "Roclore, it is you who is there?" He says, "Yes, sir, it is me who is there." "Well," the king says, "didn't I drown you some time ago?" "Well, sir," he says, "you threw me right in the herd of mules, right in the middle," he says, "I left with them and now I'm selling them," he says. "If I had only stayed there a little while longer, there were big Texas mules that were there."

"So," the king says, "come throw me there so that I can catch them." Roclore says "Sure," and he throws him in the bag, he goes and drowns the king.

The Frog and the Princess

Type 440, The Frog King or Iron Henry. *This is the first story in the Grimms' Household Tales, well collected in Europe, but not in Asia or Africa. Five texts have been reported for North America, four in French-American and one in English-American tradition.*

Told to Calvin Claudel by Mrs. Leota Claudel of Avoyelles Parish.

Once there was a king who was very rich. He was a great personage and had a daughter who was very pretty. It was her fifteenth birthday, and her father wanted to give her a present. He bought her a pretty ball, a golden ball.

Ha! she was proud of her ball! She played with it all the time. She would throw it into the air. She played and played with it. One day she came with the ball into the yard, where there was a fountain. She threw it into the air, and it fell into the fountain. An old frog came out of the water while she was crying.

"Will you give me my ball?" she asked.

"No," replied the frog. "I will give it back to you only if you will marry me."

"Oh!" exclaimed the princess, "I can't do that!"

"Ah, well! you will not get your ball."

"Well then, yes, I'll marry you . . . all right."

The frog gave her the ball. He came out of the water. Little did the girl think that what she had said was anything more than a mere promise. She had no idea of marrying him. Yet the frog began to follow right behind her—splish splash, splish splash. She looked back and saw this. At first it was a joke to her. As the day went by, the frog followed her more and more closely.

That evening, when she sat at the dinner table, the creature sat down next to her. Her father asked, "Why, what is that old frog doing there?"

"Well, I let my ball fall into the fountain. I promised to marry him if he gave it back to me. He's been following me ever since."

"Ah, then, you shall have to marry him if you promised. Go off into your room! Take your frog along. Go away from here!"

She took him and left, going into her room weeping. She went to the mirror to see herself and powder her face. He stood close by, powdering himself, too.

Her father came and said, "You shall have to marry him. You promised him that, and now you must go through with it." Ah, she was sad! She did not want to hear any such thing. She grew angry. Every once in awhile she would step on the frog, trying to kill him. She did not succeed. Splish splash, splish splash, he followed her. She would look back, and she was enraged when she saw this. Just imagine! What was she to do?

Well, her father began to prepare for the marriage, arranging a great celebration, a great ceremony. Ah, she wept! Ah, the frog was proud! He would jump all about and into the air— splish splash, splish splash—as happy as could be. He strutted all around the place, puffing himself up, so much was he elated. She would go to the mirror to look at herself, he would climb upon it, admiring her. Ah, she was vexed! Every time she turned around, she would try to put the heel of her shoe upon the frog, but could not. Every now and then she would send him a kick, still unable to kill him.

So they fixed up for the marriage. Now the hour for the wedding was at hand. It was almost time for her to get married. She began to descend the stairs. She looked back, saw him coming—splish splash, splish splash—after her. He was excited. She was furious when she saw this. Tears were in her eyes. Suddenly she let him have a kick, trod upon him as hard as she could. Then she heaved another kick. He fell from above, all the way down, landing at the foot of the stairs, plop!

The ugly creature then changed into a young man, the most handsome young man ever seen.

So in the end, things turned out quite well for the princess. She married a young man instead of a frog. And there was a great celebration.

The Mouse, the Sausage, and the Bird

Type 85, The Mouse, the Bird, and the Sausage. *This is Grimm No. 23, known in nine European countries. Only one North American text is reported, in the French tradition.*

Told to Calvin Claudel by Mrs. Leota Claudel of Avoyelles Parish.

Once there were a mouse, a sausage, and a bird that kept house together. The mouse would sweep, the bird would carry wood, and the sausage would cook.

Now every day after they had done their work, the bird would leave, fly into the air, joining the other birds to play all about with them. The other birds would say to him: "My, but you are foolish! Why don't you come to stay with me, enjoy the life for which you were intended, not follow the sausage and the mouse and keep house with them? Come, have a good time with us in the open air, fly around at night, amuse yourself all the time."

The bird made up his mind. So one day he returned home, telling the mouse and sausage he would quit keeping house. They were very disappointed, but nevertheless there was no way of stopping him. He left.

The sausage and the mouse kept house together after that. The sausage went outside, saying she would carry in the wood. She went to get the wood, but never returned. The mouse waited and waited for her. Now the dog had seen the sausage outside, picked her up, and eaten her.

Finally the bird came back that night, saying he was sorry. "I have come back," said he. "I was lonesome for you."

"Well," replied the mouse, "I am waiting for the sausage, but she has not returned with the wood."

"Wait," said the bird. "I shall go see about her."

He went outside to go look for the sausage. He asked the dog if he had not seen the sausage.

"Why," explained the dog, "I saw a sausage in the yard there. I picked it up and ate it."

The bird returned inside, telling the mouse that the dog had eaten up the sausage. "Do you think you can cook?" asked the bird.

"Why yes," agreed the mouse. "I shall do as the sausage did."

So the mouse put a big pot of water to heat. Now the

sausage used to heat the water, get into the pot, and as it boiled, gumbo was made. The mouse had seen that, thinking now that she could do the same. After the water was boiling, she jumped into the pot. Poor thing! It scalded and killed her.

So the bird had to quit keeping house. This broke up the household for good.

3. FOLK DOCTORS

DESCRIPTIONS OF FAITH HEALERS in Arkansas and Michigan can be found in "The Power Doctors," in Vance Randolph, *Ozark Superstitions* (New York, 1947), pp. 121–41, and "Bloodstoppers," in R. M. Dorson, *Bloodstoppers and Bearwalkers* (Cambridge, Mass., 1956), pp. 150–65.

"Traiteurs" or Folk Doctors in Southwest Louisiana

By ELIZABETH BRANDON

Popular medicine is still very much practiced in southwestern Louisiana, and the observer may well ask why these old concepts, discarded by modern science, have survived so vigorously in this age of electronics and atomic physics. Until 1920, the utter isolation, lack of roads or means of transportation, and scarcity of schools were instrumental in preserving the Cajun's old way of life. The sociologists T. Lynn Smith and Homer L. Hitt commented in their study *The People of Louisiana* (Baton Rouge, 1952, p. 107) that "These Acadian people until a quarter of a century ago have preserved one of the purest examples of a 17th century folk culture to be found in the United States."

The low economic and educational standards of the population did not encourage doctors to settle in this region, or patients to seek the doctor's help. The sick had to obtain whatever help was available close to them, and consequently they turned to the unlicensed healers and therapists known as *traiteurs*.

While illiterate Cajuns constitute the major part of the clientele of *traiteurs*, educated people also use their services. I know of high school and even college graduates who go to them. A young elementary school principal confided to me that treaters had done more good for him and his family than doctors. The lack of written material on the subject is not at all surprising when one knows that information on the healers and their practices are difficult to obtain. It seems that everybody conspires to hide all evidence, especially when the person seeking information is a stranger whom the Cajun greatly mistrusts. A social worker from southwestern Louisiana wrote me in 1954:

> People will not "give." Even persons with whom I was associated socially, persons who lived in Abbeville all their lives, either could not or would not give more information than that which is generally known.

There are three kinds of *traiteurs* in lower Louisiana: those who heal by prayers and incantations; those who use medicines of their own preparation, and so are called "*remède-men*," and those who profess to have supernatural powers, the hoodoo-men or conjurers. These hoodoo-men resemble the witch doctors described in major folklore works by Puckett, Randolph, Dorson, Hurston and others. The conjurers not only fabricate conjuration charms, malevolent *gris-gris*, or protective good-luck charms, but they also pretend to perform cures by means which are suspect, such as that of diabolical intervention.

The *remède*-man does not profess to have supernatural powers. He does not scoff at known cures like ice packs for fevers and compresses for swellings. However he claims to have secret formulas for his own remedies, which he distributes to his patients in the form of pills, powders, brews and ointments. Gossip has it that sometimes he even buys patented drugs in the pharmacy and resells them as his own. He uses anything and everything, from medicinal herbs and sheep manure to spider webs, strings with seven or nine knots, wire rings, and innumerable other means. To make the treatment more impressive, this sort of empiricist does not neglect the metaphysical aspect of treating in the form of prayers and incantations. Here is an account of how a *remède*-man removes worms:

The *traiteurs* can cure worms. They give to the patient a little ball made of garlic which he wears on his neck, then they say prayers. I saw them do it many times. The worms are afraid of the smell of garlic, it suffocates and kills them. The only case when a *traiteur* cannot cure worms is when the patient vomits. This means that the worms have already gone to the heart and the *traiteur* cannot help any more.

This kind of healer does not have scruples as to what disease he treats or how much money he takes. Time and again reports appear in the newspapers of criminal cases in court where a *traiteur* is involved. In March 1954 a *traiteur* was arrested in the Parish of St. Landry. He was accused of practicing medicine illegally and of causing the death of a young man of eighteen whom he had treated with herbs and iron tonic pills. At the moment of his arrest there were eight cars of patients in front of his house. He was charging $2.00 per visit and $1.00 per remedy. In October 1956 a *traiteuse* from New Iberia was indicted for having performed an abortion on a seventeen-year-old Negro girl. The fee paid the *traiteuse* was $15.00.

The most arresting group of *traiteurs* is the faith-healers. The faith-healer disclaims knowing anything about medicine; he insists that he effects cures by prayers and incantations alone. These *traiteurs* have a profound faith in the efficacy of their treating and the power of their healing. Most, although not all, of them are deeply religious and assert that they are only the intermediaries of God, and God permits the healing that their faith and prayers have invoked. According to them, God bestows the privilege of healing on the man he chooses, who in turn will heal those sick people who have faith in the healer's power. These treaters limit their practice mostly to external ailments and wounds and to a few internal diseases. They undertake to treat rashes, swelling, boils, warts, sprains, sores, bites of insects or snakes, toothaches, aching ears and throat; fevers, sunstroke, shingles, stiff neck, lumbago, sprains of all kinds; rheumatism, tonsils, hemorrhages, worms, liver and gland troubles. They will not touch bone fractures, nor do they treat heart disease, cancer or any other serious illness. Testimony bears out their claims of proficiency. An informant related the following case:

One day when we were working in a rice field I was bitten by a water moccasin. The leg started hurting and swelling. My father took me to a *traiteur,* an old guy named Bergeron who lived on the road between Abbeville and Lafayette. By the time I got there, my leg was swollen up to the knee. Mr. Bergeron treated me with prayers. We left 50 cents for him. Two or three days later the swelling disappeared.

A schoolteacher friend told how under her very eyes a *traiteur* cured worms in a pupil of hers; a young couple swore by a certain *traiteur* who miraculously saved their child wasting away from a fever; the prosperous owner of a fine Creole restaurant sang the praises of a healer whom he and his wife always consulted; one of my informants assured me that her octogenarian parents had a new lease on life since they found a very remarkable *traiteur.*

The healers proceed as follows. They place their hands on the ailing part of the body and rub it slightly. Sometimes they anoint the spot with oil before laying on their hands. All the while they recite prayers and mutter charms in such a low voice that no one can hear or understand them. Several treaters can heal or stop blood at a distance. The stories of these feats are legion.

A healer will never undertake to treat a patient who has no faith in him. Those that were not cured receive the explanation that the treatment failed because they did not believe in the treater's power of healing. To those who accuse the *traiteur* of healing by hypnosis, the believers cite examples of patients who had lost consciousness, and of the treater's working with closed eyes or with his eyes raised to the sky. They also describe healing from a distance, where hypnosis is impossible.

There are several rules to observe when consulting a treater. One should not pay him, for he will never take money. There is a belief that if a healer takes money, he will lose his healing powers. Some won't take money under any circumstances, but others will not object to the patient's leaving a dollar or two on the table. A gift takes occasionally the place of money. The treater should not be thanked either, or the treatment will not bring desired results. It is important that water never separate the healer from the object of his attention. As a result, one does not consult a *traiteur* who lives on the other side of a river. Some healers refuse to take care of a person of the opposite sex, insisting that the treatment would fail.

One kind of *traiteur* is known to treat certain objects which subsequently are supposed to have healing powers. The object most commonly treated is a handkerchief. A clean, used handkerchief should be left with the power doctor for a certain time. When picked up and placed on the ailing part of the body, the treated handkerchief is said to have the miraculous power of relieving strong headaches, sun strokes, rheumatic pains and other aches. Treated strings tied around the waist, neck, ankle or wrist will help in case of sprains or cricks. If before treating the string the healer puts three or nine knots on it, the results are still better. A charmed new nail helps a toothache, and a charmed piece of money attached to a string and tied around painful joints relieves arthritic and rheumatic pains and sprains. Here is how a charmed string works:

> Once my wife had a milk leg and someone told me to go to see Jean Mouton to have him treat it. My wife could not walk so I went to call Jean Mouton to come to see her. But he said that he could not go because he was too old and that I could treat her myself. So he took me to a room and showed me all this *traitment*. When I came home, I took a string, I said my *traitments* over it and tied it around the sick leg. Three days later, when I came home from work, my wife was up, walking around holding on to a chair. After nine days she could work again. Her leg was cured.

It is of interest to know how a treater starts his career. Some persons are destined to be *traiteurs* from birth because they came into the world after the death of their father, or they were born with a veil, or they were the seventh son of the seventh son. Other healers do not know how the power came to them. One day they simply realized that they had the miraculous ability and it never failed them. Many will admit that older *traiteurs* conveyed to them their knowledge.

The rules governing the transmission of the knowledge of a healer are very strict. He must confide in a younger person,

never in an older one. The successor must be highly trust-
worthy. Parents and grandparents have the right to teach their
formulas to their children and grandchildren. Occasionally
something happens that suggests to the old *traiteur* that a certain person deserves his confidence and should learn from him
the art of healing. Then he does not hesitate to divulge his
secrets to him. Before his death, the *traiteur* has a moral ob-
ligation to convey at least part of what he knows, but this does
not always happen. Some *traiteurs* do not divulge any secrets
because there is too much suffering involved in their use. Here
is an example of a secret charm I was able to obtain:

> For an earache: Put the finger in the ear until it has been "con-
> jured" and say five times the Lord's Prayer and Hail Mary.
> Then repeat three times: "Saint Nestor Guidry [the *traiteur*],
> Great God alive, St. Antoine, my Patron, chase away this cruel
> pain that Saint [give the name of the person] feels, which was
> caused by the cold or by the wind or by the air. I conjure you
> by the words of Jesus Christ." Then say five Lord's Prayers
> and five Hail Marys.

4. CONJURE, HOODOO, AND GRIS-GRIS

THE COMMENTS ON these terms in the classic work of Newbell N. Puckett, *Folk Beliefs of the Southern Negro* (Chapel Hill, 1926), are pertinent. Speaking of the ingredients of conjure charms Puckett says "the charms are seldom made twice in the same manner; the materials used and the way of putting them together depending almost entirely upon the momentary whim of the individual conjurer" (p. 239). On page 232 he describes a "Tricken-bag" recipe reported by Mary A. Owen in *Voodoo Tales* (New York, 1893), p. 174, which called for jaybird wing and rattlesnake fang tied up in a little bag of new linen or cat skin. Snake bones may be used for curing toothache (p. 373).

For a description of the southern hoodoo-doctor see Puckett, pp. 200–206. On page 207 he mentions that a conjurer must be able to locate buried treasure, and describes a method involving the use of a divining rod. A conjure-doctor may also use cards to help him in his work (p. 296).

On the term *gris-gris,* Puckett states that *grigri* when used as a noun means "charm" and when used as a verb means "to bewitch" (p. 16). He believes it to be of African origin and cites N. W. Newell, "Reports of Voodoo Worship in Hayti and Louisiana," *Journal of American Folklore,* II (1899), 44, on its use in Senegal as a name for amulets. Elsewhere (p. 218) Puckett quotes Florence Cronise and Henry W. Ward as saying "What is called 'gree-gree' is a fetish that is employed by its owner to revenge any wrong received by him" (*Cunnie Rabbit, Mr. Spider and the Other Beef,* London, 1903, pp. 26–27). All Puckett's examples of *gris-gris* come from Louisiana, chiefly from New Orleans.

The statements below on conjure and kindred practices were obtained by Elizabeth Brandon in southwest Louisiana in 1954. See her "Superstitions in Vermillion Parish," *The Golden Log,* pp. 108–18.

Conjure

(HENRY SALTZMAN, *Gueydan*)

There are people who have a supernatural power, it is the gift of the devil; they have a power that they can give a power to someone else. They sell them little things. They call it conjure.

A guy was telling me for instance that he had found a conjure that someone wore in his pocket. He says that it was a little bag of linen and it had like nerves and then bones. So he asked someone what sort of nerves it was and from where it came and he said it is supposed to be nerves of wings of a vulture and the bones are supposed to be snake bones. And they put a little cinders over there and it makes a luck-piece. It is a conjure, you know, and when you have that you can have power over someone else, that's what it is. It is sold. There are hoodoo men who make it, it is hoodoo.

There is a Negro in Crowley who sells conjures. Then there is that old man Le Jeune and he sold to a guy a conjure. He tells him, he says, "Jacques, now as you go out, if there is a woman you want, all that you need to do is to take what I give you, then go around her three times," he says, "and the third time she'll follow you." This guy Jack gave him $5.00 for that hoodoo.

Hoodoo

(HENRY SALTZMAN, *Gueydan*)

There are people who make a living like that. There was a Negro here, he was called Girouard. He was very smart this Negro. Well, this Girouard sold to an old man, old man LeMague, right here on the corner, a little bottle and the old man gave him $5.00 for this. It was, he said, for to be able to find lost treasures. So he believed that there was some place on the canal where the treasure was, but naturally there was not anything there. They brought Girouard to court and they put him to the penitentiary for taking advantage of a weak-minded person and obtaining money on false pretenses.

There was another hoodoo man here, on this side, he is dead now. His name was Broussard. He did not sell anything but he dealt cards in order to find lost treasures. People would give him $5.00 for that.

Gris-Gris

(MRS. COURTNEY LA BAUVE, *Abbeville*)

I have a friend who told me once that his wife was very sick because she had been given a *gris-gris*. One of her neighbors gave her a *gris-gris*. She had something against her. I asked how come they knew that she had been given a *gris-gris*, and he said, because they found packages of pins and some hair inside under the mattress and in the corners of the yard, behind beds and everywhere. And he said that his wife was very sick so they took her to the doctor's and the doctor didn't help her at all and the husband, he knew that this woman gave her a *gris-gris*.

So he said to his wife that they had to do something. In order to do away with this *gris-gris* it was necessary to give her another *gris-gris* to counteract the first *gris-gris*. So they asked another man outside of the village to come and to give her another *gris-gris*. And the man came and gave her another *gris-gris* and the woman is well today. They believe in these *gris-gris*, they believe in them truly.

5. RIDDLES

IN HIS MONUMENTAL work, *English Riddles from Oral Tradition* (Berkeley and Los Angeles, 1951), Archer Taylor defines riddles as "descriptions of objects in terms intended to suggest something entirely different" (p. 1). Other types of puzzling questions are not true riddles, but may be classified as neck-riddles, arithmetical puzzles, or clever queries such as biblical questions or conundrums. For a discussion of these other types of enigmatical questions see Taylor, "The Riddle," *California Folklore Quarterly*, II (1943), 129–47.

The following riddles told by Cajuns were collected by Elizabeth Brandon in 1954 in southwest Louisiana. Footnote references are given to those true riddles having parallels in Taylor.

This form of entertainment in French is not very much in vogue today, particularly among the young people. Few of them could give me any examples of riddles. However, the older informants provided me with 70 riddles, a few of which I am quoting below. Some of the riddles collected are direct translations from English which sound bizarre in French: "What is the worse time for rats and mice?" Answer: "When it rains cats and dogs." The expression *"Il pleut des chats et des chiens"* is nonexistent in France but does not seem to shock the ear of the French Louisianian. Twelve representative riddles follow:

1. If the first man was called Adam, what was the name of the first woman? *Madame.*
2. If a man can lift two hundred and fifty barrels of rice when it is not raining, what can he lift during a rain? *An umbrella.*

3. Before whom do the villagers take off their hats?
   Before a barber.
4. What goes to the bayou laughing and returns crying? *A bucket.**
5. What is green when thrown in the air and red when coming down? *A watermelon.*†
6. What is always under shelter but always wet? *The tongue.*‡
7. What has a tongue and does not speak? *A shoe.*§
8. What has teeth but does not bite? *A comb.*¶
9. What is it that was given to you that belongs to you only but that your friends use more than you? *Your name.*||
10. How can you stop a rooster from crowing on Sunday morning? *By killing him Saturday evening.*
11. How are a book and a king alike? *Both have pages.*
12. What is the difference between a bachelor and a married man? *A bachelor has no buttons on his shirt, a married man has no shirt.*

* Taylor discusses the contrast of weeping and laughing in the headnote to Nos. 768–769, pp. 278–79 of *English Riddles from Oral Tradition.* Nos. 768*a* and 768*b* parallel this Louisiana riddle in solution and theme, but the form in which the riddle is asked is not the same. See Taylor, p. 765, for the comparative note.

† The headnote to Nos. 1547–1549, p. 632, says that this riddle is found mainly in a few West Indian versions. Nos. 1547*a* and 1547*b*, p. 632, are examples of the "up green, down red" riddle type, and they were reported in oral tradition from South Carolina Negroes. For Spanish and Hungarian parallels see the comparative note, Taylor, p. 854.

‡ Taylor states, No. 1150, that "riddlers have often used the idea of an object that is always wet to describe the teeth or the tongue" (p. 485). In English he has noted only two instances, Nos. 1150*a* and 1150*b*, p. 488, but the solution to these two riddles is teeth rather than tongue. Taylor adds that "a weakened and perhaps degenerate version is embodied in two forms which do not clearly suggest an animal, a person, or a thing. 'What is covered and yet wet,' and 'What is wet all the time'" (see refs. in Taylor, note 2, p. 485).

§ Versions are listed from Nova Scotia and Newfoundland, p. 96, No. 296*a.* The note, Taylor, p. 716, refers the reader to Nos. 311–312*c*, p. 99, for texts containing the same theme in greater elaboration.

¶ A South Antrim parallel is listed, Taylor, p. 97, No. 299*b.* Comparative notes to Welsh, Swedish, Russian, Spanish, and Chilean examples are found on p. 716.

|| Nos. 1582–1585, pp. 644–45 contain the theme of "Have It; Others Use It." The comparative note, Taylor, p. 858, gives references in nine European traditions.

6. NICKNAMES

By ELIZABETH BRANDON

Nicknames are very popular in French Louisiana. They are so popular, in fact, that often the real name of a person is completely forgotten. In the devoted Cajun family and among friends, a nickname, "*un tit nom*," is an expression of affection. Husband and wife call each other *Tit Nègue* (Little Nigger), *Tit Bec* (Little Snoot) ; parents call their children *Bèbe, Bébé* (Baby), *Tit* Boy, *Catin* (Doll), *Suc'* (Sugar), *Douce* (Sweet), *Cœur* (Heart), *Tit Doux* (Little Sweetheart). Members of families rarely call each other by their names. It is *Da, Nona, Noune, Nounou, Nana, Did, Babou, Choume, Bi, Fifine, Ya-Ya, Ya-You, Bleu,* nicknames that seldom have anything to do with the first name of a person. And the adjective *cher, chère* (dear), is constantly on the lips of the Cajun. It is "Good-by, *chère,*" "See you soon, *cher,*" "Come in, *chère,*" and so on.

Occasionally a characteristic mark, a physical defect, or a feeling of derision suggest a name: Big Liar, Sport, Flat Nose, Short Leg. Sometimes a name will originate from an accident or a special event. Thus *Cou de Canard* (Duck's Neck) became a nickname of a family in Fork Island as a result of a brawl during a dance while a duck gumbo was being prepared in the kitchen and pieces of duck were used as missiles.

In the past, Cajun families frequently gave to their children rare names or names taken from classical mythology and history. In the older generation one hears names like Symphorion, Onésiphore, Sosthène, Cléophas, Cléobule, as well as Ulysse, Ophélius, Eurydice, Alcibiade, Ovide, Homère, Télémaque, Déus, Déussa. There was also a marked tendency to give all children of the same family names beginning with the same vowel or syllable. In one family on Vermilion Bayou the names of all the children began with "Clo": Clothilde, Cloma, Clophé, Clopha, Clodias, Clophée (feminine), Clomé, Clodice. In the family of Lastie Broussard of Abbeville there were fifteen sons and daughters, all of whose names started with "O": Odile, Odilia, Odilon, Olive, Ovide, Onésia, Octavie, Ophelia, Otto, Otis, Opta, Oméa, Olita, Olivier, Odalie.

Today the names of the children are more conventional and most often very English. There are Kenneths and Willards and Willys, pronounced by the French-speaking population Kenes, Vilard, and Veelee.

7. FOLK CELEBRATION

Country Mardi Gras

By HARRY OSTER

Usually in thinking of Mardi Gras in Louisiana one visualizes the somewhat commercialized celebration of New Orleans, copied by several other cities in the state, featuring spectacular floats and lavish balls, extending over several weeks and culminating on Shrove Tuesday. There is, however, a rural celebration of Mardi Gras, which is more traditional and more folk than its sophisticated and gaudy New Orleans cousin. Today only the people of Mamou and a few surrounding towns celebrate Mardi Gras in this fashion.

Its origin in Louisiana goes back to the 1780's when bands of French and Spanish settlers in the Opelousas Country gathered together a week or so before Ash Wednesday to make elaborate plans for celebrating Mardi Gras (*courir Mardi Gras*). Today as in the eighteenth century, mothers, wives, and sweethearts work feverishly on their men's costumes the week prior to Shrove Tuesday. Favorites still are tacky, motley one-piece uniforms, topped with a high conical cap, resembling a dunce hat, and masks of coarse screen with holes cut out for eyes, nose, and mouth. Currently, hideous manufactured rubber masks are supplanting the weird, homemade old masks. The uniforms are called *"le suit de Mardi Gras"* and the headgear, *"le capuchon."* At the organizing meeting at one of the local bars, the men from eighteen to sixty-five plan the route (sometimes as many as sixty miles in cold and mud), to curry their ponies, and to elect or re-elect *"leur capitaine,"* who in recent years has been Paul Tate, a lawyer; an aide also is chosen by the group to assist the captain. These two are the only members of the troop who are not allowed to mask, for no farmer would tolerate a band of drunken masked riders on his premises unless led by a leader of integrity. Hence, the captain and co-captain have been civic or religious leaders, highly respected citizens.

By five A.M., come Mardi Gras morning, every rider has saddled and bridled his horse and had a few drinks at the neighborhood bar where the maskers assemble. The captain "frisks" all the riders to make sure none of them has guns or knives. As the sun is coming up, the captain blows his primitive trumpet, a *"corne a vache"* (cow's horn), and *"la course des Mardi Gras"* is on its boisterous way to visit farmhouses all around the town, which is the hub (*le moyeu*) of their circular route. Neither weather nor treacherous, slippery, and muddy dirt roads stop them, and since Shrove Tuesday generally comes around the end of February, many a masker shivers with cold until he has been warmed by frequent swigs of straight bourbon. To protect themselves further from the cold, they wear one-piece suits which are large enough to cover several layers of clothing. The *"paillasse"* or clown, nicknamed after a straw mattress, is stuffed with pillows or cotton until he resembles a ball. Like the jester of the Middle Ages, he has the duty of entertaining with his comic antics and acrobatics. It is not unusual to see him climb a tree, stand on his head, or come riding up on a decrepit mule or donkey. When the *"capitaine"* sees a farmhouse he thinks suitable, he rides up to it and asks the master and mistress if they will receive his followers. If they are willing, he waves his white flag, and the maskers come dancing into the yard, singing the weird Mardi Gras song, begging for food for the evening gumbo. Seizing the people of the house by the arms, they sweep them into the wild dance. The master and mistress usually oblige with rice or a big fat chicken, which the tipsy maskers have to pursue through the gumbo mud—a wild and hilariously funny chase. At a signal from the captain, his lieutenant blows a blast, and the maskers mount their horses to resume their trip.

"La course" generally ends around four in the afternoon with the tired, hungry, muddy, drunkenly gay riders parading through the town, bringing their haul for the day (generally forty to fifty assorted chickens, guineas, ducks, or geese and enough rice to feed a small Chinese army) to the women who will flick the fowls and cook out of doors a vast amount of gumbo in huge black iron pots. Before their evening gumbo, many of the saddle-sore riders take advantage of the free drinks granted them by all the bars in town. Somehow they manage to arrive at the evening masquerade and even to fling themselves into the foot-stamping gyrations of the lively dancing until dawn.

The singing of a begging song, *"La Chanson de Mardi Gras,"* is one of the unusual features of the celebration, not characteristic of Mardi Gras in France or Canada.

The two principal variants we have recorded in Mamou are sung to the same melody, which is probably ancient since it has a gapped and modal scale. Unlike Variant A, Variant B refers to Mamou specifically and mentions the name of a local citizen who is going to be the host for the big gumbo.

"La Danse de Mardi Gras"

Spoken: All right *z-hommes, allons se mettre dessus le chemin et allons courir Mardi Gras. Ehu le capitaine? Capitaine, voyage ton "flag."*

1. *Capitaine, capitaine, voyage ton "flag."*
   Allons se mettre dessus le chemin.
   Capitaine, capitaine, voyage ton "flag,"
   Allons aller chez l'autre voisin.

2. *Les Mardi Gras se rassemblent une fois par an*
   Pour demander la charité.
   Ça va-z-aller-z-en porte en porte.
   Tout à l'entour du moyeu.

"LA CHANSON DE MARDI GRAS"

Sung by Bee Deshotels, accompanied by Angelus Manuel, fiddler, and Savy Augustine, triangle player, during Mardi Gras, February, 1958, at Grand Mamou, Louisiana. Collected by Harry Oster.

1. Ca-pi-taine, ca-pi-taine, vo-yage ton "flag". Al-lons se mettre des-sus le chemin. Ca-pi-taine, ca-pi-taine, vo-yage ton "flag". Al-lons al-ler chez l'autre voi-sin.

2. Les Mar-di Gras se ra-ssembl(ent) une fois par an Pour de-man-der la cha-ri-té. Ça va-z-al-ler-z-en porte en porte, Tout à l'en-tour du moyeu.

3. Les Mar-di Gras de-vient de tout par-tout.— Oui, mon cher bon ca-ma-rade, Les Mar-di Gras de-vient de tout par-tout; Mais tout a l'en-tour du mo-yeu.

4. Les Mar-di Gras de-vient dé tout par-tout; Mais prin-ci-pale-ment de Grand Ma-mou; Les Mar-di Gras de-vient de tout par-tout; Mais à l'en-tour du mo-yeu.

3. *Les Mardi Gras devient de tout partout.*
   Oui, mon cher bon camarade,
   Les Mardi Gras devient de tout partout;
   Mais tout à l'entour du moyeu.

4. *Les Mardi Gras devient de tout partout;*
   Mais principalement de Grand Mamou.
   Les Mardi Gras devient de tout partout;
   Mais à l'entour du moyeu.

5. *Voulez-vous reçoir mais cette bande des Mardi Gras?*
   Mais voulez-vous reçoir mais cette bande des grands
   *   soulards?*

6. *Les Mardi Gras demandent mais la rentrée-z-au-maître*
   *   et la maîtresse.*
   Ça demande mais la rentrée-z-avec tous les politesses.

7. *Donnez-nous autres une 'tite poule grasse*
   Pour q'on se fait un gombo gras.
   Donnez-nous autres une 'tite poule grasse;
   Mais à l'entour du moyeu.

8. *Donnez-nous autres un peu de la graisse,*
   S'il vous plaît, mon carami.
   Mais donnez-nous autres un peu du riz;
   Mais tout à l'entour, mon ami.

9. *Les Mardi Gras vous remercient bien*
   Pour votre bonne volonté.
   Les Mardi Gras vous remercient bien
   Pour votre bonne volonté.

10. *On vous invite tous pour le bal à ce soir;*
    Mais là-bas à Grand Mamou.
    On vous invite tous pour le gros bal;
    Mais tout à l'entour du moyeu.

11. *On vous invite tous pour le gros gombo;*
    Mais là-bas à la cuisine.
    On vous invite tous pour le gros gombo;
    Mais là-bas chez John Vidrine.

12. *Capitaine, capitaine, voyage ton "flag."*
    Allons se mettre dessus le chemin.
    Capitaine, voyage ton "flag."
    Allons aller chez l'autre voisin.

Spoken: All right boys, let's go! *Allons courir Mardi Gras.*
    Capitaine, voyage ton "flag." Passe-moi la bouteille,
    Adam. Je suis sec. Let's go!

Spoken: All right men, let's get on the road and run Mardi
    Gras. Where's the captain? Captain, wave your flag.

1. Captain, captain, wave your flag.
   Let's get on the road.
   Captain, captain, wave your flag,
   Let's go to the other neighbor's place.

2. The Mardi Gras riders get together once a year
   To ask for charity;
   They are going to go from door to door.
   All around the hub.

3. The Mardi Gras riders come from everywhere
   Yes, good old comrade;
   The Mardi Gras riders come from everywhere.
   All around the hub.

4. The Mardi Gras riders come from everywhere,
   But mainly from Grand Mamou.
   The Mardi Gras riders come from everywhere,
   Now, all around the hub.

5. Will you welcome this band of Mardi Gras riders?
   Will you welcome this band of big drunks?

6. The Mardi Gras riders ask permission to come in from
   the master and mistress.
   They ask permission to come in with all politeness.

7. Give us a little fat hen
   So that we can make a fat gumbo.
   Give us a little fat hen.
   All around the hub.

8. Give us a little bit of lard,
   If you please, my friend.
   Now give us a bit of rice.
   All around the hub.

9. The Mardi Gras riders thank you a lot
   For your good will.

10. We invite you all to the dance tonight,
    Over there at Grand Mamou.
    We invite you all to the big dance.
    All around the hub.

11. We invite you all for the big gumbo,
    Over there in the kitchen.
    We invite you all for the big gumbo,
    Over at John Vidrine's place.

12. Captain, captain, wave your flag.
    Let's get on the road.
    Captain, wave your flag.
    Let's go to the other neighbor's place.

Spoken: All right boys, let's go! Let's run Mardi Gras. Captain, wave your flag. Pass me the bottle, Adam. I'm
dry. Let's go.[1]

[1] Sung by Bee Deshotels, accompanied by Angelus Manuel, fiddler, and
Savy Augustine, triangle player, during the celebration of Mardi Gras,
February, 1959, and included in a long-playing record, *Folksongs of the
Louisiana Acadians Recorded in Grand Mamou* (May, 1959), collected
and edited by Harry Oster.

Although there is no French or French Canadian Mardi Gras begging song, the obvious antiquity of the melodies of the Louisiana variants and the nature of the texts suggests that they originated in France. Probably these variants, and in fact several features of rural Mardi Gras, come from *"La Guignolée,"* a begging song formerly and perhaps somewhere still sung in France, French Canada, and St. Genevieve, Missouri on New Year's Eve. *"La Guignolée"* is both the name of the song and the name of a custom of great age (see Henri Davenson, *Le Livre des Chansons,* Boudry, 1946, p. 48).

Thus, as in country Mardi Gras, the participants in French Canada went from door to door, singing a begging song, and they were received with special ceremony by the master and mistress of the dwellings they approached. This going around from door to door was called *"courir la Ignolée,"* just as the people of Mamou speak of their celebration as *"courir Mardi Gras."*

8. CHANSONS

Acculturation in Cajun Folk Music

By HARRY OSTER

> *Adapted from the* McNeese Review, X (*Lake Charles, La., Winter, 1958*), *12–22.*

Because of their isolation and their pride in their French heritage, descendants of the Acadians in Louisiana, now usually called "Cajuns," have retained a fundamentally French culture. A generation ago, a French visitor to southwest Louisiana—the area along the Lafourche, Teche, and Vermilion bayous—could easily have imagined himself in a province of southern France. He would have noticed that the people spoke French almost exclusively, in a dialect much like that of the provinces, that they still practiced many French customs, and that some of the people sang ancient French folksongs.

During the past thirty years, however, the strength of the French influence has been waning because of a variety of forces. When the public schools came into general existence many of them forbade the speaking of French on the premises, to force the children to speak English. The widespread building of roads during the nineteen-thirties brought these communities into contact with the rest of the world. The rise of the phonograph, radio, motion pictures, and most recently television has had the double effect of changing the tastes of this traditional people in the direction of conformity and substituting mass-produced, homogeneous entertainment for the old folk dances and songs. In addition, the return of veterans of World War II after years elsewhere, the discovery of oil on many Cajun farms, industrialization and the consequent influx of executives and workers from other states all have upset the traditional agricultural and fishing way of life.

The changes that took place in the Cajuns' choice of music constitute a particularly interesting example of acculturation, that is the modification of the minority culture by the dominant culture. As Cajun society is in a highly transitional state, one can still find music representing the three most important stages of development of the Cajun community. The music now being performed includes (1) the folk music of seventeenth-century France, still circulating in a relatively pure form; (2) hybrid folksongs which combine lyrics in Cajun French with elements from one or more outside sources (southern mountain folksongs, commercial popular music of the country-and-western type, and Negro folk music of the blues variety) ; and (3) current popular music of the times.

When settlers from the southern mountains, inheritors of the tradition of the British Isles, made their way into the Cajun country, they often brought with them Anglo-Saxon and southern mountain songs. Some of these found so much favor with the Cajuns they translated them into the French idiom. Some followed the original texts quite closely with little or no modification to make the French words rhyme. For example, "A Paper of Pins" became *"Un Paquet d'Épingles"* and "Billy Boy," "Billy *Garçon."*

However, variant versions that are typically Cajun will be found as in the song "My Good Ol' Man" which appears as *"Eyouss Que T'es Parti."* In the original, it begins comically, but ends with a mock supernatural note. Except for a difference in rhythm, the opening bars of the Cajun variant are identical with those of the southern mountain one. The supernatural element, wherein the wife answers that he cannot haunt her because she is already a ghost, has disappeared in the Cajun version, and instead love, liquor, and food are given strong emphasis, because the typical Cajun has no inclination to sing about the supernatural. Here is that version.

"Eyòuss Que T'es Parti"

1. Eyòuss que t'es parti, oué, mon bon vieux mari?
Eyòuss que t'es parti, ce qu'on appelle l'amour.
Eyòuss que t'es parti, oué, mon bon vieux mari,
Le meilleur buveur du days?
(Parlé)
Parti m' souler!

2. Equand tu vas r'venir, oué, mon bon vieux mari?
Equand tu vas r'venir, oué, qu'on appelle l'amour?
Equand tu vas r'venir, oué, mon bon vieux mari,
Qu'il est le meilleur buveur du pays?
Demain ou un aut', jour!

3. Qui tu vas ram'ner, oué, mon vieux mari, etc.
Qu'il est le meilleur buveur du pays?
Cinq douzaine d'œufs et un gallon d'couche-couche!

4. J'ai peur ça va te tuer, oué, mon bon vieux mari, etc.
Qu'il est le meilleur buveur du pays.
Oh, ça! J'veux mourir quand même.

5. Eyòuss tu veux j' t'enterre, oué, mon bon vieux mari, etc.
Qu'il est le meilleur buveur du pays?
Enterre-moi dans l' coin d' la cour et tous
les temps en temps passe-mon une patate chaude.[1]

1. Where are you going, my good old husband?
Where are you going, the one they call love?
Where are you going, my good old husband,
The best drinker in the country?
Spoken: Going to get drunk!

2. When are you coming back, my good old husband?
When are you coming back, the one they call love?

[1] Sung by Mrs. Rodney Frugé and Savy Augustine of Mamou. Recorded in 1957 by Harry Oster.

When are you coming back, my good old husband
Who is the best drinker in the country?
Spoken: Tomorrow or another day!

3. What are you going to bring back, my good old husband?
   etc.
   Spoken: Five dozen eggs, and a gallon of porridge!

4. I'm afraid that will kill you, my good old husband, etc.
   Spoken: Makes no difference. I want to die anyway!

5. Where do you want me to bury you, my good old husband?
   etc.
   Spoken: Bury me in the corner of the yard and every so
   often pass me a hot potato!

"LE MARIAGE ANGLAIS"

An interesting example of a Louisiana ballad which shows a
creative local variation is this variant of *"Le Mariage Anglais,"*
as sung for me in 1957 by Alma Bartholomew in Lafourche
Parish, Louisiana:

1.   *C'était la fille d'un roi français,*
        Son père voulait la marier
        Avec un bon Anglais.
                Refrain:

"Car moi, j'estime un bon Français
Que toi, maudit Anglais."

2.   *Quand c'est l'heure de souper,*
L'Anglais voulait couper son pain.
"Oh coupe ton pain et laisse
Le mien, maudit Anglais."

3.   *Quand c'est venu l'heure de se coucher*
L'Anglais voulait la déchausser.
"Oh déchausse-toi et laisse
Moi, maudit Anglais."

4.   *Quand c'est venu sur les onze heure et demie,*
L'Anglais pensait à ses amours.
"Oh tourne-toi, embrasse
Moi, maudit Anglais."

5.   *"Oh belle, laissez-moi dormir,*
Car tout à l'heure je vais être hors du lit;
Vous avez l'argent dans votre pays
Pour vous faire servie, et moi une dame de
Lafourche pour me faire l'amour."

1.   It was the daughter of a French king;
Her father wished to marry her
To a good Englishman.
    Refrain:
"As for me, I prefer a good Frenchman
To you, cursed Englishman."

2.   When it was the hour of eating,
The Englishman wished to cut her bread.
"Oh cut your bread and leave
Me alone, cursed Englishman."

3.   When the hour to go to bed arrived,
The Englishman wished to take off her shoes.

"Oh take off your shoes and leave
Me mine, cursed Englishman."

4.   When it came to be around eleven-thirty,
The Englishman was thinking of his love-making.
"Oh turn around,
Embrace me, cursed Englishman."

5.   "Oh, pretty one, let me sleep,
For soon I must be out of bed.
You have money in your country
To see to it that you are served,
And I have a lady of Lafourche to make love to me."

> *A variant which is typical of those of France and
> Canada has been printed by Achille Millien,* Chants et
> Chansons Populaires Receuillis et Classés, *I (3 vols.,
> Paris, 1906–10), 218–19.*

The basic plot of the ballad deals with the marriage of an
English king to a French princess who patriotically hates the
English. She rebuffs all his efforts to be kind, but finally when
they are in bed together, she decides that her patriotism has
been carried far enough. The song probably originated as a
reaction to the marriage of Henriette of France, daughter of
Henri IV, with Charles I of England in June, 1625.

The typical variant given by Millien has some dramatic
details which the Louisiana text lacks—the ladies of the city
weeping to see the princess with an Englishman; the princess
angrily rejecting his kind offer to blindfold her to spare her
some of the terrors of crossing the sea; the princess angrily telling the trumpets and violins of the accursed English to be
silent because they are not like those of the king of France. On
the other hand, the Louisiana variant has other picturesque
incidents—the princess at dinner insisting that she will cut
her own bread, and at bedtime refusing to let her husband take
off her shoes. These details are not unique to Louisiana, but the

ending represents a creative addition; the conclusion is even more sophisticated than in the variants from France. The Englishman replies to his French bride's final practical acceptance of the marriage with a rebuff; he needs to be fresh for his mistress, who is a native of Lafourche Parish in Louisiana.

V

ILLINOIS EGYPTIANS

🌿 SOME AMERICAN FOLK REGIONS are well known in the public mind as reservoirs of traditions, while others are relatively obscure, like Egypt in the southern triangle of Illinois. No sensational volume of old English ballads or European folktales has called attention to the lore of Egypt. The sensationalism of Egypt concerns violence, feuding, and mob massacres.

Still, diligent collectors have placed on record substantial sheaves of tradition. In concentrating on Egypt, they have followed the custom of the inhabitants, who recognize their part of Illinois as somehow distinctive and different. This self-awareness of a regional identity, often symbolized by a nickname, may indicate the existence of a regional culture more surely than any markings on the physiographic or population map. The spirit of a common tradition clearly unites Egyptians, even though they are not bound together by striking affinities of racial stock or religious creed, or obviously segregated by mountains or sea.

The Egyptians occupy a country set apart in various ways from the adjacent territory in midland America. Baker Brownell calls it *The Other Illinois* in his book of that title (1958), assessing its poverty and promise and personality. Egypt begins when the flat prairie lands of grain-rich central Illinois turn to foothills; at about the 41st parallel the debris where the ancient glacier stopped rises to modest mountain slopes. Egypt ends at the confluence of the Mississippi and the Ohio rivers, an American spectacle, viewed by the citizens of Cairo (pronounced Kerro). Bounded on the west by the Mississippi River and the state of Missouri, on the east and south by the Wabash and Ohio rivers and the states of Indiana and Kentucky, Egyptians can feel some sense of natural zoning. Particularly has the clay soil and hilly terrain affected the society and economy of Egypt; this is a submarginal area, with relief rolls 50 per cent higher per capita than in the rest of Illinois. The coal mines are played out, and ex-miners travel long distances, even to neighboring states, for their daily jobs. There are oil wells, but they are poor cousins to those in Texas. Truck farming in apples and peaches, corn and wheat provides the only subsistence. Yet there is vitality in Egypt, and Southern Illinois University at Carbondale has grown into a giant, rising in student enrollment from less than 5,000 in 1951 to more than 13,000 four years later. From this faculty has come a vigorous group of folklore collectors.

Who are the Egyptians? Their core is a hardy Scotch-Irish strain of southern upland farmers who moved into southern Illinois from the hills of Virginia, Kentucky, and Tennessee following the War of 1812, contributed to the statehood of Illinois in 1818, and continued to emigrate till about 1830. One strong inducement for western migration was the cheapness of land; in 1806 an acre cost $50.00 in Kentucky and $3.00 in Illinois. Another motive was the desire to leave behind a slaveowning culture; Quakers, Baptists, Methodists, and Presbyterians rejected the peculiar institution and yet retained a southern outlook. This outlook was reinforced by some lowland planter families bringing with them the ideas of the Old South.

Preceding this main emigrant body were colonial trappers and hunters, and before them a few French voyageurs, following in the wake of Marquette in 1671, who founded such still enduring posts as Kaskaskia. Succeeding clumps of newcomers came directly from overseas: educated Germans settling in St. Clair County following the abortive German revolutions of 1830 and 1848; impoverished Irish gathering in Monroe County in the 1840's; late nineteenth and early twentieth-century waves of Italians, Poles, and Slavs massing in the coal towns. Freed Negroes congregated in lusty river cities such as Cairo.

Certain lurid events have given Egypt its own historical narrative. In the years from 1843 to 1850 a creed of lawlessness dominated the four southeastern counties, Pope, Hardin, Johnson, and Massac, lying in the crook of the Ohio River; civil strife blazed between a band of outlaws known as the Flat-Heads and a self-appointed citizen's group, the Regulators, who came to outdo their enemy in acts of destruction and gunplay. The Civil War tested the loyalties of Egyptians, as well as their self-interest, since river commerce flowed both north and south, but they responded to the national appeal of Stephen A. Douglas, and only one regiment fought for the Confederacy out of Cairo's sixteen heavily Democratic, pro-southern, largely rural counties. Cairo gave the Union navy its south-ernmost town on the Mississippi, and here Grant took over his first command in April, 1861. After the Civil War, feuds continued be-tween Democratic and Republican family clans, in the pattern of southern fratricide, and flamed into one notorious conflict between 1868 and 1876 known as the Bloody Vendetta of Williamson County. During the 1870's the Ku Klux Klan was active in deeds of terrorism and murder, until routed by an ambush in 1875 at a farm where the Klan had gone to intimidate the owner.

The coal mines contributed to this litany of bloody killings. When Samuel T. Brush, owner of the successful St. Louis and Big Muddy Coal Company near Carterville, imported Negro miners in 1899 to counter a union strike, rioting ensued in which five strike-breakers were killed, and the militia had to restore order. In 1922 some fifty strikebreakers and mine guards working the Southern Illinois Coal Company in Williamson County were attacked by and surrendered to a force of the strikers, who brutally and sadistically murdered nineteen captives near Herrin. The St. Louis *Globe-Democrat* called the Herrin Massacre the most brutal and horrify-ing crime that had ever stained the garments of organized labor. Two trials failed to bring any convictions, in spite of prosecution wit-nesses who identified killers.

Prohibition brought a new cause for turmoil, and the Klan came again into prominence, being now dubiously on the side of the law, to assist federal authorities in suppressing moonshine operations in the hills of Egypt and along the Mississippi. But the Klan's dictator, S. Glenn Young, succeeded chiefly in stirring up riots, until he stopped a bullet at Herrin in 1925. Bootlegging continued to flour-ish, and in a lethal gang struggle for control of the illicit liquor traffic, Charlie Birger offered evidence against the Shelton Brothers that led to jail sentences for them on charges of armed robbery. But Birger was finally executed in 1928 for the murder of the mayor of West City.

So plentiful is the mayhem in just one county of Egypt that Paul M. Angle devoted an entire volume to *Bloody Williamson* (1952). Such pages of lawlessness and vengeance have given Egypt a sordid character and a tarnished name. Yet the passions of Egyp-tians derive from the clannishness of southern hill folk rather than from any innate bloodthirstiness. Today, Charles Neely has written, this clannishness appears "in a fairly strong local patriotism, in a deeply ingrained provincialism, and in a distrust of outsiders." Recognizing these traits, Paul Angle yet asserts ". . . in friendliness and hospitality the people of this region are unsurpassed." *

Does the folklore of Egypt, assiduously collected by half a dozen fieldworkers, display special Egyptian qualities? The first collector to recognize Egypt as a separate folk region was Charles Neely, whose *Tales and Songs of Southern Illinois* was published in 1938, the year after his premature death. The assistant professor of English at Southern Teacher's College (as it was then called), in Carbondale, contributed an original and perceptive volume to the shelves of American folklore. Neely obtained varieties both of folk narrative and folksong, contrary to the usual practice by collectors of specializing in one genre; he printed literal texts and supplied data on informants; he gathered supernatural and local legends. For texts of ghost and witch tales, Neely's work is indeed meritorious, since such tales are usually summarized, paraphrased, or printed in literary form. Thus for New England, where printed sources testify to a deep-rooted and persistent supernatural lore, oral examples are almost completely lacking.

A number of other collectors followed Neely's lead, organizing the Illinois Folklore Society centered at the university in Carbondale. Grace Partridge Smith, mother-in-law of the folklore scholar Alexander H. Krappe, whose valuable *The Science of Folklore* (1930) pointedly ignored the United States, redressed her son-in-law's neglect by dredging up scattered items of Egyptian folkstuff until her death at ninety-one in 1959. A school teacher, Lelah Allison, used her classes and personal contacts to record extensive lists of folk beliefs, children's games, and folk sayings. David S. McIntosh of the Music department at Southern Illinois University collected folksongs, and Jesse W. Harris and Frances Barbour of the English department concentrated respectively on humorous tales and proverbs. During the 1940's and '50's this group published, chiefly in journal articles, a considerable body of Egyptian folklore.

There is nothing very unusual about this recorded lore. Of all the regions presented in the present volume, the traditions of Egypt are the least distinctive, although by the same token they are the most representative. The games, the superstitions, the sayings, the tall tales, the ballads and lyrics, are commonly found in all sections of the country. There is little of the nationality coloring that marks German Pennsylvania, the Spanish southwest, or French Louisiana,

---

* Charles Neely, *Tales and Songs of Southern Illinois* (Menasha, Wis.: George Banta Publishing Company, 1938), p. 7; Paul M. Angle, *Bloody Williamson* (New York: Alfred A. Knopf, 1952), p. viii.

nor the religious hue that shapes Mormon Utah, nor the richness of the Anglo-Saxon oral style evident in coastal Maine and the southern Appalachians. What does characterize the recorded lore of Egypt is its density, its variety, and its prevalence. A living folk culture is visible in Egypt, where all the customary forms of tradition cluster and lie close to the surface of daily life. Egypt reflects the general American patterns of oral lore.

In one form, however, the folk materials of Egypt do stand out. This is the tale of supernatural belief. Ghostlore can and has been reported from all over the United States, but the ghost-and-haunt tale carries such conviction in southern Illinois towns, where it is widely known and accepted by the neighborhood, that it becomes a local legend. Witchlore, more magical and demonic than belief in revenants, endures in Egypt and further attests to a heritage of English supernaturalism. The ghost and the witch, so familiar to Americans, are English traditions, found in American pockets of Anglo-Saxon settlement on the New England coast or in the southern mountains—and in Egypt. European, Asiatic, and African peoples possess their equivalent concepts, but they do not correspond exactly to the English spirit-of-the-dead and malevolent sorceress.

Further collecting in depth would certainly alter the present picture of Egyptian lore. Only a hint is afforded of immigrant strains in a few Irish tales and ballads and German proverbs. The Italians and Slavic peoples are still untapped. On the Negro population of Cairo there is at present only one short paper. Occupational lore of the coal miners, or of river traders, is wholly untouched. A large, fertile topic that needs to be cultivated in all regions, and one in which Egypt is bound to be rewarding, is that of historical tradition. Bloody Williamson, the Ku Klux Klan, the Civil War, the outlaws of Cave-in-Rock, all have generated thick skeins of legend.

In *Tales and Songs of Southern Illinois,* Charles Neely presents eighteen texts of "Local Legends." These deal with such matters as the decimation of the Tamaroa Indians of Turkey Hill by the Shawnees after they disregarded the cautionary advice of a mysterious stranger; frights of early settlers from wolves and panthers; the trip of two countrymen after the Mexican War to the land office at Shawneetown; the disappearance of a fat hog later found looking pretty lean inside a hollow poplar tree; the curse of a priest—sometimes an Indian—on the town of Kaskaskia, whose inhabitants set him adrift on a raft on the Mississippi, a curse fulfilled when the overflowing river washed away the town; the escape of a Confederate sympathizer with the help of a pretty servant girl; the ambush of an informer who had betrayed deserters to the Union provost marshal, and whose ghost has subsequently been sighted at Dug Hill; the attempted theft of a fine stallion from a farmer at New Liberty by Flat-Head outlaws. These legends prove the existence of oral narratives based on supposed events of pioneer, Revolutionary, and Civil War history. None of them are reprinted here, in spite of their intrinsic interest and value, for two reasons. As texts these historical traditions are not particularly well told; they lack drama and structure, even though the elements of a dramatic story are clearly present. Also, the folklore character of these texts cannot be sufficiently established. They may be in some cases accurate or garbled reminiscences of more or less trivial pioneer incidents. What is needed are variant examples of the same episode, or analogous instances from other regions and other countries, in order to demonstrate their traditional nature.

Balladry even less than legend, as thus far collected, reflects the turbulent history of Egypt. Neely did secure one ballad piece on "The Death of Charles Burger" (see p. 406), which deals briefly with the career of the convict, bootlegger, and gangster. The elements of a Jesse James legend are clearly indicated in Paul Angle's account of Birger (the correct spelling), a child of Russian-Jewish emigrants, who served in the Spanish-American War, worked as a cowhand in South Dakota, and returned to his home in southern Illinois to idle as a saloonkeeper and gambler until Prohibition gave him his chance. In spite of his crimes—he killed two men in three days in 1923, but was acquitted on pleas of self-defense—Birger posed as a public benefactor, buying schoolbooks for children and coal for needy families, and urging the local citizens of Harrisburg to stay away from his gambling joints. On the reverse of the coin are such acts as Birger's cold-blooded murder of policeman Lory Price, on whose bullet-ridden but conscious body he sat while his gang drove out to find an abandoned coal mine in which to dump the victim.

Oral folk history awaits its scribes and recorders. That such a traditional history exists in Egypt is beyond question. Meanwhile, the following selection of Egyptian folk traditions still reveals an ample and well-stocked larder.

1. PLACE NAMES

THE NAMES OF LOCALITIES frequently attract or inspire folk etymologies. "Egypt" itself is a legendary place name, as the following article makes clear. Remarks on "Illinois Place-Name Lore," by Jesse W. Harris, are in *Midwest Folklore*, IV (1954), 217–20. An historical treatment is W. D. Barge and N. W. Caldwell, "Illinois Place-Names," *Journal of Illinois State Historical Society*, XXIX (1936), 189–311.

The following account is from *Midwest Folklore*, IV (1954), 165–68. The notes are by Herbert Halpert, the author.

"Egypt"—A Wandering Place-Name Legend

By HERBERT HALPERT

That Southern Illinois has the nickname "Egypt" is attested to by folklorists, popular writers, historians and place-name students. Mrs. Grace Partridge Smith has recently demonstrated that the name is one that is fully accepted and used with pride in the area.[1]

There is an approved historical explanation of the nickname. In 1818 a St. Louis business man platted the town of Cairo at the junction of the Ohio and Mississippi rivers. He probably gave it the Egyptian name because of the popular analogy between the Mississippi and the Nile, each its coun-

---

[1] Two articles reprint or summarize nearly all the published references to the Illinois stories of the naming of Egypt: Grace Partridge Smith, "They Call It Egypt," *Names*, II, (March, 1954), 51–54; Harold E. Briggs, "Folklore of Southern Illinois," *Southern Folklore Quarterly*, XVI (Dec., 1952), 208–9.

try's major river; possibly also because the regular inundation of the area around Cairo, Illinois, resembled the annal overflow of the Nile river. The naming of Karnak and Thebes, two other southern Illinois towns, reinforced the Egyptian flavor of the region and helped to fix the popular name.

The historical explanation for the name is neither as popular nor as colorful as the traditional yarn, which ascribes the nickname to events in the first third of the nineteenth century. One writer states that as the result of the "winter of the deep snow" (1830–1831) not all of the corn in northern and central Illinois was harvested. Then a late spring was followed by a killing frost on September 10, 1831, which ruined the immature corn. Southern Illinois, however, had a plentiful supply of corn.[2] Neely's brief reference to the story mentions a drought on the prairies, rather than frost, as the cause for the shortage of corn in the north.[3] Mrs. Smith cites two references to early shortages in upper Illinois. One gives 1824 as the date; the other mentions that such shortages were frequent in the first part of the century. Both references mention that men went down to fertile southern Illinois where there was plenty of corn for sale.[4]

Nearly all references to the popular story stress that the Illinois pioneers noted the parallel between their plight and trip to the south and that of Joseph's brethren, in the story in Genesis, who were driven by famine to travel to Egypt to buy corn from the huge stocks stored there. Southern Illinois, therefore, became known as "Egypt." The corn which figures in the Biblical story is not, of course, the maize or Indian corn of this country.

The minor variations in detail are proof that this story is traditional in Illinois. So far as I know, however, no one has yet called attention to the fact that southern Illinois is not the only area about which this story is told. Two other regions, one in New Hampshire and one in Texas, are also called

---

[2] "How Egypt Got It's [sic] Name" (anon.), Egyptian Key, II (March, 1947), 31.
[3] Charles Neely, collector, and John Webster Spargo, editor, Tales and Songs of Southern Illinois (Menasha, Wis., 1938), p. 3.
[4] Smith, op. cit., p. 52.

"Egypt," and each has much the same traditional explanation of its name. Furthermore, two small towns, New Egypt in southern New Jersey and Egypt, Mississippi, have place-name legends that are variants of the "going to Egypt for corn" story.[5]

The New Hampshire story sets the time of the corn shortage as 1816:

> On the road from Lancaster to Mt. Orne, or South Lancaster as it used to be called, just a short distance from the village, is "Egypt," so called because of the failure many years ago of the corn crop in this town save that which was planted in this vicinity of Egypt which grew in a remarkable way and yielded abundantly.
>
> As the people were obliged to come here for corn, they were reminded of the story in the Old Testament of Joseph's brethren who were sent to Egypt to buy corn. In this way the name was acquired, and ever since 1816, the drive in this direction has been called "going to Egypt." [6]

The Texas story dates the bad year as 1834, which is close to the year given in one of the Illinois versions:

> The yarn goes that about 1834 a group of colonists east of the Colorado River, in what is now Wharton County, raised a bountiful corn crop while planters elsewhere raised none. That fall from the Navidad, the Lavaca, the Brazos and the San Bernard they came to buy corn from the well-stored cribs on the Colorado. Generally well read in the Bible, these colonists knew the story of how Joseph's brethren found corn in Pharaoh's land, and they called the place of the corn crop amid the wilderness of Texas— Egypt.[7]

Although there is no mention in either the New Hampshire or the Texas report of any contact between the region and southern Illinois, these two regional place-name stories ob-

---

[5] There is besides a village named Egypt in Plymouth County, Massachusetts, and another in eastern Pennsylvania.

[6] Mrs. Moody P. Gore and Mrs. Guy E. Speare, *New Hampshire Folk Tales* (n. p.: New Hampshire Federation of Women's Clubs, 1932), pp. 234–35.

[7] J. Frank Dobie, "Stories in Texas Place Names," in *Straight Texas* (*Publications of the Texas Folk-Lore Society*, No. 13, Austin, Texas, 1937), p. 51.

viously belong to the same tradition as the Illinois version. Apparently both the New Hampshire and Texas regions are quite small; neither has achieved the dignity of being listed in a national gazetteer.

The two village stories introduce a different element: wartime shortages. Here is the version given in the New Jersey volume of the *American Guide Series:*

> At the time of the Revolution the village was known as Timmons Mills. After the victory at Trenton in December, 1776, Washington needed grain for his army. Benjamin Jones, one of the General's New Jersey advisors, had a large quantity of buckwheat flour and cornmeal stored at the mills; he sent his secretary, Joseph Curtis, to bring the milled grain to Trenton. Hailing the welcome arrival, Washington said: "Joseph has been in Egypt and gotten the corn." The village was Egypt until 1845, when the prefix "New" was added to avoid confusion with other Egypts. Center of a fine farm and dairy section, New Egypt still has a never failing corn crop.[8]

The story is so delightful that I regret having to point out that the 1845 date for the "New" in Egypt is an error. It was certainly "New Egypt" before 1834, according to the listing in Thomas F. Gordon.[9] Gordon also states: "The name is derived from the excellent market the mills afforded for corn."

We have no reason to be surprised at finding a discrepancy between the "historical" explanation and the legendary one. We have observed it in the Illinois story. A similar lack of agreement between the historical and legendary origin tales is found in Mississippi. According to the state guide: "Egypt . . . was established just prior to the War between the States. . . . It was named for the variety of corn grown here. During the war corn was hauled here to await shipment to the Confederate army, but before this could be accomplished Federal troops passed through and burned it."[10]

We are indebted to William Faulkner, the distinguished

---

[8] Federal Writers' Project, *New Jersey, A Guide to its Present and Past* (New York, 1939), p. 617.

[9] *A Gazetteer of the State of New Jersey* (Trenton, 1834), p. 197.

[10] Federal Writers' Project, *Mississippi, A Guide to the Magnolia State* (New York, 1938), p. 274.

novelist, for the knowledge that Egypt, Mississippi, got its name "because there was corn there when it was nowhere else in the bad lean times of the old war." [11] Mr. Faulkner's version, though it lacks a narrative, implies a popular knowledge of the Bible story, and assumes the parallel of men going from the region of shortage to the area of plenty to get corn.

What conclusions can be drawn from the existence of these five versions of the corn in Egypt story? The Illinois, New Hampshire, and Texas forms are so strikingly similar as to make one tradition; the New Jersey and Mississippi reports seem to be a related but variant form in which a wartime shortage replaces a shortage from natural causes.

To the social historian the legend offers new, if limited, evidence that the American pioneer was very familiar with the stories in the Bible. For the folklorist this legend raises a familiar problem: has this place-name story been re-invented three separate times, or five times if we include the last two versions? Or did the explanation of the name start, let us say, in New Hampshire and travel south and west with the pioneers, to be reapplied in similar situations? Although I must submit the case as "Not Proven," I favor the latter theory. Such a pattern of adaptation to new surroundings is true of many other localized legends.

[11] "Mississippi," *Holiday*, XV (April, 1954), 42.

2. GHOSTS

Ghost-Stories in Egypt

By CHARLES NEELY

From Tales and Songs of Southern Illinois, *collected by Charles Neely. Edited with a foreword by John Webster Spargo (Menasha, Wis.: George Banta Publishing Co., 1938), pp. 69–71. Hereafter cited as Neely.*

Ghost-stories have a wide currency in Egypt. They are perhaps more frequently told than any other kind of folktales. For most Egyptians they have been the terror and the delight of childhood and are likely to be the chief stock-in-trade of storytellers. One narrator, recalling her own experience, observed that the children "sat spitless as if turned to stone," while they listened to ghost-stories that were told at neighborhood gatherings. These tales are most popular in the rural communities of the Ozark foothills, but one finds them also in a highly industrialized city like Belleville.

One is inclined to associate the ghost-story with an ancient dame in a chimney-corner, but men tell them more often than women. Nor can one say that the narrator is an unlettered farmer; very often he is, but the best teller of ghost-stories I met was a college-bred man who was at the time serving as county superintendent of schools in Hardin County. In most cases the narrator takes pains to disclaim belief in the ghosts that he delights in telling about, but now and then the collector finds one who is inclined to be credulous though he may hesitate to admit the fact.

The apparitions in these ghost-tales appear in various guises, sometimes as a man of natural or heroic size, sometimes as a woman, in one instance as a hand. Frequently, they take the form of an animal—a dog, with or without a head, or a cat. More often they assume the form of an inanimate object: a laundry-bag, a bolster, a carpet-bag, a coffin, or a light. In one tale, the apparition appears as a rumbling wagon drawn by a team of horses and driven by a man. Most frequently, however, it makes its presence known by sound. Perhaps the most common sound is footsteps; occasionally, it speaks or screams or meows like a cat. In one story, the apparition pounds on a barrel or makes a noise that resembles the sound of a rolling barrel. In another story, it taps on all of the windows of the house. Sometimes it makes its presence known by the rattling or the dragging of a chain on the floor, or it may reveal itself by a noise that resembles the scratching of chickens upon a floor. One ghost causes a clock, which had long stood silent, to strike; another stirs the fire; and still another sets an invisible milkpail on the floor. Some ghosts seem to have only one sound at their command; others appear to be masters of a whole array of sound-effects.

In about half of these stories the ghost has no motive for appearing, unless it is prompted by an impulse to mischief; in the rest it has a clearly defined purpose. Several of these ghosts play benevolent roles; in three stories they lead people to treasure-troves; in two they warn of impending danger. A number of them presage death to a friend or relative or give notice that death has occurred.

Supernatural visitations in which the apparition appears to give notice of impending danger or death are usually spoken of as warnings or "tokens." Warnings do not always give rise to stories; now and then one hears only the bald statement that a certain person once received such a visitation. "Three nights before the brother of my mother died," one woman said, "a little wagon travelled around the house and over the wooden walk." A daughter of the narrator mentioned in the last sentence observed: "I was sitting in the house reading. Someone came into the hall and set a milkbucket down. I went all over the house, thinking that it might be Grandmother. I went up to the attic. Then I went out to the barn, where I found Grandmother milking." A person with a rich imagination would be sure to see a causal relationship between the sound of the milkpail and some later misfortune.

The Ghost and the Sewing Machine

> Motif E236.4, "Return from the dead because last will was not fulfilled."
> Informant, Mrs. Cordelia Kelly, Carbondale. Text from Grace Partridge Smith, "Folklore from 'Egypt,'" Hoosier Folklore, V (1946), 49.

A man was dying. He was in bed downstairs. His wife was upstairs doing her spring sewing. The racket of the sewing machine annoyed the dying man. He wanted to get up and go upstairs. He fought to get out of bed, but they didn't let him, and he died.

"Now, if I'd a been there," said a neighbor, who later spent a night in that same house, "I'd a helped him up and I'd a helped him down. What causes people to come back and hant us is an uneasy, unsatisfied mind. If you go out of this world satisfied, you're not going to come back, but if you go out unsatisfied or uneasy, you're going to come back. Why, I couldn't sleep at night in that house. He drug the machine back and forth across the floor all night so I couldn't sleep a wink for the racket."

The Avenging Voice

> Motifs E292, "Ghost causes storms," E230, "Return from dead to inflict punishment," and E402.1.1.3, "Ghost cries and screams," are all found here.

Informant Mrs. Emma Rexroat of Iowa City, Iowa, a former resident of upper Egypt. Text from Smith, Hoosier Folklore, V (1946), 49–50.

After a woman died, each night she came wailing down the hills. They could follow her by her cries around the bends and curves of the road, but could never catch up with her. People thought she was trying to avenge a wrong against her daughter, and a family with three girls was suspicioned.

One night one of the girls slipped out of an upstairs window and went up into the hills back of the house trying to locate the voice they had heard, but without success. Next night, all three planned to go out together. A big storm was coming up as they planned to start out, and they hesitated to go. Finally though, they went.

The old folks knew nothing about this; they thought the girls were safe in bed in their room. As the storm raged, the mother said, "I never had a storm skeer me like this before, I just feel like something was a-going to happen." Just as she said this, there was a terrible crash; the lightning lit up the room and through the storm came the most awful inhuman laughter that anyone ever heard.

Frightened, the father and mother went up to the girls' room. Not one of the three was there! All night they searched for them. Everyone around had heard the crazy laughter. After a while, they found a big tree that had been struck by lightning. All three girls were lying there dead. "After that," said the mother, "never a wail came out of them hills. It was all finished."

The Dutchman's Ghost Story

Motifs E236.4, "Return from the dead because last will was not fulfilled," and E402.1.5, "Invisible ghost jingles chains," are present, and there is a curious twist to E766.1, "Clock stops at moment of owner's death."

Charles Neely, the collector, writes: "This story was written down from the lips of the late Isaac J. Hartline

*of Carbondale in his eighty-fourth year. Formerly he
had lived in Union County near the scene of this story.
The tale is not widely known; apparently it was a family legend well on the road to oblivion. In the winter of
1938 when I secured this story, Mr. Hartline had not
told it for a good many years."*
Text from Neely, pp. 87–88.

Joe Kiestler was a German right from the ole country. My ole
Uncle Ike—he was an ole bachelor—kept him. He told the
Dutchman to come there to live as one of the family. Uncle Ike
didn't pay him a regular salary. He gave him money to live
on an' hogs an' cattle to git a start on.

Joe was a great lover of cats an' dogs. The Dutchman
slept upstairs an' the cats would sleep with him. Finally Joe
got sick an' he was bad off. They had to carry him downstairs.
He had an ole silver watch he thought a great deal of, an' he
wouldn't consent to go down unless the watch went. They finally
got him down an' he died. He requested that the watch be
buried with him. They didn't do it.

Well, they had an ole-fashion clock that stood in the hall
—a grandfather clock about eight feet high. But the clock
hadn't run for twenty-odd years. So one day those cats—the
Dutchman had about two dozen of them—they got out in the
hall and circled around the clock, an' the clock began to strike,
an' the cats began to meow. An' they counted the strokes, an'
if it struck onct it struck two hundred an' eighty times.

The nex' thing, they could hear something scratchin' like
an ole hen. They looked under the bed an' they never seen anything. An' the nex' thing sounded to them like a noise made by
a big log chain bein' drug down the stairway. The cats got
bunched again around the ole clock an' begin to meow. An' then
my ole uncle, that lived there, he stepped out in the hall with
the cats meowin' an' the clock strikin', an' he says, "Joe, what
is it you want? If they's anything you want, say so." He talked
to him like he was a live man. Right then the cats stopped, an'
the clock stopped, an' it never struck any more.

The Ghosts of Dug Hill

*These two encounters took place at an infamous spot,
Dug Hill, where the ghosts of Civil War soldiers were
believed to roam. Thus the ghost tales localized around
Dug Hill have become neighborhood legends.*

*The first text, collected by La Donne Deadmond in Wolf
Lake west of Dug Hill, contains Motif E422.1.1.3.1,
"Headless ghost rides horse." The second text, collected
by Katherine Dougan in Jonesboro, contains Motifs
E235.2, "Ghost returns to demand proper burial,"
E272, "Road ghosts," and E459.3, "Ghost laid when its
wishes are acceded to."*

*Texts from Jesse Harris and Julia Neely, "Southern
Illinois Phantoms and Bogies,"* Midwest Folklore, *I
(1951), 175.*

This Dug Hill is a huge hill and there is a cut through it. The
road passes through this cut.

People used to go through there, and it was real spooky.
The headless horseman rides through there. This man was
coming through there, and he saw a man laying in the road,
and he thought it was a drunk. He stopped his horse, got out
of the buggy, and went up to the man and tried to pick him up.
He put his hands down and lifted, and his hands came right
through. He walked away and looked back and still he saw the
man. So he went back again and tried to pick him up. His hands
still went through the body. By this time he was really frightened. He ran and jumped in the buggy. He started driving
right toward the body. When he came to that spot in the road,
he could feel the body as the wheels rolled over it.

Before the highway was built through Dug Hill, the old road
went by the cemetery (the new one goes through it). This hill
is located east of Ware. Used to be a woman who would come
out of the cemetery at night and walk up the hill with anyone

who came along the road. Most people were afraid to travel the road at night because of her. No one ever had enough nerve to ask what she wanted. One night a drunk from Jonesboro came by and asked her what she wanted. She told him to cover up the end of her baby's casket which had been washed out when Clear Creek overflowed. It sobered him up, so the next day he and some fellows came out and found the casket. The woman was never seen any more.

The Flying Wagon

The Dug Hill neighborhood is also the scene of this apparition, which suggests the well-known European legend of the aerial Wild Hunt. See the cluster of motifs around E501.13.1, "Wild Hunt heralded by stamping of horses." More prosaic is E535.2, "Ghostly wagon." Informant John H. Treece, Jonesboro. Text from Neely, pp. 80–81.

A feller by the name of Bill Smith told me this story. Bill ain't jest exactly in his right mind; he's a sort o'half idiot, I guess. He's still a-livin' at Jonesboro, and you might see him on the street. If you'd ask him about it, he'd tell you the same thing I'm a-tellin' you if he'd talk to you.

Bill was a-haulin' off corn one day. It's been a long time ago. He'd hauled off three loads of corn that day and was a-goin' home after dark. He had to pass through Dug Hill fer he lived over in the bottoms. He'd jest about got half-way down the hill, goin' west, when the neck-yoke of one of his horses come off, and Bill had to stop the wagon right there on the grade and git out to fix the yoke.

The ground was froze hard, fer it was in December when he was a-haulin' the corn off. And the wagons that come over the roads done a heap of rattlin' on account of the shape they was in. You could hear the wagon comin' a long way off.

As Bill was down there a-fixin' the yoke, he 'eared the awfulest racket a man ever did hear. It sounded like some drunk man a-drivin' an empty wagon over the road as fast as the horses could go. Bill thought maybe it was one of his buddies that was a-haulin' off corn with him, comin' home drunk. It scared Bill to death nearly, fer he knew that there wasn't enough room fer the wagon to git by on account of the road bein' so narrow, and Bill knowed he couldn't git out of the way. It looked like him and his horses might git killed. Bill looked back up the hill and hollered as loud as he could, but it didn't do no good. The racket kept gittin' nearer and nearer. Bill didn't know what to do. He knowed that the driver couldn't stop the wagon in time.

The noise was on the brink of the hill. Bill looked up, and he realized a few minutes later that the noise of the wagon was in the air above him and not on the road a-tall.

Bill looked up in the air, and he seed comin' over the crest of the hill a heavy pair of black horses a-pullin' a heavy wagon with side-boards on. A man was a-settin' in the wagon a-drivin.' The horses were a-runnin' up there in the air jest like they was on the ground, and the wheels of the wagon was a-turnin' jest like they was on the ground, and the wagon was makin' a awful lot of racket like a wagon does when it's drove over rough, froze ground. The wagon and team passed right over Bill's head and struck the crest of another hill, and Bill couldn't see it any more, but he heard the noise of the wagon after it had got two miles away.

The Dutton Hill Ghost

The poignant Motif E221, "Dead spouse's malevolent return—usually to protest with survivor because of evil ways," is present here, in the subform of E221.1.4.2, "Dead wife rides on horse behind man as he goes to court another." John Greenleaf Whittier used the theme of E221.1, "Dead wife haunts husband on second marriage," in his poem "The New Wife and the Old," and the same motif is found in Japan (Dorson, Folk Legends of Japan, "The Ghost of the First Wife," pp. 99–101.)

> *"Secured from Miss Millie Barnard, Shawneetown, daughter of Mrs. Ollie Barnard. The Barnard and Lowry families—Mrs. Barnard was a Lowry before her marriage—tell a number of ghost-stories, some of which concern their own relatives and ancestors. Certain members of the family believe in ghosts, and all of them like tales of a ghostly character." Text from Neely, p. 89.*

There was a young man and his wife who lived near Dutton Hill in Hardin County. The wife was a lovely woman, and she had a beautiful black horse. The man was a two-timer; he was slipping over across the graveyard to see another woman. When the wife found it out, she grieved herself to death. On her death-bed she begged him to take care of her horse. She was buried in the cemetery that he went across.

After her death, he rode the horse across the cemetery to see the woman. And as he crossed, his wife's ghost would come out of the grave and get on behind him. He would dig his spurs into the flanks of the horse, trying to get away from the ghost. But it would stay with him till he was past the cemetery.

He didn't take care of the horse at all but mistreated it and kept its sides sore with the spur. One night as he was racing through the cemetery, trying to escape his wife's ghost, the horse fell and threw him against a tombstone and killed him.

The Miser's Gold

> *The tale of a bold man staying overnight in a haunted house is widely told in the United States, both as a believed event and as a humorous fright story. Its central motif is H1411 "Fear test, staying in haunted house," here joined to another extremely popular motif, E371.4,* "Ghost of man returns to point out buried treasure," for which Baughman cites nine examples from Great Britain, one from Canada, and fifteen in the United States.*
>
> *Informant Mrs. Mary U. Stallion, Elizabethtown, who came from Tennessee, but localized the story in Hardin*

County, Illinois. Text from Neely, pp. 86–87, who also gives two other, longer variants.

There was a haunted house out here in the hills. The reason it was haunted was because an old miser had been killed there. The old miser had lots of money, and one night some men came there and tried to make him tell where he hid it. He wouldn't tell them; so they slashed his throat. Ever since the house has been haunted. People claimed that if you'd go there and stay all night, the old miser would come back and tell where he kept his gold, but nobody was brave enough to spend the night there.

Finally, there was a man who was brave enough to stay there. He went to the house one evening and went to bed. He hadn't been in bed long before he was sound asleep. Along in the night he was awakened by a bump, bump noise. He sat up in bed. The noise continued. It was something coming down the stairs. Whatever it was at last reached the floor and came to the door, opened it, and came into the room. The man was almost scared to death at what he saw. There stood the old miser with his throat slashed and bleeding horribly, with a coffin in his arms. The man was so badly frightened that he couldn't speak.

The ghost said: "You are the only man who is brave enough to stay here all night, and I'll show you where my gold is hid."

The old man took the man to a tree, and he found a rich **treasure.**

The Girl Who Died of Fright

Variants of this legend are listed by Baughman from nearly all parts of the country. In a text told by a German lady in Milwaukee, a Prussian soldier pins himself to the grave by unwittingly sticking his bayonet through his cape (Dorson, "Folklore at a Milwaukee Wedding," Hoosier Folklore, VI, 1947, 5). This is Motif N384.2, "Death in the graveyard; person's clothing is caught;

person thinks something (ghost) is holding him, dies of fright," and Type 1676B, Clothing Caught in Grave-yard.

Informant Mrs. Mary U. Stallion, who enjoyed a local reputation as storyteller in Elizabethtown on the Ohio River in southeastern Illinois. Text from Neely, pp. 64–65, who gives three other variants from other parts of Egypt.

One time there was a girl who said she didn't believe in haints. She said she wouldn't be afraid to go to a graveyard at night by herself. They told her she'd better not, but she claimed she wasn't afraid. Some one dared her to go. One evening about dark she started.

As the girl got close to the graveyard, she began to have a creepy feelin'. By the time she got to the cemetery she was about scared to death, but she went on in. She decided that she'd stick a stick in a grave to prove to them that she'd been to the graveyard.

She hunted around and found a stick and went up to a grave for to put it in as proof. But when she went to job it in the ground, she got her apron underneath the point of the stick. It jerked her down, and she thought a ghost had reached up out of the grave and was pullin' her in. It scared her so bad that she just dropped over dead right

Next morning her folks got uneasy about her not comin' home, and they got out to lookin' for her, and they found her lyin' across a grave with her apron pinned under a stick that she'd stuck in the ground.

I guess maybe the sudden scare caused her to have heart failure. Anyhow she was scared of ghosts.

Buried Alive

Type 990, Seemingly Dead Revives, and Motif K426, "Apparently dead woman revives when thief tries to steal from her grave." This migratory legend is reported

77 times in the Irish folklore archives and has entered the English, French, and Spanish traditions in North America. A Negro text is in Dorson, Negro Tales from Pine Bluff, Arkansas, and Calvin, Michigan, p. 219.

"Miss Irene Mache, Belleville, told this tale, which she had obtained from a Mrs. Shrimp, also of Belleville. Belleville is an industrial city near St. Louis with a large German population. Inhabitants of that city have preserved folktales and ballads to a degree that is surprising when one considers all of the resources of entertainment at their disposal." Text from Neely, pp. 61–62.

Before the time that embalming of the dead was practiced, many people were pronounced dead, only to come alive again. This story has to do with a middle-aged woman who had been ill for two weeks and then died. After a wake had been held, as was the custom, she was buried.

It happened the night of the day of her burial that a group of grave-robbers visited the cemetery and noticed the new grave and decided to rob it. The chief object of these robbers was not to steal the bodies, but rather any jewelry that might have been buried with them.

When the lid of the coffin was raised, they were glad to see a ruby ring as well as a plain gold ring on the victim's second finger of the left hand. They were disappointed when they found that it was impossible to remove the rings over the first joint. At last, as they hated to leave these two valuable rings, they decided to cut the finger.

As the knife pierced the flesh, the robbers were startled by a slight movement of the hand. At about the same time the corpse sat up in the coffin—and the robbers took to their heels.

The woman climbed out of her coffin and went home, where she explained that she had been conscious of the fact that she had been pronounced dead but was unable to move or speak to prevent being buried.

3. BOGIES

Chat Garla

> *From French settlers who came to western Illinois early in the seventeenth century has descended this belief in a demonic cat. Relevant motifs are B147.1.2.2, "Cat as beast of ill-omen," E423, "Revenant in animal form," and C58, "Tabu: profaning sacred day."*
> *Informant Mary Louise Garner, Kaskaskia. Text from Neely, pp. 92–93.*

There's a story about the old Governor Bond property. When the river washed Kaskaskia away, they tore the old Bond House down and moved it to the island. Folks claimed that it was a hainted house. It was a big house with lots of rooms, and it would hold a lot of people. A woman and her two sons once lived there. She was a widow.

The oldest boy wanted to go hunting one day, but she wouldn't let him go because it was All Souls' Day. People believed that it was wrong to hunt on that day because they thought that the birds and animals might be the souls of dead people who had returned to earth. But the boy stole the gun and slipped out of the house with it. He had hitched the team to the wagon to get some wood. When he was climbing over the fence with the gun, it went off and killed him. The gun scared the team and it started to running away. The younger boy fell out and was drug to death.

The chain traces made a rattling noise, and a black cat

at the house ran upstairs screaming. The woman said that she knew that something had happened, for she heard the cat and the chains. She always said that the cat had warned her.

After that, people on the island wouldn't go hunting or fishing on All Souls' Day because they said that they were afraid of the *Chat garla*. People who lived at the Bond House after that said that they heard noises of a cat screaming and of chains rattling.

The McConnall Banshee

> *Irish immigrants in Egypt brought with them their spe-
> cial tradition of the banshee, a fairy woman attached
> to a family. See Motif M301.6.1, "Banshees as portents
> of misfortune," and Sean O'Sullivan, A Handbook of
> Irish Folklore (Folklore of Ireland Society, 1942),
> "Banshee," pp. 490–91.*
>
> *Informant Gordon Lowry, Shawneetown. Text from
> Neely, p. 96.*

Before any one of the McConnall family died, a benshee [*sic*] would scream, and it would take the route that the family would go to the cemetery. The neighbors along the route would hear it.

When old lady Brown died—she was a McConnall—the benshee came into the house and got in bed. It looked like a little old woman about a foot high, with a rag tied around its head. John Gentry was going to kill it, but Mrs. Brown said, "Don't bother that. That's my baby."

Some folks said that the benshee was a curse sent by the church, for the McConnalls had once burned a church.

When Walter Fraley's baby died, the benshee cried all over the place, but no one could see it.

4. WITCHES

The Witch Who Stole Milk

Several familiar motifs are present here. The witch's powers are seen in D1520.16, "Magic transportation by chair," D2083.3.1, "Milk transferred from another's cow by squeezing an ax-handle (or the like)," and G211.2, "Witch in form of cat." A common method of combating the witch is D1385.4, "Silver bullet protects against giants, ghosts, and witches." Neely cites the classic work of George Lyman Kittredge, Witchcraft in Old and New England (Cambridge, Mass., 1929), pp. 163–66, for instances of witches stealing milk.

Informant Miss Esther Knefelkamp, Belleville, who obtained the story from Mr. Henry Juenger, Sr., of the same city, with this additional comment: "Years ago some women were witches and could take any form they pleased. This lady (the witch of the story) was my neighbor—I know. I was the son who took a shot at her. This is not just a yarn; it really happened. It's so!"
Text from Neely, pp. 109–10.

Once upon a time there was an old woman living on a farm. The neighbors said that she was a witch. This old woman moved from her place to her son's some distance away. In those days the neighbors helped do the moving. The old woman had a high-backed rocker on her front porch, and she was seen sitting there very often. When one of the last movers saw her sitting on her front porch, rocking to and fro, he asked her if he could not take her and her rocker along as it was some distance to her new home. Then the old lady said, "Oh, no, my boy. I and my rocker will be there ahead of you-all." And lo and behold, when the wagon arrived at the new home, the old lady was calmly rocking on the front porch of her new home.

After a time everybody's cows in that neighborhood gave no milk. This old lady had several towels hanging on her back porch. With a towel hanging before her, she would milk the neighbors' cows from the lower two corners; when she was finished she would have several large foaming buckets of wholesome milk. This same lady used to bewitch the neighbors' horses and make them sick. They would see a black shadow, and when they go to the barn they would see a cat. The son took a shot at her. The next morning the old lady's hands were all crippled up.

At another time this old lady went into another's corn crib to steal corn. Some one of the boys decided to take a shot at her. He didn't kill her, just crippled her. So he took a dime and broke it into pieces and used that for a shot. A black cat ran away meowing like the devil. The next day some one called on her. The old woman had to stay in bed, for she was all shot up, and blood trickling in streams down her face.

The Dried Footprint

> *Neely cites Motif D1266, "Magic book," and Kittredge,* Witchcraft, *pp. 146, 465, nn. 66, 67, 70, on the Sixth and Seventh Books of Genesis (Moses), which have already played a part in Pennsylvania Dutch sorcery (see below, p. 111). See also the general Motif D2063.1.1, "Tormenting by sympathetic magic."*
> *Informant Miss Esther Knefelkamp, Belleville, whose source was Mrs. Louis Stein. Text from Neely, p. 106.*

Once upon a time there was a farmer who planted seventy-five acres of young fruit trees. The next morning all of the trees were pulled up. He asked his hired man to replant the trees. Again the trees were pulled up. Then the third time the farmer told his hired man to plow and harrow the ground well so that not a footprint could be seen. The hired man did this, and the third time the trees were pulled up.

This time the farmer found a footprint near one of the trees. As carefully as he could he carried the ground with the footprint to the house and very slowly began to dry the ground. He had his suspicions, and since he owned the Sixth and Seventh Books of Genesis and therefore had magical powers, he felt that he could find the culprit. He said, "The fellow who did this will get sick." He let the ground with the footprint dry for several days, and then he went to the house of the man he suspected. The man was very sick in bed. The farmer left and returned the next day. The fellow was worse the next day, and his family thought he was dying. The farmer said that when the footprint was thoroughly dry, the fellow would die. The fellow promised never to do it again, and the farmer let him go.

The Witch Hare

> *Baughman suggests Motif G271.4.2ba, "Shooting witch picture or symbol with silver bullet breaks spell," and gives references from six states. Jesse W. Harris, in "Some Southern Illinois Witch Lore"* (Southern Folklore Quarterly, X, 1946, 186), *tells of Charley Lee, a Hamilton County witchmaster, who shot pictures of witches with a silver bullet.*
>
> *Informant a lady of 82 living in Carbondale. Smith cites Motifs D655.2, "Witch transforms self to animal so as to suck cows," and G211.2.7, "Witch in form of hare," and Kittredge,* Witchcraft, *166, 497, n. 495, for milk sucking and 134, 139, for the witch-ball. Text from Grace Partridge Smith, "Folklore from 'Egypt,'"* Journal of American Folklore, LIV (1941), 52–53.

There was an old lady and her daughter who were witches and they tried in every way they could to plague the neighborhood. A cow belonging to some of the people around would suddenly go dry, or one would take sick and die. This old woman would come around in the shape of a hare. The hounds couldn't catch her. When they turned the dogs on her, the hare would run into a sinkhole in the holler, and when they built a fire all around, it would run into the hole. No trap could catch this hare, for it would snap every trap they set without getting caught. Well, they tried to trap her three times with a steel trap, so they finally got a witch doctor to help. He told them to take silver and melt it, then to draw the witch's picture and shoot it. If they wanted to break the spell without killing her, to shoot her in the leg. Then they drew the picture and shot her in the leg.

Soon, the old woman's son came running on his feet [*sic*] and wanted someone to go for the doctor as his mother had fallen and broken her leg while sweeping the house! Well, when the bewitched cattle died, they would always find a witch-ball under their skin, one made of dog-hair, horse-hair, and rabbit-hair.

The Wreath in the Pillow

> *Forty-five instances of this belief are reported by Harry M. Hyatt in* Folklore from Adams County, Illinois *(New York: Memoirs of the Alma Egan Hyatt Foundation, 1935), "Hoodoo and Witchcraft Wreaths," Nos. 9309–9354, pp. 488–98.*
>
> *Informant Irene Mache, Belleville, whose source was Mrs. John Becker, Belleville. Text from Neely, pp. 105–6.*

Doctors seemed to be at loss as to just what was troubling Clarence Manners. The child had been ill for a period of five weeks, getting weaker day by day.

One day a neighbor came in to see Clarence and told his mother doctors could do the child little good, for he was bewitched. She suggested they look into the pillow upon which Clarence rested his head. Upon opening the pillow a wreath formed by the feathers was found. The wreath was not entirely finished, the neighbor explained, and for that reason Clarence was still alive. At the suggestion of the neighbor the wreath was placed on a chair and a rope was used to beat it until it was demolished.

The next day an old lady living in the neighborhood was confined to her bed with a bruised body. Mrs. Manners realized then that it was she who had bewitched her son. Clarence recovered soon after the wreath was destroyed.

Snakes in the Hole

> *Here is a fusion of White and Negro tradition. This wizard is primarily a treasure-finder; see Motif D1314.2, "Magic wand (twig) locates hidden treasure." The notions in N556, "Treasure-finders always frightened away," and N582, "Serpent guards treasure," are firmly established in southern Negro folk belief, viz. Dorson, "Buried Treasure and Hants," in Negro Folktales in Michigan, pp. 133–35.*
>
> *"Related by Mr. Charles Neely, Sr., Carbondale. This tale was formerly generally known in the southern part of Pope County. Tom Kaylor and Bill Dotson were both local 'characters.'" Text from Neely, p. 120.*

Uncle Tom Kaylor was a wizard, people said. People in the neighborhood used to go to him when their milk wouldn't make butter. Uncle Tom would tell them to melt a piece of silver. Uncle Tom also had a mineral rod with which he located buried treasure.

It was believed among the people of that community that money was buried on Aunt 'Liza McGhee's place. Uncle Tom took his mineral rod one moonlight night and located the buried treasure. He marked the spot. The next night he hired a Negro well-digger, old Bill Dotson, to dig down to the money.

They went to the place and Bill began to dig. It was fall and pretty cold. Bill got down a few feet and the snakes began to crawl out the sides of the hole and coil about Dotson's feet.

The deeper Dotson dug, the more numerous the snakes were.
Finally, Dotson couldn't stand it any longer. He pitched his
spade out of the hold and climbed out.

If Kaylor ever went back to hunt the money, no one ever
knew, but Dotson never went back.

Water Witches in Egypt

A stimulating analysis of Water Witching U.S.A. *has
been written jointly by an anthropologist and a psy-
chologist, Evon Z. Vogt and Ray Hyman (Chicago,
1959). In a spirited essay-review, R. Carlyle Buley,
professor of history at Indiana University, and a firm
believer in his own and other persons' powers to divine
water, challenges the authors' conclusions; they contend
that water witching is socially useful but not scien-
tifically verifiable. See his "Water (?) Witching Can Be
Fun,"* Indiana Magazine of History, *LVI (1960), 65–
77.*

*The following account of "Water Witching" in southern
Illinois, by Lelah Allison, is from* Hoosier Folklore, *VI
(1947), 88–90.*

Water witching is not new, and no matter where one goes, he
will find someone who can witch water in that community. The
methods used are almost the same everywhere, but there are certain techniques which differ. A small fork from a green tree,
with limbs long enough so that the fork can be held upside
down over one's head, with the ends held in each hand, seems
to be used by all who have the power of locating water underground. Other than that, each witcher has his own method.

Southern Illinois has many wells which have been dug at
places designated by a water witch. Other regions have many
such wells also, but the methods herein described are those used
by southern Illinois water witches.

John Todd Spruell of Wayne County likes a fork from a
live peach tree, but he can use a fork from any tree, so long
as the tree is alive, or "green." He cuts the fork from the tree

just below the point where the limbs branch. He then trims the limbs, leaving them long enough to turn the fork upside down over his head, and holds on to the ends of the limbs with each hand. The remainder is cut off from the ends of the limbs. He holds the fork in front of his body with the apex of the V extending away, grasps the end of each limb in each hand, and raises his arms up to each side of his head so that the limb is over his head. The witcher is now in position to walk about until he feels the force of an underground stream pulling on the fork.

He walks back and forth across a lot or field in which the owner would like to have a well, to see if the fork will pull downward. If there is no feeling of "pull" on the fork, there is no water underground in that area. If the owner is insistent on digging a well, especially at a dry time when he must have water for his stock, he selects the next desired lot or field. The witch walks back and forth here until he is sure that he has covered all the territory. When he feels the fork pulling downward, he walks back and forth until he locates the exact spot at which there is a stream of water underground. He then turns each way and follows the vein of water so that the most desired spot can be located for the owner.

To locate a vein is not enough. The witch must be able to tell the power of the underground stream. If there is a heavy pull on the fork, there is much water. If the pull is slight, the vein is a small one. The owner will not locate his well at that point.

As the witch approaches the vein, the fork begins to pull downward. At the point at which he stands directly over the vein the apex of the stick will point directly downward. He approaches the vein at right angles from both directions to be sure that he has located the exact spot. When that is located, it is easy to follow the vein toward its source and toward its destination.

After he has located the vein and estimated its strength, he estimates the depth by walking back at right angles until he feels the first pull on the fork. He then walks to the vein counting the feet. That is the number of feet it will be necessary for the owner to dig to find a good supply of water. Mr. Spruell says that he has witched dozens of wells in several counties of southern Illinois, and that there has always been water at the spot he has designated, when the owner has dug, and the depth of the water has never missed but a few feet of the measurement he has foretold.

Al Snowdell, now of Iowa but a native of Edwards County, Illinois, says that any green fork will serve, but he likes a peach fork. His method is the same except for the means of locating the depth. After he locates the vein and its direction and force of water supply, he estimates the depth by standing over the vein. Holding the fork in position in front of his body, he counts the number of times that it is pulled downward, each time turning it back, of course. The number of times that it is pulled down is the number of feet to the water.

He says that he witched wells in the panhandle of Oklahoma, when it was so dry that settlers left their homes to move back to regions where water was plentiful. He says one well he witched in that dry region was strong enough to keep a deep pond filled for a rancher's herd of cattle and that a large windmill pumped that water twenty-four hours a day. He witched many wells in southern Illinois before he felt the urge to move westward. He has also used the fork in southwestern Iowa, where he now lives.

John Mossbarger used to witch wells, if he were asked to do so; but he did it with a sly grin on his quiet face. He insisted on using a peach fork, but it had to be green. He estimated the depth of the water by the force of the "pull" on the stick.

This method of locating underground water sounds fantastic, but it is surprising how common is the use of these and other water witches when a landowner wants to dig a well. If he spends money to dig a well, he wants a supply of water. He needs water, or he would not go to the bother and expense of digging a well. In order to be sure that his venture is successful, he asks a water witch to come to his farm and use his power to locate the hidden stream that can supply the needed liquid. He may do it on the sly when he asks the water witch to come, but the latter is almost sure to point to the well, when it is done, as another of his "finds."

The owner may give the man a dollar or two for his trouble. The witcher likes to show his power and tell what he has located.

Water witching has turned into another type of witching in southern Illinois. Some have used their power to locate the hidden pools of oil common in much of that area—and "black gold" is even more sought after than water.

5. FOLK MEDICINE

THE FOLLOWING PAPER was printed in *Illinois Folklore*, II, No. 1 (April, 1948), 3–7. I have referenced items of medical folklore to *The Frank C. Brown Collection of North Carolina Folklore*, VI, *Popular Beliefs and Superstitions from North Carolina*, 1–4783, edited by Wayland D. Hand (Durham, N.C.: Duke University Press, 1961). Hand provides extensive comparative notes for each entry.

Folk Medicine in Southern Illinois

By DR. BEN FOX

At the mention of the term "Folk Medicine" most people smile benignly, serene in the belief that folk medicine is something that is practiced by the tribesmen of Jesse Stuart's county in Kentucky, or by American Indians, or by unlettered people who are remote—conveniently remote. It is hard for moderns to realize that folk medicine is practiced all around them in both rural and urban districts, and that all social levels employ it in some degree.

Folk medicine is made up of the empiricisms which are employed for the prevention or cure of disease, without the background of investigation, by people without adequate training. It is closely related to superstition. Often it represents experience of the race in some far off and long forgotten time; sometimes it has value. As the precursor of modern or investigative medicine it has been long discussed by medical historians; Howard W. Haggard's *Devils, Drugs, and Doctors* (1929) is probably the most popular work on the subject.

I shall confine my remarks to the less emetic types of therapy, and to those which I have personally encountered or of which I have reliable information. Probably the most commonly employed folk drug in our locality is sassafras. This has been used so long that most of you have come to regard a decoction of sassafras root as a spring variant on the tea-and-coffee theme of breakfast, but by your ancestors and many of your contemporaries it was consumed with a definite purpose—to "thin the blood." Why the blood was supposed to be thick at the end of winter is not explained, nor is it given that thick blood really needs thinning, but on the basis of this observation a considerable tonnage of sassafras root has been excavated and unnumbered quarts of the brew have been consumed. I suppose no one was damaged thereby.

In this connection the use of sulphur and sorghum may be mentioned. It was and is used for the same purpose as sassafras—thinning the blood. It acted as a purgative which was not too violent, and I trust none was killed by it.*

Some medications were employed for their very repulsiveness; I have had a young man tell me that his father made a custom of putting a small snake in a pint of whiskey each spring. This viper vintage was then set on the shelf and a few spoonfuls of the stuff were taken from time to time as a treatment for rheumatism. I have encountered this on only one occasion, but I was given to understand that it was common enough practice among friends of this particular family, and they could not understand that the ingestion of the alcoholic serpent soup should do violence to anyone's sensibilities. I know the whiskey guzzling was a part of their ethos, and perhaps the snake was a logical consequence.†

Among the cases of repulsive agents to treat illness must be mentioned that of fastening a dirty sock about the neck

---

* The *Brown Collection*, VI, 127–29, lists specific blood purifiers and tonics in Nos. 890–904. See Nos. 895–96 for the use of sassafras and 902–3 for sulphur and sorghum.

† No. 1991 in the *Brown Collection*, VI, 258, states: "For rheumatism, try a Chinese remedy: behead a rattlesnake, put it into a jar and cover with rice whiskey and leave for a year; then drink the whiskey." The note reports other variations such as rattlesnake flesh in corn whiskey (American backwoodsmen) and dried rattlesnake in corn whiskey (Kentucky).

for the relief of tonsillitis, or even a cold. I have seen this used, and by people who would not want it on them. This mode of therapy belongs in the same category as does tying a small bag of asafoetida about a child's neck to ward off diphtheria,* and presumably the underlying belief was that no self-respecting germ would remain within miles of the wearer.

Twelve or fifteen years ago I had occasion to visit a man who was very ill with a mass of ulcers halfway round his ribs; he had shingles. When I told his relatives that treatment for the condition was not dramatically successful one of the neighbors volunteered the information that the proper thing to do in such a case was to slice off the tip of a black cat's tail, and using the portion still attached to the cat as a brush, paint the ulcers with feline blood. I do not know whether this ceremony is effectual or not; the man died.

By this same family I was informed that snake bite can be best treated by splitting a chicken the long way and binding half the fowl, raw side down, to the bitten area. It was solemnly stated that in the course of two or three days the chicken meat "drawed so much pisen out of the bite that the chicken turned plumb green." † It had not occurred to my informant that even in the absence of snake venom a chicken carcass decomposes in a few days and that the change in color which was observed was produced by the ordinary process of rotting.

The greasing of the chest for respiratory infections is such ingrained practice that every family physician has to bow to it. I can well remember having a woolen cloth saturated with melted tallow, beeswax, turpentine and camphor tied on my own diminutive thorax. The procedure had value, since the mess was always applied hot, and always contained some mild skin irritant. Heat and counter-irritation are demonstrably helpful in inflammatory processes, since they stimulate blood flow, and in some measure hasten repair.

In connection with the local application of heated greases for inflammatory processes, I have known a community in which a piece of fried tablecloth was used in the treatment of "weed

---

* Given in the *Brown Collection*, VI, 170. No. 1281, with one Iowa reference.
† This belief is listed as No. 2130 in the *Brown Collection*, VI, 276. See Nos. 2131–33 for the use of other parts of the chicken, such as the heart or the egg yolk, to draw out poison.

in the breast" or mastitis in the nursing mother. This piece of heavy linen was fried in a mixture of lard, butter, tallow, and as I remember cheese parings, along with a dash or two of camphor and a jigger of turpentine, and applied to the swollen and painful mama. Oddly enough, no one seemed to realize that this was again heat and counter-irritation; the comfort given was ascribed to some mystic effect of the linen. This same piece of material was kept in the neighborhood for a long time, and was passed from bosom to bosom with a fine impartiality and a splendid disregard for the fastidious; it was said to have a wonderfully "drawing" effect.

As an addendum to the folklore of human lactation may be mentioned a method of suppressing milk flow at weaning time. This required the expression of the mother's milk directly on a hot rock; some held out for a stove lid. As the milk struck, sizzled, steamed and dried, the secretion of the breast also dried, according to the firm belief of many a southern Illinois mother. The belief that something outside the body—a hot rock—can have an effect on a part of the body—the mammary gland—with which it has no relationship, has many parallels. I have been gravely asked if the placing of a pan of cold water under the bed at night would stop night sweats, and this query did not come from an illiterate.

An equally ridiculous belief, prevalent in my early childhood, had to do with the treatment of a sty, in which the sufferer went to the nearest crossroad, and intoned, "Sty, sty, come off my eye and go to the next one that passes by." *

A companion piece in absurdity was the belief that recovery from venereal disease could be accomplished only by transmitting the infection to someone else.

Among the Negroes of Jackson County, the eating of meat after receiving a laceration of the skin was avoided; it was said to delay healing and caused the growth of proud flesh. This is another belief that I have not heard mentioned in a long time, and it may now be lost.

* See the *Brown Collection*, VI, 296–97, Nos. 2295–2302. In each item a slight verbal difference occurs in the charm text. Also, some believers recommend going to a fork in the roads (Nos. 2300–1) and some to a street corner (No. 2302).

Among the vaporings of the human psyche should be catalogued the magic power ascribed to a child who has never seen his (or her) father. This is the power to cure thrush in infants by blowing in the mouth.* I have been under the impression that it is because the child has never beheld the parent that the dramatic effect or *oïdium albicans* is so pronounced; it is not necessarily because of posthumous delivery. I have often wished to find someone whose parents had been divorced early enough to prevent male parent and offspring seeing each other; it would be interesting to check the anti-*oïdium* effects of such a one against those of a proven posthumous son or daughter. One of my sisters, then about eight years old, came home one hot afternoon and announced that old lady such and such had asked her to blow into Dorothy's mouth. Dorothy was about two and had whooping cough. Dorothy's mother had made her request because my sister was a seventh child. I never heard a report on the success of the treatment.

A final paragraph must be devoted to warts. Many methods have been suggested for their removal, and all have their adherents. There are the methods of the knotted string, the method of the heated needle, the method of stump water, and many dozens more. I always preferred the one in which the wart is gouged with a thorn until it bleeds. A drop of blood is placed upon each of seven grains of white corn. Each day, one of these grains is fed to a black hen. On the seventh day the wart is alleged to disappear.†

Folk Remedies

Introduction by Grace Partridge Smith, from "Folklore from 'Egypt,'" Journal of American Folklore, LIV

* This belief is listed in the *Brown Collection,* VI, 66, Nos. 413–16. The person who does the blowing might be someone born after the death of his father, an illegitimate child, or someone who had never seen his father. The idea that thrush can be cured by a seventh child is given in No. 418, p. 66.
† Seventeen items in the *Brown Collection,* VI, 323–26, Nos. 2501–17, describe wart cures in which blood from the wart is put onto grains of corn. Corn shucks, corn stalks, and cornbread are also thought to be efficacious (Nos. 2518–20, p. 326).

*(1941), 57–58. The list of home remedies there given
is combined below with another list by Smith, under the
same title, in* Hoosier Folklore, *V (1946), 68–70.*

*Notes I have added under particular entries refer to the
extensive, annotated listing of folk medical beliefs in*
Popular Beliefs and Superstitions from North Carolina,
*1–4783, edited by Wayland D. Hand (The Frank
C. Brown Collection of North Carolina Folklore, VI;
Durham, N.C.: Duke University Press, 1961).*

Remedies used by early-day Egyptians are still resorted to
back in the hills of lower Egypt. Old granny brews of those
days took the place of modern prescriptions. Fortunately
enough, the Illinois terrain produced roots, barks, and herbs
that were of help to pioneer settlers and doctors in treating
many mild physical upsets of either adults or children. First
aid in such cases were brews of different sorts.

For teas, there was a choice of catnip, horehound, pump-
kin-seed, Jerusalem oak, pinkroot, rattlesnake weed, plantain
root, sage, smartweed, white-oak bark, slippery elm, milkweed
root, sumac bark and berries, boneset, raspberry or mullein
leaves, dandelion, tansy, sassafras, sarsaparilla, sycamore chips,
"sheeps pills," and red-root, to say nothing of that seemingly
all-purpose plant, the pokeweed (*Phytolacca americana*). This
is a coarse perennial with white flowers and really evil-looking
berries. It has many uses in the Egyptian domestic pharmaco-
poeia, while the leaves, wilted and lightly sautéed, are said to
be a delicious substitute for the more frequent delicacy, turnip
greens. The medicinal potency of the pokeweed may be noted
below.

Cures

aching feet: carry a double cedar knot in your pocket or tie a
   salt mackerel on the sole of your foot.
boils: apply peach-tree leaf poultice.
catarrh: kiss the nostrils of a mule.
colitis: put a chicken in the pot, feathers and all, and give the
   tea drawn from it. A sure cure.
common cold: use camomile tea, sipped hot at bedtime, followed

up by quinine which has been wrapped or disguised in slippery
elm.

corns: spit on the corn and later you can pick it out.

> 1198   To remove a corn, rub it with spittle before you get up in the
> morning.
> 1199   If you have a corn on your toe, you can take it off by spitting
> on your finger and rubbing your finger over the corn. Do this
> for nine mornings before you speak to anyone.

croup: put a black silk string around the neck of the child.

> See No. 1258 and references. The object used in this cure can be a
> black silk cord (North Carolina), a black silk thread (Maryland),
> a homespun woolen thread (Pennsylvania German), or a string
> with three knots in it (Nebraska).

earache: a drop of buttermilk in the ear.

fever: split a black live chicken and put it on the patient's feet.

> No. 1415 is similar, and refers to the Ozark practice of burning
> feathers of black hens under the bed.

fever blisters: the next time you see a billygoat, grab some of
his whiskers and apply to the sore; it will vanish.

freckles: wash your face in the dew of the first day of May and
they will disappear.

> Nos. 1508–17 demonstrate how elaborate this belief has become.
> Some of the simpler variations are: wash your face in May Day
> dew and walk backward into the house; wash your face in dew for
> the first ten (nine) mornings in May.

gas: raise your right arm up and down three times; this will
cure the gas.

hives and shingles: any hot tea. Smear on the blood of a black
chicken.

> For the use of black cat's blood as a cure for shingles see No. 2096.
> The blood should be applied to the patient's breast (Indiana) or
> put on a lump of sugar and swallowed (southern Negro).

measles: gather sheep droppings ("sheeps' pills") and make a
tea of them. The measles will then come out.

> The note to No. 1809 indicates that this cure is widely known over
> the entire United States and in Ontario and Nova Scotia.

neuritis: thread a needle three times and tie it around your
neck at night; in the morning, the pain will be over.

nosebleed: tie a coin or piece of lead around your neck.

> "Wear a dime around your neck to stop the nosebleed" (No. 1906).
> Other cures involving coins are given in Nos. 1902–5.

pain in side: spit under a rock and the pain will go to the rock.

> In Nos. 2104–7 occur such variations as: spit on the rock three times; spit under a flint rock; spit under a rock and run away without looking back.

rabies: the stomach of every deer contains a "madstone" which will cure you if bitten by a mad dog.

rheumatism: carry a bull's eye (horse chestnut) in your pocket; let bees sting you; walk barefooted in the morning dew; carry an Irish potato in your pocket; cross your stockings before you go to bed, then get up at midnight and cross them the other way; carry the shank bone of a hog; soak pokeberries in whiskey and drink the concoction—sure cure!

> Carry a horse chestnut, Nos. 2001–2; let bees sting you, No. 1969; carry an Irish potato, Nos. 2017–23; soak pokeberries in whiskey, Nos. 2015–16.

scarlet fever: keep away from trees; the Indians told the people that scarlet fever was everywhere in trees.

skin blemishes: rub the skin with the afterbirth.

sore throat: wear a woolen sock, wrong side out, around the throat or put on a poultice of salt pork, or make a tea of wild cherry bark mixed with shag-bark (called "scaly bark" in Egypt). Tie a string around your neck at night.

> Nos. 2209–13 list sore throat cures which involve tying a stocking around the neck. No. 2211 specifies a stocking from the left foot, and No. 2213 prescribes that the heel of a wrong side out black stocking be tied over the Adam's apple.

stuttering: at hog killing time, take the melt (milt) and throw it on the child who stutters.

sty: repeat the following jingle:
> Sty, sty, leave my eye,
> Catch the first one that comes by.

T.B.: drink goat's milk.

teething: hang a mole's foot around the baby's neck on a black string; split child's gum with penknife; rub thimble over gums; make a necklace of elderbush joints.

> Some of these beliefs found in North Carolina are: mole's foot on a string, Nos. 361–64; thimble rubbed over gums, No. 375; necklace of elderbush joints, No. 376.

toothache: pick the aching tooth with a hickory splinter, then stick the splinter into a newly made grave.

No. 2337 simply says "To cure toothache, pick the tooth with a splinter," but mentions the widespread idea that it should be made from a tree struck by lightning.

thrush (thrash): in mouth, have a person who has never seen his father blow into the baby's mouth; in stomach, do the same in the rectum.

tisic [*sic*]: Measure the baby's height on a tree and make a hole at this point in the tree. Then cut off a lock of the baby's hair and put it in the hole. When the bark of the tree grows so as to cover the place, the baby will be well.

No. 328 gives a detailed description of this cure which dates from 1880 or earlier, and was widely used by people in Watauga County, N. C.

tonsilitis: have a horse blow in your mouth or wear an old dirty sock around your neck, the dirtier the better.

warts: take a string and tie a knot in it for every wart, then take the string to the crossroads and bury it; catch a katydid, put it on the wart and it will eat it off.

For examples see No. 2439 (knots tied in string) and p. 317, No. 2455 (katydid or a grasshopper).

whooping cough: let the patient crawl under a mule and the cough will go away.

Cutting the Fever

Informant Dr. Sherman Barnes of Carbondale. From Grace Partridge Smith, "Folklore from 'Egypt,'" Hoosier Folklore, *V (1946), 58.*

Motif D1206, "The magic ax," is cited by Smith. Cf. Popular Beliefs and Superstitions from North Carolina, *1–4783, edited by Wayland D. Hand, No. 45, p. 10, "Put an ax under the bed to cut the pain in two during childbirth," and No. 1463, p. 191, "Place steel under the bed for fever; it draws out the electricity from the body."*

A doctor was called to visit a patient back in the "sticks." He was a favorite with the hill-folk of Egypt since he never laughed at their customs or superstitions. When he arrived at the man's cabin, he found him in bed and burning up with fever. He turned down the bedcovers to examine the man's chest and there was an ax in bed with him.

"What's the ax for?" questioned the doctor, trying not to show his surprise.

The patient replied weakly, "It's to cut the fever."

Instead of throwing out the ax and scolding, all the doctor did was to reverse the position of the ax, saying as he did so, "But you've got it in the wrong way." Then he gave the patient some pills and left. The man got well.

6. FOLK BELIEFS

Weather Signs

From Grace Partridge Smith, "Folklore from 'Egypt,'" Hoosier Folklore, *V (1946), 61–62.*

I have annotated these weather beliefs with references to comparable ideas in Vance Randolph, Ozark Superstitions *(New York: Columbia University Press, 1947).*

Egyptians live, in a measure, by their weather lore. Since the community is essentially agricultural and, unfortunately, droughts are common, rain is often fervently wished for by farmers for the fruitful yield of crops. The townsman likewise scans the heavens—or the almanac—for propitious or unpropitious signs for his undertakings. The Egyptian agriculturist, like his parents and grandparents, plants and reaps by phases of the moon and by signs of the zodiac; with the same care he breeds his stock and poultry. Some of the weather signs which are found in Egypt are:

1.   Sun red at morning,
     Sailor's warning;
     Sun red at night,
     Sailor's delight.*

2.   Morning red and evening gray,
     Helps the traveler on his way.

---

* See *Ozark Superstitions,* pp. 14–15, for a discussion of the "red" sun at sunrise and at sunset.

Evening gray and morning red,
Brings down rain on the traveler's head.

3. Rainbow in the morning, a shepherd's warning:
Rainbow at night, a shepherd's delight.*

4. Blest be the bride the sun shines on;
Curst be the bride the rain falls on.

5. Between one and two,
We'll know what it's going to do.

6. A mottled sky means:
Never long wet and never long dry.

7. Thunder before seven, rain before eleven;
Rain before seven, stop before eleven.†

8. When mare's tails are seen in the sky, it is a sign of foul or falling weather.

9. If you kill a spider, it will rain.‡

10. If you kill a snake and hang it on the fence, it will rain.§

11. If a cock crows before three o'clock in the morning, it will rain or be bad weather for three days.||

12. If it rains on Monday, it will rain for three days that week.**

* *Ozark Superstitions,* p. 15, notes that a rainbow in the morning indicates a storm within twenty-four hours.
† *Ozark Superstitions,* p. 17, contains the second line of this verse.
‡ See *Ozark Superstitions,* p. 32, for the belief that if you kill a spider it *won't* rain for seven days. Randolph comments that some children will not kill spiders during a dry spell, but that this is generally a childish game believed by few children.
§ *Ozark Superstitions,* pp. 30–31, discusses methods used by Ozark hillmen to produce rain. One of these is to hang dead snakes belly-up on fences.
|| *Ozark Superstitions,* p. 12. A rooster's persistent crowing at nightfall means that rain will come before morning.
** For beliefs concerning rain on Monday see *Ozark Superstitions,* p. 18.

13. If a cat eats grass or the fire pops, it will rain or snow.

14. If the smoke floats west or if there is no dew, it will rain.

15. If the sun sets behind a bank on Sunday night, it will rain on Wednesday night.

16. If the sun sets behind a bank on Thursday night, it will rain the next day.*

17. Rain standing on the leaves of a tree is a sure sign that it isn't over.†

18. Stars in the moon's circle mean rain.‡

19. If a tame swan flies against the wind, it will rain.

20. If a pigeon washes itself, it will rain.

21. If a horse paws the ground or neighs, the weather will soon change.

22. If the weather clears during the night, it won't stay clear very long.

23. If a hen crows, there's going to be a flood.

24. For every fog in summer, so many snows in winter.§

25. If corn shucks are heavy, it's going to be a hard winter.‖

26. If the bark on the north side of a birch tree bursts in summer, the winter following will be bad.

---

* See *Ozark Superstitions*, p. 19, for the belief that if the sun "sets cloudy" on Thursday, heavy rain will come before Saturday night.
† For another instance of this belief, see *Ozark Superstitions*, p. 17.
‡ People in the Ozarks believe that you can tell how many days will elapse before a storm by counting the stars in the moon's circle. See *Ozark Superstitions*, p. 15.
§ Ozark hillfolk say that the number of fogs in August is equal to the number of snows the following winter. See *Ozark Superstitions*, p. 23.
‖ *Ozark Superstitions*, pp. 25–26.

27. On whatever day of the month the first snow falls, there will be so many snows that winter.*

28. If animals have heavy pelts, 'tis the sign of a hard winter.†

29. If smoke floats to the south, there will be snow.

30. If it thunders a certain day in December, it will frost the same day in May.

31. If a turtle snaps at you, it won't turn loose until it thunders.

32. Lightning does not strike twice in the same place.

33. Lightning in south, sign of drought.‡

Beliefs Connected with Birth and Infancy

> *From Lelah Allison, "Folk Beliefs Collected in Southeastern Illinois,"* Journal of American Folklore, *LXIII (1950), 321. The complete article is on pp. 309–24. I have annotated entries that correspond to items in* Popular Beliefs and Superstitions from North Carolina, 1–4783, *edited by Wayland D. Hand (The Frank C. Brown Collection of North Carolina Folklore, VI; Durham, N.C.: Duke University Press, 1961).*

Folk beliefs are found in all regions. This collection was made in the Wabash region in southeastern Illinois, but some of these

* Related beliefs from the Ozarks are: the number of days the first snow stays on the ground equals the number of snows during the winter. Or, multiply the number of the day that the first snow falls on times the number of the month, and double this figure if it is under fifteen; then you will know how many snows will fall during the winter. See *Ozark Superstitions,* pp. 23–24.

† The Ozark hillman expects a hard winter if the hair on muskrats, skunks, coons, and possums is unusually thick. See *Ozark Superstitions,* pp. 25–26.

‡ *Ozark Superstitions,* p. 15, states that lightning in the south is a dry-weather sign, but in any other direction is a rain sign.

beliefs are widespread over the country. Although southeastern Illinois has some folk beliefs that belong to that region alone, today's fast and easy methods of travel do spread folkways farther and more rapidly than was possible in the old days.

Most of the pioneers of southeastern Illinois came from England, or from the southern states, which were settled by the English, and so many folkways can be traced to that mother country. Some of the beliefs, however, have grown out of the condition under which the early people lived, such as weather conditions, which vary greatly in southern Illinois. People of thinly settled territories, where there were few doctors, necessarily sought cures when illness came. Poor transportation meant little intercourse, and so the individual was left to his own resources to solve the unusual happenings in his life.

These beliefs and practices are numerous and cover all phases of life, because they are a part of the life of an early people: household, weddings, relatives, animals, birds, religion, lucky and unlucky days, personal appearance, weather, cures, wishes, plants, and dreams. They have been passed on by word of mouth from generation to generation.

Birth and Infancy

1.   A baby speaks with angels when it smiles.*

2.   You make a baby stammer by tickling its feet.†

3.   If a pregnant woman is frightened, her baby will bear a birthmark of the object that frightened the mother.‡

4.   If a pregnant woman is hungry and does not eat the food

---

* No. 262. This belief has been recorded in six southern states, six midwestern states, and in New Mexico, Washington, and Ontario. In the Ozarks, the sleeping child's smile is regarded as a bad omen.

† No. 343. Some variations of this belief are: tickling the sole of the feet (South Carolina and Iowa); tickling the feet before the child is a year old (Pennsylvania German and Illinois); and tickling under the chin (Ozarks).

‡ Nos. 97–99, 101, 104, 108, 112–13 concern women who were frightened in pregnancy and whose children had corresponding birthmarks. Some of the frightening objects were a bear, a police dog, a dead hog being eaten by a buzzard, and a snake.

that she wants, her baby will have a birthmark of that food.*

5. Baby will cry for food its mother wanted before its birth; give it that food, and it will stop crying.†

6. An ugly baby makes a pretty adult.‡

7. It is bad luck to name a first child after its parents.

8. It is bad luck to cut a child's fingernails before it is a year old.§

9. A baby will die if you let it look in a mirror before it is a year old.||

10. A child has worms if it picks its nose.

11. You should not cut a baby's hair before it is a year old.**

12. A baby will be a prophet if it is born with a veil over its face.††

* Nos. 86–96. Some state that the child will never be able to eat the desired food (No. 86, German) and that the birthmark may be removed by rubbing it with the object it resembles (No. 87).

† No. 199 gives references to two German parallels from Pennsylvania and another from Illinois.

‡ No. 163 adds that a pretty baby makes an ugly grown person, and cites the German notion that "pretty cradle babies become ugly street gamins."

§ No. 252. The child will not live (No. 253) or you will not be able to raise him (No. 254). You should bite the nails instead. Nos. 232–34 indicate that the child will become a thief if his nails are cut too early.

|| No. 255. The references cited state that some misfortune will befall the child or he will be sickly. For the belief in death caused by a child looking into a mirror, see Nos. 4892 ff. Nos. 228–29 aver that the child will become a robber.

** No. 250. Most references cited in the notes specify bad luck if the child's hair is cut before its first birthday. However in one case it is good luck to trim a child's hair on Friday when the moon is growing (Illinois).

‡‡ Nos. 244–45. The special powers which may come to a person born with a caul over his face are varied. For instance, the person may see spirits (Georgia), see the dead (Louisiana), have the gift of healing (Illinois), be a genius (Oregon), be insured against drowning (Maryland, Illinois, and Oregon), or be an eloquent lawyer.

13.   Shorten a baby's dress in May and shorten its life away.

14.   A baby will die if you put its dress on over its head before it is a year old.

15.   A baby born after its father's death has occult power.*

16.   It is bad luck to change a baby's name.

Beliefs Connected with Dreams

From Lelah Allison, "Folk Beliefs Collected in Southeastern Illinois," Journal of American Folklore, LXIII (1950), 322. I have annotated entries that correspond to items in Popular Beliefs and Superstitions from North Carolina, 1–4783, edited by Wayland D. Hand.

1.   Dream of a funeral and attend a wedding.

2.   It is bad luck to tell a dream before breakfast.†

3.   It is bad luck to dream of muddy water.‡

4.   You will have enemies if you dream of snakes.

5.   It is bad luck to dream of black horses.

6.   Count seven stars for seven nights, and you will dream of the man you will marry.§

---

* No. 414 says that a child born after the death of its father can cure thrush, and No. 1963 states that he can cure rash.
† No. 3135 cites references to the same belief in Illinois, California, England, and Germany.
‡ No. 3108. Related beliefs hold that to dream of muddy water is an omen of sorrow (3109) or a sign of disappointment (3110).
§ No. 4462. Cf. No. 4464: if you count seven stars for seven nights and eat a thimbleful of salt before going to bed you will dream of your future husband giving you water.

7. It is good luck to dream of clear water.*

8. To dream of the man you will marry, take a thumbful of salt the night before Easter.

9. It is good to dream of bananas.

10. Marry soon if you dream of a corpse.

11. If you dream of a cellar, you will have an inheritance.

12. You will be successful if you dream of being dead.

13. Dream of tears is consolation.

14. You will have good news if you dream of letter writing.

15. You will have unexpected joy if you dream of sorrow.

16. You will make true friends if you dream of ivy.

17. Dream of letters and receive good news.

18. If you have a snake dream, an enemy is plotting against you.

* No. 3107 gives references for six states, New England and New Brunswick.

7. FOLKTALES

Tales from Ireland

"How Death Came to Ireland"

> *"Told by the late Frank Schumaker, Grand Tower, who learned it at either first- or second-hand from an Irish immigrant who had settled in that town and worked at the iron foundry that used to be there."* Text from Tales and Songs of Southern Illinois, *collected by Charles Neely (Menasha, Wisconsin: George Banta Publishing Company, 1938), pp. 121–23.*
>
> *This curious narrative is a Märchen or fairy tale in modern colloquial idiom. Some of the best known motifs in fairy tales appear, such as D361.1, "Swan Maiden," D1521.1, "Seven-league boots," K1335, "Seduction (or wooing) by stealing clothes of bathing girl (swan maiden)," H324, "Suitor test: choosing princess from others identically clad," and C321, "Pandora's box." The storyteller has localized this tale and given it an Irish-American twist ending.*

An Irishman told this story about a king of France. He said the King of France he wanted to get married, but he couldn't find no one that suited him. So he went travelin' through the country huntin' a wife. He come to a wilderness where an old hermit monk lived. The king he stayed there awhile with the old monk, and they'd go huntin'. One day they was out a-huntin' and they saw three white swans. The king he wanted to kill them, but the old monk he said: "No, don't kill them." The king asked him why, and the old monk he said: "They ain't swans. They're the girls who come to the lake every day to swim." The old monk had lived a thousand years, and he knew all about them things.

The king he wanted to catch the three girls. But the old man said that the only way they could catch them was to git their clothes, and that would be hard to do, for the three women swam so fast that he couldn't git the clothes. But the king kept on insistin' about catchin' the three girls; so the old monk give him a pair of ten-mile boots to put on. The king he put on the ten-mile boots and slipped up the bank of the lake and stole the three girl's clothes before they knowed it.

Then the girls swam to the shore where they saw what the king had done, and they begged for their clothes. But the king wouldn't give them back without they'd take him along with them. The three women they agreed to. The oldest girl took the king first, and she flew away with him, and her sisters followed. She carried the king a long way till she came to a mountain, and then she dropped him. The second sister she caught him and carried him across the mountain and on a long way till she got tired; then she dropped him. The youngest sister she caught the king and carried him the rest of the way. She was the one the king was goin' to marry.

When they got to the home of the three sisters though, the king he couldn't tell them apart, but the youngest she give him a sign. She held her knees close together, and the other two they held their knees apart. And they were married and lived very happy. But the king wanted to go back to France. His wife told him that he couldn't, for he'd die if he did. He kept on insistin' on goin' back. His wife she fixed up a flying-ship to take him back, but she told him that he'd die if he got out. The king promised not to git out of the ship, but come right straight back.

When the king got to France, he forgot all about what he'd promised his wife. He stepped out on the ground and Death was right there, and he nabbed him.

"Don't take me, Death," the king said. "Take those old men around here, I'm young."

"I want you," said Death holdin' on tight to the king.

FOLKTALES 343

The king saw that Death was goin' to take him anyhow; so he said all right he'd go if Death would get in that box he had along also. Death got into the box, and the king slammed the lid shut and fastened it tight, so he couldn't git out. Then the king got in his machine and flew back to his wife.

When the king got back to his wife, he told her what had happened, and he started to open the box Death was in. His wife stopped him and said: "Don't open the box here. If you do, we'll all die."

They didn't know what to do with Death, but a big storm come up over the ocean, and they took the box with Death in it and dropped it into the ocean. The box floated a long time in the ocean until it came to Ireland, and was washed on shore. Men got the box up on the shore and began to wonder what was in it. Two big Irishmen got sledge-hammers and broke the box open. Death flew out and killed every man of them. And he started to killin' people all over Ireland. That was why the Irishmen left Ireland and come to America.

"The Village Fool"

"The two numskull stories below were brought to Illinois straight from County Downs, Ireland, by immigrants in 1840. They settled in and around Chester, where they built up an Irish community. Informant: Miss Lulu Kelly, Carbondale, who heard the stories from her Scotch-Irish father when a child. An example of Type 1696, Motif J2461, What Should I Have Said?" From Grace ·Partridge Smith, "Folklore from 'Egypt,' " Hoosier Folklore, V (1946), 52–53.

A full discussion of British and American variants is given by Herbert Halpert in a note to the Ozark text of Vance Randolph, The Devil's Pretty Daughter (New York, 1955), pp. 72–73. Baughman cites texts from Virginia, North Carolina, Louisiana, Kentucky, Illinois, and Missouri.

Jack was sent to the store to buy liver, lights, and hearts. He kept saying over to himself on the way, "Liver and lights, and heart," so he wouldn't forget what he was to buy. Pretty soon he came to a man who was drunk and sick at the side of the road. Jack was still saying aloud, "Liver and lights and all." The man heard him and said, "Don't say that!" Jack stopped and said, "What shall I say then?" And the man answered, "Say 'Some come up; hope that never more come up.' "

So Jack went along saying this and pretty soon he came to where a farmer was sowing grain. The farmer heard Jack saying as he passed, "Some come up; hope never more come up." Then the farmer called, "Don't say that!" and again Jack asked, "What shall I say then?" "Say 'I hope they come up by thousands.' " Well, Jack went along saying this and pretty soon he met a funeral and the undertaker, hearing him, said, "Don't say that; say, 'God rest all poor souls!' "

So Jack went along saying "God rest all poor souls!" After a while some men came along, leading a dog to be hung. When they heard Jack saying, "God rest all poor souls!" they called to him, "Don't say that! Say 'I'm leading a bitch to be hanged!' " Lastly Jack met a wedding party on their way to church. When they heard him say, "I'm leading a bitch to be hanged," they chased him and gave him a thrashing and when he got home he got another.

"Jack and the Sheep's Head"

> *"Informant: Miss Lulu Kelly. The incident of the sheep's head appears in Joel Chandler Harris, Told By Uncle Remus (New York, 1905), in the story, 'The Hard Headed Woman,' p. 287." Note and text from Grace Partridge Smith, "Folklore from 'Egypt,' " Hoosier Folklore, V (1946), 53–54.*
>
> *Two texts, with references to other examples in England and North America, are in Dorson, Negro Tales from Pine Bluff, Arkansas, and Calvin, Michigan, pp. 56–57, "Hoghead and Peas" and "Sheephead and Dumplings." Baughman assigns Motif J1813.8 * to the story.*

Jack was left at home to mind the house while the rest of the family went to church. He was to tend the fire and watch the pot in which a sheep's head with dumplings was boiling. All went well for a time, but after a while the pot began to bubble and to boil over. Jack didn't know what to do. Finally, he ran to church, motioned to his mother from the door and beckoned to her to come outside. All she did was to shake her head. Jack kept on with his motions, but the mother paid no attention.

At last Jack called, "Now, none of your winkin' and blinkin'. The sheep's head is butting all the dumplings out of the pot!"

"When Death Comes"

Informant: Mrs. Cordelia Kelley, of Carbondale. Text from Grace Partridge Smith, "Folklore from 'Egypt,'" Journal of American Folklore, LIV (1941), 57.

Baughman proposes Motif J217.0.1.1, "Trickster overhears man praying for death to take him." The theme is popular in southern Negro tradition; see the similar text in Dorson, Negro Folktales in Michigan, "Efan Prays," p. 61, and note 31, p. 212.

A man and a woman, husband and wife were both sick abed. He said he wasn't ready to die; she said she wasn't ready to die neither. Both of them were afraid they were going to die.

A wag of a feller in the neighborhood came and sat up with the old couple. The old man was worse sick than the old woman. The wag said to the wife, "I hope he'll get better," and she said, "If he dies, I don't know what I'll do. I hope I'll die first."

After this, the wag went away and he got a rooster and picked its feathers all off. Then he tied a string to its leg and he put it in through the window onto the table by the old woman. Then he mumbled in a hoarse, groaning voice, "O-o-o-h, O-o-o-h, I'm after you, I'm after you!" The old woman was terribly frightened, and when she heard this a second time, she said, "There he is, right over there in the bed." But the voice insisted, "I've come after *you*, I've come after *you*." And the old wife said again, "There he is, right over there in the bed in the corner. Git *him!*"

By this time, the wag had pulled the rooster back again out the window and the woman said to her husband, "John, he's gone!" He answered, "I thought you wanted to die first." "Yes," hesitated his wife, "but when Death comes, *that* is different!"

Lies

What the folklorist calls "tall tales," the folk are apt to call "lies," "windies," "whoppers," or "gallyfloppers." In We Always Lie to Strangers (*New York, 1951*), *Vance Randolph synopsizes Ozark tall tales.*

Lowell Thomas prints texts, and lists the localities of variants sent him in response to his radio broadcasts, in Tall Stories (*New York and London, 1931*).

"The Cold Snap of '83 in Thebes"

"Informant: Wendell Margrave, of Thebes. The story [as he heard it] was told by Jim Harbell, a seventy-five-year-old farmer in the vicinity. Variations of this amusing tale are scattered about Southern Illinois." Text from Grace Partridge Smith, "Folklore from 'Egypt,'" Journal of American Folklore, *LIV (1941), 50.*

This is Type 1896, The Man Nails the Tail of the Wolf to the Tree and Beats Him, *and Motif X1132, "Animal whipped out of skin." A Finnish-American text from Michigan is in Dorson,* Bloodstoppers and Bearwalkers, *p. 144.*

Motif X1606.2, "Lies about quick change in weather from warm to cold," is also present.

Every time the boys in the grocery store complained about the cold, he—Jim Harbell—would say, "It's not a patch on the cold snap of 'eighty-three.'" And then he would tell his story, as follows:

"I was out a-cradlin' wheat in the North Forty (I was a mighty good hand to cradle when I was a young feller), an' I heard Clint Henderson's dogs mouthin' in the holler. An' I thinks to myself, sez I, 'Clint's dogs has got up a deer.' An' sure enough, before long, the deer came runnin' across the wheat field an' I drapt an' ran over to the fence where I left my gun, an' I picked it up, an' I drawed a bead on that there deer, but I didn't shoot, for I thinks to myself, sez I, 'it's been a long spell since I run down a deer!' (I was a mighty fast runner in those days when I was a young feller.)

"Before long, I'd got ahead of all the dogs, an' I was gainin' on that there deer at every jump. It jumped the fence an' so did I. I finally came up to him just as he was wadin' into Miller's Creek to throw the dogs off the scent. An' just then, *the cold snap struck!* It got so cold and so fast that that there deer's feet froze fast in the ice. Three times I drawed a bead on that there deer's heart an' three times I put my gun down, for, thinks I to myself, sez I, 'If I shoot that there deer out in that there ice, I'll have to chop him out of the ice, an' skin him, an' pack him home.' (I was a right lazy feller in them days when I was a young feller.) So I thought quite a spell and finally I got an īdy [idea]. So I went over in the brush an' cut a long hickory switch, an' I got out on that there ice with that there deer an' whipped him until it scared him so bad he jumped plumb *out of his skin,* an' then I shot him."

"Davy Crockett and Old Bounce"

"Informant: Mrs. W. F. Lamb, Cairo. Stories attached to Crockett are still told by persons on the Illinois-Kentucky border." Text from Grace Partridge Smith, "Folklore from 'Egypt,'" Hoosier Folklore, V (1946), 55.

Motif X1215.11, "Lie: the split dog." See the examples in Dorson, American Folklore, pp. 44, 81, 108, 229.

Davy used to hunt with hounds. One day the dogs got to running hard and fast through a thicket of saplings. Old Bounce was with the dogs. He ran so fast that he split hisself wide open on a sapling. What did Davy do then? Well, sir, he stopped just long enough to pick up the two pieces and slap them together. This worked just fine except that he got one half of Old Bounce one way and the other half just opposite. He was in a desperate hurry not to let the other dogs get too far ahead. So Old Bounce went on this-a-way: When his one half got too tired running, he just flopped over and the other half began running.

"The Cat with the Wooden Paw"

> "Told by Mr. Wendell Margrave, Carbondale. The story is one that Mr. Margrave learned from his father, whose home was at Thebes, Illinois. It is a well-known story in that neighborhood." Text from Neely, pp. 48–49.
>
> Type 1912 and Motif X1211.1, Crippled Cat Uses Wooden Leg to Kill Mice, reported only for the United States.

Jack Storme was the local cooper and blacksmith of Thebes. He had a cat that stayed around his shop. The cat was the best mouser in the whole country, Jack said. He kept the shop free of rats and mice. But one day the cat got a forepaw cut off. After that he began to grow poor and thin and didn't take any interest in anything because he wasn't getting enough to eat.

So one day Jack decided to fix him up a wooden paw. He whittled one out with his knife and strapped it on the maimed leg. After that the cat began to grow sleek and fat again. Jack decided to stay at the shop one night to see how the cat managed it with his wooden paw.

After dark the cat got down in front of a mouse-hole and waited. Pretty soon a mouse peered out cautiously. Quick as a flash the cat seized it with his good paw and knocked it on the head with his wooden one. In no time that cat had eighteen mice piled up before the hole.

"Beating the Storm"

> *"Informant: Mrs. Ray Lybarger, of Carbondale. The story with variations is common in the vicinity. For a version from Carterville, a town near Carbondale in the Crab Orchard Lake district, see Neely, p. 48." Text from Grace Partridge Smith, "Egyptian 'Lies,'" Midwest Folklore, I (1951), 94.*
> *Motif X1796, "Lies concerning speed."*

My grandpap told me about a man in his settlement who had the fastest team of buggy-mares in the district. He said one day as they were coming home from the County Fair there came up an awful rain storm. "It sure came a gully-washer," said the farmer and went on: "My team started for home as fast as they could go and when they reached the barn, the two young shoats I had in the back of the buggy in a crate were drowned, but d'ye know, that team never got wet."

"The Gregarious Turtle"

> *Informant: Carl Blood, of Carbondale, who heard the story from a bus driver in Williamson County. Text from Grace Partridge Smith, "Egyptian 'Lies,'" Midwest Folklore, I (1951), 96. Smith refers to variants in Hoosier Folklore Bulletin, I (1942), 16, and Lowell Thomas, Tall Stories, pp. 66–68.*
> *A lengthy text, "Grant's Tame Trout," is reprinted from a 1904 Maine pamphlet in Dorson, Jonathan Draws the Long Bow, pp. 120–21.*

A cat adopted a turtle and raised it. The turtle tried to arch its back, hiss, and spit like its foster-mother. It even tried to climb a tree when it saw the cat run up a tree to escape a barking dog. One time there was a flood, and the back yard where the cat and the turtle lived was full of water. So the cat climbed a tree and was safely out of danger. The turtle did its level best to follow but could not make it. Unhappily, it had just started up the trunk when it fell back into the water and was drowned.

"The Power of Rich Soil"

> *Informant: Mrs. Ray Lybarger, of Carbondale, who heard the story from her mother in Makanda. Text from Grace Partridge Smith, "Egyptian 'Lies'," Midwest Folklore, I (1961), 93–94.*
>
> *Baughman gives numerous United States references for Motif X1532, "Rich soil produces remarkable crop." Cf. Motif X1532.1, "Rich land: corn grows so fast that it pulls up its own roots."*

Two old-timers were arguing about whose soil was the richer. After several exchanges, one old codger said, "Why, one day a man was crossin' my back forty and he dropped some seed corn as he was walkin' along. That there ground was so rich that the corn sprung right up and the man was caught by the seat of his pants on an ear of corn. Yes sir! And what could we do! We had to shoot him sour-milk biscuit in a scatter-gun to keep the poor critter from starvin' to death."

"Cornfields in Arkansas"

> *"Informant: elderly mother of a Jackson County resident whose family stories often include unflattering references to 'Arkansaw' of old-time jokes." Text from Grace Partridge Smith, "Egyptian 'Lies'," Midwest Folklore, I (1951), 95.*
>
> *Motif X1523.2, "Lies about farming on steep mountain"; and see Vance Randolph, We Always Lie to Strangers: Tall Tales from the Ozarks (New York: Columbia University Press, 1951), pp. 14–40.*

A man was running for the State Legislature in Arkansas. One day he was going down a rough road when he saw a cloud of dust at the foot of a very steep hill. When he got to the bottom

of the hill, he found an old man picking himself up out of the
dirt and busily pounding the dust from his clothes.

"What's the matter, Grandpappy?" asked the politician.
No answer. The old man kept on pounding his still dusty
coat and pants. After awhile he spat and said, "W-a-a-l, it's
like this—I just fell out of that there gol-danged corn field up
on that there hill."

Anecdotes

> *Anecdotes are told as supposedly actual incidents at-*
> *tached to local characters or celebrated personalities.*
> *Jests are the unattached fictions of oral humor. The*
> *same plots are continually crossing back and forth be-*
> *tween the status of anecdotes and of jests or jokes.*
> *When the jest is made specific, by hooking onto to a*
> *named individual in a named locality, it becomes an his-*
> *torical happening. Where the actors are neutrally de-*
> *scribed as "a man" or "a clerk," the story wavers be-*
> *tween firm anecdote and floating joke.*

"You Haven't Packed the Saddle"

> *Professor David S. McIntosh of Southern Illinois Uni-*
> *versity has told how he obtained this text. "I heard*
> *Miss Una Keeling tell this story at the last meeting of*
> *my extension course, Music 307, at Pinckneyville, Illi-*
> *nois, on January 16, 1947. I asked her to write it out*
> *and send it to me. In her letter, she says: 'It is an old*
> *story my mother tells, told to her by her mother. As to*
> *its origin I haven't the slightest idea of where, when or*
> *how. The last phrase* you haven't packed the saddle *is*
> *an expression which has been used in our family for*
> *many years to calm the younger folk when we got to*
> *expressing ourselves too forcefully as to what we would*
> *or wouldn't do.'"*
>
> *Stith Thompson points out the resemblance of an*
> *orally told yarn to Shakespeare's* Taming of the Shrew.
> *"The tale," writes Thompson* (The Folktale, *New York,*

*1946, p. 105), "goes back to the Exemplum literature
of the Middle Ages, where it appears in Juan Manuel's
El Conde Lucaner. It was also retold by Straparola in
the sixteenth century. Whether from these literary
forms or otherwise, it is popular in the folklore of the
Baltic states and Scandinavia. It has also been reported from Scotland, Ireland, Spain, and Russia, and
has been heard from a Zuni Indian in New Mexico."
This folktale, Type 901, has since formed the subject
for a doctoral dissertation in folklore at Indiana University, "The Taming of the Shrew" (1961), by Jan H.
Brunvand. Dr. Brunvand supplies the following information on American texts. He has accumulated thirty-
one variants in English in the United States, of which
twelve are in the Indiana University Folklore Archives,
twelve in his private collection, and seven are printed.
Besides the text below, which Brunvand considers the
most complete American version, and the one closest to
a Scandinavian original, others in print are in Richard
Chase, American Folk Tales and Songs (New York,
1956), pp. 226–27; Vance Randolph, Sticks in the
Knapsack (New York, 1958), pp. 71–73; Max Rezwin,
ed., Sick Jokes, Grim Cartoons and Bloody Marys (New
York, 1958), p. 14; J. H. Brunvand, "Folktales by
Mail from Bond, Kentucky," Kentucky Folklore Record, VI (1960), 70–71. American versions are distinguished by the expression "That's once" or the like, and
by a simplified anecdotal form.
Text communicated to Illinois Folklore, I, No. 1 (Oct.
1947), 17–19, by David S. McIntosh.*

"Experience is the Best Teacher" you have heard, and the
young girl of our story finds out the truth of the matter.

Many years ago 'most every home was the center of a
large, happy family. In this one particular family there were
several grown daughters. First one, then another married and
went away to establish a home of her own until only the youngest was left.

Then one day a young man from a neighboring community
came to the father asking for her hand in marriage. The father
readily gave his consent but warned the young man that this

girl, being the youngest, had grown up to be impetuous, head-strong and hard to manage. However, the young man was un-daunted by this warning and plans were made for the wedding.

Most people, in those early days, traveled either on foot or on horseback. So when the wedding day arrived the young man came for his bride on horseback, bringing along his faith-ful dog and his gun in the hope of bagging some game on the return trip through the woods.

Late in the afternoon, after the wedding festivities were over, the young man and his bride set out for their home. They had not gone far on their journey until the old dog treed some-thing. The young man stopped, cocked his gun and waited . . . but the old dog was mistaken and there was nothing at all. "That's the first time," he said. On they rode a little farther and again the old dog treed. Again the young man got ready to fire, but this, too, proved to be a false alarm. "That's the sec-ond time," said he. After crossing a ravine the performance was repeated and the young man cried in vexation, "Now that's the third time you've fooled me, and you'll not do it again." With that, he pulled the trigger on his poor dog.

By this time the sun was getting low and the path through the forest was becoming dim, so the horse stumbled. Up spoke the young man, "That's your first time," and on they went. Down the road a ways a small branch had fallen from a tree, over which the old horse again stumbled. "That's the second time." On they went a mile or so till they came to a place where there was much loose rock and shale on the road. There again the old horse stumbled. "Now that's the third time," cried the young man. "I'll teach you to be always falling down with me. This time you'll not get up." So he lifted his gun and shot the old horse.

Now they would have to walk the rest of the way home. Besides, there was the saddle. "Wife," said the young man, "pick up the saddle and tote it home." (But this wife was stormy and headstrong!)

"I'll not do it, sir," said she.

"That's the first time," said he. "I said for you to pick up the saddle and pack it home."

"But I'll not do it, sir," she repeated.

"Now that's the second time," said he. "I say, pick up that saddle and pack it home!"

She remembered the dog, she remembered the horse, and without another word she picked up the saddle and carried it home.

Sometime later all of the sisters with their husbands and families met together at their father's home for a reunion. Of course, the sisters had a great many things to tell and talk over, now that each had her own home and they were not able to see one another very often, so that the day slipped by all too quickly. Before they had half finished talking, our young man came in and announced to his wife that it was time to start home. "Whenever you say," said the wife.

Her sisters, remembering how wilful she had always been, forthwith began to object, saying, "Oh, don't go yet! Tell him you're not ready. I'd sure not go till I got good and ready!"

"Yes," she smiled calmly, "*you* might, but *you* haven't packed the saddle." *

Substituting for the Off Ox
By JESSE W. HARRIS

> *A popular form of American anecdote is the story of eccentric behavior credited to a notorious town character. Many such alleged events turn out to be migratory legends. The following anecdotal legend discussed by Professor Harris has been known in Illinois since 1883, and is current in other states. A Maine variant is in Robert E. Gould,* Yankee Storekeeper *(New York and London: Whittlesey House, 1946), pp. 138–39.*
>
> *From the* Journal of American Folklore, *LX (1947), 298–99.*

* Professor McIntosh, who first heard the above tale recited orally, noted some variations in the style of the oral and the written versions. The written "impetuous, headstrong and hard to manage" was "headstrong and kinda tempery" in the oral recital. "Besides, there was the saddle" was "He happened to look at the saddle and thought it was too good a saddle to leave." The written " 'I'll not do it, sir,' she said," was the less formal "I'll not do it." Other variations of this kind indicated that in its oral form the tale was somewhat less formal in tone than in the written text.

The incongruous situation created by the substitution of a man for one of the members of an ox team formed the basis of a type of oral humorous yarn during the pioneer age. Three stories of this type that I have found in southern Illinois belong to the tradition of oral humor, although two of them have been recorded in county histories dating back to the early 1880's. The third story of the group is rooted in the oral tradition of the Possum Trot area in western Saline County where it was still part of the local store of yarns as recently as the early 1900's, a period close enough to the ox-team age to enable local people to appreciate the humor of the story. Like most other pioneer yarns, this one is no longer on the active list. Recent inquiry, however, has revealed that the story is still remembered by local residents.

With the exception of locality, names of characters, and a few minor details, the three southern Illinois versions of the story are identical. As recorded in *The History of Effingham County* (Chicago, 1883), the story runs as follows:

John I. Brockett vows and declares that when he was a good sized lout of a boy, their extremity in the line of bull calves was so great that he conceived the happy expedient of yoking himself up with the only one his family possessed. The idea was no sooner conceived than it was executed, with a younger brother to drive. But John made such a sorry-looking calf that his mate refused to pull, and wheeled his rump around and turned the yoke, and thus they stood with their heads in opposite directions. . . . John had heard of tying oxen's tails together to keep them from turning the yoke. So he got a cob and gathered it up in the seat of his leather breeches, and tied the rope fast below the knot formed by the cob, and this was securely tied to the calf's tail, and the difficulty was overcome and the team rehitched to the "lizzard." The calf again tried to thrust himself around and turn the yoke. He pulled till John's suspenders "popped," and his leather breeches stretched out until they were as long and slim as the calf's tail, when John ordered his brother to give them the gad. The bull calf looked at John, its mate, and bellowed and plunged and pulled its tail nearly off, and finally, in agony and fright, it ran off at full speed, John doing his best to keep up, and check the calf, and keep his neck from being broken. Over the brush, the briars, logs and everything pell-mell, the frightened calf bellowing, and now worse frightened John roaring at his mother, as the runaways approached the house. "Here we come, d——n our fool souls! stop us! we're running away."

A Jefferson County version of the story makes one Buck Casey the central character. This version is preserved in Perrin's *History of Jefferson County* (Chicago, 1883), and, at that date, was already earmarked as a traditional yarn. Buck was the son of a "settler," and he yoked himself with the only bull calf "the family possessed, for the purpose of hauling wood from the adjacent forest." Buck's younger brother Abram did the driving, and, as the runaways approached the house, Buck yelled: "Here we come, head us off, pop, damn our fool souls, we are running away." The hero of the Saline County oral version of this story was also called Buck; he was identified as the son of a family that occupied a local log house which was still standing in the first years of the present century. This version of the story corresponds in every way with those above except a slight variation in what Buck yelled as he and his mate came plunging past the home cabin. He said, "Stop us, dod dammit; we're runnin' away."

How widely dispersed this story was in the earlier period of our history is now difficult to determine. The three versions mentioned above happen to be spaced over a territory ranging something more than a hundred miles from north to south. The fact that two of them made local histories in the same year (1883) probably indicates that they were rather well known local stories at that date. About a dozen years ago I heard a story of this type told by a native in east Tennessee. Since there were still a few ox teams about, the story had retained, perhaps, an element of authenticity there that it had lost in other places. In this version of the story, a man named Buck had substituted himself for an ox that had balked, and his wife, who was doing the driving, interpreted his order to give them the gad literally by applying the whip to the back of Buck himself. Thereupon, the exasperated husband is said to have yelled: "Dod dammit, don't hit me, hit him; I'll pull."

The Draper and the Bible

> "Informant: Mrs. Lollar, Carbondale. An almost word-for-word analogue was recently sent to the writer by Mrs. Elva Kimball Walker, from Mascoma, N.H." Text from Grace Partridge Smith, "Folklore from 'Egypt,'" Hoosier Folklore, V (1946), 57.
>
> Motifs J1115.7, "Clever merchant," and J1262, "Levity regarding Biblical passages."

A man kept a general store. His clerk was told that he must be on the "up and up" in everything. One morning, a woman came into the store and wanted to purchase some cloth. The clerk brought out the material asked for and priced it at $1.50 a yard. The customer said it wouldn't do. So she began to look around at other goods displayed on the counter. While she was looking, the clerk busied himself at the shelves, apparently looking for something to suit. After a while, he took up the *same* piece he had showed her at first, spread it out and commented, "Cheap at $7.00 a yard!" The woman took the goods, now satisfied.

Later the clerk told the owner of the store about his little ruse. "How in the world can you justify such a sale?" said he. "You know you were to make no sale that you could not square by the Bible." The clerk replied, "She was a stranger, and I *took her in!*"

Too Busy to Lie

> "Informant: Miss Tina Goodwin, Carbondale. Text from Grace Partridge Smith, "Folklore from 'Egypt,'" Hoosier Folklore, V (1946), 54.
>
> Type 1920B, Motif X905.4, The liar: "I have no time to lie today"; lies nevertheless. See Dorson, American

> Folklore, *pp. 132, 229, for examples, and above, p. 68,*
> *for a Maine text.*

Some men were going by our house, one of them noted as a storyteller. My mother called out to him "John, come in and tell us a story." "No," answered John as he hurried along, "I haven't got time. My wife is sick and I'm on my way to the doctor's house. I'd rather lose my best cow than lose her . . ." and he was gone.

Later they found out his wife was hale and hearty.

8. FOLK SPEECH

SELECTED AND EDITED from the article by Lelah Allison, "Folk Speech from Southeastern Illinois," *Hoosier Folklore,* V (1946), 93–102.

I have annotated parallel phrases and expressions found in *The Frank C. Brown Collection of North Carolina Folklore,* I, "Proverbs and Proverbial Sayings," edited by B. J. Whiting, pp. 329–501 (Durham, N.C.: Duke University Press, 1952); Archer Taylor and B. J. Whiting, *A Dictionary of American Proverbs and Proverbial Phrases, 1820–1880* (Cambridge, Mass.: Belknap Press of Harvard University Press, 1958); and Vance Randolph and George P. Wilson, *Down in the Holler, A Gallery of Ozark Folk Speech* (Norman, Okla.: University of Oklahoma Press, 1953).

Folk Sayings and Expressions From Southeastern Illinois

By LELAH ALLISON

> *The following idiomatic speech, proverbs, proverbial phrases, and sayings are a collection by the writer, written in the interest of folklore of three counties—her home region—in southeastern Illinois: Wayne, Edwards, and Wabash. Knowing them the author wishes to make it clear that the people, though of the rural districts and small towns, certainly cannot be classed as ignorant because they use their own folk expressions in preference to standard speech. The wide variety of this folk speech shows the tenacity of its hold upon the*

people, many of whom are university graduates who slip into the vernacular, especially when living in their home region.

"Weather"

Even the safest of all topics, the weather, has its expressions. If it rains very hard, "It's rainin' nigger babies" or "It's raining' pitchforks," or perhaps "Pitchforks with nigger babies stickin' on the ends of 'em." * It may "Rain cats and dogs." † It may be "A *pourdown*." ‡ A cloudburst "Beats anything" or is "A toad strangler." If it does not rain enough, "We've not been payin' the preacher," or "All signs fail in dry weather." § Either very dry or very rainy weather may be "A humdinger." Very cold weather may "Freeze your snout," or "Freeze the tail off a brass monkey." ‖ Very hot weather may cause you to "Melt and run down." It is either "A roaster" or "A scorcher." "You pant till your tongue hangs out." Frost "Nips their tails," or "Wilts them down," or just plain "Nips." Ice is "Slick as glass," ** or "Slick as greased butter." Hail, as well as many other things, may "Beat the band." ††

"Time and Speed"

Time expressions are numerous: "Since Heck was a pup, and he died an old dog," or "As old as Ann," or "Since the year

---

* See Taylor and Whiting, *Proverbs*, p. 288, No. 2 s.v. "Pitchfork," for three references, the earliest dated 1856.

† See Taylor and Whiting, *Proverbs*, p. 62, No. 60 s.v. "Cats," for ten references.

‡ Randolph and Wilson, *Down in the Holler*, p. 273, cite this term in Ozark usage. It is also common in southern Indiana.

§ Taylor and Whiting, *Proverbs*, p. 333, s.v. "Sign," gives four references.

‖ Taylor and Whiting, *Proverbs*, p. 264, No. 8 s.v. "Nose," gives "hot enough to melt the nose h'off a brass monkey," and cites uses of "cold enough to freeze."

** See Taylor and Whiting, *Proverbs*, p. 153, No. 2 s.v. "Glass," for the phrase "slippery as glass."

†† The *Brown Collection*, I, 365, s.v. "Band," reports the phrase "raining to beat the band."

one," or "Slow as the second coming of Jesus," or "Slow as pond water," or "Slow as molasses in January," * or "Slow as a snail." † "Not seen you in a coon's age," ‡ "Slow as seven years' itch," "So slow he don't earn his salt." § "Quick as a cricket," "Quick as a flash," ‖ and "Faster than greased lightning" ** are all favorite phrases. "Be done in two shakes of a black sheep's tail" is an expression often used to express extra speed, as well as "a lamb's tail." †† He is a "slow poke" when he does not like his task and shows it by his action and is "Jumping around" when he puts on speed when he wants to go somewhere. "Twist your tail" is a warning to hurry. "Shake a leg" is another warning for speed. "Old as Methuselah" and "Old as Adam" are expressions of age, often applied to such objects as butter.‡‡

"Appearance"

Physical appearances have their share of sayings. These may refer to mental ability, social position, aspirations, moral defects, or personal traits. An ugly woman's face "Would stop a clock." She is "As ugly as a mud fence," §§ or "Ugly as

* See the *Brown Collection,* I, 445, item 1 s.v. "Molasses," for similar expressions such as "slow as cold molasses," "as slow as molasses in winter," "as slow as molasses running up hill."

† Taylor and Whiting, *Proverbs,* p. 340, No. 1 s.v. "Snail." The earliest source reported (1851) used the following phrase: "We ought . . . not to be creeping along like a snail."

‡ The *Brown Collection,* I, 529, "Folk Speech" (ed. G. P. Wilson), defines coon's age as "a long time"; and the saying is also listed, *ibid.,* p. 386, "Proverbs," s.v. "Coon."

§ See Taylor and Whiting, *Proverbs,* p. 316, No. 4 s.v. "Salt," for references to the phrase "You don't earn your salt."

‖ See Taylor and Whiting, *Proverbs,* p. 137, s.v. "Flash." No. 1. "Quick's a flash."

** See Taylor and Whiting, *Proverbs,* p. 221, No. 3 s.v. "Lightning," for "Quicker 'n greased lightnin' "; pp. 221–22, No. 14, for "Like a streak of greased lightning."

†† See Taylor and Whiting, *Proverbs,* p. 323, No. 3 s.v. "Shake." The animal in the references listed may be a sheep, a mutton, a donkey or a monkey.

‡‡ Taylor and Whiting, *Proverbs,* p. 242, No. 2 under "Methuselah."

§§ See Taylor and Whiting, *Proverbs,* p. 254, s.v. "Mud fence," for the phrase "As ugly as a mud fence in a thunder storm."

‖‖ See Taylor and Whiting, *Proverbs,* p. 335, No. 8 s.v. "Sin." One variation given is "as ugly as original sin."

sin." ‖ ‖ An attractive one is "Pretty as a picture," * or
"A peach." † She is "Sweet as honey," or she is "A honey." ‡
She "Favors her mother's family," or is "A pretty little trick."

A tall person is "Long for this world even if he should die
tomorrow." A thin person is "Skinny," "Thin as a rail," §
"Thin as a toothpick," or "Skinny as a picket." A little person
is a "Gimlet." The overly large person is "Fat as a hog," ‖
"Fat as a fool," ** or "Fat as a butterball." †† A large shape-
less person may be "Built like a stove" or "Like a sack of
wheat." A person large about the waist is "Big as a barrel."
The obese one is "Big as all outdoors." ‡‡ The woman with
large legs "Has legs like fence posts." It may be said of a person with red hair, "If you cut his hair he will bleed to death."
A hooked nose is "A parrot nose." "You could hang him over
a limb by his nose."

A strong person is "tough," "Strong as an ox," §§ "Tough
as a pine knot," ‖ ‖ "Strong as a horse," *** or "Tough as shoe
leather." A freckled person is "Speckled as a turkey's egg."
A clumsy person is "Awkward as a cow," or "A blunderbuss."
If he refers to using his hands it is "My fingers are all
thumbs." ††† The man who has lost his hair has a "Bald pate,"
or "It is slick as a peeled onion." ‡‡‡ The one with a pug nose
"Has turnips for sale." The one with big ears is "Donkey" or
"Donk." The person with a small sharp face is "Rat face."

* See Taylor and Whiting, *Proverbs*, p. 283, No. 4 s.v. "Picture." The
earliest reference cited is Louisa M. Alcott's *Little Women* (1869).
† See Taylor and Whiting, *Proverbs*, p. 278, No. 2 s.v. "Peach," where "as
fair as a peach" is reported.
‡ See Taylor and Whiting, *Proverbs*, p. 187, No. 3 s.v. "Honey."
§ See Taylor and Whiting, *Proverbs*, p. 302, No. 1 s.v. "Rail," which cites
Mark Twain's use of "As thin as a rail" in *Roughing It* (1872).
‖ See Taylor and Whiting, *Proverbs*, p. 184, No. 1 s.v. "Hog." No. 2 is
"Fat as a nigger's hog."
** See Taylor and Whiting, *Proverbs*, p. 142, No. 12 s.v. "Fool."
†† See the *Brown Collection*, I, 378, No. 1 s.v. "Butter-ball."
‡‡ See Taylor and Whiting, *Proverbs*, p. 272, No. 1 s.v. "Out doors."
§§ See Taylor and Whiting, *Proverbs*, p. 273, No. 2 s.v. "Ox." Note the addi-
tional phrase: ". . . and ignorant as strong."
‖‖ See Taylor and Whiting, *Proverbs*, p. 386, s.v. "Pine knot."
*** See Taylor and Whiting, *Proverbs*, p. 190, No. 11 s.v. "Horse."
††† See Taylor and Whiting, *Proverbs*, p. 133, No. 2 s.v. "Finger." An elab-
oration is that men's (or seamen's) fingers are all thumbs.
‡‡‡ See Taylor and Whiting, *Proverbs*, p. 270, No. 1 s.v. "Onion," where a
bald head is likened to a peeled onion.

"*Health*"

If a person is asked how he is, he may say "Middlin'," "Fair to middlin'," * "Just tol'able," "Out of kelter," "Out of shape," "Poorly," or "Dawnsey" † if he is not well. He may refer to his ill health by saying, "I feel like something the cat's drug in," "I feel like something sent for that couldn't come," or "I feel like a cent piece with a hole punched through it." He may look as if he "Had been through the flint mill." ‡ The person who is not strong is "Weak as a cat." § If he has not had enough sleep, his eyes may look like "Two burnt holes in a blanket." A thin or undernourished person is "As big as a cake of soap after a week's washing."

The well person may be "Pert as a cricket," ‖ "Right pert," "Fat and sassy," "Fine as silk," ** or "Fine as frog hair." Often he is "Fine and dandy," or "Fine as a fiddle." †† If he is joyous he is "Happy as a lark." ‡‡

Some German Proverbs in Southern Illinois §§

By FRANCES M. BARBOUR

A search for proverbs in behalf of the American Dialect Society several years ago turned up a number of foreign proverbs in southern Illinois. These are mainly German, for I was very

* In Randolph and Wilson, *Down in the Holler*, p. 265, "middlin'" is defined as "tolerable."
† In Randolph, *Down in the Holler*, p. 238, the word "dauncy" is used to mean "lacking appetite," or "fastidious about food." One of the references defines the term as "in poor health."
‡ See Taylor and Whiting, *Proverbs*, p. 244, No. 1 s.v. "Mill," for "He's been through the mill." Lincoln used this common phrase.
§ See Taylor and Whiting, *Proverbs*, p. 59, s.v. "Cat," No. 29.
‖ See Taylor and Whiting, *Proverbs*, p. 84, No. 6 s.v. "Cricket." Harriet Beecher Stowe used "peart as a cricket" in *Uncle Tom's Cabin* (1851).
** See Taylor and Whiting, *Proverbs*, p. 334, No. 2 s.v. "Silk." This phrase also appears in *Uncle Tom's Cabin*, in the form "fine as floss silk."
†† See Taylor and Whiting, *Proverbs*, p. 130, No. 1 s.v. "Fiddle," for the more customary "Fit as a Fiddle."
‡‡ See Taylor and Whiting, *Proverbs*, p. 214, No. 6 s.v. "Lark." Other comparisons to a lark are "bright, cheery, chipper, gay, joyous."
§§ From *Midwest Folklore*, IV, (1954), 161–64.

fortunate in enlisting the interest and help of Mrs. Cansuelo Volkert, a newspaper editor in the German community around Columbia and Waterloo. I am quite aware that the possibilities for finding proverbs of French origin around Prairie du Rocher and of Italian origin around Herrin and West Frankfort are as yet practically unexplored. So this report deals largely with unfinished business—with only those foreign proverbs which came to me incidentally in a general quest for proverbial material.

A seventeenth-century definition assigns to a proverb the attributes of brevity, sense, and salt. Since I consider salt the principal source of charm, I have perhaps overburdened some of the sayings listed below with both a literal and a free translation in order to preserve the flavor of the original phrasing. For help in the free translation of the rather corrupt German I am indebted to two colleagues who are familiar with colloquial American German, "*die schoenste Lengvidge,*" as I am not.

What impresses one most as he examines the German proverbs is that practically every one has its English equivalent. I shall mention a few of these parallels:

1. *Ende gut, alles gut.*

   All's well that ends well.

2. *Regends [Regnet's] nicht, dribbles noch.*

   Even if money does not rain, dribbles help.

   (*Every little bit helps.*)

3. *Stilles Wasser ist tief.*

   Still water runs deep.

4. *Die Dummen werden nie all'.*

   All the fools aren't dead.

5. *Kurtzes Haar ist schnell geburst'.*

    > Short hair is quickly brushed. (*A short horse is soon curried.*)

6. *Wenn die Mädchen pfeifen, weinen die Engel.*

    > If girls whistle, the angels weep. (*Whistling girls and crowing hens always come to some bad ends.*)

7. *Feine Kleide', feine Leute.*

    > Fine clothing, fine people. (*Fine feathers make fine birds.*)

8. *Geld regiert die Welt.*

    > Money rules the world.

9. *Was ich nicht im Kopf hab', das muss ich in die Füsze haben.*

    > What I don't have in my head I must have in my feet. (*You should make your heels save your head.*)

10. *Wenn das Pferd fort ist, dann macht man den Stall zu.*

    > One locks the stable after the horse is stolen.

11. *Was ich nicht weiss, macht mich nicht heiss.*

    > What I don't know does not make me hot (*won't hurt me*).

12. *Wer zuletzt lacht, lacht am besten.*

    > He laughs best who laughs last.

13. *Verschiebe niemals das auf Morgen
    Was du heute kannst besorgen.*

Never put off until tomorrow what you can do today.

14. *Mal' nur nicht den Teufel an der Wand;*
Wenn man den Teufel nennt
   kommt er gerant.

> *Do not paint the devil on the wall; if one even names him, he comes running. (When you speak of the devil, he appears.)*

15. *Morgenrot ist dem sein Tod.*

> *Red sky in the morning is deadly (is the sailor's warning).*

16. *Abendrot, gute Wetterbot'.*

> *Red sky at night means good weather (is the sailor's delight).*

17. *Schnell und Gut geht nicht zusammen.*

> Fast *and* good *do not go well together. (The more haste, the less speed).*

9. GAMES AND GAME RHYMES

I have annotated the following games according to Paul G. Brewster, American Nonsinging Games *(Norman, Okla.: University of Oklahoma Press, 1953); and Leah Jackson Wolford's* The Play-Party in Indiana, *edited and revised by W. Edson Richmond and William Tillson (Indianapolis: Indiana Historical Society, 1959).*

Children's Games in Egypt

By LELAH ALLISON

From Hoosier Folklore, *VII (1948), 84–93. The author, a teacher at McKendree College, Lebanon, at the northwestern tip of Egypt, comments: "My students wrote these games for me; they had played these games many times. In general, I have kept the wording of the writers."*

Children's games are numerous, but nearly all of them have one thing in common: they will accommodate any number of players. Children like numbers, and usually they are happier when several join their group. That is very likely the reason why their games can be adapted to any number of players. There are two general divisions, the outdoor games and the house games. Because it is natural for children to like to play outdoors, the outdoor games are more numerous than the others. Weather conditions, cold and rain, make the inside games a necessity.

Simplicity is a marked characteristic of the games. They are so simple that the most naïve can understand them and the very young can participate. It is remarkable how many games a very young child can remember and even direct.

Some games are very old; children from generation to generation seem to enjoy them and never tire of them. Some of them differ slightly; the difference may be caused by misunderstanding by some director in the group who "starts" the game in his own group, or the difference may be the result of some clever player's own initiative.

These games are only a few which any collector will find if he observes children at play. All of these are played by child groups in Illinois. Perhaps all of them are played in all states of the Union.

Outdoor Games

"Poison Tag"

> Brewster includes a text from Indiana, pp. 63–64, entitled "Chinese Tag." He gives references to this particular tag game and to tag games in general, p. 64.

Any number of people may play poison tag. One player is chosen to be "it," and he must tag another player before he can become one of the regulars. The one tagged then must become "it." The one who is tagged must hold his hand on the spot that was tagged by "it" and keep it in that position until he tags someone else. The fun of the game consists in "it" tagging a player in an unusual place for him to hold his hand. For example, if "it" tags a player's heel, it is not easy to keep a hand on the heel and chase another player to tag him.

"Drop the Handkerchief"

> Brewster prints a text from North Carolina, p. 91, and discusses the game as it is played in Hungary, Switzerland, Greece, and the Dominican Republic. He supplies additional references on pp. 92–93.

*Richmond and Tillson print an Indiana text with words
and music, pp. 216–18. They note, p. 299, that Itisket
is not, strictly speaking, a play-party game, and that it
recently has lost the song and become a game of chase.*

This old game of drop the handkerchief differs slightly from
some of the older games of this name. The children form a circle
holding hands and singing. "It" is outside the circle holding a
handkerchief, running around the circle as the song is sung.
This is the song:

> A tisket, a tasket, a green and yellow basket,
> I sent a letter to my love, and on my way I dropped it.

On the word *dropped*, "it" drops the handkerchief behind
a player and continues running. The one behind whom the
handkerchief was dropped picks it up and runs around the
circle in the opposite direction. The first reaching the empty
space in the circle remains there; the other is "it."

"London Bridge Is Falling Down"

*Richmond and Tillson describe this game, p. 221, and
comment, pp. 301–2, that "London Bridge" is reputedly
very old and that some scholars, such as Lady Gomme,
believed that the game is a vestige of ancient foundation
sacrificial rites.*

Two players "take the game." They select two objects of
similar type, such as apples and pears or spring and autumn;
but they do not tell the players which object represents which
person. All other players form a circle joining hands. "The
takers" join hands and hold them high, one standing inside the
circle, the other outside, allowing the players to pass under the
hands as they go around in a circle singing:

> London bridge is falling down, falling down, falling
>   down;
> London bridge is falling down and caught my true love
>   in it.

At any point in the song the "Takers" may drop their hands around a player, and the circle stops. The one caught is whispered the two chosen words and asked which he will take. He selects one, and the "taker" who is represented by that chosen object tells the caught player to get behind him. The caught player stands directly behind the "taker," and the game continues until no one is left in the circle. Instead there are two lines, one line behind each "taker." Then each player puts his arms around the waist of the person in front of him and holds his hands tight. The two "takers" hold their hands tight, and a tug of war begins, each line trying to outpull the other. If one player breaks hands, all the line behind him is out of the game.

The side that can pull the other side away from the starting place is the winner.

"Andy Over"

> *Brewster prints a version from Kansas and supplies references, p. 84, to additional versions, noting that the game is sometimes called "Anthony Over," "Handy Over," or "Anty Over."*

Andy Over is played around a building which is not too large to throw a ball over and which is so situated that any number of players may run around it. A barn is a good building, for there are likely no windows for the ball to accidentally break. A string ball or a soft rubber ball is necessary. The players choose sides, one side taking one side of the building. The players cannot see each other. One side has the ball and throws it over the roof to the other side saying, "Andy over," as he throws the ball. The object of the game is for some member of the other side to catch the ball. If one does catch the ball before it touches the ground, all on that side start to run to the other side of the building. They go in opposite directions so that those on the other side will not know who has the ball. The one who does have the ball touches a player with or throws it at a player. All touched by the ball go to the other side.

If the ball is not caught, the side failing to catch the ball

throws it over the roof to the other side, calling, "Andy over."
The game continues until all on one side are caught.

"Red Rover"

*Brewster prints a version from Montana, describes
similar games played in Czechoslovakia and Greece, and
gives notes to other variants, pp. 170–71.*

Two captains choose the players who form two lines facing each
other, the lines about fifty feet apart. Each team stands in a
line holding hands. A captain calls, "Red Rover, Red Rover, let
(Mary) come over." He names any person on the other side
that he wishes to come over. The person named comes over and
tries to break through between two hands of any of the players.
If he breaks through, he chooses one player to take back with
him. If he cannot break through, he stays on that side.
    The game continues until no one is left on one side.

"Too Late for Breakfast"

All players, except two, form a circle holding hands. The two
hold hands and run around the circle, hitting the hands of a
couple. The first couple continues running around the circle.
The couple whose hands hit runs around the circle in the opposite direction. The object is for the couples to race for the
empty space. The losers must then be "it."

"May I?"

*Brewster classifies this game as a "little girls' game"
and prints a version from Georgia. He also describes a
similar Jugoslav game, p. 164.*

One person is "it." The others stand in a straight line. "It"
tells players they may take so many steps; they are not ordinary steps but are called scissors, elephant, baby, pin, giant,
side steps, and so on. If players remember to say, "May I?" they

take the steps. If they forget, they go back to the starting line. Sneaking steps are allowed, if "it" does not see the sneaker. If he is caught, he goes back to the starting line. The one who reaches the goal first is winner, and he is "it" for the next game.

"Kick the Can"

On pp. 47–48 Brewster prints a version from Arkansas and gives references to British and North Carolina variants.

Kick the can is similar to hide and go seek. Boundaries may be placed on possible places to hide. "It" hides his eyes and counts to a hundred by fives. While he counts, the others run to hide. If "it" sees a player, he touches the can (any tin can), calls the person by name, and that person must come to the can. If a player sees a chance to slip to the can, he kicks it as far as possible, and everyone has a chance to hide over, the same person taking the game.

"Bicycle Tag"

Each player must have a bicycle. Limited areas are named, and if one goes beyond that area, he is "it." One is chosen "it" to begin the game; he gives the others time to get away. The point is for "it" to touch any part of another's bicycle with his front wheel. His foot must not be on the ground as he catches the other player. The one tagged is then "it."

"Ring Around the Rosey"

In the Brown Collection, I, 150–51, six versions of the verse are printed and references are given to additional variants.

Children like to sing this simple game. "It" is in disgrace and is in the center of the circle. The circle goes around singing, "Ring around the rosey, pocket full of posey. Last one to stoop

is a dirty red nosey." On the last word all are to squat. The last
one to squat is "it."

Indoor Games

"Hangman"

> *Brewster prints a New Jersey variant, p. 132, entitled*
> *"Hang the Butcher," in which the game is played by*
> *only two children.*

Give each player a sheet of paper and pencil and instruct him
to draw a scaffold, a right angle with one end in the ground and
a brace across the angle with a rope dangling from the end of
the angle left in the air. The leader chooses a name, a person,
place, or thing: as a bird, a river, or air. One player writes the
name of the article on a piece of paper, folds it, and places it
before the other players. They have six guesses. If *trees* were
the category, and the word was *walnut*, the game would go like
this: first player may ask, "Is there an *a* in the word?" The
answer is, "It is the second letter." The players would then
write the letter A on the second blank. Second player may ask,
"Does it have an *e?*" The leader would say, "No, draw your
head on the rope." Each player draws his head. This is repeated
around the players until each hangs himself or the word is
guessed. For each wrong answer, the players add parts to the
hangman: body, two arms, and two legs.

"Ring on a String"

> *A Pennsylvania version is reported by Brewster, pp.*
> *19–20. He discusses the game as played in Germany,*
> *Switzerland, Spain, and Scotland, and gives further*
> *references.*

"It" is inside a ring of people who hold a string which is as large
as the circle of players. A ring, or two or three rings, are on the
string. The point is to keep the rings hidden under the hands

but to pass them along on the string. The players work their two hands together and apart as far as the neighbors' hands on each side. That action is done all the time so that "it" cannot know where the rings are. He may guess as often and as fast as he wishes. If one is caught with a ring, he becomes "it."

"Fig Mill"

> Cf. Brewster "Paper and Pencil Games," pp. 127–33. This seems to be a variant of Tic-Tack-Toe, pp. 130–32, or "Noughts and X's" p. 128.

Draw three squares inside each other on a cardboard. Give two players nine buttons each, players to have different colors as one white, one red. Draw a cross through the square. Intersections of the lines are places to put buttons. The object is to get three buttons in a row. Three is a fig mill. The player who gets three in a row takes a player's button.

Singing Games in Southern Illinois

By DAVID S. McINTOSH

> A full treatment of the songs in this form of American traditional entertainment is Benjamin A. Botkin, The American Play-Party Song (Lincoln, Neb., 1937). An older work of 1916 brought up to date with comparative notes is W. E. Richmond and William Tillson, Leah J. Wolford's The Play-Party in Indiana (Indianapolis: Indiana Historical Society, 1959), which deals with a southern Indiana county similar to "Egypt." "A Finding List of Play-Party Games" was presented by Altha L. McLendon in Southern Folklore Quarterly, VIII (1944), 201–34.
>
> The discussion, texts, and dance formations that follow are taken from a pamphlet written and published by David S. McIntosh, Southern Illinois Singing Games and Songs (Carbondale, 1946), pp. v–viii, 1–49.

The Singing Game is at home in southern Illinois and has been a vital part of our culture since the coming of the earliest white settlers. The people that came into "Egypt" in the early days were mostly of English, Scotch or Irish ancestry and they brought with them a large store of folksongs, singing games, and dance tunes. In many areas all that remains of this folk music and folklore is to be found in the memories of some of the older people.

Last summer, on a research trip, Mr. John Allen and I were on our way to Bay City, Illinois, and we stopped for a visit with Mrs. P. M. Buchanan, whose home is about four miles north of Bay City. We had been traveling through a timbered area for several miles on one of these southern Illinois roads where the trees, elderberry bushes, and weeds almost "take" the road, and we had come upon a cleared field off to our left that led up to a clump of trees shading a very old house. Three large and beautiful oak trees, a pecan tree, and a very ancient catalpa tree sheltered a large log house with a long front porch. The "dog trot" had been made into an extra room.

After finding out what we wanted, Mrs. Buchanan joined us on the porch and patiently began to answer my questions. "Yes, I went to play-parties, but they were always with one of the neighbors—we went horseback or sometimes in a buggy but we always had to be in before twelve, not like the young folks now-a-days. We played 'Buffalo Girls,' 'Prince Charlie,' 'Snap,' but I don't remember how the songs went or how we played the games; my folks didn't like for me to go to places where they had kissing games; they like to have 'sings' when the young folks came to our home. We would have quartets, duets, guitar trios, and such things, mostly church songs." Mr. Allen came back from sketching the house and asked about the bell chained to the catalpa tree. "Oh, that! It came from a steamboat that burned over on the river years ago. My grandchild has a lot of fun playing with it. The river is just a few miles away."

On the fourteenth of December, 1945, we were in the home of Henry Dudenbostel, Campbell Hill, in the northwest part of Jackson County, learning more about the play-party in the early days. This time the man of the house sang a number of singing games and explained how they were played. He said, "The play-parties were held outdoors in the summer and in the winter were held in the homes of the neighborhood, usually in the kitchen. There would be fifteen or twenty couples present, the more the better. The parents would join right in with us and they had as much fun as we did. There was no drinking; if the girls knew we drank anything at all, they wouldn't have anything to do with us. We occasionally had square dances with fiddle music, or one or two of the boys carried a french harp with them, or maybe a jew's-harp. We'd make up a surprise party at school and pick out some family in the community that had some young people—a good-looking girl—and all go out after supper. I remember one time we went out about a mile from town and the lady of the home said, 'Glad you came—have all the fun you want; go out in the kitchen; you can quadrille all that you want to, but we don't want you to dance.' Of course that was what we wanted."

Some time ago, we made the acquaintance of Mr. Robert Wilson of McLeansboro, Illinois, and discovered that he remembered a great many of the old songs and singing games. In a letter that I received from him, he gave the following description of his boyhood life in his father's pioneer home in southern Illinois: "My father was an old-time fiddler with a considerable reputation in his day. His mother's people had moved to southern Indiana from North Carolina in an early day. They had brought slaves with them. These, of course, were automatically freed when they crossed the Ohio River. Some of them, however, stayed with the family as long as they lived. One old Negro, of whom my father used to tell stories to us children, was named Hawk. That was all the name he had. Hawk was a fiddler, and he taught my dad to play the old tunes he knew, and it seemed he had an almost inexhaustible supply.

"My father and mother settled in a thickly wooded region in Saline County and cleared a farm, built log buildings, reared a large family, and lived real pioneer lives. When I was small, as early as I can remember, the young people from far and near would gather at our house and have an old-time dance. My father would play the fiddle and my mother would often take part in the dances. They danced mostly the square dance, though they sometimes danced the waltz, the schottische, or occasionally a little different form they called the cotillion. They also danced different versions of the Virginia Reel. Sometimes the fiddle would be laid aside and they would sing for their dances. Occasionally some of the young people who had recently been converted at an old-time protracted meeting would refuse to dance with the fiddle but would dance with singing."

It is quite evident that when the folks of this region wanted to have a good social time together, they would turn to the square dance or to the singing game for their fun. The singing game was considered respectable by almost everyone, but the square dance, except in some communities, was not patronized by the church folks who had very definite convictions that dancing to the fiddle was bad. The singing of the music was apparently the redemptive feature of the game: that, and the fact that most of the singing games were familiar to the parents, as they had played them all their lives. Some few families, such as the Wilson family, were able to combine the singing games with other types of country dancing, but usually the play-party or singing-game party and the dance were separate forms of entertainment.

The singing game is also distinguished from the dance in the greater freedom of movement allowed the individual and in the opportunity for the improvisation of words to fit the mood of the players. This improvisation accounts for the great number of verses to such games as "Skip to Ma Lou," "Old Dan Tucker," and "Roll That Brown Jug Down to Town," and also accounts for the many different tunes.

Another advantage was that the music for the game was always at hand, and was good or bad, depending entirely upon the voices of the group. The singing was done by those taking part in the game, although in some communities there were occasionally some restrictions on the singing. Mrs. Elsie Parrish McNeill said that in her neighborhood the singing was done by the boys, and if some girl would start to sing, the other girls would show their disapproval.

Note: For a description by Leah Wolford of the play-party as played in Ripley County, Indiana, see The Play-Party in Indiana, *pp. 113–22, a section entitled "The Play-Party and Its Environment." There Wolford discusses the critical attitude of the ministers, the favorable sentiment of the younger people, and the mixed feeling of parents towards the playing of these games. She describes a typical evening's entertainment, telling who gave the parties, how the guests arrived, what they wore, and what they had for refreshments, and she notes the differences between her generation (ca. 1900) and her parents' generation [R. M. Dorson].*

Let's Go Down to Rowsha's

The dance formations accompanying the following songs are thus described by McIntosh.
Double circle: Partners facing counterclockwise with boys on the inside.

"LET'S GO DOWN TO ROWSHA'S"

Sung by Mrs. Mabel Tudor, Rockwood, Illinois. Collected by David S. McIntosh, 1945.

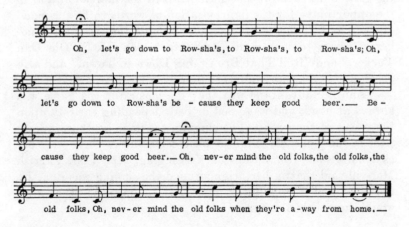

Oh, let's go down to Row-sha's, to Row-sha's, to Row-sha's; Oh, let's go down to Row-sha's be - cause they keep good beer. — Be - cause they keep good beer. — Oh, nev - er mind the old folks, the old folks, the old folks, Oh, nev - er mind the old folks when they're a - way from home. —

Single circle: All facing toward center with girls standing to the right of the boys.

Contra, or longways formation: Two lines of players face each other, the men on one side and the other side, opposite their partner.

McIntosh prints three variants of this drinking song, pp. 11–14. The name of the beer parlor is alternately Rowsha's, Rowser's, and Rowster's. A text from Versailles, Indiana, is printed in The Play-Party in Indiana, *pp. 139–40, which specifies lager beer. In her note Wolford commented that this dance was not considered proper for church members, but was highly popular among schoolchildren at the noon recess (ca. 1900).*

This kind of game song today becomes a college beer-bust singing game. See Dorson, American Folklore, *pp. 265–66. Richmond and Tillson add to Wolford's note, p. 272, that the song is still sung on college campuses, but that the game is not so widespread as text and tune. They refer to variants in Missouri and Oklahoma.*

Informant: Elsie Parrish McNeill, Carbondale, Illinois.

"We'll All Go Down to Rowser's"

1. We'll all go down to Row-ser's, to Row-ser's, to Row-ser's.
   We'll all go down to Row-ser's, to where they keep the "B."

2. We'll nev-er mind the drink-ing, the drink-ing, the drink-ing.
   We'll nev-er mind the drinking, for drink-ing is a sin.

3. For drink-ing is a sin, for drink-ing is a sin.
   We'll all go down to Row-ser's, for drink-ing is a sin.

4. We'll all go down to Row-ser's, to Row-ser's, to Row-ser's.
   We'll all go down to Row-ser's, to where they keep the "B."

5. We'll nev-er mind the old folks, the old folks, the old
    folks.
    We'll nev-er mind the old folks, for they're away from
    home.
6. For they're away from home, for they're away from
    home.
    We'll never mind the old folks, for they're away from
    home.

Formation: Two couples form a circle, girls standing at the
    right of their partners. Boys join right hands across and
    the girls join right hands across, under the hands of the boys.
Action: 1. Circle left. 2. Change hands and circle right. 3. Turn
    partner by the right hand then turn lady by the left. Repeat
    action to end of verse. Each couple now takes in a new couple,
    forming two wheels. 4. The two wheels circle left as in 1st
    verse. 5. Change hands and circle right. 6. Repeat the action
    of verse three.
The song is repeated from the beginning and each of the four
    couples invites a new couple on the floor. This procedure con-
    tinues until all couples are on the floor.

Bingo

*McIntosh names as informant Milo Richmond, Cutler,
Illinois, and cites Beatrice A. Hunt and Harry Robert
Wilson, Sing and Dance (Chicago: Bell and McCreary
Co., 1945), p. 45.*

*A legend is embodied in this play-party song. See Dor-
son, American Folklore, pp. 98–99, for the tale and
song of "Johnny Verbeck," who was ground into sausage.*

1.   The Mil-ler's big dog lay on the barn floor,
        And Bin-go was his name.
        The Mil-ler's big dog lay on the barn floor,
        And Bin-go was his name.

"Bingo"

Sung by Lottie Hendrickson, Marion, Illinois. Collected by David S. McIntosh, 1945.

The Mil-ler's big dog lay on the barn floor, And Bin-go was his name. The Mil-ler's big dog lay on the barn floor, And Bin-go was his name. B-I-N-G-O, B-I-N-G-O, B-I-N-G-O,—— and Bin-go was his name.

CHORUS:

B-I-N-G-O, B-I-N-G-O
B-I-N-G-O, and Bin-go was his name.

2.   They cut him up into sausage meat,
And Bingo was his name.
They cut him up into sausage meat,
And Bingo was his name.

CHORUS

3.   They whistled to that sausage meat,
And Bingo wagged his tail,
They whistled to that sausage meat,
And Bingo wagged his tail.

CHORUS

Formation: Double circle.
Action: Promenade with partner for twelve measures. On measure 13 begin a grand right and left. Right hand to partner on "B," left to next lady on "I," right to next on "N," etc. After

"O" hold joined right hands high, and on next phrase promenade with new partner, counterclockwise. Repeat for second and third verses.

Old Dan Tucker

> *This is one of the best known folk rhymes and dance tunes in the United States. For a version of the song and a description of the game as played in Ripley County, Indiana, see The Play-Party in Indiana, pp. 180–82. In their note, pp. 286–87, Richmond and Tillson state that "Old Dan Tucker" was originally a minstrel song, composed around 1840 by Dan D. Emmett, and that it may have been based on an older Negro folksong. The song "has assimilated dance directions as well as having picked up additional stanzas from similar songs . . ." and verses of it have been used as a "knee-bouncing" song in the nursery.*

> *"The first three verses came from Mrs. Lessie Parrish, Carbondale, Illinois" [D. S. McIntosh].*

"OLD DAN TUCKER"

Sung by Mrs. Lessie Parish, Carbondale, Illinois. Collected by David S. McIntosh, 1936.

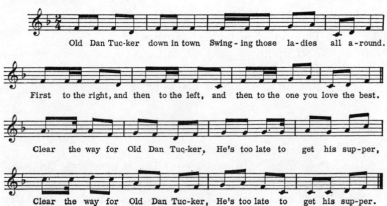

Old Dan Tuc-ker down in town Swing-ing those la-dies all a-round.

First to the right, and then to the left, and then to the one you love the best.

Clear the way for Old Dan Tuc-ker, He's too late to get his sup-per,

Clear the way for Old Dan Tuc-ker, He's too late to get his sup-per.

1.   Old Dan Tucker down in town
Swinging those ladies all around.
First to the right, and then to the left,
And then to the one you love the best.

CHORUS:

Clear the way for Old Dan Tucker,
He's too late to get his supper,
Clear the way for Old Dan Tucker,
He's too late to get his supper.

2.   Old Dan Tucker, he got drunk
He jumped in the fire and kicked up a chunk
Red hot coals got down in his shoe,
And Lordy, how his coat tail flew!

3.   Old Dan Tucker climbed a tree
His Lord and Master for to see,
The limb did break and he did fall
And he didn't get to see his Lord at all.

> *"The following verses came from Mr. John Allen of Carbondale, Illinois; 1945."*

Old Dan Tucker was a man of sense
Wore his shirt outside his pants,
Combed his hair with a wagon wheel,
And died with the toothache in his heel.

Supper's over, dishes washed;
Can't get supper here, by gosh.

> *"The following verses came from Professor Troy Felts, Carbondale, Illinois; 1933."*

1.   Old Dan Tucker was a mighty fine man,
He washed his face in the frying pan,

Combed his head with a wagon wheel,
And died with the toothache in his heel.

CHORUS:

Git out of the way for old Dan Tucker,
He's too late to get his supper:
Git out of the way for old Dan Tucker,
He's too late to get his supper.

2. Breakfast's over and dinner's cooking,
Old Dan Tucker is out a-looking;
He looked to the East, and he looked to the West,
And saw a little shike-poke running his best.

Formation: Single circle with extra boy in the center, who is
old Dan Tucker.

Action: At the start of the song, "Old Dan" starts swinging
the girls, going from one girl to another as he wishes. He
times his swinging of the girls so as to bring him to the girl
of his choice at the right time.

As the chorus is begun all promenade in counterclockwise direction and the boy who is left without a partner goes to the
center and becomes "Old Dan Tucker."

Rope-Skipping Rhymes

> *For a discussion of rope-skipping as played in England
> around 1900 and for texts of skipping rhymes see Alice
> Bertha Gomme,* The Traditional Games of England,
> Scotland, and Ireland, *Vol. II (London, 1898), pp.
> 200–204. A brief bibliography of skip-rope rhymes and
> six rhymes from North Carolina are printed in the
> Brown Collection, I, 170–72.*
>
> *For a variant of No. 1, "Johnny Over the Ocean," see
> Paul G. Brewster, "Rope-Skipping, Counting-Out, and
> Other Rhymes of Children," Southern Folklore Quar-
> terly, III (1939), 173, Nos. 2 and 3. The note refers
> to other versions from Massachusetts, Pennsylvania,*

*and Nebraska. Two other verses which begin with
"Johnny over the ocean/Johnny over the sea" are listed
on p. 178, Nos. 39 and 40.*

*A variant of No. 3, "Old Man Daisy," is printed by
Brewster, p. 176, No. 26. In this text the character
is "Old Man Lazy," and the last line is "H-O-T spells
hot" instead of "Zîder, zîder/Billy-goat rider!" The
note refers to Massachusetts and Pennsylvania versions
and states that this verse is also used as a counting-out
rhyme.*

*Warren E. Roberts prints an Indiana text of No. 4,
"Down in the Valley," and gives references to other
versions in "Children's Games and Game Rhymes,"
Hoosier Folklore, VIII (1949), 9–10.*

"If a rope were stretched from the Atlantic to the Pacific and
all the little children in the country were jumping it, many of
them would be chanting identical or similar rhymes to those
below. That little Egyptians know some of these widespread
jingles will be evident from a few following representatives from
the Carbondale and the Makanda area. Most of those repro-
duced here are through the courtesy of Miss Tina Goodwin,
teacher in the primary grades of the Carbondale Brush School.
The last two have been contributed by Betty Mott of Makanda,
herself a rope-skipper." Grace Partridge Smith, "Folklore from
'Egypt,' " *Hoosier Folklore*, V (1956), 58–60.

1.   Johnny over the ocean,
            Johnny over the sea,
            Johnny broke a milk bottle,
            And blamed it onto me.
            I told Ma,
            Ma told Pa;
            Johnny got a whipping,
            Ha, ha, ha.
            How many whippings
            Did he get?
(*Count until there is a miss.*)

2. Changing bedrooms one by one
    Changing bedrooms two by two
    Changing bedrooms three by three.

(This goes on until no more can get "in." After the rope is full, they are let out, one by one.)

3. Old man Daisy *(skip)*
    He went crazy *(skip)*
    Up the ladder *(skip to right)*
    Down the ladder *(skip to left)*
    Zîder, zīder,
    Billy-goat rider!

(Skip until there is a miss.)

4. Down in the valley,
    Where the green grass grows,
    There is ———— *(girl's name)*
    Sweet as a rose.
    Along came ———— *(boy's name)*,
    And kissed her
    On the nose.

(Skip until there is a miss.)

5. I was born in a frying-pan,
    Just to see how old I am.

(Count as long as you can.)

6. Sally drank marmalade,
    Sally drank beer;
    Sally drank everything
    That made her feel queer.

    CHORUS:
    A-whoopsie went the marmalade,
    A-whoopsie went the beer,
    A-whoopsie went everything
    That made her feel queer.

Sally ate a pickle,
Sally ate a pie
Sally ate everything
That made her feel queer.

CHORUS:
A-whoopsie went the pickle,
A-whoopsie went the pie,
A-whoopsie went everything
That made her feel queer.

(*After each "A-whoopsie," jump forward a foot or so.*)

Jingles

> *A comprehensive and richly documented collection of English children's rhymes which also circulate freely in America is Iona and Peter Opie's* The Oxford Book of Nursery Rhymes (*Oxford: Clarendon Press, 1951*), *and further specimens are found in their subsequent volume,* The Lore and Language of Schoolchildren (*Oxford: Clarendon Press, 1959*). *The variety and imagery of Negro rhyming is seen in Thomas W. Talley,* Negro Folk Rhymes (*New York, 1922*).
>
> *Texts from Grace Partridge Smith, "Folklore from 'Egypt,'"* Hoosier Folklore, *V (1946), 60–61.*

Occasional Jingles

"The geographical distribution of these jingles is indicated in parentheses."

1.   Snow or blow,
        I'm bound to go,
        With my beau.

                            (*from Centralia*)

2.   Rain or shine,
        This girl's mine.

                            (*from Centralia*)

3. Under the window in stormy weather,
    I marry this man and woman together.
    Let none but him who rules the thunder,
    Put this man and woman asunder.

    (from Cobden)

4. Happy is a cat,
    Happy is a kitten,
    Happy is the boy
    Who never gets the mitten.

    (from Cobden, 1868)

5. Little head, little wit;
    Big head, not a bit.

    (from Cobden)

6. When you get married,
    And live on a hill,
    Send me a kiss,
    By the whip-poor-will.

    (from Eldorado)

7. Remember well
    And bear in mind,
    A jay-bird's tail
    Sticks out behind.

    (from Mt. Vernon)

8. Rabbit in the rail-pile
    Punch him out quick.
    Get a twister on him,
    With a long prong stick.
    Watch him on the north side,
    Watch him on the high;
    There he goes. Sic him, Tige.
    Yi, yi, yi!

    (from Stonefort)

10. FOLKSONGS

Songs from Great Britain

> *The following comments are from David S. McIntosh,*
> *"Southern Illinois Folk Songs," Journal of the Illinois*
> *State Historical Society, XXXI (1938), 299–300.*

In this paper I am presenting a few of the folksongs that I have collected in southern Illinois in the last five years. In my use of the term "folksongs" I refer to those songs that have been dependent upon oral tradition for their existence.

My memory goes back to my boyhood and a visit to my grandparents, who lived in Mt. Erie, Illinois. One particular evening has stuck in my mind; my mother sat at the old reed organ and chorded while the group sang many old songs. My uncle sang "Oh See That Watermelon Smiling on de Vine," and my father and mother sang "Dutch Courtship." I judge that this type of entertainment was rather common in the early days of the twentieth century in homes that contained an organ or piano.

It was my pleasure to visit a few years ago in the home of William Jones, who lives south of Carbondale. He sang "Froggie Went A-Courtin'," "God Knows I Been All Around This World," "Come All You Texas Rangers," and a number of other songs that I recorded. I asked Mr. Jones how many songs he knew, and he said he believed he could sing all night and never sing the same song twice. Mrs. Jones said that the young folks used to get together during the winter months and spend entire evenings singing songs and playing games. In all my contacts with folksong singers in southern Illinois in the last six years, during which time I have heard more than two hundred songs, I have yet to note any accompaniment of any sort except a tapping of the foot or a swaying of the body.

In just two instances did I find songs that required group participation. One was the "Froggie Went A-Courtin' and He Did Ride. Um, huh!" The other was the song, "The Twelve Apostles."

"Lady Isabel and the Elf-Knight"

> *This is No. 4 in the canon of English and Scottish popular ballads established by Francis James Child. For American texts and commentary see Tristram P. Coffin, The British Traditional Ballad in North America (Philadelphia, The American Folklore Society, 1950), pp. 32–35. In common with other American variants, the McIntosh text printed below has kept no trace of the supernatural character of the elf-knight. There is in this text, as Coffin notes, a curious substitution of "golin" (colleen) for the parrot who customarily threatens to reveal the maiden's murder, and is bribed to keep silent by promise of a golden cage. The collector vainly inquired for the parrot. This text, unlike some American ones, is not squeamish about referring to the girl's nakedness.*
>
> *Text and comments from McIntosh, "Southern Illinois Folk Songs," pp. 300–303.*

"Lady Isabel and the Elf-Knight," an old English ballad, was sung by Mrs. Lottie Hendrickson of Marion, Illinois. She was past eighty years of age at the time and was a very interesting and intelligent old lady. She had a wonderful memory and was able to sing eighteen songs for me, which I recorded. She was very patient, and was willing to repeat so that I could write the tunes accurately. She was unusual in that she rarely made any variation in the songs. She had a deep contralto voice and pitched the songs very low.

I asked her to explain the meaning of the last stanza, since

"Lady Isabel and the Elf-Knight"

Sung by Lottie Hendrickson, Marion, Illinois. Collected by David S. McIntosh, 1934.

I fol-lered her up and I fol-lered her down, to the
cham-ber where she lay. She nei-ther had the heart for to
flee from me, Nor the tongue for to tell me
nay,—— nay, Nor the tongue for to tell me nay.

it seemed to have no definite connection with the last of the song, but she was unable to do this. I suggested that the young lady might be addressing her parrot and was making promises of reward to the bird in return for its secrecy. Mrs. Hendrickson said that the song about the parrot was another song and did not go with this song. Unfortunately she was unable to recall this song.

Early one Saturday morning I drove to Marion after Mrs. Hendrickson and brought her to my home in Carbondale. We spent the entire day setting down songs. Late in the afternoon she told me that she could not recall any more. So we began looking through Campbell and Sharp's book, *English Folk Songs from the Southern Appalachians,* and we came upon this song. As soon as I had read a few lines she said, "I know that song." Then she began to sing. After singing the entire song without hesitation, she said: "I haven't sung that song in twenty years." I asked her where she learned it, and she said, "Poppy and Mommy used to sing it to us kids."

I follered her up and I follered her down,
To the chamber where she lay.
She neither had the heart for to flee from me,
Nor the tongue for to tell me nay, nay,
Nor the tongue for to tell me nay.

"Git up, git up, my pretty 'golin,'
Come go along with me.
Come go with me to old England,
And there I will marry thee,
And there I will marry thee."

"Go take the best part of your father's gold,
Likewise of your mother's fee.
Take two of the best steeds out of your father's stable,
Where-in there is thirty and three,
Where-in there is thirty and three."

He mounted her on the bonny brown,
He led the dappled gray,
And away they rode to the old seashore,
Just in the length of a long summer day,
Just in the length of a long summer day.

"Git down, git down, my pretty 'golin';
Git down, git down, by the sea.
For here I've drowned six kings' daughters,
And you the seventh shall be,
And you the seventh shall be."

"Turn yourself all around and around,
With your face to the greenest tree.
For I never thought it right,
A naked woman a man for to see,
A naked woman a man for to see."

He turned himself all around and around,
With his face to the greenest tree.

She caught him around the middle so small,
And tripped him into the sea,
And tripped him into the sea.

"Lie there, lie there, you false William;
Lie there instead of me.
For you have stripped me as naked as ever I was born,
Not a thread have I taken from you,
Not a thread have I taken from you."

She mounted herself on the bonny brown;
She led the dappled gray.
And away she rode to her father's hall,
Just three hours before it was day,
Just three hours before it was day.

"Hush up, hush up, my pretty 'golin';
Don't tell no tales on me.
I will build you a house with the beating wings of gold,
And your door shall be silvery,
And your door shall be silvery."

"I Have Four Brothers"

> *Sung by Mrs. Mabel McGowan, Carbondale, Illinois.*
> *Text from David S. McIntosh, Southern Illinois Sing-*
> *ing Games and Songs (Carbondale, 1946), pp. 45–47.*
> *This is "The Elfin Knight," No. 2 in Child. Coffin cites*
> *and discusses the American texts in The Traditional*
> *Ballad in America, pp. 30–31. As is characteristic of*
> *American examples, the supernatural love story has*
> *dropped out and only the riddles remain.*

1. I have four brothers over the sea,
    Perry, merry, dictum, dom a dee.
    They each sent a present into me.
    Perry, merry, dictum, dom a dee.
    Quartum, quartum, perry dee sentum,
    Perry, merry, dictum, dom a dee.

2.   The first sent cherries without any stones,
Perry, merry, dictum, dom a dee.
The next sent chickens without any bones,
Perry, merry, dictum, dom a dee.
Quartum, quartum, perry dee sentum,
Perry, merry, dictum, dom a dee.

3.   The third sent a blanket without any thread,
Perry, merry, dictum, dom a dee.
The fourth sent a book that could not be read,
Perry, merry, dictum, dom a dee.
Quartum, quartum, perry dee sentum,
Perry, merry, dictum, dom a dee.

4.   Cherries in the blossom have no stones,
Perry, merry, dictum, dom a dee;
Chickens in the eggs have no bones,
Perry, merry, dictum, dom a dee
Quartum, quartum, perry dee sentum,
Perry, merry, dictum, dom a dee.

5.   Blanket in the fleece has not thread,
Perry, merry, dictum dom a dee;
A book in the press cannot be read,
Perry, merry, dictum, dom a dee.
Quartum, quartum, perry dee sentum,
Perry, merry, dictum, dom a dee.

"The Hold-Up"

"Prospects for discovering Irish traditional lore in 'Egypt' rest, to a certain extent, upon a knowledge of early settlements in Illinois and of the location of centers where Irish families gathered in the first decades of the 1800's. In Illinois, the first European colonists were Irish, settling on the Ohio River in 1804. In the 1840's, or a few years earlier, three hundred Irish

*families located in Monroe County, bordered on the
west by the Mississippi River and adjacent to St. Clair
and Randolph counties. These newcomers built up an
Irish-Catholic community in the five eastern sections of
Monroe County. In the following years, other Irish
groups had come to Illinois so that by 1850 the federal
Census reported the Irish population of the state as
27,786.*[1]

"*With these facts in mind, the collector should be able
to pick up here and there in Illinois, especially in the
tri-counties mentioned, various old-time Irish traditions.
The original Monroe County settlement undoubtedly
sent offshoots to bordering areas, if not farther afield.
Fortunate circumstances have enabled the writer to obtain four Irish ballads, three of them from Randolph
County, so far as noted probably unreported in American folksong; the fourth is a transient in Jackson
County. All four have been heretofore lacking in the
scant roster of Illinois balladry.*

"*The Randolph County ballads were in the repertoire
of an old-time resident in the neighborhood of Red Bud,
familiarly known as 'Peg.' They were reclaimed by the
writer's informants from a relative, Mrs. Carrie Lohrberg, of Red Bud, who heard the songs from Peg herself at her father's home, more than seventy years ago.
Peg was then a grown woman and married. It is prob-
able that she was a 'stray' from the original Monroe
County colony. These facts and suppositions warrant
setting the age of her songs at not less than one hundred years. They have, it is obvious, all the flavor as
well as the phrasing of the Irish vernacular.*" So writes
Grace Partridge Smith, "*Four Irish Ballads from
'Egypt,'*" Hoosier Folklore, *V* (1946), 115–16. The
text of "*The Hold-Up*" is on pp. 116–17. Mrs. Smith
further notes: "*The verses were transcribed as they
sounded from Mrs. Lohrberg's recital. She herself was
uncertain about a few of the words. The peculiar phrasing of the lines is in character with an English-speaking
Irishwoman. See P. W. Joyce,* English As We Speak
It In Ireland, *Dublin, 1910.*"

[1] John Reynolds, *My Own Times* (Chicago, 1879), pp. 182–84.

This ballad plot suggests the initial episode in "The Undaunted Female," L3 in G. Malcolm Laws, American Balladry from British Broadsides (Philadelphia: The American Folklore Society, 1957), p. 166.

(*Tune: The Irish Washerwoman*)

Faith in me cuttle and stick in me buttle,
    Brog and the letters in the measere,
Sen off to Dublin town to trip,
    To sail upon the say, sir!

To see if I could get employ,
    To cut me corn and hay, sir;
To pick the pence upon the say,
    The cockle and I may clarens, sir!

As I was travelin' along the way,
    To sell my corn and hay, sir,
I met an honest gentleman a-travelin'
    Along the way, sir!

An' "How d'ye do, an' how's your health?"
    But he proved to be a mighty rogue, sir;
For down at the foot of the lane,
    A pistol he pulled out, sir.

He pits the very nozzle,
    Into my very mouth, sir,
And swore that if I would bawl or cry,
    My brains he'd blow out, sir!

Three steps I did retire,
    "Money?" says I. "Your Irish eye, sir!"
My shellallah never misses fire——
    His pistol flashed; his head I smashed, sir!

Muckle-a-rooh, this song so true,
    To the bottom of the say I'll go, sir;

You promised to take me over to Pargate,
An' I'll make it an' stick to the bargain.

Native American Ballads

> *The standard work discussing, identifying, synopsiz-*
> *ing, and citing ballads original to the United States is*
> *G. Malcolm Laws,* Native American Balladry *(Phila-*
> *delphia: The American Folklore Society, 1950). Laws*
> *identifies 185 American ballads, and groups them from*
> *A to I under the headings War Ballads, Ballads of*
> *Cowboys and Pioneers, Ballads of Lumberjacks, Bal-*
> *lads of Sailors, Ballads about Criminals and Outlaws,*
> *Murder Ballads, Ballads of Tragedies and Disasters,*
> *Ballads on Various Topics, and Ballads of the Negro.*

"Brother Green, or The Dying Soldier"

> *Text taken from David S. McIntosh, "Southern Illinois*
> *Folk Songs,"* Journal of the Illinois State Historical
> Society, *XXXI (1938), 309–10. McIntosh writes: "I*
> *heard this sung first by Mr. R. H. Finley; he called it*
> *'The Dying Soldier." Mr. Finley lives southeast of*
> *Carbondale. When I asked him to sing this song, he*
> *said, 'Here's the way it goes—the way my dad sang*
> *it.' " The singer used the same tune he employed for*
> *his rendering of "Barbara Allen."*
>
> *Subsequently Professor McIntosh recorded a second,*
> *longer and even more sentimental version, from a Mrs.*
> *Wilmore of West Frankfort. She informed him that*
> *the song was composed by Reverend L. J. Simpson,*
> *late chaplain in the army, on the death of a brother*
> *killed at Fort Donelson, February, 1962.*
>
> *Laws excludes this song from his syllabus, because of*
> *its weak narrative, but lists it in his Appendix III,*
> *"Ballad-like Pieces" (p. 263), with a reference to*
> *Henry M. Belden,* Ballads and Songs Collected by the
> Missouri Folk-Lore Society *(Columbia, Mo., 1940),*
> *p. 377. Belden has only the first stanza of "this pious*

and patriotic song"; he cites texts from six east-central states

"THE DYING SOLDIER"

Sung by R. H. Finley, Carterville, Illinois. Collected by David S. McIntosh, 1934.

Oh, Brother Green do come to me,
For I am shot and bleeding,
And I must die, no more to see
My wife and my dear children.

A southern foe has laid me low
On this cold ground to suffer.
Dear brother, stay; lay me away,
And write my wife a letter.

Tell her I am prepared to die
And hope we'll meet in Heaven;
For when I believed in Jesus Christ,
My sins were all forgiven.

My little babes, I loved them well.
Oh, could I once more see them
And bid them both a long farewell,
Till we shall meet in Heaven

But here I am in Tennessee,
And they are in Illinois.

And I must soon to be buried be,
No more to hear their voices.

Dear Mary, you must treat them well
And train them up for Heaven.
Teach them to love and fear the Lord,
And they will be respected.

Two brothers yet I can't forget,
That's fighting for this Union,
For which, dear wife, I gave my life
To lay down this rebellion.

Oh, I am dying, Brother Green,
Oh, do I die so easy,
And oh, that death has lost its sting,
Because I love my Jesus.

"Pearl Bryant"

> *"Secured from Miss Edna Dunn, Metropolis, Illinois, who got it from her aunt, Mrs. Minnie Trovillian of Brownfield. Mrs. Trovillian learned it from her mother, Mrs. A. B. Bland, also of Brownfield, whose family brought it from Tennessee. The music was furnished by Miss Dunn." Text from Neely, pp. 157–60, who adds the following note (p. 178):*
>
> *"Two variants of this ballad are known in Egypt, the second one under the title, 'Drooping Willows.' The usual name of the piece seems to be 'The Jealous Lover' or 'Pearl Bryan.'*
>
> *"[John Harrington] Cox, Folk-Songs of the South [Cambridge, 1925, pp. 200–201], No. 38, quotes a letter from Mr. Clifford R. Meyers, State Historian and Archivist of West Virginia, which explains why the ballad sometimes has the title 'Pearl Bryan.' According to Mr. Meyers, a girl of that name, residing in Greencastle, Indiana, was murdered January 31, 1896, as a result of a criminal operation performed by two young doctors or dental students, Scott Jackson and*

Alonzo Walling. The girl's body was found near Fort Thomas, Kentucky. This variant of the ballad made its way into Tennessee and then into Pope County, Illinois. Somewhere along the route Bryan became Bryant."

Two ballads have mingled in the present text, a highly popular native piece of uncertain origin, "The Jealous Lover," and the composition describing the murder of Pearl Bryan at Greencastle, Indiana. Laws points out that one form of the Pearl Bryan ballad (the present one) is simply a variation of "The Jealous Lover," with the names of Pearl Bryan(t) and Scott Jackson substituted for Florella and her murderous fiancée Edward.

Accordingly, Laws calls the present song type "Pearl Bryan II" and associates it with "The Jealous Lover (b)" in his category F1, Murder Ballads. Under F2 and F3 he places two other forms of Pearl Bryan.

Deep, deep in yonder valley
Where the violets fade and bloom
There lies my own Pearl Bryant
In the cold and silent tomb.
She died not broken-hearted,
Nor lingering sickness fell,
But in an instant parted
From a home she loved so well.

One evening the moon shone brightly,
And the stars were shining, too.
Up to her cottage window
Her jealous lover drew.
"Come, Pearl, let's take a ramble
O'er the meadows deep and gay.
There, no one can disturb us,
And we'll name our wedding day."

Deep, deep into the valley
He led his love so dear.
Says she, "It's for you only

That I am rambling here.
The way seems dark and dreary,
And I'm afraid to stay;
Of rambling I've grown weary
And would retrace my way."

"Retrace your way you'll never;
These woods you'll never more roam.
So bid farewell for ever
To parents, friends, and home.
From me you cannot hide;
No human arm can save you;
Pearl Bryant, you must die."

Down on her knees before him
She pleaded for her life,
But deep into her bosom
He plunged a fatal knife.

"What have I done, Scott Jackson,
For you to take my life?
You know that I have always loved you
And would have been your wife.

"Good-bye, dear loving parents;
I'll never see you more,
Tho' long you'll wait my coming
At the little cottage door.
But I will forgive you, Jackson."
These were her dying words.
Her pulse had ceased their beating
And her eyes were closed in death.

The birds sang in the morning
Their awful, weary song.
They found Pearl Bryant lying
Upon the cold, cold ground.
She died not broken-hearted,

Nor lingering sickness fell,
But in an instant parted
From a home she loved so well.

"William Stafford"

> *"Secured from Mr. Dave H. Adamson, Jr., Belleville, who learned from his mother, Mrs. D. H. Adamson, Sr., of Belleville." Text from Neely, pp. 210–11.*
>
> *See Laws H1, "An Arkansas Traveller," for references. In Dorson, American Folklore, p. 93, a verse is given about the miserable Arkansaw gent. Five texts are printed in Vance Randolph, Ozark Folksongs, Vol. III (Columbia, Mo., 1949), No. 347, pp. 25–31, "The State of Arkansaw," with an extensive headnote.*

My name is William Stafford,
    Was raised in Boston Town;
For nine years as a rover
    I roved the wide world 'round;
Through all its ups and downs
    Some bitter days I saw,
But never knew what misery was
    Till I struck Arkansaw.

I started on my journey,
    'Twas the merry month of June;
I landed in New Jersey
    One sultry afternoon.
Along came a walking skeleton
    With long and lantern jaw.
He asked me to his hotel
    In the state of Arkansaw.

I followed up a great long rope
    Into his boarding place,
Where hunger and starvation
    Were printed on his face;

His bread it was corn dodger;
　His beef I could not chaw;
He taxed me fifty cents for that
　In the state of Arkansaw.

I rose the next morning early
　To catch the early train.
He said, "Young man, you'd better stay;
　I have some land to drain.
I'll give you fifty cents a day,
　Your washing, board, and all;
You'll find yourself a different lad
　When you leave Arkansaw."

Six months I worked for this galoot;
　Charles Tyler was his name;
He was six feet seven in his boots
　And thin as any crane.
His hair hung down like rat tails
　Around his lantern jaw;
He was the photograph of all the gents
　That's raised in Arkansaw.

He fed me on corn dodgers
　As hard as any rock;
My teeth began to loosen;
　My knees began to knock.
I got so thin on sassafras,
　Could hide behind a straw,
So I sho' was a different lad
　When I left Arkansaw.

"Casey Jones"

> *"Miss Dorothy Westwood, Belleville, gave me this ballad, which she learned from her father." Text from Neely, pp. 169–71.*
>
> *Laws G1 gives full references to this celebrated ballad describing the death of engineer John Luther Jones of*

the Illinois Central at Vaughan, Mississippi, April 30,
1900, in a train crash. Casey Jones is the tragic hero
of the railroaders, dying in action as he nobly takes on
an extra run and tries to make up for lost time. The
key verse has the phrase "You got a white eye," spoken
by the fireman when he sees the fatigue in Casey's face.
A useful biographical sketch is Fred J. Lee, Casey
Jones, Epic of the American Railroad (Kingsport,
Tenn., 1939).

Come, all you rounders, I want you to hear
The story of a brave engineer;
Casey Jones was the rounder's name
On a big eight-wheeler of a mighty fame.

CHORUS:
Casey Jones, he pushed on the throttler;
Casey Jones was a brave engineer;
Come on, Casey, and blow the whistler,
Blow the whistles so they all can hear.

Now, Casey said, "Before I die
There's one more trail that I want to try,
And I will try ere many a day
The Union Pacific and the Santa Fe."

Caller called Casey about half-past four;
He kissed his wife at the station door,
Climbed in his cab and was on his way,
"I've got my chance on the Santa Fe."

Down the slope he went on the fly
Heard the fireman say, "You got a white eye."
Well the switchman knew by the engine's moan
That the man at the throttle was Casey Jones.

The rain was a-pounding down like lead;
The railroad track was a river bed;

They slowed her down to a thirty-mile gait,
And the south-bound mail was eight hours late.

Fireman says, "Casey, you're running too fast,
You run the black board the last station you passed."
Casey says, "I believe we'll make it through.
For the steam's much better than I ever knew."

Around the curve comes a passenger train,
Her headlight was shining in his eyes through the rain;
Casey blew the whistles a mighty blast,
But the locomotive was a-coming fast.

The locomotives met in the middle of the hill,
In a head-on tangle that's bound to kill;
He tried to do his duty, the yard men said,
But Casey Jones was scalded dead.

Headaches and heartaches and all kinds of pain,
They all ride along with the railroad train,
Stories of brave men, noble and grand,
Belong to the life of the railroad man.

"The Death of Charlie Burger"

> *"During the prohibition era, two bootlegging gangs,
> the Shelton Gang and the Burger Gang, fought for
> supremacy in southern Illinois. Burger finally drove
> the Sheltons to East St. Louis and from his stronghold
> at Shady Rest controlled the liquor traffic in several
> counties. He maintained his position for several years
> by bribery of officials and murder. Brought to trial at
> last in Franklin County for the murder of the mayor
> of West City, he was convicted and hanged." Note by
> Neely, p. 268. Informant Alice Story, Harrisburg. Text
> from Neely, pp. 266-68.*
>
> *This is a purely local ballad. For the vicious career of
> Charles Birger (sic) see Paul M. Angle, Bloody Wil-
> liamson (New York: Alfred A. Knopf, 1952), chaps.
> 12-14.*

I'll tell you of a bandit,
Out in a Western state,
Who never learned his lesson
Until it was too late.
This man was bold and careless,
The leader of his gang,
But boldness did not save him
When the law said, "You must hang."

This bandit's name was Burger;
He lived at Shady Rest,
And people learned to fear him
Throughout the Middle West.
'Twas out in old West City
Joe Adams was shot down,
And then the cry of justice,
"These murderers must be found."

Then Thompson was captured
And turned state's evidence.
Burger was found guilty,
For he had no defense.
He asked for a rehearing,
But this he was denied.
In the county jail house
To take his life he tried.

On the 19th day of April in 1928
Away out west in Benton
Charles Burger met his fate.
Another life was ended;
Another chapter done;
Another man who gambled
In the game that can't be won.

The Ten Commandments show us
The straight and narrow way,
And if we do not heed them
Sometime we'll have to pay.

We all must face the Master,
Our final trial to stand,
And there we'll learn the meaning
Of houses built on sand.

Songs of Sin, Politics, and Love

> *In lieu of indexes for non-ballad folksongs in the
> United States, the "Index of Titles" and "Index of
> First Lines" in Randolph, Ozark Folksongs, Vol. IV
> (Columbia, Missouri: State Historical Society of Mis-
> souri), pp. 418–46, are useful finding lists.*

"Young People Who Delight in Sin"

> *"This song was sung by Mrs. Lottie Hendrickson, and
> you will notice in the music a slur indicated at the end
> of each phrase. This upward slur is characteristic of
> the singing of many old people. In the case of Mrs.
> Hendrickson, she made use of this device on very emo-
> tional songs. The slur does not always extend the
> octave, but usually gives this impression." Text from
> McIntosh, "Southern Illinois Folk Songs," pp. 316–18.
> Five variants, with references, are under the title
> "Wicked Polly" in Randolph, Ozark Folksongs, Vol.
> IV, No. 596, pp. 16–20.*

"Young People Who Delight in Sin"

Sung by Lottie Hendrickson, Marion, Illinois. Collected by David S.
McIntosh, 1934.

Young peo-ple___ who___ de-light in___ sin,___ I will___
tell to you what has late-ly___ been.___ A___ la-dy who was
young and___ fair, She___ died in sin___ and sad des-pair.___

Young people who delight in sin,
I will tell to you what has lately been,
A lady who was young and fair,
She died in sin and sad despair.

She would go to frolics, dance and play,
In spite of all her friends could say.
"I'll turn to God when I am old,
And then He will receive my soul."

On Friday she was taken ill;
Her stubborn heart began to yield.
"Alas, alas, my days are spent,
Too late, too late, now to repent."

She called her mother to her bed;
Her eyes were rolling in her head.
"When I am dead, remember well,
Your wicked daughter screams in Hell!!!"

"My earthly father, fare you well,
My soul is lost and doomed to Hell.
When I am dead, remember well,
Your wicked daughter screams in Hell."

"Don't You Know"

"*This is an old political campaign song and was sung by Mr. R. H. Finley, who gave the following description of the big political meeting that took place in his home town when McKinley was running against Bryan for president* [*in 1896*].

"*'Of course, there were no cars. There were sixteen white horses in the parade and one yellow one. (This was a dramatic presentation of Bryan's silver policy, 'Sixteen to one makes the gold bugs shiver.') Each white horse was ridden by a girl dressed in white, but the girl riding the yellow horse was dressed in yellow. The teams of horses were hitched to band wagons—*

*big wagons with seats around the sides facing the
center of the wagon, much like bleachers at a football
game. Each wagon could seat about thirty people.'"
Text from McIntosh, "Southern Illinois Folk Songs,"
pp. 318–20. For the political background see Paul W.
Glad,* The Trumpet Soundeth: William Jennings Bryan
and his Democracy 1896–1912 (*Lincoln, 1960*).

"Don't You Know"

Sung by R. H. Finley, Carterville, Illinois. Collected by David S.
McIntosh, 1934.

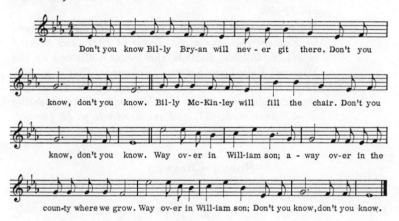

Don't you know Billy Bryan will never get there?
Don't you know? Don't you know?
Billy McKinley will fill the chair.
Don't you know? Don't you know?
Way over in Williamson, away over in the county where
    we grow,
Way over in Williamson, don't you know? Don't you
    know?

Don't you know Henry Jones will be our next clerk:
Don't you know? Don't you know?
For H. P. Crain is big enough to work.
Don't you know? Don't you know?

Way over in Williamson, away over in the county where
    we grow,
Way over in Williamson, don't you know? Don't you know?

. . . .

Sixteen to one makes the gold bugs shiver.
Don't you know? Don't you know?

"Sober Quaker"

> *Sung by Art Johnston, Fairfield, Illinois. Text from McIntosh, Southern Illinois Singing Games and Songs, pp. 47–49.*
>
> *McIntosh refers to another southern Illinois text, heard by Frances Barbour at St. Louis in 1917, and printed in H. M. Belden, Ballads and Songs Collected by the Missouri Folk-Lore Society (Columbia, 1940), p. 265, "The Quaker's Wooing." A variant is in Randolph, Ozark Folksongs, Vol. IV, No. 362, "The Courting Song," text B, 56–57, and see headnote p. 55 for references.*

"SOBER QUAKER"

(*Girl*)
1.   Where art Thou going, Sober Quaker?
    Ti um a tu dee a,
    In the early dawn of morning,
    Ti um a tu dee a.

(*Boy*)
2.   I'm hunting for a lovely creature,
    Hay hi ho hum.
    And can you tell me where to find her?
    Hay hi ho hum.

(*Boy*)
3.   I have a ring worth twenty shillings,
    Hay hi ho hum,
    And you may wear it if you wish to
    Hay hi ho hum.

(*Girl*)

4.
I neither want your ring or money,
Ti um a tu dee a,
I've got a beau as sweet as honey,
Ti um a tu dee a.

(*Boy*)

5.
I'll move my chair a little closer,
Hay hi ho hum,
And gently lay my arms around you,
Hay hi ho hum.

(*Girl*)

6.
You move your chair up any closer,
Ti um a tu dee a,
I'll kick you straight into the fire,
Ti um a tu dee a.

"Dutch Courtship"

> *David S. McIntosh comments on this song: "My father and mother would sing this song after much coaxing, and we children never tired of hearing it. Mother would sit at the piano and chord, and father would stand beside her. The first verse would be sung by father, the second by mother. This would continue to the last verse which was sung by both.*
>
> *"My mother's people came into southern Illinois from Pennsylvania shortly before the Civil War, and settled at Mt. Erie in Wayne County. They were known as Pennsylvania Dutch, and I suppose this song came into southern Illinois with them. I have never heard it sung except as my folks sang it. It was sung to the tune of 'Maryland, My Maryland.'*
>
> *"This is the only song in my collection that had an accompaniment."*
>
> *Text from McIntosh, "Southern Illinois Folk Songs," pp. 303–5. Sung by W. D. McIntosh.*

"Dutch Courtship"

Sung by W. D. McIntosh, Carbondale, Illinois. Collected by his son, David S. McIntosh. Remembered from childhood and transcribed in 1934.

Thar ware a time, a good old time I ware in Dutch-land far a-way; and I'd go thar to be a-gain, if you go dar mid me. What! Go so long way off and live from sis-ter and from brud-der,— Oh, no! dear Hans, I can-not leave mine fad-der and mine mud-der.—

Thar ware a time, a good old time,
I ware in Dutchland, far away
And I'd go thar to be again,
If you go dar mid me.

What? Go so long way off and live
From sister and from brudder?
Oh, no, dear Hans, I cannot leave
Mine fadder and mine mudder.

Then, Hailey, dear, why smile so sweet?
You break my bleeding heart in two.
You know I'd leave de peoples all,
To go along mid you.

Oh, Hans, mine udder fear would be,
Mid hearts so full of pain,
That all the young men in the town
Could never smile again.

Then, Hailey, dear, good-by, good-by,
I've noting more just now to speak.
My heart is broke, good-by, my love,
I'd drown me in the creek.

Oh, Hans, oh, Hans, come back, I pray,
And I will leave mine mudder.
I'll leave mid you this country quick
And fly into anudder.

Then married we will buy a farm
And cabbage we will cultivate,
And sauerkraut in a barrel big,
With plenty of smearcase, we will make.

Oh, limbergar, dar limbergar,
How many a ting them cheese mid tell,
To people who the house go by
Mid noses turned up at the smell.

"The Old Girl of Cairo Town"

> "An old river town with a large Negro population,
> Cairo was for many years a gay and wicked city of
> Egypt.
> "Secured from Miss Hazel Towery, Olney, who learned
> it from her father, Mr. B. F. Towery, Marion." Text
> from Neely, p. 268.

"THE OLD GIRL OF CAIRO TOWN"

There was an old girl who lived in Cairo town,
And I wish to the Lord that she was dead.

She puts so many notions into my girl's head
That we can't get along, we can't get along,
We can't never get along no more.

REFRAIN:
Great God ain't that hard?
Me to love a girl who don't love me.

Come all the way from Cairo town,
And I never had but one dime to spend.
All the money I ever had
I done spent it on that little girl of mine,
Spent it on that little girl of mine,
Done spent it on that little girl of mine.

VI

SOUTHWEST MEXICANS

🌿 THROUGHOUT THE STATES of the southwest, Mexican-Americans now comprise a permanent and increasingly substantial segment of the population. Their Latin-American culture, derived from Spain and refashioned in semitropical Mexico, has taken root north of the Rio Grande in Texas, New Mexico, Arizona, southern Colorado, and southern California. There it confronts the cultures of the southern white, the southern Negro, the Pueblo and Plains Indian, and the European immigrant.

Natural growth and migrant streams have more than tripled the population of Mexican-Americans from 1950 to 1960. Their number rose from 450,562 to 1,735,992, of whom nearly 90 per cent live in the Southwest. The two great centers in the 1960 census are Texas with 655,523 (196,077 in 1950) and California, which has now jumped ahead with 695,643 (162,309 in 1950). Arizona, in third place, jumped from 24,917 to 105,342. Although most of the scholarly writing on Mexican-American folklore has focused on New Mexico, less than 10,000 Mexicans lived in that state in 1950, as contrasted with 34,459 in 1960, out of a total population of under a million.

These figures graphically illustrate the swift and spectacular upsurge within the past decade of the oldest European civilization in the United States. The first fingers of Spanish exploration in New Mexico reached out from old Mexico in expeditions launched as early as 1539, the most famous being led by Coronado in search of the Seven Cities of Cibola. Mexico severed her political ties with Spain in 1821, and New Mexico broke with Mexico in 1846, but other bonds remain. There is incessant travel, legal and illegal, across the Rio Grande border, and constant visiting, emigration, correspondence, and cultural contacts through the mass media. The effect on folklore is doubly invigorating, for sixteenth-century traditions receive twentieth-century injections. Thus one student writes: "The legend of the Weeping Woman in Arizona is continually refreshed by contact with Mexican sources, either social or literary—by visiting back and forth across the border and then among Arizona and California families; by a motion picture; by a play." * Introducing a collection of New Mexican Spanish riddles, Aurelio M. Espinosa pointed out the vitality of this riddle tradition which dated from the time of Spanish colonization in New Mexico.† Soledad Pérez found that the birthplace of her Mexican informants in Austin, Texas, were about evenly divided between Mexico and the United States.‡ In the mountain pockets of northern New Mexico, Helen Zunser uncovered an isolated community with curiously ambivalent attitudes:

> Our friends called themselves Spanish Americans, but called their language Mexican. There was deep antagonism in their attitude towards the people and country of "Old Mexico," and they resented being called Mexicans. "Bad country, old Mexico. Too many bandits. Kill all the time, have long knives. Like to fight." . . . they always spoke of temperamental differences, as if the Mexicans were much more violent than they were. Yet we knew of individual cases where Old and New Mexicans had been friends, and we were told that their language differences were slight.§

Of all the distinct nationality groups in the United States, the Mexican-Americans are the one most explosively on the march. There is no question in their case of folklore being a matter of relics and survivals; their folk traditions are dynamic and expansive. Consider the places in American life held by the *curandero,* the *corrido,* and the *santo.*

. . .

* Betty Leddy, "La Llorona in Southern Arizona," *Western Folklore,* VII (1948), 272.
† *Journal of American Folklore,* XXVIII (1915), 319.
‡ *The Healer of Los Olmos and Other Mexican Lore,* ed. W. M. Hudson (Dallas and Austin, 1951), p. 72.
§ *Journal of American Folklore,* XLVIII (1935), 141. Cf. Arthur L. Campa, "Spanish, Mexican, Native: The Problem of Nomenclature," in *Spanish Folk-Poetry in New Mexico* (Albuquerque, 1946), pp. 12–16; and the terms used by John H. Burma, *Spanish-Speaking Groups in the United States* (Durham, 1954), p. 35, note 1.

In the institution of the *curandero,* religious faith and medical science meet at the folk level. He is the faith healer who cures by special powers, when ordinary doctors are helpless. His counterparts are universal, and in the United States we have already encountered them as *traiteurs* among the Louisiana Cajuns and *brauchers* among the Pennsylvania Dutch. Customarily the healer also possesses gifts of clairvoyance, second sight, and white magic that overcome dark forces of evil.

An example of a *curandero* whose fame and feats have spread widely through south Texas and entered into local tradition is Pedro Jaramillo, known as the healer of Los Olmos. Some sixty accounts of his cures and powers were collected and printed, first in Spanish in 1934 and then in English translation in 1951, by Ruth Dodson of Nueces County.* Jaramillo was born in Guadalajara, Jalisco, Mexico (the date is not known), and died at Paisano, Starr County, Texas, in 1907. He came to Texas in 1881 and settled at Los Olmos Ranch, situated between the Nueces River and the Rio Grande near present day Falfurrias. There he announced himself as a *curandero,* and treated the Mexican families scattered through the ranches over an area of several hundred square miles. At the height of his fame, Mexican families came to him from as far away as New York and Mexico City, and Americans too sought his succour. When a poor laborer in Mexico, Jaramillo suffered some ailment to his nose, and in distress buried his face in mud at the edge of a pool. After three days of such treatment, the malady disappeared, though a scar remained permanently on his nose. The third night he heard a voice saying that God had given him the power to heal, and that he should immediately treat his ailing master. Pedro prescribed a tepid bath for three days running, as the first idea that popped in his mind, and it worked. So runs the story, attributed to Don Pedro himself. The scar on his nose always identified him, together with his long white beard and big felt hat.

The numerous belief tales of Don Pedro's cures follow a regular pattern. In phase one, an afflicted person visits Pedro, or a friend writes him, or Pedro calls on the patient, usually after recourse to conventional doctors has failed; in phase two, the healer offers his prescription, which always involves some eccentric action, perhaps coupled with a perfectly reasonable suggestion like taking warm baths; and phase three is the unfailing recovery.

The number nine always figured prominently in the remedies.

---

* "Don Pedrito Jaramillo, The Curandero of Los Olmos," in *The Healer of Los Olmos and Other Mexican Lore,* pp. 9–70.

So Don Pedro prescribed a can of tomatoes for an insane man for nine consecutive mornings. For a woman with a stomach ailment he recommended that she put a glass of water at the head of her bed and drink it next morning "in the name of the Lord." Another woman with a pain in her side was to wet and soap the soles of her feet for nine nights at bedtime and sleep lathered up. A sick ranchman was instructed to eat raw egg for nine mornings before breakfast; he did so for eight days, but on the ninth morning, not finding a hen's egg, he substituted a turkey egg and failed to recover. For a little girl with a swelling on her neck, Pedro prescribed that her mother dip a chicken feather in olive oil and rub the soles of the girl's feet with it, from the toes back to the heels, for nine consecutive days. A thin, pale American woman on her way to see a doctor in Laredo met Pedro, who told her to drink a bottle of beer for nine consecutive days while taking a bath; she was well and almost too fat before the period was up.

Occasionally a patient failed to follow instructions. A vaquero blinded by a tree limb was told to do heavy ax work for nine days running, with no siesta; on Sunday he rested and consequently was blind for the rest of his life. A man suffering from bad teeth was instructed by Don Pedro to eat salted onions for nine days; after the first day, finding the onion intolerable, he threw it over his left shoulder, saying "In the name of God." His teeth stopped hurting and fell out one by one. Pedro said the man's faith had affected the cure.

Some of Pedro's cures verged on the miraculous. He recommended that a paralyzed man near death be placed on a *zalea*—a sheepskin with the wool still on—and dragged to a creek, where a strong fellow picked him up and threw him in the water. The paralytic barely crawled out. Each day when the treatment was repeated he grew a little stronger, until finally he could walk perfectly. A sick shepherd named Monico Hinguanza traveled sixty miles to the Los Olmos Ranch, arriving at dark after a heavy rainfall. Pedro took the shepherd to the swollen creek near his hut, threw a piece of a heavy canvas into an eddy swirling around the creek's edge, and tossed a pillow on the canvas. Then Pedro lifted Monico on top of the canvas, which supported him, and the eddy rocked him into a pleasant sleep. In the morning he was well. In gratitude Monica presented the bachelor *curandero* with one of his sons, to wait upon and serve him. (This account was told Ruth Dodson by an old man who walked nine miles to return fifty cents he had borrowed from her to buy some medicine.)

The *curandero* also exhibited powers of clairvoyance. A skeptic once came to him pretending that he was sick. Pedro prescribed a bale of hay. Then he said, "When one brings a lie, he will take a lie." Another time a horse dealer named Chat Vela who suffered from a mule kick on his shin was prevailed upon by fellow vaqueros to visit Don Pedro. The *curandero* prescribed a porous plaster to be placed on the uninjured leg. Because he had little faith in Pedro's powers, Chat never tried the cure until, during a bad spell with his leg, a relative urged him to put on the plaster. "If that old *brujo* [wizard] cures me," he laughed, "I will give him ten dollars and a fine pair of gloves." The leg healed. Chat called on Pedro and presented him with the gloves and ten dollars. "You are forgetting something," the *curandero* reminded him. "You should say, 'Here, old *brujo,* is ten dollars and a pair of gloves.'"

These are some specimens of the hundreds of traditional stories told by Mexican-Americans in south Texas, forming a cycle of saint's legends comparable to those circulating in the Middle Ages. People expect indeed that Pedro Jaramillo will be canonized. Pictures and statues of Don Pedrito adorn the homes of Mexican families in Texas, resting among those of already recognized saints; votive offerings are daily brought to his grave, at Los Olmos Ranch; a Laredo firm labels its curative herbs with his picture and the trademark "Don Pedrito." At the height of his fame as many as five hundred people were said to have camped on Los Olmos Creek awaiting his return, having traveled by foot, horse, wagon, buggy; and mailcarriers, first on horse and then by stagecoach, brought him two hundred letters a week.

Other *curanderos* in south Texas have learned from Don Pedro the power to *recetar* (prescribe), and always place on their altars a picture or an image of Don Pedro, even if they lack one of the Virgin. A *curandera* who was launched on her profession by Don Pedro is black-eyed Doña Maria Pérez on Sinton, Texas, a specialist in curing *susto,* or fright. She prescribed doses of seed oils and baths in herbal teas. Doña Maria gained her power of *recetando* from Don Pedro, and a photograph of the dignified *curandero* hangs on the wall above her chair. While working as a midwife in the little Texas town of Delfina, about 1882, she fell down a steep stairway, and lost consciousness for days, until taken by her parents to Don Pedro.*

* Brownie McNeil, "Curanderos of South Texas," in *And Horns on the Toads,* ed. M. C. Boatright, W. M. Hudson, A. Maxwell (Dallas, 1959), pp. 43–44.

The attitudes of Mexican-Americans to Don Pedro are expressed in the reply of an old chap from Falfurrias who, when asked if he believed in the *curandero,* murmured softly, *"¡Sí! Era Dios"* (Yes! He was God).

. . .

What the ballad is in Anglo-American folksong, the *corrido* has become in Mexican-American—with the important difference that ballads are seldom newly composed in the United States, while *corridos* are constantly and publicly created and sung. As it evolved in the mid-nineteenth century in Mexico, from the older Hispanic form of the *romance,* the *corrido* combined lyrical and narrative elements in a basic stanzaic form of four eight-syllable lines, usually with consonantal rhyme. The singer offers an opening salutation and a closing leave, and dates the topical event which he describes in his verses. His language is colloquial and idiomatic, he employs popular refrains and stock phrases, and he tells a realistic and earthy story. While *corridos* are written by known composers and printed in cheap broadsides—facts that would ordinarily give two strikes against their folk character—they arise so directly from popular attitudes and often pass so quickly into oral currency that they do in many cases qualify as folk products.

Since World War II a number of collectors have brought together *corridos* sung by Mexicans in the United States. A graduate student at the University of Texas, Brownie McNeil, prepared a sheaf of them under the title "Corridos of the Mexican Border." *
In his volume on *Spanish Folk-Poetry in New Mexico* (1947), Arthur L. Campa devoted one section to "The Corrido," printing twenty-three texts. So too did Aurero Lucero-White Lea in *Literary Folklore of the Hispanic Southwest* (1953), in which she included fifteen texts, and discussed New Mexican modifications of the *corrido*. Lea found less need in New Mexico for the use of *corridos* to purvey historical and political news, such news being regularly printed in Spanish; consequently the New Mexican *corrido* tends to be more a song of entertainment than of information, sung to a borrowed *corrido* tune with violin and guitar accompaniment. From his own field collecting and musical transcriptions John D. Robb published *Hispanic Folk Songs of New Mexico* (1954), containing two *corridos*. In a richly documented study, *The Mexican Corrido as a Source for Interpretive Study of Modern Mexico (1870–1950)* (1957), Merle E. Simmons devoted the final chapter to "Mexico's

* *Mexican Border Ballads and Other Lore,* ed. M. C. Boatright (Austin, 1946), pp. 1–34.

Relations with the United States and North Americans," and analyzed emotional grievances and resentments of the *pueblo* against the *gringo* as openly revealed in *corrido* texts. The same border theme stimulated Américo Paredes to undertake a book-length biographical study of a legendary hero and the *corridos* of his exploits, *"With His Pistol in His Hand"* (1958), dealing with Gregorio Cortez, who defied the Texas Rangers.

A border separating—and connecting—two alien cultures is a fertile breeding ground for folk traditions, and the Texas-Mexican border has bred a dense and spirited border lore, of which the *corridos* are one manifestation. They celebrate Mexican outlaw heroes, trail rides of Mexican cowhands up to Kansas, petty border raids, and occasionally, as in "El Contrabando del Paso," a highly personal life story, in this case of a young Mexican smuggler caught in El Paso and committed to Leavenworth, who rues his false *amigos*.

· · ·

Santos are the sacred images fashioned by Spanish-Mexican folk artists, or *santeros*, whose handiwork flourished from about 1775 to 1900 in New Mexico and southern Colorado. Both as the products of a peasant folk art, and as objects linked with supernatural forces, the *santos* attract the attention of the folklorist.

The *santero* was a carver and a painter. From cottonwood he carved statues of Christ, the Virgin, and the saints, and these sculptures are called *bultos*. On pine tablets he painted similar figures and scenes, called *retablos*. A third form is painting in tempera on deer, elk, or buffalo skin. The history of *santos* in North America presumably begins with Coronado's entrance into New Mexico in 1540, although actual mention of Catholic religious images and ornaments being transported into the area does not occur until the Oñate expedition of 1598. Historical narratives, personal wills, and church inventories of the seventeenth and eighteenth centuries give evidence of numerous images present in churches, chapels, and homes. Late in the eighteenth century a spirit of original design seems to have replaced the mechanical copying of existing models by image-makers. The need for *bultos* and *retablos* on the part of unlettered farmers and villagers arose from the neglect of the mother country to furnish the desired ornaments, and the deep folk-religious piety of Spanish New Mexicans that required statues and paintings.

North American travelers along the Santa Fe trail opened in 1822 failed to note the *santos*, but from 1845 on, with the outbreak of the Mexican War and the resulting incorporation of New Mexico into the United States, the comments from Yankee Protestant visitors and settlers multiply. They are uniformly uncomplimentary. Already in 1841 one traveler to Santa Fe, George W. Kendall, gibed at a wax figure of the patron saint San Miguel, in the village of San Miguel del Bado, carried in a procession to ward off a body of invading Texans. Kendall called it a grotesque and comical sight; its ill-fitting wings and lace cap covered with feathers provoked uncontrollable merriment among the Americans. Even the perceptive ethnologist John G. Bourke reacted in 1881 with unalloyed disgust to the "idols" of "barbarous execution," which "vied in hideousness with the tin-framed, painted and begrimed daubs of San Antonio, San Juan and San Diego." *

A century following the admission of New Mexico, the attitude of United States citizens toward the *santos* has undergone a complete reversal. Local collectors and curio dealers first showed interest in them, and gradually art critics and art historians and museum curators gave them recognition, all contributing to a vast polemical and devotional literature that extends from popular magazines to learned journals and handsomely illustrated art books. Some eighty-two publications can be found on New Mexican religious folk art, chiefly written in the last twenty years; one specialist, Elizabeth Boyd, has produced twenty-two articles, monographs, and a full-dress volume, *Saints and Saint Makers of New Mexico* (1946). The climactic hagiography is by José E. Espinosa, *Saints in the Valleys. Christian Sacred Images in the History, Life and Folk Art of Spanish New Mexico* (1960). Here is a meticulous and commanding work of scholarship, assembling all the documentable facts about the history and technique of the *santos,* furnishing plates of pictorial specimens, providing a detailed bibliography and catalogue, analyzing the styles of individual *santeros.* What is missing is a consideration of the folk beliefs and folk practices centered around the *santos.* The author points out that of the sixty-three saints identified in the images, three—Acacius, Liberata, and Barbara—are spurious intruders, unrecognized by the Church and consecrated only in "fanciful and melodramatic legends." But the folk culture that believes in the powers of the *curandero* makes no such learned distinctions among *santos.*

* As quoted in José E. Espinosa, *Saints in the Valleys* (Albuquerque, 1960), 83-84.

1. CUENTOS

Ignez Was a Burro

This tale joins together full versions of Type 851, The
Princess Who Cannot Solve the Riddle, *and Type 570,*
The Rabbit-herd, *both widely distributed in Europe.
Type 851 is Grimm No. 22, "The Riddle," well re-
ported in Spanish-American tradition both in the United
States and in Latin America. Of the four riddles in
the present text, two are variants of Motif H802,
"Riddle: one killed none and yet killed twelve," and
H792, "Riddle of the unborn"; and two are suggestive
of Motif H804, "Riddle: from the eater came forth
meat and from the strong sweetness," and Motif H793,
"Riddle: seven tongues in a head." Type 570 is incident C in Grimm No. 165, "The Griffin Bird." Both
tale types are also known in French- and English-
American tradition.*

Text from Helen Zunser, "A New Mexican Village,"
Journal of American Folklore, *XLVIII (1935), 161–
64. Informant: Mrs. Lorenz, who narrates in "Mexi-
canized" English.*

Once there was a woman, have a tonto for a son. He too dumb.
There's a king who have a daughter who spend all her time
reading books of riddles. The king say anyone can marry her
who makes three riddles she can't guess. If she guess, man get
hung. So this tonto decide to go try marry the princess. His
mother very mad, she say: "What for you go die far from home?
Better stay here, so we can bury you." But he say he want

to go. So he go bake some biscuits to take along and his mother put poison in so that he should go a little way, eat it, and die, and they can come pick up the body. Now he had a female burro named Ignez, and he get on her and ride a little way. After a while he think to eat some biscuits. Get off burro and hunt some manure to make a fire. While he's gone Ignez the burro eat up all the biscuits and die right away on account of the poison.

This tonto come back and see the burro dead, make some coffee and drink it and go on to foot. He go about a quarter of a mile when he see three coyotes coming to where the burro is. They smell it. So he turn back to see what they do and he see them eating the burro. But the meat of the burro poison on account of the biscuits, and the three coyotes die. Then the tonto turn and go on, when he see six crows flying to where is the burro and the coyotes. So he turn back to see and he see the six crows sitting on the heads of the coyotes, picking out the eyes. But the coyotes poison too, and they die all six. So this tonto make that for his first riddle. "Ignez was dead. Kill three who kill six."

Then this tonto go a little way on foot. Now he's hungry and see a doe feeding. I guess he have a rifle or a pistol, and he shoot the doe. Bullet go right through and she die. He go up to skin it and eat the meat, and he see that she has a baby in her, and he take that out to eat, the meat fresher. Now he have no wood or manure to make a fire, so he take out a book out of his pocket, lots of paper, and burn that. Then he makes that for his second riddle. "I see what I shoot, but kill what I don't see. I eat meat still unborn, and I cook it with words."

Then this tonto go more far and he come to a mesa where a lion was chasing some wild horses, and they run so fast that the sweat run down from them. So he very thirsty and take a cup and hold it to the side of one of the horses and catch the sweat. Then he drink it, and he make this the third riddle. "I drank water not from the sky, not from the earth."

Now when he's coming to the king's palace he go over a bridge; there lots of rain so the river full, and there's a dead burro in it, turning around and around and a crow sitting on his head picking out the eyes, and saying "Caw caw." So just for a joke he make the fourth riddle. "Something turning in the water, and something on top singing."

When he come to the palace he call the king, and the king says, "You know what happen if my daughter guess?" And he say, "Yes, I be hung." Then the king call his daughter and he tell her the riddles and the king say, "How long you need to guess this?" and she say, "Oh probably till tomorrow." But she can't guess. Next day she come to the king and say, "I can't guess." "Then you must marry this fellow." "Oh no, he so bad and ugly. Give me three days to guess." So this tonto say, "All right."

Now the king had three daughters besides this one and she go to her sister and say, "You go to this fellow tonight and promise him lots of money, gold and silver, if he tell you the riddle." And the sister go to the tonto and say, "How much you want to tell me the riddle?" "I don't want no money, but I tell you for one thing." "What that?" (You know the skirt the womans wear under their dress, the petticoat?) "You give me your petticoat, and sleep with me one night, and I tell you." "You fresh ugly tonto, what you think I am?" and she go to her sister and say, "What you think he want?" and tell her. And the sister say, "O sister, do what he say or I have to marry him." And she talk and talk till the sister do what she say. So he take her petticoat and roll it up and put it under the mattress, and then sleep with her. In the morning he tell her, "Ignez was a burro." She want to hear the rest, but he won't tell her. "No, I just promise you the first part."

So the same with the other two sisters, and he only tell them a part of the riddle, so she only know the first riddle, but no more.

So she feel very bad and go to the king her father and say, "I don't want to marry this man. You get me out of it." So the king say to the tonto, "You can only marry my daughter if you do three things what I say." So the tonto say, "I thought if she couldn't guess the riddles." "O no, you got to do what I say."

So he give him twelve jackrabbits and say, "You put these

in the pasture, but at night bring them back to the corral." *
So he bring them to the pasture, and as soon as they there,
pft! they all away, one here, one there. So he feel bad and
put his head on his hands, and a fairy come up to him. That's
the same as an angel, only she has a stick, and wherever it hits
fire comes out, and she can make anything she wants. So the
fairy say, "Why you feel so bad?" And he tell her and the
fairy say, "Here, I give you a whistle, and when you whistle
each time a jackrabbit come." So he take it and whistle one
time and a jackrabbit come up, and he whistle twelve times
and twelve jackrabbits come into the corral.

Now the king feeling too worried his daughter has to marry
such a ugly tonto, so he say to the compadre of the tonto, "You
go buy a jackrabbit for so much money as he want."

So the compadre go down and make a sad face and when
the tonto see him he say, "Whatsa matter?" "O I feel too bad.
My wife sick, and the doctor say she can't be cured unless she
eat a jackrabbit. You sell me one, compadre." "O no, I can't
do that. These jackrabbit belong to the king. If you want, go
buy from the king." So the compadre go and tell the king,
and the king go hisself to buy it. "Sell me one jackrabbit,
and I give you all the money you want." "Why don't you take
one, they yours? I can't sell it." "No, you sell me one." "All
right, I sell you, but I don't want no money, just give me a
piece of your nose." The king get mad, but his wife say, "You
better do that or our daughter have to marry this tonto." So
the king say all right, and go and get a knife, and cut off a
piece of his nose and the tonto put it away in his vest pocket.
Then he give him a jackrabbit, but in the night he blow
twelve times and get twelve rabbits. When the king see this
he say, "I thought you sold me one rabbit." "Yes, but that
was mine. I don't sell you yours."

Then the king get mad and say, "All right, but now you
can't marry my daughter unless you get a sackful of lies and
a sackful of truths." He think the tonto never do this, but he
say, all right, and just ask for two fifty-pound flour sacks,
and the king give it to him. The next day they build a big

* Here Type 570 begins.

scaffold, and all the people come to see because they think he surely get hung, the king, the queen, and all the daughters. And this tonto get up and take out the two bags and the king say, "Well, where is the lies and the truths?" So the tonto take out one petticoat and say to the daughter, "Is this your petticoat? Did you give it me?" and she get mad and say, "No, you dirty old thing, what you think I am?" and so the boy say, "This go in the bag of lies." The same thing with the second. He put that into the sack of his too. Now comes the youngest one's turn, and he go up to her and say in a strong voice, "Now you tell me the true. You better look out. Is this your petticoat or no?" And the king say loud, "Yes, tell the true," thinking she lie like the others. But the little one she scared and say in a little voice, "Yes, that's mine." So he put that in the bag of truths. Then he open up his vest pocket and take out the piece of nose and go to the king and say, "Is this yours?" The king had a black plaster on his nose, think it make it well. So he put his hand on his nose and holler, "No, no, that not mine. Put it away. You can marry her."

So they build him a big house and he send for his mother, build her a house and treat her good, and his wife want to know the answer to the riddle, but he say, "No, not till after our first baby is born." So he got that too, and that the end.

The Three Lovers

Type 1361, The Flood, *best known in Chaucer's version in "The Miller's Tale," but also collected in Scandinavia and east Europe. An Ozark text is in Vance Randolph,* Sticks in the Knapsack, *"Tote Out the Big Trunk," pp. 99–100; and see note p. 159. The Randolph and Rael texts are the only ones reported in the United States. Motifs present are K1225, "Lover given rump to kiss," and K1557, "Second lover burns paramour at window with hot iron."*

Text from Juan B. Rael, Cuentos Españoles de Colorado y de Nuevo Méjico, *Vol. I (Stanford: Stanford*

University Press, 1957), No. 43, pp. 105–9. Translated from the Spanish for this volume by Merle E. Simmons.

Once there was a woman who lived in a city and was married to a man named José Pomuceno. This man owned sheep. He was obliged to look after his business in the country. And whenever he would go out of the city, his wife never missed a chance to betray him. So it was that things got so bad that she had three lovers.

It so happened that one night when the husband wasn't at home the three were going to come the same night. That's the way this woman had things arranged when the first one came. Then the second one arrived. He knocked at the door. The wife said to the first one who was there:

"My husband."

"Where shall I hide?"

"Hide in that wardrobe."

The man hid in the wardrobe. The other man entered. A little while later the third one arrived and knocked at the door. The woman says * to the second one:

"My husband."

"No," he says. "If it is your husband, let him kill me. I'll do as I please. I am sure that it isn't your husband. You are giving several of us the run-around."

When the woman saw that he didn't believe that it could be her husband, she tried to drive the other one off, telling him to go away, that everything was off, that he should return some other time.

Then this fellow said to her from outside, "Since you can't do anything else, why don't you at least give me a kiss?"

"Yes," the one who is with her tells her. "It's all right. Tell him to come to the window."

The latter (i.e., the one outside) comes to the window and the other one holds up his rump for him there, and the fellow outside kisses it.

* Note: In order to preserve the flavor of the original texts, historical present tense has been kept in the English translations, even in instances where the past tense might have made for a smoother narrative.— M. E. Simmons.

Saint Peter immediately went and carried the complaint to the Lord. Then the Lord sent for Peter. As soon as he went there, the Lord said, "Well now, throw this fellow into Hell. That's the only place where they can put up with him."

So they took him there. Some festivities were being planned and they put him to work cutting wood. In each load of wood that he brought in, he brought a plant with turpentine. And the day of the party, they gave him the job of serving the meal and of arranging the chairs, and he began to put turpentine on the chairs.

When they finished dinner, they said to him, "Peter, clear the table."

"I can't do that until I sing the *Bendito* [a prayer that begins with the word *bendito*, i.e., blessed]. Everywhere that I have been I have followed this custom."

"Well, don't sing it."

"*Bendito y alabado* and hail Holy Mary."

And the devils jump up with their chairs sticking to them bumping into each other and hitting each other trying to get out through the windows. The doors were locked tightly and he kept shouting at them louder and louder, "Hail Holy Mary!" Until finally one got out and went to complain to Saint Peter. Then Saint Peter went and told the Lord that the devils could no longer put up with Peter. Then the Lord told Saint Peter to bring Peter.

When Saint Peter came with him, the Lord said, "Put this fellow to looking after some sheep."

They took him to look after some sheep. There in the field where he was walking, he could see a very pretty house, and he began to walk all around it but without finding a way to look in. And when he turned around, he found Saint Peter at the door with a very large key. Then he asked Saint Peter what was there. And Saint Peter told him that it was Glory. Peter begged his namesake to let him look in. But with a sudden lunge Peter squirms loose and went in. Then he began to look all around. Saint Peter begged him to leave, but Peter wouldn't do it. Finally Saint Peter sent a page to summon the Lord. Then the Lord told Peter to come out.

Peter told him, "Lord, I won't come out. Aren't you the one who told me and granted me the reward that not even God the Father could throw me out of a place where I had entered and from which I didn't want to leave?"

"Very well, Peter, with your tricks, stay in Glory, for you will be turned to stone."

"Yes, Lord," he said, "but with eyes." [1]

The Two Witches

> *Type 325*, The Magician and his Pupil, *episode III, Trick Sale of Son. Motifs present are C837, "Tabu: loosing bridle in selling man transformed to horse. Disenchantment follows"; D610, "Repeated transformation. Transformation into one form after another"; D641.1, "Lover as bird visits mistress"; D615.1, "Transformation contest between magicians." This is Grimm No. 68, "The Swindler and His Master," a well reported European tale, also known in India, South America, and the West Indies. A southwest Spanish-American text is in Rael, II, No. 259, 192–96. A United States Negro story using Motif D615.1 is in Dorson, Negro Folktales in Michigan, No. 29, "The Mojo," pp. 59–60; and see note, pp. 211–12; and two others are in J. Mason Brewer, Dog Ghosts and Other Texas Negro Folk Tales (Austin: University of Texas Press, 1958), pp. 9–14, 20–21.*
>
> *Text from Zunser, "A New Mexican Village," pp. 167–68. Told by Antonio.*

One time there two man witches and they make a bet. This a long time ago. They say they change themselves into a horse, and run a race. The witch that lose the race, he stay a horse all the time. So they run a race and one witch lose, and he have to stay a horse because of his bet.

So the other witch takes this horse and sell him to a man. But he say, "Don't you ever take off the halter off of this

---

[1] Some versions of the tale add phrases such as "in order that I may see everything that happens there."

horse, or else it be too bad." Now one day a little boy take this horse down to the river for water and a priest come by. This priest say, "What for you water a horse with the halter on? That horse can't drink; you take off the halter." So the boy take off the halter, and the horse change right away into a fish.

Now that bad witch is flying around like a hawk, and he see what happen, and he change hisself into a big fish. That little fish see this, and he change into a bird. The bad witch change into a hawk again, and this little bird fly, fly, until he too tired, and he see a princess sitting in a garden. Quick he fly to that princess and hide hisself in her lap. She take that poor little bird and put it in a cage, no one can get him now. He too happy, that bird, and sing all day long.

Now something wrong with the princess, she too sad all the time, never laugh. This witch he change into a physician and he come along and say he can cure her, but he need the blood of that bird. All right, the king give him the bird, and he cut its throat. But when the blood run out, it change to seed. That witch change into a hen and eat up the seed. But when he come to the last seed, he can't find it, and that seed change into a coyote and eat up that hen!

There's a man sees that coyote and take him home to mind his store. A witch woman comes along and she wink at that coyote. She see that coyote a witch. So that night the coyote think to go to her, and he take a big leg of mutton from the store, put it on his shoulder, and go to see her. But the town dogs they smell him when he go by, and they jump on him and tear him all apart. That the end of those two witches.

2. LEYENDAS

The Weeping Woman

> *"Probably the legend of 'La Llorona'—'The Weeping Woman'—has permeated Mexican folklore more thoroughly than any similar theme," Bacil F. Kirtley has written in a study of the legend, " 'La Llorona' and Related Themes," Western Folklore, XIX (July, 1960), 155–68. Kirtley considers La Llorona to be largely of European origin.*
>
> *The following comments on and text of the legend are from Soledad Pérez, "Mexican Folklore from Austin, Texas," in* The Healer of Los Olmos and Other Mexican Lore, Texas Folklore Society Publications XXIV, *ed. Wilson M. Hudson (Dallas: Southern Methodist University Press, 1951), pp. 73–74, 76. Informant: Mrs. Barbara Salinas.*

The tale of the Weeping Woman (La Llorona) is not new. It is essentially a Mexican tale that has existed since Aztec times. According to Thomas A. Janvier [1] and Luis González Obregón,[2] the tale is based on Aztec mythology.

Both Janvier and Obregon refer to Bernardino de Sahagún [3] to point out the connection existing between the Weeping Woman and the Aztec goddess named Civacoatl, Chihuacohuatl, or Tonantzín who appeared dressed in white and bearing a cradle on her shoulders as though she were carrying a child. The

[1] *Legends of the City of Mexico* (New York, 1910), pp. 134–48, 162–65.
[2] *Las Calles de México*, I (7th ed.; Mexico, D. F., 1947), 37–40.
[3] *Historia de Nueva España*, I (Mexico, D. F., 1890), Bk. I, 32–33.

goddess mixed among the Aztec women and left the cradle abandoned. When the women looked into the cradle, they always found an arrowhead shaped like the Aztec sacrificial knife. At night the goddess went through the cities and towns shrieking and weeping and disappeared in the waters of lakes or rivers.

Later, the myth became merged with the story of real tragedy, usually a story involving a crime, such as infanticide. Vicente Riva Palacio and Juan de Dios Peza retell a sixteenth-century tale of Luisa, a beautiful peasant girl who fell in love with Don Muño Montes Claros and bore him three sons.[4] When Don Muño abandoned Luisa to marry a woman of his own class, Luisa murdered the children and then went through the streets shrieking and sobbing. Don Muño committed suicide.

Today, the tale of the Weeping Woman is current throughout Mexico. In the United States it is also known in Texas, California, Arizona, and possibly other states. Betty Leddy has listed forty-two versions in her study, "La Llorona in Southern Arizona."[5]

The Weeping Woman is well known in Austin. Most of my informants had come from Mexico and had known it before they came here. In some instances the tale has become localized. The Weeping Woman is often said to be someone who lived in Austin many years ago; she killed her children, and now her spirit wanders about.

In Austin, La Llorona appears in many shapes and forms. Some informants contend that she is a woman with a seductive figure and horse face. Others hold that she is a woman dressed in black, having long hair, shiny, tin-like fingernails, and a skeleton's face. A few believe that she is a vampire that sucks its victim's blood. The majority insist that she is a woman dressed in white, with long black hair, long fingernails, and the face of a bat. The Weeping Woman's failure to repent and confess her sins has become affixed to two of the stories.

An unlimited number of personalized stories can be built on La Llorona. The following is a typical encounter.

---

[4] *Tradiciones y Leyendas Mexicanas* (México, n.d.), pp. 127–49.
[5] *Western Folklore*, VIII (1948), 272–77; and "La Llorona Again," *Western Folklore*, IX (1950), 363–65.

My brother had a very good friend who was a shoemaker. The two were heavy drinkers, and they liked to go out together to eat and drink.

Well, one night my brother went to see his friend about twelve-thirty and prevailed on him to go out to drink with him.

Shortly after the two had started out for their favorite saloon, they noticed that a very attractive woman was walking just ahead of them. They decided to follow her. The two followed for a long time, but they couldn't catch up with her. When it seemed that they were coming up even with the woman, she suddenly seemed to get about half a block ahead of them. Finally, my brother and his friend decided to turn back, but as a parting gesture they said, "Good-by, my dear!"

At the same time that the two said, "Good-by, my dear!" the attractive woman whom they had followed turned around. She had the face of a horse, her fingernails were shiny and tin-like, and she gave a long, piercing cry. It was La Llorona.

My brother would have run, but his friend had fainted, and he had to revive him. The two reformed after that encounter with La Llorona.

The Hermit of Hermit's Peak

> *A number of motifs regularly associated with saints' legends are found here: V223.6, "Saint as prognosticator"; D2105, "Provisions magically furnished"; F933.1, "Miraculous spring bursts forth for holy person"; V221.12, "Saint cures blindness." The best folkloristic study of saints' legends is C. Grant Loomis,* White Magic: An Introduction to the Folklore of Christian Legend *(Cambridge, Mass.: Medieval Academy of America, 1948).*
>
> *Text from Zunser, "A New Mexican Village," p. 174.*

Juan Maria de Castellano lived on the peak for three years, in a cave whose entrance had in-pointing nails, so that he cut himself going out. He knew everything. He slept on a rag on the ground. He had a chest full of religious things, so heavy that no one could lift it. No animal touched him, and wild animals would come up to be stroked. He wore out a trail walking backward and forward. He built a cross too heavy for anyone to carry. He left the peak because he knew that a man wanted to kill him. When he met this man he said, "I know you will kill me." He walked to France and died there.

Once twelve men came up to Hermit's Peak to make the fourteen crosses for the stages. They worked all day very hard. For dinner he, the hermit, cooked only a little bit of mush, as big as a fist, and put it on a plate. The men felt bad, and thought they would be hungry, but the little piece made them full and they worked all day.

This happened to an old man, still living, whose name is Jesus, and lives nearby. He is now very old.

The hermit used to haul water in a five-pound lard pail. He had to walk down all the way to town, they up to the top again, because there was no water. One day all the people in Gaillnas decided to go up and get him some water. He was very glad to see them and said to this man Jesus, then a young man; "Jesus, go, and near a certain rock you find three does and a young buck. Take your gun and go there." Jesus went and found the animals. He got down on his knee to shoot, but saw in front of him water shooting out. He ran to call all the people to see, and the does went away.

This water is very cold. Good to drink, but if fifteen or twenty cans of it are poured slowly on your face and neck, it will burn. But it is good for curing. A boy they knew was led barefoot up the mountain by his mother. He was blind. They all prayed rosaries. Twenty cans of water were trickled on the boy, who was cured of blindness.

A girl took a picture of all the people praying there. When it was developed Maria de Guadalupe, the angels and hell were visible. It's in Gaillnas now.

A Dead Cowboy Speaks

For the cycle of comic tales in United States Negro tradition about a dead man on the "cooling board" see

Dorson, Negro Tales from Pine Bluff, Arkansas, and Calvin, Michigan, *pp. 82–86, 217. Motif E235.2.1, "Dead man speaks demanding proper funeral rites," is pertinent.*

Text from Pérez, "Mexican Folklore from Austin, Texas," pp. 94–95. Informant: Mrs. Charles G. Balagia.

My cousins Andrés, Francisco, and Santiago had wanted to come to the United States for a long time. They were coming to see us, but they got on the wrong train, and instead of coming to Austin they went to Oklahoma. While there, they worked as cowboys.

Once while the three were out on the range, one of their fellow cowboys became ill. They took the cowboy to the nearest house, which was a two-room abandoned shack. The cowboy died, and the others put his body on some planks in one of the rooms and placed a candle at the head of the body and another at the foot.

Then one of the cowboys suggested a game of cards to while away the time. My cousin Francisco objected. He said, "There's a dead man in the next room. We can't be disrespectful."

The others refused to hear. They began to play cards and drink whiskey. One of the candles began to burn very low, and they had no other, so Andrés told Francisco, "Go into the other room and get one of the candles."

Francisco went into the room where the dead man lay. As he clutched the candle, the dead man raised himself up slightly. Francisco tripped, threw down the candle, and fell against the planks. The candle at the head of the body blew out and the planks flew up into the air. As they did so the dead man was thrown forward on Francisco. His elbows pricked Francisco, and he heard a shrill voice say, "You must respect dead men."

At this, Francisco screamed, "Help, the dead man is killing me!"

When the cowboys heard this, they ran out of the shack. Andrés was the first to recover, and he went back to see what had happened to Francisco. Francisco had fainted. The cowboys revived him, but they didn't go back to the cards and whiskey. They never again played or drank when they were around a dead man.

From the Folk Bible

For American Negro examples of folk-biblical tales see Dorson, Negro Folktales in Michigan, pp. 156–63; and Dorson, Negro Tales from Pine Bluff, Arkansas, and Calvin, Michigan, pp. 239–42.

Texts from Zunser, "A New Mexican Village," p. 169.

"Why the Mule is Childless"

Why can't the mule have children? Because once when a king want to kill God, José take Maria to Egypt, and a bird (the turtle dove) scare it and it shy and frighten Maria. That why.

"The Devil and Whiskey"

Who first made whiskey? The devil. When God first sent him out of heaven, he ask one favor. "Just let me make a little soup, I drink it, not feel so bad." That's whiskey. When men drink they fight. I see many men fight with whiskey, never seen hardly any fight without. Comes from the devil.

"The Crow and Noah"

Why can't the crow eat all winter? Because when Noah sent two crows away to see if the rain stop, they find some people and pick out their eyes. Since then they work all summer, bury corn, but no find it in winter. Fat in summer, *muy flacca* in winter. Bluejay bury corn in summer, but find it.

"John Baptist"

What's the one thing God couldn't do for hisself? Baptise him. He had to call John Baptist.

3. CUENTOS HUMORISTICOS

Don Peanut and Doña Peanut

This cycle belongs to the groups of stories concerned with simpletons, dolts, numskulls, and noodles, as of Jean Sot (see below, pp. 250–53). A good comparative collection is William A. Clouston, The Book of Noodles (London, 1888). See Section J1700–J2749 in the Motif Index, "Fools (and other unwise persons)." A specific motif is J1805.1, "Similar sounding words mistaken for each other." But the fool is often also a clever rogue, as in Motif K1766, "Trickster's boasting scares his powerful opponent from contest."

Variants of eating-the-railroad-track and asking-for-coffee-with-milk are in Zunser, "A New Mexican Village," p. 171.

Text from Juan B. Rael, Cuentos Españoles de Colorado y de Nuevo Méjico, Vol. II, No. 323, p. 357. Translated for this volume by Merle E. Simmons.

Once there was a woman and a man. The man's name was Don Peanut and the woman's Doña Peanut. When they had Little Peanut, the woman didn't know what name to give him. She wanted to give him an American name and she asked Don Peanut what she should call the child [saying] that she wanted to give him an American name and she couldn't remember a single American name. And he told her:

"Well, call him Sanmagán" (i.e., Son of a Gun).

Finally they called him Little Peanut.

One day Little Peanut was crying and Don Peanut asked Doña Peanut why the child is crying so much and she says that it is because he is hungry.

And he tells her, "Well, give him a *tortilla*."

"But he doesn't want a *tortilla* all by itself."

"Well, then, put two of them together," he tells her.

On another occasion the three of them were tramps and were walking down the railroad track and Doña Peanut said to him: "Oh, how hungry I am, Don Peanut! I'd like to eat something so that I would have something substantial on my stomach."

"Well, eat a rail from the track, but just don't tell the company because it will bill me for it."

"No, you don't understand; I mean rather something *ligera*."

"Well, eat a hare, that is *ligera*." *

Another time Don Peanut was in jail and was very hungry and he said to Doña Peanut: "Why don't you bring me a cup of coffee?"

And she didn't have any coffee in the house nor did she have any money to buy it, and she says to him, "But with what, Don Peanut?"

"With milk, you know how I like it."

Another time Don Peanut went off to work and stayed away a year working, and when he returned he brought Doña Peanut only one peso, and she says to him, "It has been a year, Don Peanut, and you brought only one peso."

"Don't you think that's enough? Just imagine, if I had been away a thousand years I would have brought you a thousand pesos."

Another time they were very poor and couldn't find any way to make enough money to drink wine, and he put a sign there

* Note: The joke here involves a play on the word *ligero* (feminine form, *ligera*). With reference to food it means something *light,* but with reference to an animal it means *swift-footed.*—*M. E. Simmons.*

on his house: *Don Peanut, the Strong.* And then whenever he asked people for money, they would give it to him because they were afraid of him. One day a very strong bully arrived at the square and saw the sign on Don Peanut's house, and he said, "I am going to see that Don Peanut, the Strong."

And he came to Don Peanut's house and says to him, "You are Don Peanut, the Strong?"

"Yes, what do you want?" Don Peanut says to him.

"Well, I want to fight with you," he says.

"Very well," Don Peanut says to him, "wait just a minute."

And he called Doña Peanut and says to her, "Bring me my cap that wards off blows and my shoes for leaping backward."

And Doña Peanut brought him a cap and some old shoes, and Don Peanut puts them on and says to her: "Now, then, read me the list."

"You have ninety-nine; you just need one more to make one hundred."

"Well, mark down the hundred; this one will make it."

And when the bully heard that, what he was going to do to him, he ran away and refused to fight.

Once they were playing cards and they began to bet a lot of money against him, and he had only one peso left to bet, and they had a lot, and he says to Doña Peanut:

"Bring me my money bag so that I can cover the bets of these fellows and they can cover mine."

"Which one do you want, the little one or the big one?"

"The little one. Do you think you could carry the big one?"

And then those fellows lost heart and he won the money.

Cavacato (Mr. Peanuts)

> *Text from Zunser, "A New Mexican Village," pp. 171–72. Informants: Antonio and Mrs. Lorenz.*

You ever hear about Mr. Peanuts, Cavacato? He too funny, lots of tales about him, can't remember all. He's not in a book.

Now one time he go on the railroad with a partner, and the track curve, bend on one side, and he have his bag on his back on one side. His partner say, "O Mr. Peanuts, your load is curvy." "O that because the road curvy. I have to be curvy too."

This Mr. Peanuts have a wagon with a blanket on top. He like to go fast, so one time he tie this wagon in back of the train, and tie one burro on each side of the locomotive, and tie the goat in back of the coal car. His wife asleep in the wagon. Mr. Peanuts he go in the locomotive with the engineer. That train go fast. Mr. Peanuts look out the window. He see the burro's head on each side the locomotive, with his ears down like running too fast. He look out in back, see the goat's head. He glad, think they run fast. Now they come into a town and stop. Mr. Peanuts go out. O! O! He see only the heads of his burros and his goat, no more body. Where his wife? She in the cow catcher another locomotive. He run fast to flag that other train, but it go off on another switch. Poor Mr. Peanuts left all alone.

The New Mexican and the Californians

Type 1567F, Hungry Shepherd Attracts Attention, reported in Spain, France, and Germany (Motif J1341.6). Text from Juan B. Rael, Cuentos Españoles de Colorado y de Nuevo Méjico, Vol. II, No. 421, p. 532, "The Man Who Told About the Calf." Translated for this volume by Merle E. Simmons.

A New Mexican went to California and came to a house where two men were eating and they didn't invite him to eat. And one of them said to him:

"What kind of country is it where you live?"

"Oh, that is a great country, a rich country!"

"What's rich about it?"

"All the families in New Mexico, when they eat, use one spoon for each mouthful."

And those fellows were astonished that for each mouthful there was a spoon, but he didn't tell them that the spoon was a *tortilla*.*

"But in addition to this," he told them, "The cows there are not like the ones here."

"Why?"

"Because the ones here give birth to one calf at a time and those there give birth to two."

"And how do they manage to feed two calves?"

"Why, just the way you are doing now. While one of them is sucking, the other one just watches."

And from that those men knew that that man was hungry and they invited him to eat.

The Smart Indian Lawyer

> Motif J1191.2, "Suit for chickens produced from boiled eggs," is known in Dutch and Jewish examples.
> Text from Zunser, "A New Mexican Village," p. 175.
> Informant: Antonio.

A man running for election, but he very poor. He go to an old woman and say, "Give me half a dozen eggs on credit. When I get rich I pay you." Now this old woman she have boiled eggs, and she give him half a dozen boiled eggs on credit. Long time passes and he get elected, but still too poor, and he don't pay that old woman for her eggs. So after a while she start thinking: "Suppose I have those eggs, maybe they hatch and I have little chickens. By now I have lots and lots of hens." So she go and sue him. Now the man is very worried. He sit and think all day, "I lose the case, go to the penitentiary." He very worried. One day a friend of his come up, an Indian. "Hello." "Hello." "Why you so worried?" "O, I'm worried because my case come to court and I surely go to the penitentiary." So the Indian say, "You let me be your lawyer," and the man say, "All right."

* Note: The Mexican tortilla is a flat cake made of corn, thinner than but about the same size as a pancake. Rolled up it serves very well as a spoon.—*M. E. Simmons.*

Next day he come to court. Every one there, judge and everybody, but the Indian not there. O the man awfully worried. The judge say, "Where your lawyer? I put you in the penitentiary if he don't come pretty soon." The man say, "My lawyer not here yet, give me ten minutes." The judge give him ten minutes. They wait, but the Indian don't come. So he says, maybe he get sick; to give him ten minutes more. So they give him ten minutes more. Then just as they ready to start, the Indian come in.

"Where you been?" say the judge. "Why you so late, when we all wait?"

"O," say the Indian, "I was just toasting hava beans to plant."

"What you mean, toasting havas to plant? You can't grow from toasted havas."

"O, sure. I can grow the same as the old woman can raise chickens from boiled eggs."

So when they hear that, they laugh, and they throw the case out of court.

The Mean Rich Man

Type 1561, The Lazy Boy Eats Breakfast, Dinner and Supper One after the Other. *Although collected in a dozen European countries, the tale has not been reported in Spanish or Spanish-American tradition. Baughman cites English-American texts from Kentucky, Indiana, and Wisconsin.*
Text from Zunser, "A New Mexican Village," p. 177. Told by Antonio.

Once there were a rich man, very mean, and he think all the time how to fool the mens who work for him, and get them to work too hard for little money. So one day he goes to the town, and he sees a simple man standing in the street, not doing nothing, so (with his mouth open). He go up to him and say, "You want to work?" and the simple man says sure, and he

say, "Come up to my place, and I give you fifty cents a day."
And the simple man he says sure, and the rich man laugh to
hisself, and think, "O, now I get this simple man to work
hard."

So they get to this rich man's house, and it too late to
work, so in the morning he wake him up and say, "Hey, you
got to go to the fields to work." So the simple mans get up
and he eat a good breakfast, the rich man's wife give it to him.
And the rich man say, "You got to go far to work, over fields,
too far to come home for lunch." So the simple man say, "You
give me my lunch now. I want it now so no one have to come
after me with my lunch." And the rich mans too glad, he give
him the lunch so that no one has to stop work to go give the
simple man eat. And when the simple man finished, the rich
man say, "O, why don't you eat your supper now so you don't
have to come home early?" He think he can't eat much now,
and then his wife don't have to give him to eat after.

So the simple mans said, "All right," and he eat his supper.
Then the rich man say, "Now go to the field to work," and
the simple man say, "O no, all my life after supper I go right
to sleep. All my life I have a habit, not change now." And he
go to sleep, and the rich mans too mad.

Confession

> Type 1804, Imagined Penance for Imagined Sin. Scat-
> tered examples come from France, Italy, Yugoslavia,
> and Czechoslovakia. A Spanish-American text, the only
> New World example, is reported from Cuba.
> Text from Zunser, "A New Mexican Village," p. 175.
> Told by Fernán.

One time, a man steal a cow, and he go to the priest confess.
Priest too mad, and say he only excuse him if he pay fifteen
dollars. (Just a story, not true.) Then he say: "You mustn't
steal, but you musn't have the intention to steal, that the
same thing. Just as bad."

"All right," the man say. Then the priest say, "Give me the fifteen dollars or I not excuse you." "All right."

He take the fifteen dollars out of his pocket and make to give it over the screen, but then he put it back in his pocket. "Say, why you not give me the fifteen dollars?" "O, I have the intention to do so, same as giving you!" He no pay.

The Apple Tree

> *Type 1423,* The Enchanted Pear Tree, *known in literature as the Merchant's Tale in Chaucer, and in Book 7, the ninth Night, in Boccaccio's* Decameron. *A long, elaborate version involving three island castaways currently circulates as a "dirty joke." Reported in scattered instances in Europe, and in Spanish and English-American tradition.*
>
> *Text from Zunser, "A New Mexican Village," pp. 177–78. Told by Fernan.*

Once there was a fellow who go to California to look for work. He get a job with a farmer, picking apples. Now this farmer have a fine daughter, and the boy want to kiss her, but the father never go way, always around. She willing too. So he thinks him a way.

One day he way on top of the apple tree picking apples, throwing them down. Farmer and his daughter on bottom, they pick up the apples, put them in baskets. Now all of a sudden the boy runs down from the tree, very fast, very quick.

"What's the matter?" the farmer say.

"O, I quit, I no stay here any more."

"Why you quit? What the matter?"

The boy a good worker. Farmer don't want him to go way.

"O, I don't like to stay in a place where I see such things."

"What do you see?"

"I look down from the tree and see you kiss your daughter. I not like that."

The farmer say, "O, no, that not true."

"Well, if you don't believe me, go see yourself."

So the farmer climb on the top of the tree and look down. The boy and girl kissing. He holler down, "Yes, what you say is true." They two have a good time.

The Countryman

> *Motif J1811, "Animal cries misunderstood." Referred to in Dorson, American Folklore, p. 108.*
>
> *Text from Juan B. Rael, Cuentos Españoles de Colorado y de Nuevo Méjico, II, No. 434, 537. Translated for this volume by Merle E. Simmons.*

Once there was a Mexican who had come to the United States to look for work and he returned to Mexico. Then a fellow countryman asked him how he had liked it. And he said:

"Well, I didn't like it at all. Even the animals there speak English. Once a rooster stopped and sent me on my way saying, *"Get out of here."* * Soon I met a sow with a piglet and she said to me, "Go on, go on." And then a duck with a flock of ducklings comes up and says to me, "Quick, quick."

The Fool

> *This jest is a reversal of Type 1322, Words in a Foreign Language Thought to be Insults. The insults in the foreign language are misinterpreted as polite remarks.*
>
> *Synopsized in Dorson, American Folklore, p. 107. Text from Juan B. Rael, Cuentos Españoles de Colorado y de Nuevo Méjico, Vol. I, No. 51, p. 119. Translated for this volume by Merle E. Simmons.*

Once there were two brothers. One was named John and the other's name was José. This John was little bit stupid. One day his brother sent José to buy some gloves of the kind that have blue thongs. And John went off and came to the store.

* Note: In Spanish the call of the rooster is conventionally represented by *quiquiriquí*, which sounds vaguely like the English expression.— *M. E. Simmons.*

The clerks were Americans and the clerk says to him, "What do you want?"

"*Sí, guante,*" he says to him.

"What do you say?" he says to him.

"*Sí, pa José.*"

"Oh, you fool!"

"*Sí, de esos de la correita azul.*"

"Oh, you go to hell!" he says to him.

"*Sí, de esos me mandó él.*"

Then the clerk got mad. He couldn't understand him and he ran him out.*

The Two Farmers

> Type 1699, Misunderstanding Because of Ignorance of a Foreign Language, *is reported in single instances from Germany, France, Hungary, Slovenia, Serbocroatia, India, Africa, Chile, and Michigan (Negro). Five examples are cited from Russia and six from Puerto Rico.*
>
> Text from Juan B. Rael, Cuentos Españoles de Colorado y de Nuevo Méjico, *Vol. I, No. 81, p. 131. Translated for this volume by Merle E. Simmons.*

This is the story of José Maria and Don Antonio. They lived near to each other and had animals and sold butter, eggs, meat, and milk. Now these two farmers said they were pals. Once some Americans came. That fellow José Maria didn't know even one word of English. The Americans asked him to sell them some eggs and milk. He made out with them as best he could by sign language. And the American tells the fellow that they are going to sleep on the other side of the river and for him to go for his pay the next day.

* Note: The humor of this tale is based, of course, upon the similarity of sounds between certain key words spoken by the American clerk and the Spanish words which the Mexican thinks he hears. His Spanish phrases could be translated approximately as follows: "Yes, a glove." "Yes, for José." "Yes, those with the blue thongs." "Yes, he sent me after those."
—M. E. Simmons

But since he didn't know any English, he says to his wife, "I am going to see my pal so that he can go to interpret for me. He knows English very well."

So he leaves and goes over that way and says to him: "Well, I have come to tell you that some Americans came yesterday afternoon to my house and bought some milk and eggs. We made ourselves understood as best we could and they said that they were going to sleep over there and there they are. Now I want you to go with me so that you can interpret for me."

"Very well," Don Antonio says to him. "Let's go."

And Don Antonio says to the Americans when they arrive: "Gur mornin (*Good morning*), thieving gringos. Al * pay my pal José Maria. You no al pay my pal José Maria, I'll *breque* (*break*) you *neque* (neck) with a palo *esteque* (stick)."

Well, the American couldn't understand, but finally he paid; and when they were on their way back, Don José Maria says to Don Antonio, "If it hadn't been for you, the Americans wouldn't have paid me."

"I," Don Antonio says to him, "know English perfectly. I'm not ashamed to speak it."

No Estiendo

Another example of Type 1699, Misunderstanding Because of Ignorance of a Foreign Language. *The same theme occurs in "The Colored Man and the Mexican," in Dorson,* Negro Folktales in Michigan, *p. 79, although this conversation takes the more specialized form of Type 1700, "I Don't Know."*

Contributed by Américo Paredes, who heard the joke in Texas-Mexican border country in 1926 from a cousin, Ignacio Manzano.

Once a Mexican and an American were grubbing stumps by the day. They camped together and decided to divide their

---

* Note: The *Al* used here and in the following line is not clear. It may be the Mexican's attempt to pronounce the "y'all" (i.e., you all) that is so widely used in Texas.—*M. E. Simmons.*

chores. The American didn't know much Spanish; he just nodded and said "*Sí*" to everything the Mexican said.

When they went back to camp the first evening, the Mexican said, "We'll have *tortillas de harina* (wheat-flour tortillas) tonight." The American didn't understand a word, but he nodded and said, "*Sí*."

"*Yo amaso*," the Mexican said. ("I will knead the dough.")
The American nodded and said, "*Sí*."

"*Tú estiendes*." ("You roll the dough flat.")
The American pricked up his ears at that. He thought the Mexican had said, "You understand." ("*Tú entiendes*.") He shook his head and said, "*No estiendo*."

"What?" the Mexican said. "You won't do it? Why not?"

"*No estiendo*," the American said.

"You're a stubborn one," the Mexican said. "All right, we'll switch jobs. *Tú amasas, yo estiendo*."

"*No estiendo*," the American said.

"If you say once more that you won't do it, I'll whack you over the head with this ax handle."

"*No estiendo*," the American said.

So the Mexican hauled back and gave the American a lick with the ax handle, and then another and another. And no matter how much he beat him, the American kept saying, "*No estiendo! No estiendo!*"

So they had no *tortillas de harina* that night.

Moochers

Contributed by Américo Paredes, who heard these jokes in Brownsville, Texas, and Matamoros, Mexico, when he was attending Brownsville Junior College, 1934–36.

A moocher walked into a saloon in Matamoros which was crowded with Texas-Mexicans from Brownsville, just across the river. He wormed a place for himself at the bar, put his elbows down on it, and held his head in his hands.

When there was a lull in the noise he said loudly, "Poor Mr. Thomas!"

Nobody paid him any mind, so at the next lull he said again, "Poor Mr. Thomas! *Pobrecito!*"

He kept this up until the man next to him turned around and said, "*Qué* Thomas, *hombre?*"

"The same thing you're drinking," the moocher replied, signaling the bartender, "and thanks." *

Another moocher pun is embodied in a saying rather than an anecdote. Of a cigarette sponger it is said, "*Fuma Loques Strais.*" This is a play on "Lucky Strikes," uttered in a strong Spanish accent, and "*lo que trais*" (i.e., whatever kind you have on you). Hence "He smokes Lucky Strikes" signifies "He smokes whatever brand you have in your pocket."

La Flora y la Fauna

> *Contributed by Américo Paredes. Motif J2496.2,* "Mis-*understandings because of lack of knowledge of a different language than one's own.*"

The customs, immigration, and Department of Agriculture officials who work on the bridges across the Rio Grande are not extremely popular with Borderers, who feel that they are obstacles to free intercourse between the Texans and Mexicans. These dignitaries are frequently the butt of anecdotes such as the following, which was told of a Mexican official at the Matamoros bridge in the 1930's.

The official received a letter from Mexico City which said: "In view of the international situation it is imperative that you report all that you know about the flora and the fauna (*la flora y la fauna*) in your area."

The official went to work on the matter. In a week he wired Mexico City: "In answer to your query about La Flora and La Fauna. La Flora works in a whorehouse down the street, but nobody here knows La Fauna. You may locate her in the Reynosa red light district."

* Pun on "*Qué* Thomas?" ("Which Thomas?") and "*Qué tomas?*" ("What will you drink?")

4. MAL DE OJO AND SUSTO

The Evil Eye

An instance of the evil eye among Greek-Americans is described in Dorson, American Folklore, pp. 163–64. Current traditions in Ireland dealing with the evil eye are given in Dorson, "Collecting in County Kerry," Journal of American Folklore, LXVI (1953), 19–42. Louis C. Jones has written on "The Evil Eye Among European-Americans," Western Folklore, X (1951), 11–25. A recent popular book by an eye-doctor is Edward S. Gifford, The Evil Eye: Studies in the Folklore of Vision (New York: Macmillan Co., 1958), and an older standard work is Frederick T. Elworthy, The Evil Eye: An Account of this Ancient and Widespread Superstition (London, 1895).

The following experiences are given by Soledad Pérez, "Mexican Folklore from Austin, Texas," pp. 108–9. Informants: Mrs. Barbara Salinas, Mrs. Charles G. Balagia, and Gloria Prado.

When a person suffers from the evil eye, he says, "I was given the eye." To cure this an unbroken egg is passed over his face. Afterward, the egg is broken in a saucer, and it is placed under the bed.

Another remedy is to find the person who cast the evil eye; the egg placed under the bed must be examined after the cure has been administered. If a white membraneous film appears over the egg, it means that the person who gave the evil eye is a man. If only an eye appears on the egg, it means that the person who cast the evil eye is a woman.

When Chita was small, I took her downtown on one occasion. She was a pretty little girl, and people admired her. While I was standing at the counter of one of the department stores, a little Mexican woman approached me and wanted to touch Chita. She said, "What a pretty baby! Won't you let me touch her hair and eyes?"

I didn't like for people to be touching the baby; so I said, "No, please don't touch her!"

The woman left, and I didn't believe in the evil eye; so I thought no more about it.

The next day Chita became ill. She had a very high fever and was flushed and uneasy. I called the doctor. He came and looked at her. Two or three days went by and Chita didn't improve. She just seemed to get worse. We went from one doctor to another, but it didn't do any good.

Finally one day my comadre Mrs. Ramos came over, and she looked at Chita and said, "This child is suffering from the evil eye. I can cure her if you will let me try."

I told her to go ahead; and she did. She asked for two eggs and a cup. One of the eggs she passed over Chita's whole face. Then she took the egg, broke it, put it in a cup, stirred it, and made a cross with some of it on Chita's forehead. While doing this she pronounced several prayers. The other egg she placed on the mantelpiece in the living room and asked that no one touch it.

The next day Mrs. Ramos came back. Chita's fever was gone, and you could tell that she was better. Mrs. Ramos then took the egg from the mantelpiece and broke it. If I hadn't been there, I wouldn't believe it, but my husband and I both saw it. The egg looked as if it were hard-boiled. Mrs. Ramos said, "Chita will get well now. The evil eye has gone into the egg; that's why it looks like this."

Chita got well.

In my home, whenever anyone became ill my aunt was called. On one occasion it was believed that my little brother had the evil eye. My aunt came and passed an unbroken egg over my little brother's face. Then she broke the egg, and taking some of it, she made a cross on his forehead. After that she said several prayers and swept my brother from head to foot. She took another egg, broke it, put it in a saucer, and left it under the bed. Later, when my aunt took the egg out from under the bed, she said that she could tell my brother had been suffering from the evil eye because an eye had formed in the egg.

A Case of "Susto"

Susto *is the term for the state of shock which ensues from a malevolent spell cast on a victim by a practitioner of black magic. Persons afflicted with* susto *will customarily seek the services of a* curandero, *or professional healer. Children's scare stories are called* "Cuentos de Susto" (*see the examples printed under that title by Baldemar A. Jiménez, in* The Golden Log, *ed. M. C. Boatright et al., Publications of the Texas Folklore Society XXXI, 1962, 156–64).*

The following eyewitness account is from Soledad Pérez, "Mexican Folklore from Austin, Texas," pp. 110–12. Informant: Mrs. Cecilia G. Vda de Hernández.

On one of my visits to the home of an informant, Mrs. Cecilia G. Vda. de Hernández, I witnessed the curing of Lily Hernández, her daughter. The treatment lasted three days, and Mrs. Hernández administered it. It was begun on Friday afternoon soon after my arrival.

First Mrs. Hernández went out to the kitchen and placed a small *comal* [a flat iron grill for cooking tortillas] on the stove. Then she placed a dump of alum on the *comal* and came back into the bedroom. She made Lily undress and lie face down on the bed with her arms outstretched in the form of a cross. Then covering Lily with a sheet and taking a small broom made of green twigs and shaped in the form of a cross, Mrs. Hernández proceeded to sweep Lily from head to foot.

As she swept, Mrs. Hernández recited three credos. After this she took me out to the kitchen, where we looked at the alum. Something resembling foam had risen to the surface, and Mrs. Hernández gazed intently and then asked me to look at it.

"Don't you see the forms of two men fighting?" she asked.

"Well, yes," I hesitated, "but it's not very clear. Won't you show me exactly where it is that you see those two forms?"

She peered down and patiently outlined what appeared to be two forms of men with outstretched arms and doubled fists. "I thought that was what had shocked Lily and now I am sure," she said. "She never told me, but I found out that a man tried to assault her and her boy friend. Her boy friend had to fight with this other man, and it frightened Lily very much."

Mrs. Hernández then gave Lily a tea that she had brewed, and I left after obtaining permission to come back to witness the rest of the cure.

On Saturday afternoon I returned. Mrs. Hernández again placed the alum on the stove, swept Lily just as she had done on the previous day, and gave her some more tea. Then Mrs. Hernández and I went to look at the alum. She was very pleased.

"The cure is going to be very effective," she said. "Today, the figures of the men are barely visible."

When she asked me about it, I affirmed her statement.

On Sunday afternoon the cure was completed. As she had done previously, Mrs. Hernández placed the alum on the stove and swept Lily from head to foot, but she did not give her any tea. After this she said that she would be gone for a short time. I noticed a small bundle under her arm, but I did not ask what it contained. About forty-five minutes later she reappeared and told what she had done.

"I had to take the lingerie that Lily was wearing on the day when she was frightened to the exact location where the attempted assault took place," she explained. "I have dragged the lingerie across the exact spot three times in one direction and three times in another so as to form the sign of the cross. Now I shall put the lingerie on her, and we shall know whether the cure is complete or not."

She then dressed Lily in the lingerie, and we sat and

chatted amiably for about half an hour. She asked Lily how she felt, and she replied that she was sweating profusely. Mrs. Hernández covered her with a blanket, and immediately afterward we went into the kitchen to look at the alum. Nothing could be seen.

"I am very happy," said Mrs. Hernández. "The two men who were visible on the first and second day have disappeared, and that means that the cure is successful."

When I left, Lily was asleep, but she was still sweating profusely. Now Lily is well and has returned to her work.

5. PROVERBIOS

THE FOLLOWING PROVERB TEXTS are from Soledad Pérez, "Mexican Folklore from Austin, Texas," pp. 118–25. I have annotated them according to comparable sayings in Burton Stevenson, *The Home Book of Proverbs, Maxims and Familiar Phrases* (New York: The Macmillan Co., 1948).

1. *Ahora es cuando, yerbabuena, le has de dar sabor al caldo.*

> Now, mint, is when you must give the soup flavor. (Strike while the iron is hot. Now's your chance.) *

2. *Dar atole con el dedo.*

> To give gruel with the finger. (To deceive with words or acts, especially to deceive one's husband.)

3. *El que no quiere ruido que no críe cochinos.*

> He who doesn't want noise should not raise hogs. (Don't make trouble if you don't want trouble.) †

4. *El que para tonto nace haste guaje no para.*

> He who is born (to be) a fool will not stop until

---

* See Stevenson, *The Home Book of Proverbs*, Section II, p. 1255, for proverb texts centered on the idea of striking while the iron is hot.
† See Stevenson, *The Home Book of Proverbs*, p. 1692, No. 11, for a positive statement of this saying, "He that loves noise must buy a pig." Stevenson's sole reference is to an 1813 collection of Spanish proverbs.

*he becomes an (empty) gourd. (He who is born
a fool is never cured. Once a fool, always a fool.
Note: The* guaje *is a dry empty gourd; it is often
used to keep a person afloat in water.)**

5. *El que por su cuenta es buey hasta la coyunda lame.*
    *He who allows himself to be made into an ox will
    even lick the (yoking) straps. (He who desires
    to be made into a cuckold must wear the horns
    for all to see.)* †

6. *Entre menos burros, más olotes.*
    *The fewer donkeys, the more cobs. (The fewer,
    the better [cheer]. Note:* Olotes *[corncobs], dried
    as well as green, are given burros to eat.)* ‡

7. *Las doce en punto y el buey arando.*
    *It is twelve o'clock and the ox is (still)
    plowing. (It is twelve o'clock and all is
    well).*

8. *Le dan en el codo y aprieta la mano.*
    *They ask him for some money and he closes his
    hand.*

9. *Más vale sucio en casa y no limpio en el camposanto.*
    *It is better to be dirty at home than clean in the
    cemetery. (It is better not to overwork and live
    longer than to overwork and die quickly.)*

---

* "He who is born a fool will not stop until he becomes an (empty) gourd."
This proverb type is cited by Stevenson on p. 843, No. 3, of *The Home
Book of Proverbs.* The earliest reference Stevenson cites is to an Indian saying dated around 100 A.D., which reads "A cure has been ordained for everything, but there is no medicine for the cure of a fool." Stevenson does not
include an example which uses the gourd as a symbol.

† Stevenson lists this proverb type under "Let every cuckold wear his own
horns" on p. 467, No. 9, of *The Home Book of Proverbs.* Two references
are cited; both are English, one from 1670 and one from 1762.

‡ In *The Home Book of Proverbs,* p. 1566, No. 13, Stevenson cites Cicero's
use, in 67 B.C., of "The more the merrier." The full form "The more the
merrier; the fewer, the better fare" made its first appearance in English
in 1530.

10. *Ni tanto que queme al santo, ni tanto que no le alumbre.*
    Not so much candlelight as will burn the saint,
    nor so little as will leave him in the dark. (Be
    moderate.)

11. *No hay más amigo que Dios ni más pariente que un peso.*
    There is no better friend than God, no better
    relative than a peso.

12. *No tener ni saliva.*
    Not even to have saliva. (Poor as a church
    mouse.) ⃰

13. *No todos los que chiflan son arrieros.*
    Not all who whistle are mule drivers. (This say-
    ing means that appearances are deceiving.) †

14. *Traigo bastón en la mano y frecuento la fiscalía.*
    Me llamo Don Apolonio y me apellido García,
    I carry a cane in my hand and I visit the Minis-
    terial office frequently, my name is Don Apolonio
    and my surname is García. (This expression is
    used to show contempt for persons who pry into
    other's affairs or who attach undue importance to
    themselves. The surname García seems to be used
    only for the sake of rhyme.)

15. *Un garbanzo de a libra.*
    A chick pea that weighs one pound. (This ex-
    pression is used in referring to a rare or unusual
    occurrence.)

16. *Un peso vale más que cien consejos.*
    A peso is worth more than a hundred counsels.

⃰ See Stevenson, *The Home Book of Proverbs*, p. 1856, No. 12. His earliest
reference is to an English play of 1672 and the latest is to Thackeray's
Vanity Fair (1848). The examples which Stevenson prints are all of the
"poor as a church mouse" form.
† On pp. 82–83 of *The Home Book of Proverbs* Stevenson prints sayings
that warn one not to judge by appearances. Examples are included of the
"appearances are deceiving" form.

6. ADIVINANZAS

THE EIGHT RIDDLES BELOW come from Soledad Pérez, "Mexican Folklore from Austin, Texas," pp. 126–27. I have annotated them according to parallel examples in Manuel J. Andrade, *Folklore from the Dominican Republic*, Memoirs of the American Folklore Society XXIII (1930); Aurelio M. Espinosa, "New-Mexican Spanish Folk-Lore, IX, Riddles," *Journal of American Folklore*, XXVIII (1915), 319–52; and Archer Taylor, *English Riddles from Oral Tradition* (Berkeley and Los Angeles: University of California Press, 1951).

1.	*Blanca como la nieve,*
	Prieta como el carbón,
	Anda y no tiene pies,
	Habla y no tiene boca.

	White as the snow,
	Black as the coal,
	She walks and she has no feet,
	She speaks and she has no mouth.
	Solution: *Una carta—a letter.**

2.	*Blanco fué mi nacimiento,*
	Me pintaron de colores,
	He causado muchas muertes,
	Y he empobrecido señores.

---

* In *English Riddles from Oral Tradition*, Nos. 260–65, p. 87, Archer Taylor states that this riddle contains a paradox ("moves without legs") which can be applied to many objects, and he lists nineteen of these objects, pp. 88–90. See section 17, p. 90, for an example of the "moves without legs" theme applied to a letter, and references to Spanish (1880), Catalan (1882), and French (1887) versions, and one from New Mexicans in California (1915).

At birth I was white,
But I was painted with colors,
I have caused many deaths,
And impoverished many men.

Solution: Barajas—cards,*

3. Dentro del mar está un queso,
    Dentro del queso está una O,
    Dentro de la O está una T,
    Adivínemela Ud.

In the sea there is a cheese,
In the cheese there is an O,
In the O there is a T,
Tell me what it is!

Solution: Marquesote—sponge cake.

4. Lana sube, lana baja.

Wool goes up, wool comes down.
Solution: La navaja—the knife.
(B and v are pronounced the same.) †

5. Plata no es,
    Oro no es,
    ¿Que es?

It is not silver,
It is not gold,
What is it?

Solution: Plátano—bánana.‡

---

* In *Folk-Lore from the Dominican Republic* (*MAFLS,* XXIII), Nos. 51(a)
and 51(b), p. 361, Manuel J. Andrade prints two variants of this riddle,
and on p. 400 he gives references to examples found in Puerto Rico, Argentina, and Spain. In version 51(a) the card is described as being green
at birth and dressed in a thousand colors, and in version 51(b) the card
is described as a young lady of variable color over whom men waste gold
and kill themselves.

† See Taylor, *English Riddles,* Nos. 1547–58, p. 632, for a general discussion
of the "up and down contrast" used by riddlers. According to Taylor, "this
contrast which is readily adapted to various objects is freely used by
European riddlers and in countries where the European tradition of rid-
dling is known." He does not include an example of the contrast between
wool and knives.

‡ See Andrade, *Folk-Lore from the Dominican Republic,* No. 261, p. 387, for

6.   *Rita, Rita que en el monte grita*
     Y en la casa está silenciosita.

     Rita, Rita shouts in the forest,
     And at home she is silent.

                    Solution: *El hacha*—the ax.*

7.   *Una vieja larga que le escurre la manteca,*
     ¿Que es?

     Who is the tall old woman whose garments drip fat?
                    Solution: *La vela*—the candle.†

8.   *Ya ves cuán claro es,*
     Adivíname lo que es.

     You see how clear it is,
     Tell me what it is.

                    Solution: *Llaves*—keys.‡

a variant of this riddle, and p. 401 for references to examples from Puerto Rico, Argentina, and Spain. Andrade's text is not in question form and adds two additional lines: "Open the curtain (covering)/ And you will see what it is."

* Aurelio M. Espinosa prints two variants of this riddle in New-Mexican Spanish Folk-Lore, IX, Riddles," *Journal of American Folklore,* XXVIII (1915), Nos. 54(a) and 54(b), 326. In his note, p. 326, Espinosa refers to other versions from Argentina, Chile, and Spain. He states that "the New-Mexican version is in all respects the best, and is probably a faithful version of the primitive original."

† For two versions of this riddle see Andrade, *Folk-Lore from the Dominican Republic,* Nos. 320(a) and 320(b), p. 393. The table of comparative references, p. 401, cites versions from Puerto Rico and Argentina.

‡ For a New-Mexican Spanish text of this riddle see Espinosa, "New-Mexican Spanish Folk-Lore," No. 68, p. 328.

7. PASTORELA

A DISCUSSION OF THE RELIGIOUS folk drama of the Spanish-Mexican Southwest, particularly as exemplified in "Los Pastores" or "The Shepherds Play," is given in Dorson, *American Folklore*, pp. 103–6. The present selection and translation of certain scenes have been made for this volume by Américo Paredes, of the Department of English at the University of Texas, from an unpublished text, "Pastorelas." A highlight of "The Shepherds Play" is the comic interview, printed here, between Lucifer and the foolish shepherd Cucharón, a counterpart of numskull characters in folktales; his confusion of "Messiah" with the name of his cousin Matthias involves Motif J1803, "Learned words misunderstood by uneducated." The theft of Cucharón's tamales by his fellow shepherd Bato does not appear in the text of "Los Pastores" printed by M. R. Cole. Professor Paredes provides the following information on his manuscript source.

The original from which the following excerpts have been translated is a manuscript dated October 14, 1891, in the hand of Juan Manuel Pérez of Brownsville, Texas. His niece, Mrs. Sara Zamora de la Rosa, who in 1954 allowed me to copy the manuscript, told me that Juan Manuel Pérez and other uncles of hers presented the "Pastorelas" in Brownsville as late as 1913. The Pérez manuscript is that of an *ensayador* or rehearser, written down in ink with pencil notations and modifications. In view of the date of the manuscript, it would be strange indeed if Juan Manuel Pérez and his group had not presented this particular variant of the "Pastorelas" in Brownsville during Christmas of 1891, at the same time that Captain John G.

Bourke was witnessing another "Pastorela" published in 1907 as Vol. IX of the Memoirs of the American Folklore Society, with translation, introduction, and notes by M. R. Cole (*Los Pastores, A Mexican Play of the Nativity*, Boston and New York, 1907). These two manuscripts are worthy of more detailed comparison than is given here. Both come from the same folk area, the lower Rio Grande border; both were written down in 1891, although one did not come to the attention of folklorists until 1954. One was written down for a collector; the other was written by the *ensayador* for his own use. They are clearly variants of the same version of the play, and comparison of the texts clarifies many obscurities in both.

Pastorela [1]

(*To Celebrate the Birth of Our Lord Jesus Christ*)

CHARACTERS

First file	Second file
Gila	Angel
Parrado	Tebano
Meliso	Nabal
Toringo	Mengo
Tulio	Gerardo
Cucharón	Lisardo
Bartolo	Bato

Hermit, Lucifer, Satan, Asmodeus, Indian, Ranchero

(*During most of the play the characters remain on stage once they appear, "exiting" merely by walking aside and standing away from the main scene of the action. Since the stage was usually a patio,*

[1] Cole calls the Rio Grande City variant "Los Pastores" and implies (pp. x, xvi, and xxi) that "Pastorela" identifies the modern, literary adaptations of the shepherd's nativity play, while "Los Pastores" is the name of the true folk play. The title given the Brownsville variant is evidence to the contrary.

this was only logical, but the custom was kept when the pastorelas moved into neighborhood theaters. At one end of the stage is the manger scene; the shepherds come in formed in two files. Gila, the only girl in the cast,[2] and the Angel Michael, most often played by a young boy, are at the head of each file; but the leaders are Parrado and Tebano. Parrado and Tebano sing the first two lines of each quatrain, and the files answer with the second two lines.) [3]

PARRADO and TEBANO (*as file enter*):
Pleasant meadow, soft aroma,
Oh, unequaled gaiety.

ALL:
Little zephyr, soft and pretty,
Let us both as brothers be.

PARRADO and TEBANO:
Hail the country and its beauty;
Death to infelicity.

ALL:
Little zephyr, soft and pretty,
Let us both as brothers be.

PARRADO and TEBANO:
Hail the country, only gladness,
Only innocence it knows.

ALL:
Only love and quiet pleasure,
For the mortal sweet repose.

PARRADO and TEBANO:
Pleasant meadow, soft aroma,
Oh, unequaled gaiety.

ALL:
Felicity! Felicity! Felicity!
(*The play proper now begins. The shepherds sing*

---

[2] Often all three members of the Holy Family are represented by images, although the parts of Mary and Joseph may be taken by a girl and a boy. The Christ Child is always a doll.

[3] In other songs Parrado and Tebano sing the full quatrain, and the files answer with the chorus.

*a song in which they announce the coming of Christ
and their intention to fight the Devil. They start
their journey across the mountains to Bethlehem.
A hermit joins them and then Lucifer appears in
the shape of a lion-faced gentleman dressed in
black. He declares himself in a soliloquy beginning,
"From the darkest dungeons, from the most horrid
caverns, I come like a lion, roaring and thundering."
He approaches the shepherds, who are making camp,
to discover the secret which torments him, whether
the Messiah has been born. His visage frightens
them and they move off to another spot and make
camp again. Cucharón, the glutton,[4] has a wallet
stuffed with food, but he will give none to Bato, who
is faint with hunger. Cucharón taunts Bato, letting him smell the food and no more. Bato con-
vinces him that he has drunk too much already, and
that the wolf has been sighted.)*

CUCHARÓN:

> It seems you have spoken well
> For the world is upside down
> And my head keeps turning, turning.
> Look! On that mountain slope
> A black billy goat is climbing!
> I must go back and ask
> If my goats came home.

BATO:

> Yes, go. And while you are gone
> I will look after your wallet.

CUCHARÓN:

> Well, then, I am going, brother.

LUCIFER:

> From this peasant must I learn
> The matter that troubles me.
> Shepherd, where are you from?

---

[4] In the Rio Grande City variant Cucharón does not have the role of glutton.
The sequence of Bato's theft of Cucharón's tamales is found only in the
Brownsville text.

CUCHARÓN:
> From over yonder, *Señor.*

LUCIFER:
> I ask of your fatherland.

CUCHARÓN:
> My father is long deceased;
> Pray for him.

LUCIFER:
> Idle conceits.

CUCHARÓN:
> I am not idle, *Señor.*
> What's this? Let me pass.

LUCIFER:
> Perhaps.
> Whenever I wish it so.

CUCHARÓN:
> And that makes it even worse.
> What next?

LUCIFER:
> In time you'll know.

CUCHARÓN:
> If later, why not right now?

LUCIFER:
> Time enough; don't be impatient.

CUCHARÓN:
> Dressed all in black he comes,
> That is the color of death;
> It means that I die in haste
> And that this raven has smelled me
> And come for the funeral feast.

LUCIFER:
> This simpleton will I use
> The great secret to discover,
> And through his mouth shall I know
> That which Heaven has concealed;
> For to the humble has God
> All his mysteries unfolded,
> For them are His fruits and care.

Look shepherd, if you will tell me
A truth that I wish to know
I promise to let you pass;
But if you don't, your remains
Shall be a bloody reminder
And a warning to the world.

CUCHARÓN:

A risky job it will be;
Pray God that I do it well.

BATO (*at other end of the stage*):

Pray God that he be delayed;
I have played him for a fool
And now the wallet is empty,
No wine, no cheese, no tamales.

LUCIFER (*to* CUCHARÓN):

Tell me, shepherd, have you heard
If the Messiah is born
Or if they say He is coming?

CUCHARÓN:

I have a Cousin Matthias
Who left us two years ago
Because of a certain killing;
He left the country for good
But lately they pardoned him,
And I hear he's coming back
As quick as a thunderbolt;
And if he has not arrived
He will pretty soon, I hope.

LUCIFER:

I don't ask you for Matthias;
Good shepherd, what I would know
Is whether the true Messiah
Has been born.

CUCHARÓN:

And rightly so.
He's the one; I well remember
That I saw him circumcized,
And I was there at his naming;

Matthias, that was the name;
For he was the son of Matthew,
A first cousin of my father,
My grand-uncle's closest kin
Who married the cousin-german
Of this Matthias the First;
Because you will know, *Señor,*
That these Matthews and Matthiases
All come from Matthewselah,
A descendant so they say
Of Matthias and of Mattock
Used on your mother-in-law,
All of the issue of Aaron
Which is my grandfather's side;
And so the name True Matthias
Is most rightfully his own.

LUCIFER:

Imbecile! What are you saying?
Is it your pleasure to burn
Like a piece of glowing coal?

CUCHARÓN:

Coal did you say? Was it coal?
Ah, *sí, Señor,* that reminds me;
I did know within these parts
The blacksmith, Uncle Matthias,
But I couldn't rightly say
Whether or not he's the true one.

LUCIFER:

Now will I tear out your heart
For the barbarous thing you do me;
All of your history
While the fires of Hell consume me!

CUCHARÓN:

Quick, help me God for I kindle!

LUCIFER:

With that Name alone you wound me.

CUCHARÓN:

Quick, help me God for I burn!

LUCIFER:

> And for that reason I leave you,
> For if that did not prevent me
> I would entomb you here.

CUCHARÓN:

> Go along, go to the depths;
> I do not know how to conjure you;
> And here will lie Cucharón,
> Breathless for an eternity.
>
> (*Lucifer retires; Cucharón returns to camp, singing, "I will never go alone/ In the dark along this road;/ I promise it, I promise it." He relates his meeting with the Devil and finds his wallet empty.*)

CUCHARÓN:

> Friend Bato, but what is this?
> What have you done to me?
> What became of my tamales?

BATO:

> They must be strayed, or lost.

CUCHARÓN:

> With the wallet closed so tight?

BATO:

> There could be nothing inside.

CUCHARÓN:

> If those tamales were strayed
> We would find them, there perhaps.

BATO:

> And do you think they're that stupid,
> To remain just lying there?
> Perhaps they went for a walk
> Along the meadows so gay.

CUCHARÓN:

> That is ridiculous, Bato,
> For you know they have no feet,
> Then how could they run away?

BATO:

> Tell me with what kind of meat
> Were the lost tamales made.

CUCHARÓN:

> The flesh of a nanny goat.

BATO:

> And where did the nanny roam?

CUCHARÓN:

> In the meadow, like the rest.

BATO:

> Now see what a fool you are;
> Those tamales found themselves
> Inside the wallet enclosed,
> Wrapped in dough; who, do you think,
> Would find that a happy lot?
> Now, now, if you're not a fool.

CUCHARÓN:

> But the poor nanny was dead.

BATO:

> Let me put this one example
> To your hand: A soul in Hell
> Is lonely for what it stole,
> And it comes back to the world
> To haunt the scene of the crime
> Hour upon hour. Now then,
> Is this true?

CUCHARÓN:

> Of course it's true.

BATO:

> Well, then, that just goes to show
> What a foolish man you are;
> You know that you stole the goat
> From your master. Very well,
> Because it was stolen meat
> It is now haunting the meadows.

CUCHARÓN:

> Look, Bato, you go too far.
> You give me back my tamales.

BATO:

> Tomorrow, about this hour;
> It's a promise.

(Before Cucharón and Bato can fight, Nabal enters saying he has seen an angel. Lucifer, Satan, and Asmodeus then take the center and plan revenge. Michael appears disguised as a shepherd and holds a long dialogue with Lucifer, who demands his adversary's name.)

LUCIFER:

Then you must tell me your name
So I may know whom to seek.

ANGEL:

Shepherd am I, and the victor
Over dark, infernal pride.

BATO:

And I am Bato, the shepherd,
Who fought the warlike tamales,
Of all that ventured before me
Not one was left in the wallet.

CUCHARÓN:

I'm Cucharón; I am he
Who with my powerful hand
Will knock out all of your teeth
And all your molars as well
Now with the aid of this club,
Not ceasing your bones to break,
In the name of the good Gilita [5]
And the name of other names,
All of which some day or other
Will cause you impediment.

(Michael retires, though Lucifer frantically calls on him to stay. The fiends call another council of war, while the shepherds sing to Michael to return. Michael reappears and strikes down all the fiends. Now the shepherds may reach Bethlehem. One by one they cross to the farther end of the stage where the manger is located, each singing his own song or "caminata" ("journey or progress"). As each

---

[5] Cucharón swears in Gila's name because she made the tamales that Bato stole.

arrives at the manager he makes his adoration and leaves a gift. All do so except Bartolo, the sluggard, who lies asleep mid-stage. Lucifer hovers about him.)

BATO:

We must go to Bethlehem;
Arise, Bartolo, arise!
It is time that you prepare
The gift you will take the Child.

BARTOLO:

And why do I have to take it?
I'll ask for something instead;
To be cured of this debility
That keeps me tied to my bed.

LUCIFER:

My anger still burns within me,
And solicitous I'll be
To entangle this one shepherd
If I can manage the scheme;
I will spoil his hopes of Glory,
The manger he'll never reach,
Nor will he make adoration
Though they threaten and they call;
I will make use of my power
And he will not move at all.

GILA:

There in Bethlehem is Glory;
Arise, Bartolo, arise!

BARTOLO:

If Glory[6] should want to see me,
Let her come here where I lie.

PARRADO and TEBANO (*inviting* BARTOLO):

Come, before the Wise Men leave
We will manage to arrive.

BARTOLO:

Better to get there this evening,
When they serve the food and wine.

[6] A pun on *Gloria,* meaning both "glory" and a woman's name.

HERMIT:

> To Jerusalem, Bartolo;
> This pleasure do not deny us.

BARTOLO:

> Why not just give my regrets
> To the genuine Messiah?

NABAL:

> Come, and you'll see the ox
> Warming our God with his breath.

BARTOLO:

> And what if he's mean and wild?
> What if he gores me to death?

MELISO:

> A baptismal celebration
> Will occur in Bethlehem.

BARTOLO:

> No one has named me the sponsor,
> What truck should I have with them?
> If they give coins to the people
> I pray that you bring me mine.[7]

MENGO:

> Come, Bartolo; you shall see
> The loving Jesus divine.

BARTOLO:

> If you wish to introduce us
> Bring him here, where I recline.

TORINGO:

> Arise, Bartolo, arise;
> Let us go adore the Babe.

BARTOLO:

> I had just fallen asleep
> And now you have made me wake.

GERARDO:

> Do not be slothful and heavy,
> Arise, Bartolo, arise!

[7] It still is the custom among people of Mexican culture for the *padrino* or sponsor at a baptism to scatter coins among the children who gather outside the church door, crying, *"Bolo, padrino!"* as the baptismal party leaves.

BARTOLO:

    I'm tired of lying like this,
    I'll sleep on my other side. (*Turns over.*)

TULIO:

    I call on your noble spirit,
    Bartolo, please leave your bed.

BARTOLO:

    If I leave it, it will be
    In order to break your head.

LISARDO:

    The morning star has appeared
    And the day is sure to follow.

BARTOLO:

    I just heard the vespers ring,
    That's one that I will not swallow.

CUCHARÓN:

    Arise, Bartolo, arise!
    It's time we were on the road.

BARTOLO:

    You take the one that you please
    And "Bartolo" me no more.

BATO:

    Eating the blessed straw
    There is a mule, you'll see.

BARTOLO:

    And if it's a stingy mule?
    She'll share none of it with me.

PARRADO and TEBANO:

    Bartolo, your laziness
    Is more than foolish, in truth;
    You obstinately refuse
    To look on the face of God,
    Who to redeem us all
    In His awful majesty
    Saw fit to become the Flesh
    In the womb of Mary, the pure,
    The innocent, virginal.

LUCIFER:

> That Name again! It torments me!
> And still for my greater pain
> All this has been done in vain.
> You have conquered; you have conquered.
> All the Celestial Court
> Against the infernal fury
> Is today at your command.

SHEPHERDS (*singing*):

> You have no recourse,
> Bartolo, arise;
> And go to the manger
> To visit the Child.

> (*They use boards as levers to get Bartolo up. He
> makes his "caminata" and adoration; then all sing
> a lullaby to the Christ Child. The play ends with
> an appeal to the audience to pardon the many
> faults of the performance and with the actors' re-
> spects to the priest and the civil authorities.[8] They
> exit, singing, and the Indian enters, speaking in
> broken Spanish.*)

INDIAN:

> Now ending festivitation,
> All completed, all is past;
> So maybe they try to stop me,
> I stay behind for the last.

[8] The Brownsville variant makes no reference to "His Majesty," as does the Rio Grande text.

8. CORRIDOS

AN EXCELLENT TREATISE is Merle E. Simmons, *The Mexican Corrido as a Source for Interpretive Study of Modern Mexico (1870–1950)*, (Bloomington: Indiana University Press, 1957).

"Corrido de Gregorio Cortez"

> *The corrido of "Gregorio Cortez" is the subject of an engrossing work of biography, legend and balladry by Américo Paredes, "With His Pistol in His Hand": A Border Ballad and Its Hero (Austin, Texas: University of Texas Press, 1958). The following text is Paredes' Variant B, pp. 161–63. He comments (p. 190): "Variant B was recorded late in the summer of 1954, but its source, Nicanor Torres, was already fifty-eight years old in 1920, when Variant A is believed to have been recorded. Torres was about forty when the ballad first appeared. He is a bit hazy about dates and places. He says that he knows the song as it originally came out, back in 1915 or 1912 when Cortez killed the sheriffs. He also places Karnes City in the vicinity of San Benito, about twenty miles from the Rio Grande. In any event Torres was singing the corrido before 1920. He has retained a fairly long version, in spite of his years (he was ninety-two in 1954), but there is little doubt that time has made changes in his variant."*

Gentlemen, give your attention,
The misfortune has occurred;

The Major Sheriff died,
Leaving Román badly wounded.

The next day, in the morning,
When people arrived,
They said to one another,
"It is not known who killed him."

Then said Gregorio Cortez,
With his pistol in his hand,
"I don't regret that I killed you;
I regret my brother's death."

Then said Gregorio Cortez,
And his soul was all aflame,
"I don't regret that I killed you;
A man must defend himself."

Then the Americans said,
With a lot of fear,
"Come, let us follow the trail;
The wrongdoer is Cortez."

"If we catch up with him, what
        shall we do to him?
If we talk to him man to man,
If we talk to him man to man,
Very few of us will return."

He struck out toward Piedras
        Negras,
Without showing any fear,
"Follow me, don't be cowards;
I am Gregorio Cortez."

When he had reached Palo Alto
They caught up with him again;
Quite a few more than three hundred,
And there he jumped their corral.

Then said Gregorio Cortez,
Shooting out a lot of bullets,
"I have weathered thunderstorms;
This little mist doesn't bother me."

In the county of Karnes City,
According to what we hear,
They caught up with him again,
And there he killed another sheriff.

Now he has met a Mexican,
Without showing any fear,
"Tell me the news;
I am Gregorio Cortez."

"It is said that because of me
Many people have been killed;
I will surrender now
Because such things are not right."

Cortez says to Jesús,
"Now you are going to see it;
Go tell the sheriffs
To come and arrest me."

The sheriffs were coming,
Coming so fast they even flew,
For they wanted to get
The ten thousand dollars they were offered.

When they surrounded the house,
Cortez suddenly appeared before them,
"You will take me if I'm willing,
But not any other way."

Then the Major Sheriff said,
As if he was going to cry,
"Cortez, hand over your weapons;
We are not going to kill you."

Then said Gregorio Cortez,
He said and in a loud voice,
"I won't surrender my arms
Until I am in a cell."

Then said Gregorio Cortez,
In a loud and fine voice,
"I won't surrender my arms
Until I am inside a jail."

Now with this I say farewell,
With the leaves of a cypress tree,
This is the end of the singing
Of the ballad about Cortez.

"Corrido de Jacinto Treviño"

*This corrido of another Mexican border hero who mocks
the Texas Rangers well expresses Mexican attitudes of
disdain for the lordly Americans. Collected by Américo
Paredes in Spanish from Cornelio Varela Jiménez, 46,
at Matamoros, Mexico, on August 23, 1954. The taped
original is in the University of Texas Folklore Archive.
Notes supplied by Professor Paredes.*

"JACINTO TREVIÑO"

Sung by Cornelio Varela Jimenez in Matamoros, Mexico, in 1954.
Collected by Américo Paredes.

It happened once in McAllen,
In San Benito, that's twice;
Now it has happened in Brownsville,
And we have seen something nice.

In that saloon known as Baker's
The bullets started to fly;
Bottles would jump into pieces
Wherever you set your eye.

In that saloon known as Baker's
They scatter and they run;
No one is left but Jacinto
With rifle and pistol-gun.

"Come on, you cowardly Rangers;
No baby is up agin you.
You wanted to meet your Daddy?
I am Jacinto Treviño!

"Come on, you treacherous Rangers;
Come get a taste of my lead.
And did you think it was ham
Between two slices of bread?" [1]

The Sheriff was an American,
But he was shouting aloud,
"You are a brave man, Jacinto;
You make the Mexicans proud."

Then said Jacinto Treviño,
Laughing so hard that it hurt,
"Why don't you just kiss my elbow
And fold the cuffs of my shirt!"

Then said Jacinto Treviño,
Taking a drink from a spring,
"Oh, what a poor bunch of Rangers;
They didn't do me a thing!"

Then said Jacinto Treviño,
"Now it is time to retire;

[1] A reference to the Anglo-American addiction to the ham sandwich, much criticized in Border Mexican folklore.

I'm going to Rio Grande [2]
And I will welcome you there."

Now I must beg your permission,
This is the end of the chorus;
I am Jacinto Treviño,
A native of Matamoros.[3]

"Corrido de la Muerte de Antonio Mestas"

> *The discovery by John D. Robb of this* corrido, *sung
> by a blind singer near Abiquiu, New Mexico, is dis-
> cussed in Dorson,* American Folklore, *pp. 110–11. Robb
> was able to verify the historical basis of the accidental
> death of Mestas, to record additional variants, and to
> learn the name of the composer, bilingual Gino Gon-
> zales, who launched the* corrido *into tradition. The
> dream of death ascribed to Mestas follows Motif
> D1812.3.3, "Future revealed in dream."*
>
> *Text and translation from John D. Robb,* Hispanic Folk
> Songs of New Mexico *(Albuquerque: University of
> New Mexico Publications in the Fine Arts #1, 1954),
> pp. 52–57.*

1. In the year of eighteen hundred
    And eighty-nine in July,
    On the fifth day God determined
    Antonio Mestas must die;
    That he should be thrown from the saddle
    And meet his death on the ground,
    Near the ridge of El Mogote,
    And there his body was found.

2. From the ranch owned by the English
    Antonio rode at dawn,

---

[2] Rio Grande City, always called "Rio Grande" by Texas-Mexicans.
[3] The identification of the singer with the hero in the *despedida* or formal
close is common in the *corrido*.

To round up a herd of cattle
Which from their range had gone.
Though young and handsome and happy,
Antonio to fate was resigned;
To die like a man and a cowboy
Was in Antonio's mind.

3.   For as he slept in the bunkhouse
Antonio had a dream,
A dream of death in the mountains,
Beside a running stream.
The cook he did not waken,
Who was his bosom friend,
And who, they say, in a vision
Foresaw Antonio's end.

4.   The next morn all went searching,
They searched the land in vain,
They searched the mountain forests,
They searched the sagebrush plain.
They searched from early morning
Until the darkness fell,
But finding nothing, departed
Although they had hunted well.

5.   To La Cebolla came flying
The unexpected word,
To give the people notice
Of what had just occurred.
The people came out crying
With pity and alarm,
And everyone was fearful
Antonio had suffered harm.

6.   But God who watcheth and knoweth
The thing that the searchers seek,
Caused a Crow who stood on the hilltop
These bitter words to speak:

"Below me lies your servant
Among the grasses tall;
Observe the thing that I see,
It's here your friend did fall."

7.   July the seventh they found him,
And all with sorrow were filled,
As they viewed Antonio's body,
Who by a horse was killed.
They turned away in horror,
The blood within them froze,
For the body was swollen and rotting,
And torn by carrion crows.

8.   Then came Bernabal Trujillo
And saw him where he lay;
In tenderness he lamented,
And crying out did say:
"My brother, what has befallen,
And what is this I see,
So dead and still in the meadow,
Can this thing really be?"

9.   Ambrosio Espinosa,
A strong and vigilant youth,
Was sent to bear to the family
The stern and dreadful truth.
And like the agile butterfly,
He flew through the winds of the night,
And the will of God sustained him
With courage and with might.

10.   At last he came to the valley
In which his father dwelt,
And thus he spoke of the matter,
And full of sadness he felt:
"Please go, my *padrecito*,
And tell Don Agustín

His son lies dead in the mountains,
But gently please begin."

11.   Don Benito did as requested,
To bear the news he went:
"Good day, little friend. How goes it?
With a message I am sent."
"Dismount, my friend Don Benito,"
Don Agustín calmly did speak;
But though, poor man, he knew nothing,
He suddenly felt weak.

12.   "Forgive me for coming so early,
I come to bring you word
Of your beloved Antonio,
Which I have just now heard."
And Mestas, greatly excited,
Exclaimed, "What happened, I pray?"
And Don Benito responded
To Don Agustín this way:

13.   "The late Antonio Mestas"—
Don Agustín's heart was chilled,
"On the mountain called 'El Mogote'
By a bronco has been killed."

14.   Mestas cried out in anguish,
"I've lost my only joy;
I pray to God in my sorrow
That he may take my boy."
He went to tell Martinita
(She felt a sense of dread),
"Your happiness is finished,
Your husband dear is dead."

15.   The poor young woman fainted
From shock, surprise, and fears,

At the violent news he related
Which thus had reached his ears.
And sighs and moanings of anguish
Came forth from this breast so true:
"Oh husband dear of my spirit,
What has become of you!"

16.   "My father Atilano,
And father Agustín,
Oh brothers of my childhood,
My grief is very keen.
"Beloved husband Antonio,
My husband and faithful friend,
In God is my only comfort,
Antonio, 'til the end."

17.   Don Agustín saddled his pony,
Consumed with passionate grief,
To give his son the last honors
Would be his only relief.

18.   Don Agustín rode northward
With Don Atilano his friend,
Went up to the town of Cebolla
Where the cowboy met his end.
And as they climbed the steep mountain,
The father lashed at his steed,
"Today I've no pity for the horses,
For a horse has done this deed."

19.   They came at last to Cebolla
Where the cowboy had been brought,
And gazing down at his body,
The anguished father thought:
"Am I awake? Am I sleeping?
Is this a dream in my head?
An evil dream I am dreaming,
Or are you really dead?"

20.
    Don Agustín, sad and bewildered,
    Looked down at the corpse of the lad,
    And many a deep sigh escaped him,
    And these are the thoughts that he had:
    "I must take him home in a coffin,
    I must take his body down,
    And give him a Christian burial
    In his own native town."

21.
    But seeing the swollen body,
    Which would not go in a case,
    He knew they must bury the body
    At once in that very place.
    "Good-bye, beloved Antonio,
    Good-bye, my dear little boy;
    Alas, alas, you have left us
    And taken all our joy."

22.
    In great and solemn procession,
    The people from miles around
    Accompanied him to the graveyard
    And laid him there in the ground.

23.
    And then like swords of anguish,
    The heavy spadefuls fell,
    And shudders ran through the people
    Who had known Antonio well.
    They said farewell full of sorrow,
    With pity they were filled,
    At the memory of poor Antonio
    Whom a wild horse had killed.

24.
    At last, when all had been finished
    And they to their homes had returned,
    And all of the young man's relations
    His tragic fate had learned,
    Antonio's wife Martinita
    Raised up her voice in pain:

"I shall never see my dear husband
Returning home again."

"El Contrabando del Paso"

Text from Brownie McNeill, "Corridos of the Mexican Border," in Mexican Border Ballads and Other Lore, *ed. Mody C. Boatright (Publications of the Texas Folklore Society XXI, Austin, 1946), pp. 30–32. Only the English translation is reprinted.*

McNeill writes (pp. 29–30): "Some years ago the Rio Grande changed its course just below the city of El Paso and sliced off a part of Mexico, a strip of land approximately one-half mile long and a quarter of a mile wide, leaving it within the boundaries of the United States. The United States government, however, has never recognized the territory as a part of our country, and hence it has become a no man's land. The Border Patrol maintains a constant lookout from a series of towers along the bank of the old channel for anyone attempting to smuggle in contraband merchandise. Although El Pasoans refer to the place as Cordova's Island, it is known to the Spanish-speaking folk on both sides of the river as el charco seco (the dry marsh). *The term marsh refers to the dense patches of reeds with intermittent cane brakes which separate the island from the United States border. It is said that the ghost of many a* contrabando (smuggler) *walks the dry marsh on nights when there is no moon, for the area was a favorite crossing spot for smugglers during prohibition days, and many a gun battle has taken place there between the smugglers and the United States officers. It is no wonder that the phrase* andar en el charco seco (to walk the dry marsh) *has become a grim synonym for smuggling."*

The ballad of El Contrabando del Paso *is the lament of a youthful smuggler who fell in with bad company and met the inevitable end of all smugglers—Leavenworth.*

The seventeenth of August
We were in despair,
And they took us from El Paso
Handcuffed on the way to Kansas.

They put us out of the jail
At eight o'clock at night,
They took us through the depot,
They put us aboard a coach.

I direct my glances
All around the station,
To look for my beloved mother
So that she might give me her blessing.

Neither my mother was waiting for me
Nor my lady, my wife,
Goodbye, all my friends,
When shall I see you again?

There comes the train whistling,
It won't be long in arriving,
I tell all my friends
Not to cry.

I'm going to take the train,
I commit myself to the strong saint,
I shall never go back to smuggling
Because I have bad luck.

Smuggling is very good,
One makes good money,
But what I don't like
Is that they take me prisoner.

Now the train begins to move
And the bells to ring,

I ask Mister Hill
If we are going to Louisiana.

Mister Hill with his little laugh
Answers me: "No, sir,
We'll pass through Louisiana
Right straight to Leavenworth."

Run, run, little machine,
Turn loose all the steam,
Hurry and take this seagull
To the plain of Leavenworth.

I recommend to my friends
That they go give it a try,
That they get into smuggling
And see where they will land.

I recommend to my countrymen
That they stay away from the dry marsh,
Don't believe those friends,
Those pig heads.

Who, as for sticking by their word,
Friends, it's the truth,
When a person finds himself in court
They forget friendship.

But as for that there's no remedy,
Now, what's happened is past,
Some day they are bound to find themselves
In the same situation as I.

Right straight from St. Lawrence
It was about eleven o'clock in the morning
That we stepped upon the threshold
Of the penitentiary.

He who recites these verses
Has asked your pardon,
If they are not incorrigible
Well, that being your opinion.

I send you there, dear mother,
A sigh and an embrace,
Here the verses about the smuggler of El Paso
Have come to an end.

"Mi carro Ford"

*Not only border heroes and tragic deaths provide
themes for Mexican Southwest troubadours. Here is a
jaunty tribute—or lament—on a jalopy.*

Text and translation from Robb, Hispanic Folk Songs
of New Mexico, *p. 83.*

1. It's a banged-up car I'm driving;
    One who has not long been striving
    Can't begin to make it run,
    But when I'm behind the wheel-oh,
    Like a bird I make it feel-oh,
    Or a shot fired from a gun.

2. It has fenders that are dented,
    And the top will shed no rain;
    Radiator's very holey,
    The transmission is a pain.

3. At about the hour of noon, I
    Filled the batt'ry, none too soon,
    And the cables I restored;
    Then my cigarette I lighted,
    Got aboard, and quite delighted,
    On three cylinders off I roared.

4.
I had just begun my ride,
When the engine up and died,
So the motor I inspected,
Found it worse than I expected—
Only dirt and muck inside.

5.
But a friend of mine was passing,
And he gave me this advice:
Take that scarecrow far away,
Hide it from the light of day;
It was never worth the price.

VII

UTAH MORMONS

✢ THE PROBLEM POSED by Mormon folklore is the problem every folklorist must face at some point in his inquiries: how shall he distinguish between faith and legend, sacrament and ritual, piety and superstition? With the Mormons, no easy separation can be made between the theology of an official hierarchy and the folk notions of an untutored flock—as, for example, in the case of the Roman Catholic Church and New Mexican peasants—since the flock is fully tutored. The Church of Jesus Christ of the Latter Day Saints came into existence as recently as 1830, and its swelling membership of well over a million is fully acquainted with its short but marvelous history and its firmly held dogmas. The faithful believe in the Book of Mormon as a new revelation, made known to the Saints through the prophet Joseph Smith. Together with the Doctrine and Covenants and the Pearl of Great Price, it supplements the Bible as the revealed Word of God.

None of these scriptures belong to the domain of folklore, even if rejected as revelation by a skeptical non-Mormon or an apostate. The same principle applies to sacred as to secular writings in the eyes of the folklorist; the literary document, fixed and unswerving, can never be folklore, whether a romance by Hawthorne or the Book of Genesis. Yet folk traditions often swirl around the heroes and events consecrated in holy writ and celebrated in literary fiction. Nathaniel Hawthorne and the author of Genesis both draw upon oral legends. There is indeed a Bible of the folk which exists independently from the King James or other translations.* In the orally retold miracles of Christ and the apostles and the saints; in the tale-

_____

* See the detailed exposition by Francis Lee Utley, "The Bible of the Folk," *California Folklore Quarterly*, IV (1945), 1–17.

cycles surrounding the Devil in his quest for souls, or St. Peter at the Gate of Heaven, or the Wandering Jew on his tormented round; in the carols, proverbs, and parables clustering around biblical themes, the Bible can be said to flourish as a source of living folk literature. The same general motifs unite Satan with other tricksters, saints with other culture heroes and protectors, Catholic miracles and Protestant providences with the magical acts of seers, shamans, and soothsayers around the world. This universality of motif is what intrigues the folklorist.

Founded so recently in prophecy and revelation, vision and trance, the Mormon church, too, has sown a Bible of the folk among its devoted followers. The providential deliverances of Joseph Smith and Brigham Young during the westward march of the Saints form one chapter. The miraculous salvation of the Mormon settlement in Salt Lake Valley in 1848, when gulls swarmed on the crickets eating the first grain crop, is a special and oft-repeated story. Well-nigh incredible accounts of healing by elders and conversions by missionaries, and the ubiquitous appearances of the Three Nephites in time to succor Saints in distress, contribute further narrations to the folk Bible of the Latter Day Saints. To the Mormon believer they are gospel, but for the folklorist they are oral supernatural traditions that display international themes. So the legends of the Three Nephites in the course of their circulation have absorbed such other vigorous traditions as the ancient tale of the Wandering Jew and the modern one of the Ghostly Hitchhiker.

The study of folklore has attracted a number of Mormons and former Mormons. Such university professors as Wayland Hand, Austin Fife, Stuart Gallacher, and Terrence Hansen learned foreign languages as Mormon missionaries, subsequently made academic careers of their language specialties in German, French, and Spanish, and then turned to Folklore for their research interests—though not necessarily Mormon folklore. In order to assess their own tradition objectively, the degree of detachment is required which Hector Lee maintains in *The Three Nephites* (1949), and Austin and Alta Fife in *Saints of Sage and Saddle* (1956), both admirable analytical works based on extensive field recordings.

Those folklore genres which do not involve matters of belief and dogma can readily be accepted as folkstuff by believers and nonbelievers alike. The string of ripe anecdotes about Elder J. Golden Kimball, the former cowhand addicted to profanity, pleases Mormon audiences, who appreciate the references to esoteric points of church ritual and organization. No one takes offense if the folklorist demonstrates that these and other Mormon jokes are traditionally known in variant forms. Ballads fall now on one, now on the other side of the line, depending on whether they deal with sacred or secular episodes. Who would take seriously the encounter of sweet Betsy from Pike with Brigham Young in a Mormon-colored variation of the jocular ballad? But only a folklorist would pair it with the ballad of "The Seagulls and the Crickets," centering on an act of divine interposition to save the Saints.

And what is the present attitude of the Saints toward the supernatural world? One commentator, M. Hamlin Cannon, believes that as the Mormon church has waxed strong and sophisticated, the old acceptance of evil spirits and protective angels has waned, and now belongs with the heroic age of Joseph Smith and the pioneers.* But Austin Fife declares that the very fabric of Mormonia depends on its allegiance to doctrines of interceding prophets and priests and revenants, of supplicatory rites and prayers, and of abounding malignant spirits.†

In addition to folklore possessed by Mormons, there also exists a folklore about the Mormons. The internal traditions are those possessed by the Saints, which shower glory and good humor upon their church; the external traditions are those developed by the gentiles out of the hatred and venom directed against the faithful. A volume of anti-Mormon folklore could well have been collected around 1900, reflecting general American hostilities and suspicions rampant in the second half of the nineteenth century, and finding printed expression in savage and inflammatory tracts. Some relics of this earlier phase still endure, and can be found in good-natured jokes and songs which caricature the Mormon's supposed libidinous tendencies. When the flames of racial and religious friction have somewhat cooled, a minority group often absorbs the gibes of its enemy, and insider and outsider join in the laughter. This is what is happening in the United States with the once dreaded Mormon.

* "Angels and Spirits in Mormon Doctrine," *California Folklore Quarterly,* IV (1945), 343–50.

† "Folk Belief and Mormon Cultural Autonomy," *Journal of American Folklore,* LVI (1948), 19–30.

1. SAINTS' LEGENDS

GENERAL ACCOUNTS of this genre are Gordon H. Gerould, *Saints'*
Legends (Boston and New York, 1916), a literary study, and
C. Grant Loomis, *White Magic, The Folklore of Christian Legend*
(Cambridge, 1948), a study of folkloristic motifs. Legends of the
Three Nephites are discussed in Dorson, *American Folklore*, pp.
113–18.

Collecting Oral Legends of the Three Nephites

> *Austin Fife gave this account of his field methods, along*
> *with a classification for his forty-three texts, in "The*
> *Legend of the Three Nephites Among the Mormons,"*
> Journal of American Folklore, *LIII (1940), 22–23.*

The following forty-three versions were collected by the author
and his wife in several Utah communities during the summer of
1939 and during the last week of December, 1939. Less than
two weeks were spent in collecting them and only a few communities were visited. In reality it was only at St. George in the
southwest corner of the state that a sufficient amount of time
was spent to warrant the assumption that the greater part of
the common Three Nephites legends of this particular locality
had been collected. Hence it is with some assurance that we
conclude that the number of these legends which could be
gathered from oral sources by some months of extended effort
in all localities where there are organized branches of the Mormon Church would probably amount to several hundred.

In collecting our versions, the procedure was to go first
to friends or acquaintances in each locality, or to recommended
parties such as the local agents of the Federal Writers' Project,
members of local historical societies, and directors of certain
church organizations. From them, the names of people who
were known to have told versions of the legend were secured, and
such people were visited in their homes. When a version was
told it was usually taken down in shorthand by the author's
wife. In collecting the stories an effort was made to take them
down exactly as told, including grammatical errors, dialectal
expressions, and so on, although it was not always possible to
record all the local peculiarities of pronunciation. Furthermore,
a great variety will be noticed in the grammatical forms and
idiomatic expressions found in the various versions. This is
accounted for by the fact that the educational background of
the narrators varied greatly. Many were local folk with the
most meager formal education. Others were trained college people, among whom were medical men, college professors, and
other professional people. It is, however, important to observe
that the editing by the author has been limited to the omission
of asides in the narrative which had no relationship to the subject in hand. The names of the narrators, their approximate
ages, the locality in which the stories were collected, the dates
of collection, and other significant facts concerning the source
of the stories are all given in footnotes following each version.

In arranging the various versions of this legend an attempt has been made to group them according to the characteristic motifs of each. Six groups have thus been formed. The
first, composed of five versions, comprises stories in which the
bringing of a special spiritual message is the central motif. In
the second group of twelve versions the mysterious manner in
which the stranger appeared and disappeared constitutes the
principal motif. In the nine versions of the third group, some
helpful act, such as a miraculous healing or the giving of important personal advice, is the central motif. The principal item
of interest in the fourth group, which is composed of nine versions, is the miraculous furnishing of food or the giving of a
blessing of plenty in exchange for hospitality. The fifth group

is composed of eight versions which are incomplete or which do not have a characteristic central motif relating them to any of the four groups previously mentioned.

"How Mrs. Fisher's Voice Was Restored"

> *This narrative involves the theme of supernatural curing by a Nephite. Motifs V221, "Miraculous healing by saints," and D2188.1, "Ability to disappear or appear at will," are present.*
>
> *Text from Hector Lee, The Three Nephites: The Substance and Significance of the Legend in Folklore (Albuquerque: University of New Mexico Press, 1949), No. 21b, pp. 140–42. Informant: Mrs. Irvin Fisher, Bountiful, Utah. Collectors: Hector Lee and Monza Higgs, by wire recorder.*

Oh, I'm seventy-two. I've been married going on fifty-two years. And I've lived in Utah all my life. I was born in Utah, and lived here all my life. But I had a real hard trial in my life, on account of which I whispered one third of my life. And the other two-thirds it was hard to talk. Because I had to use so much force, you know, to talk. And Mother took me to doctors and had me blessed by wonderful men, and I never got one bit of help from them. And I thought there was no hope; yet I got a blessing from a patriarch in 1899, and he told me of a great work that I was to do. And I thought that would be in another life and not this one.

So I said, "Grandma, that can't come true."

She says, "Oh, yes it can, every bit of it," she says. "I know what our Heavenly Father can do." She says, "He can bless you, and I'm going to pray for you as I've never prayed in my life."

And so she started right in to praying, and she prayed. And she prayed one month, and I thought maybe she'd get weak. And she prayed another month; and then she prayed another month. And when that month was up and it was just the last day, a knock came at my door. And I went to that door and pulled the curtain up a little way and saw it was a man with a gray beard and right white hair. A little frock-tail coat and dark pants and a light shirt. I knew he couldn't hear my whispers, so I took hold of his hand and brought him into the house, because it came to me, "He's a Nephite of the living God! Let him in quick or he'll be gone!" And I knew it was one.

And then I set him down and he says, "Go get the dear old lady," he says, "that has prayed three solid months for your blessing." So I went and brought Grandma into this room, and she began to cry: "I've lived to be eighty-eight years old to behold a Nephite of the living God! Ah," she said, "how wonderful!" I kissed her on her forehead and whispered, "Don't cry."

And then I asked him if he'd like a glass of milk. And he said, "You can go and pray." And I went into the other room to pray. When I came back then he told me he had a prayer to offer that no human being had ever heard or ever would hear because it was given to him in Heaven. But he says, "It'll be literally fulfilled, every word of it." And I says, "Oh, I'm glad!" He said, "Set right down here." And I set right down by him. And he put his right hand on my head, and his left hand on my throat, and I shouted "Hosanna to God!"

The feeling that filled my soul! I pray that the ones that are listening to this will be thrilled with the same feeling. And then he blessed me; he blessed our home. . . . Then he bid us goodbye and we went right out onto the porch—I took Grandma right with me. And he walked out of the gate just as spry as a young man, and walked along. When he came to the big gate, he didn't disappear; but he went right out of sight. He wasn't in the fields nor along the road nor any place. So I set Grandma down and ran where I could see along this road a mile and a half; and no signs of him. And I said to a lady, "Did you see a man pass here?" She said, "If a butterfly'd a-went by, I could a-seen it." She says, "There was no man passed here." So then I made myself quite contented. . . .

And I pray with all my heart that the one that hears this will know that I testify unto it. And it is true as the sun rises in the east and sets in the west. And I've never whispered once since I got it. Never since my blessing, I've never whispered once. . . . Nobody is going to realize what a great joy I get, being able to sing, to holler, to laugh, and make a noise. And I thank God with all my heart for this wonderful experience in my life! Amen!

"The White Bread on the White Cloth"

> Motifs Z142, "Symbolic color: white," D2105, "Provisions magically furnished," V221, "Miraculous healing by saints," and Q42.3, "Generosity to saint in disguise rewarded," are evident here. The revised edition of the Motif-Index gives its imprimatur to Q45.1.1, "Three Nephites give blessings as reward for hospitality."
>
> Text from Lee, The Three Nephites, No. 10, pp. 137–38. Collected from Norma Schofield by Hector Lee on wire recorder June 1, 1946, in Salt Lake City.

John and Isabella lived in a one-roomed home south of Thirtyninth South on West Temple [Salt Lake City]. Their first child, John Price, Jr., was just an infant and was very very sick, and nothing they had done had helped. They prayed and prayed for help, but his condition continued to grow worse. One night after they had retired and the room was still lighted by the fire from the fireplace, there came a knock on the door. Grandpa Price opened the door, and there stood a stranger, a fine looking man dressed in a gray suit. He asked for shelter for the night. Great-grandfather Price told him that they had only one room and that there were no extra beds, but the stranger said that he'd be content if he could sit by the fire and keep warm for the night. And so he was invited in.

As the stranger settled himself by the fire, the child, who had not rested well for days, sank into a peaceful sleep. Grandpa had determined to stay awake to watch the man, but he himself seemed unable to stay awake. During the night Grandma awoke with a start, worried because she had fallen asleep with her sick child there. Then she saw this stranger sitting at the table and the table was covered with a cloth so brilliantly white that she could hardly look at it. She nudged

Grandpa, and they watched him eat bread of the same brilliant white. As they looked, they knew that he must be a heavenly being, and they said nothing. The next morning when they arose, they offered the stranger breakfast, but he refused.

The home in which they lived was surrounded by bare ploughed ground, without even a tree near. And Grandpa walked out of the house with the man, and as they turned the corner he started to say something to the stranger, and the man had disappeared entirely. As he went back into the house, Grandma Price met him and told him that the baby was absolutely well and playing in the crib. They knew that this man had been sent in answer to their prayers, and believed him to be one of the Three Nephites. . . .

Q: They had no idea where the bread might have come from?

A: No, they had no idea. They had no bread, of course, of that hue in their home. Nor the cloth. The cloth didn't belong to them at all. . . .

"The Hungry Missionaries"

> Motifs Q42.3, *"Generosity of saint in disguise rewarded,"* and D2105, *"Provisions magically furnished,"* recur. This is an especially popular tradition; Fife gives two other variants, one identifying the bread-giver as a Nephite.
>
> Text from Austin Fife, *"The Legend of the Three Nephites Among the Mormons,"* Journal of American Folklore, *LIII (1940), 37–38.* Informant: Hortense Anderson, about 40, Salt Lake City, August 12, 1939.

There were two young missionaries that had been traveling in the eastern part of the United States when the mission was first opened. They were traveling without purse or script— going without help from home, or anything at all. The poor youngsters hadn't found much help—they were just starved— just didn't find anyone that would give them anything. They were walking between two towns—it's strange that I have forgotten the place. They finally knelt down under the trees and prayed that a way would be opened up for them to get something to eat—they were so hungry. They walked a mile or two farther and a man approached them. He had a kindliness about him, a mellowness. He gave them a warm loaf of bread. Of course they were thrilled to death to have it.

One of them wrote and told his mother about it—that he just walked along toward them and then walked away from them. His mother said that it was a strange thing. She wrote back to them that the very night that they had been given the loaf of bread, she had baked bread and put it on the table, and a man came asking for bread. She gave him a warm loaf of that bread. The fellow always felt that he had eaten his own mother's bread.

"The Hitchhiking Ghost Nephite"

> *Here the Nephite legend has absorbed details of Motif E332.3.3.1, "The Vanishing Hitchhiker," the ubiquitous contemporary American legend, discussed in Dorson, American Folklore, pp. 249–50. Motif V223.6, "Saint as prognosticator," is also present. This account falls in Fife's first category, of stories in which the Nephite brings a special spiritual message.*
>
> *Text from Lee, The Three Nephites, No. 57a, pp. 147–48. Informant: Pearl Baker, Green River, Utah. Collector: Hector Lee, by wire recorder, June 3, 1946.*

This story came from Clyde Trammel, of Grand Junction, and I haven't had an opportunity to check with him about it, but it seems that a friend of his and his friend's wife were driving by truck from Montrose to Grand Junction when they picked up an old man. They hauled him for a long way and he seemed to be very much read up on the current events; he knew a great deal about the war, and he talked very interestingly. They came to a long, desolate stretch of road, and the old man wanted out, and they tried to dissuade him and told him that he should go on down to more civilization, but he insisted on being let off. And they let him out on this long stretch of road. As he got out of the truck he thanked them, and he said, "On your way back you will be hauling a dead man." And then he says, "I suppose there's something you want to know?"

"Well, maybe the end of the war." He said, "The war will end in August." This was in 1944.

Well, they went on, and they talked about the old man. And on the way back they picked up a dead man from a car wreck. There had been a wrecked car, and one of the fellows was killed, and they hauled the corpse back into Grand Junction. And of course it lent more credence to the old man's prediction of the end of the war. But August, '44, came and went, and the war still didn't end. However, in August, '45, the war ended, and they decided that the old man had been a Nephite.

Q: They didn't decide that he was a Nephite until after the end of the war?

A: Oh, yes. When they hauled the corpse back, they decided that he must have had some foreknowledge; and some of their friends had told them about Nephites, and so they made up their minds that he was a Nephite. However, they began to doubt it when the war didn't end in August.

Q: When did you first hear this story?

A: This spring, 1946. And I heard it from Mrs. Mac-Dougall, of Green River, Utah.

Q: Was Mrs. MacDougall one of the persons concerned?

A: No, she had heard the story from Clyde Trammel, who is a railroad man. And he, himself, wasn't concerned in the story. It was some friends of his that had had the experience.

"The Roving Jew"

> *Type 777, The Wandering Jew (Motif Q502.1), reported chiefly in Scandinavian and English tradition, has here become enmeshed with the Three Nephites. Motif D2188.1, "Ability to disappear or appear at will," again appears as the central theme.*
>
> *Text from Austin Fife, "The Legend of the Three Nephites Among the Mormons," Journal of American Folklore, LIII (1940), 30–31, discussed 5–6. Reprinted in Fife, "Popular Legends of the Mormons," California Folklore Quarterly, I (1942), 124–25. Informant: Charley Seegmiller, 93, St. George, Utah, December 27, 1939.*

Mr. Seegmiller, a pioneer settler in Utah's "Dixie,"
emigrated from Germany. The event he reports must
have taken place about 1870.

There was surely a queer incident of that character down
on the Muddy here. My brothers Adam and Billy was there
—it was before I went down there. One day they was settin'
around—kind of a windy day—and all at once they seen a
man comin' along the desert. This desert was a plateau above
the Muddy Valley, on the east of the valley, and it was just only
covered with evergreens, green bushes, so you could see all
over. Well, this man, he come, and they was choppin' some
wood there. He said, "How to do," and waited a few minutes
and said, "I would like if you would let me have some dry
bread and some patches to patch my clothes," and he says, "I
am goin' to cross the desert here and I would like to have
somet'ing of that kind."

My brother Billy looked at him and said: "Do you know
what kind of country you are goin' over? I don't see that you've
got much preparation. I've been over that country lots of times,
and you haven't hardly got anyt'ing to pack water wit'."

He says, "Oh, yes, but I know how to get water."

Then they says to him: "What do you want dry bread
for? We'll give you some good bread to go over there." "No, I
want dry bread, if you got it. Good bread sometimes spoils,
but dry bread won't spoil."

They talked and finally he says, "I'll be goin' soon."
They says, "Well, what might your name be?" So he talked
German to them: *"Man heisst mich den ewigen Juden"* ("They
calls me the everlasting Jew").

Well, they paid no attention to it, but when he got away it
come to them, "Well, that must be the rovin' Jew." It was
about as far as from here to the Temple (St. George Temple,
about eight blocks from Mr. Seegmiller's home), to a drop off
the valley. Everyt'ing was clear, and he couldn't make that
distance in the time since he left them. They run out to look
for him but they couldn't see him anywhere. I've often wondered why they didn't follow his tracks.

3. COMIC STORIES

ecdotes of J. Golden Kimball

The cycle of jocular tales about the cowboy who became a revered Mormon preacher and elder is a part of living Mormon tradition. For some examples of Kimball stories see Austin E. and Alta S. Fife, Saints of Sage and Saddle (Bloomington: Indiana University Press, 1956), "The Golden Legend," pp. 304–15; Wallace Stegner, Mormon Country (New York: Duell, Sloan & Pearce, 1942), pp. 190–99; and Dorson, American Folklore, pp. 120–21. Stories about Kimball customarily center on his unclerical use of profanity or stealthy violation of church taboos.

The following anecdotes and introductory remarks are transcribed from a tape recording sent to the editor of this volume by Hector Lee, dean of Sonoma State College, Sonoma, California. From his experience as a Mormon youth, and his talents as a folklore collector and a natural storyteller, Dean Lee relates them with special authority. He made this recording in January, 1951. A copy of the tape is on deposit in the Folklore Archives, Library of Congress.

These stories are about J. Golden Kimball, and there's a whole cycle of J. Golden Kimball in the Mormon country. As a matter of fact, wherever you go today where there are Mormons and you mention the name of J. Golden Kimball, somebody can remember a story about him.

In the early history of the Church of Jesus Christ of

2. LOCAL LEGENDS

A NUMBER OF PROVIDENCES and supernatural stories associated with the history of the Mormon church do not involve the Three Nephites, and take the form of local rather than personal legends.

The Devil Appears at the Site of the Mountain Meadows Massacre

No historical episode has seared more deeply into the Mormon conscience than the so-called Mountain Meadows Massacre of 1857, when Mormons wiped out an emigrant party to whom they had promised safe conduct through Utah. See the ballad printed below pp. 523–25, under "Folksongs of Mormons." Motif G303.3.1, "The devil in human form," appears here.

Text from Austin Fife, "Popular Legends of the Mormons," California Folklore Quarterly, I (1942), 121. Informant: Clara W. Stevens, Woods Cross, Utah, July 26, 1939.

My mother's sister Elizabeth lived in southern Utah, and she and her husband were coming up here and they passed the place where the Mountain Meadows Massacre had been—in that vicinity. They camped just a short distance from where that tragedy had occurred, and they built a fire and cooked their supper, and were sitting around the camp fire after supper, and looked over where that tragedy had happened and saw a man's head coming out of the ground, and it just slowly and gradually came out of the ground and sat there and smoked a pipe. That was supposed to be the devil.

A Massacred Mother Returns to See Her Child

> *Motif E323.1, "Dead mother returns to see baby," occurs here. Text from Fife, "Popular Legends of the Mormons," p. 121. Informant: Mrs. Leon Fonnesbeck, Logan, Utah, July 25, 1939.*

At the time of the Mountain Meadows Massacre, Peter B. Fife lived at Fort Cove. He took into his home one of the seventeen children who had been saved from the massacre. One day the child was sleeping, and a woman dressed in white from head to foot appeared to Mrs. Fife, who was just outside the house. The woman asked if she could see "my baby." Mrs. Fife told her that the child was sleeping and that she might go in to see it. The woman entered the house. Shortly after, Mrs. Fife also went in the house, but the woman was not there. The house where the Fifes lived is believed to be haunted.

The Miracle of the Miller's Sacks

> *Motif D2105, "Provisions magically furnished," is embodied in this providential account of how a pioneer Mormon community was saved from hunger. The celebrated providence alluded to in the text is the preservation of the first grain crop planted in the Great Salt Lake Valley in 1848 by gulls which devoured a plague of crickets.*
>
> *Text from Fife, "Popular Legends of the Mormons," p. 115. Informant: Orville S. Johnson, Salt Lake City, August 12, 1939. Paraphrased in Austin and Alta Fife, Saints of Sage and Saddle, p. 79.*

There was a family named Burnham that was a miller. He owned a mill around the full of grain. When the neighbors came he loaned them half a sack but wouldn't s run out before they got some more to come them another half a sack—he said that half to carry than a full sack. It went on until Year's. In January a neighbor came and he of the last sack in the granary. The neighbor know what they were going to do—most of going to starve. The ground was frozen. It episode of the gulls, before 1856.

At any rate, another neighbor came in was passed. He split half a sack, and put a qua in the bin. This he split several times until hi empty. A neighbor came in for meal and he sai any.

He said, "Brother Burnham, can't you d The State High Council met and asked for a spe and it's been held—something has to happen." said, "we might go out and shake a few sacks—th thing I know of." They went back out to shake and every sack was full of meal.

Latter Day Saints, commonly known as the Mormon Church, one of the most colorful characters of the second generation was J. Golden Kimball. He was born in 1853 and died in 1938, at the age of 85. He was the son of Heber C. Kimball, one of the Twelve Apostles, and Brigham Young's first councilor. J. Golden Kimball was six feet three inches tall, seventy-five inches tall, and as thin as a toothpick. And he had a high, thin voice to match his figure. The stories that I'm going to tell now are being told throughout the Mormon country by those who knew him and loved him. They were collected from oral tradition, and were told by Ranch Kimball, his nephew, and Attorney Shirley P. Jones, and Attorney Jesse Budge, and others.

"Respect for the Priesthood"

One day as J. Golden was crossing the street at South Temple and Main Street, a couple of high school boys in an automobile whizzed around and just barely ticked him. He was getting a little old and he was walking with a cane, and they came so close he was infuriated. And he raised his cane and shook it at 'em and he said:

"You son-of-a-bitch. Have you no respect for the priesthood?"

"Feeding the Calf"

One Sunday evening he was all dressed up ready to go to church. He had on his finest suit, long black coat, and his silk shirt, and his tall silk hat, and he was very handsome and well-dressed. Just as he was about to leave for church, he discovered that someone had not fed the calf, so he took the bucket of fresh, warm milk—the sudsy milk—in all his finery and he went out to the corral and fed the calf. And the calf came up and dived into the bucket very hungrily, and put its nose clear in under the foam and got a mouthful, and then the calf raised his head and shook his head, and shook milkfoam all over the good Brother. He said (*shouting*):

"If I wasn't a member of the Church, if I wasn't trying

to foreswear swearing, if I wasn't a good brother in the priesthood, if I couldn't control my temper, I'd take your goddamn head and push it through the bottom of this bucket."

"His Vocabulary"

Someone said, 'Brother Golden, is your language usually premeditated?"

"No, very seldom."

"Well," they said, "what about those two little words that you use now and then that worry the authorities?"

"Well, I never intend to cuss when I get up to speak; I'm not thinking about the words, but those words come up, they're left over from my cowboy days. They used to be my native language. I can assure you that they come from a far larger vocabulary."

"The Lord Heard Me"

He was downtown at the Rotisserie eating dinner one day with a fairly large group of friends, mostly lawyers, and he was seated at the end of the table, and the waiter came around to take his order first. As you know, being a good Mormon he was not supposed to drink tea or coffee, but he did like his coffee. Well, he ordered his dinner and the waiter wrote it down, and then he said, "What will you drink?"

Brother Golden in a very weak voice said, "Water."

And the fellow sitting next to him touched the waiter and said, "Oh, bring him coffee. He likes coffee."

So the waiter wrote it down and went on around the table. Brother Golden didn't say anything until the waiter got 'way down at the other end of the table, and then he said: "The Lord heard me say water."

"A Complaining Sister"

For a variant ascribed to Peetie Bishop, "A Prayer to the Lord," see below, p. 518.

J. Golden Kimball was down in southern Utah preaching a sermon in church one warm spring Sunday morning, and he was probably carried away a little further then he normally went. After the service he went out front and received the congratulations of the members, but there was one lady standing over under a tree by a ditchbank who was unhappy. She said:

"Brother Golden, I've just got to get this off my chest—it's bothered me a long time, and today I feel that I should speak. You members of the authorities of the Church come down and speak to us," she said, "you speak as if you were the Lord Almighty, himself. And I resent that, a little." She said, "I reserve the sacred privileges for the Lord himself. The Lord makes the sun shine, the Lord makes these beautiful trees, and this green grass and this stream of water. And you authorities of the Church couldn't compete with anything like that."

"Well, now, sister. I'll agree with you. I couldn't make the sun shine; I couldn't make the trees; I couldn't make the grass; but I'll take you up on the water."

Danish Dialect Stories of the Mormon Church

The form of humorous folktale based on mistakes of language and custom made by immigrants in the United States is described in Dorson, "Dialect Stories of the Upper Peninsula: A New Form of American Folklore," Journal of American Folklore, *LXI (1948), 113–50; and Dorson, "Jewish-American Dialect Stories on Tape," in* Studies in Biblical and Jewish Folklore, *ed. R. Patai, F. L. Utley, D. Noy (Bloomington, Ind.: Indiana University Folklore Series No. 13, 1960), pp. 111–74; and see Dorson,* American Folklore, *pp. 137–41.*

These tales were told and recorded by Hector Lee for this volume in November, 1959. A feature article including some examples of Danish dialect stories from Ephraim, Utah, appeared in the Salt Lake Tribune *(Salt Lake City), January 8, 1950.*

This is Hector Lee with some Danish stories from Sanpete County, Utah. In the 1850's and 60's one of the most fruitful vineyards for the missionary work of the Mormon Church was in the Scandinavian countries. When people would come to Utah for the sake of the church, from foreign countries, it was Brigham Young's custom to assign them to communities in different parts of Utah and Idaho and Arizona, and he tried to place the language groups together. For example, there was one colony of Icelanders, and another colony almost entirely of Welsh.

Well, it happened that in Sanpete County, two towns, Manti and Ephraim, were about 100 per cent Scandinavian, mostly Danish. And the stories I have to tell are well known in the Mormon country as Sanpete County stories. Most of them were told by a man named P. D. Petersen, whose nickname was Peetie Bishop; that's because he had once been a Mormon bishop. Although not all of these are Peetie Bishop stories, they all fit the same general pattern.

You will notice that there are two main kinds of humor in these Danish stories; one has to do with the language problems, the malapropisms and the accidental puns and other errors in diction; and the second kind comes from incongruities of character.

"Funeral Oration"

There's the funeral oration told by Peetie Bishop. It seems that two old men in the town of Ephraim lived together out by the edge of town, and they grew old together and they often argued about the mystery of death and wondered about the glories of the hereafter. Well, one night they made an agreement that the first one who died would make a tour of the place, that is, the hereafter, whatever place it was, and he'd come back in a dream and tell the survivor all about it. And in exchange for this, the survivor was supposed to preach the finest funeral sermon that was every preached.

Well, eventually one of 'em died, but I suppose it was the wrong one, because the fella who remained wasn't a very good preacher. Nevertheless, he had to keep his bargain, and when the day of the funeral arrived and the corpse was laid out and the congregation was assembled, the old brother got up in church and he did his best. He cleared his throat and looked over the audience, and then he began:

"My dear brudders and sisters. Ve are come here on dis occasion to pay our last re—well, to say few vurds [words] for our dearly departed brudder. He has now gone to de great behind. Sometimes he have not been very good in de church: he swear a little, he drink a little, and he don't go to church much; he don't do much good in de neighborhood; but I vant to say von ting, brudders and sisters. He vas not always as bad as he sometimes vas. Ant [and] now he have gone to dwell among the holy angels. Vat ve see here before us is only de shell, de nut have flew de coop. But I vant to say, brudders and sisters, dat he come from a fine long line of descendants. His great-grandfader, he fought in de battle where de bull run. And his grandfader, he vas a veteran of de Blackhawk Var, and his grandmudder, she vas a veteran of de nighthawk var. And I vant to say dat he vas a grand old veterinary himself."

"Marriage Ceremony"

Another story of this general type has to do with the marriage ceremony. It seems that a newly elected bishop was called upon to perform his first marriage ceremony, and of course he'd never done this before, but he decided to face the inevitable and go through with it. And the bride and groom stood up in church before him, and the congregation were there, so he cleared his throat and he looked at them and he said:

"Now brudders and sisters, ve are gathered here in all solemenity to lock up in holy wedlock this young couple. Now, Brother Jan August Andersen, do you take Sister Helena Rhodes for sickness and complaining and keeping you poorer? You do? Brudders and sisters, he say he do. Now, Sister Helena Rhodes, do you take Jan August Anderson for staying out late nights and vorse, and more of it? You do? Brudders and sisters, she say she do. Now you vill please take hands . . . no, no, I didn't say shake hands. You're a little excited and so am I, you vill get better 'quainted after vile [while], dat's all right. You

just take hands now. Now, brudders and sisters, if dere is anybody vitin [within] de sounding of my voice which has any reason vy [why] dese young people should not get married, let
him forever . . . shut up. And so now, by all de atority under
my vest, I pronounce you Papa and Mama for time and ma-
ternity."

"A Prayer to the Lord"

> *"A Complaining Sister,"* a variant attached to J. Golden
> Kimball, is printed above, p. 514.

Another story is told about the time they had a long dry spell
in that county. The farmers needed water very badly, and they
waited and waited, but it didn't rain. And finally they decided to
offer up a prayer and see if their prayers could induce the
Lord to send the rain. And so on the appointed day they all
gathered in church and old Brother Petersen got his turn to
preach and to make the prayer. So he got up and he says:

"Now brothers and sisters, ve are gathered here on this
Solomon occasion and ve are here for a great purpose. Ve are
here to ask the Lord for rain. Now ve must remember dat de
blessings come from de Lord. Dis vas shown in de great crossing
of de plains when our forefadders and our foremudders too, dey
came in covered vagons across de plains. But I want to remind
you von ting, brudders and sisters, dat if our prayers should
not be answered it would not be the Lord's fault. It would be
our own lack of fate. Ve must have fate, and unless ve haf fate,
maybe our prayers vill not be answered because ve cannot do
it all by ourselves. De biscup he cannot make water; Brudder
Johnson he cannot make water; Sister Petersen she cannot
make water. You cannot make water; I cannot make water. No,
brudders and sister, only the Lord can make water. In de name
of Jesus Christ. Amen."

"Sister Petersen and Brother Hansen"

Another story is told about what happened in church on Sacrament Day meeting. That was the time once a month when the

congregation was free to stand up before the group and bare their testimony of the truth of the Gospel and their own personal experiences. And one day old Sister Petersen got up and she bore her testimony to the Gospel, and attributed her long and healthy life to the fact that she did not drink tea or coffee. And when she said that she looked right straight at old Brother Hansen, and it was pretty well known that he did break the Word of Wisdom and drink some tea or coffee. And he felt a little bit guilty about this, so he got up and he says:

"Now, brudders and sisters, I would like to bare my testimony, too. And I am very careful about the remarks which I have just heard from Sister Petersen, because I tink she mean me. She tink maybe dat I ruin my healt' by drinkink tea or coffee. But I vant to say dat I am very strong to de blessings of de Lord, and ven I drink de tea or coffee, it do not hurt my healt' atall and my stomach is good. It is all right. And I vant to tell Sister Petersen right now dat I vill put my stomach up against hers any day."

"Planning a Mormon Funeral"

Peetie Bishop used to tell this one about Chris Jensen, a friend of his. He said Chris was talking to some of the boys one day and he said:

"You know, my mother-in-law, she was very sick. And, ve haf her in bed with the doctors, and ve try all of the medicine vich ve know how, but she was right at death's door, and in spite of everything that ve do, she continued to improve. Vell, one day she called me in to talk to me, and she say, 'Now Chris, how vould you like to help me plan my funeral?' 'Yeh, dat I vould,' I says. And so ve goes in and ve sits down on dat overly-stuffed furniture in de living room, and she takes my hand in her cold hand and she says, 'Now Chris, let us plan de funeral ceremonies.' And so ve decides who should give de opening benediction, and vich of de uncles and cousins should be de polar bears, and who should preach at de funeral sermon.

"And den she says, 'Now Chris, you have been a good husband to my daughter, and I tink maybe you should like to choose the closing song.' Well now, I don't know nuttin' about de songs for de church or de funerals. All I know is "I Von't Go Home Until Tomorrow" and "Vere Is My Wandering Boy Dis Evening," and tings like dat. And den it come to me right out of de blue, and if dat ain't a inspiration I don't know vat it isn't—"God be Wit You if We Ever Meet Again"."

"A Good Latter Day Saint"

One day the Mormon elders called on old Brother Petersen. The occasion was a very sad one for him, because his boy had been going a little bit wild around the community, and they pointed out that the boy was not living his religion, and something would have to be done about it. And the poor old man was very sad and he sat there in his rocking chair for a moment and his eyes glistened just a little with tears, and then he says:

"Now, brudders. I vant to say von ting though." He says, "Now, my boy, it may be true dat he don't go to church; and it may be true dat he swear too much and he drink too much; and he don't pay his tithing in the church, and he didn't go on a mission; and he play with the girls too much, and all of dis is bad. But I vant to tell you one ting, brudders. He is a good Latter Day Saint."

Missionaries and the "Spirit"

A spate of personal experiences related by youthful Mormons about their missionary service overseas follows a traditional pattern. In general the missionaries vanquish their adversaries, and in particular they discomfit fundamentalists and spiritualists.

The comments and texts illustrating this theme are supplied by John L. Sorenson, an anthropologist on the faculty of Brigham Young University, Provo, Utah, who has accumulated interview materials on the functions of folklore in contemporary Mormon society.

One of the most trying experiences for a Mormon is to spend two or more years away from home as a missionary. Today nearly 12,000 of these young Mormons are serving as missionaries, and almost that many families, wives, or sweethearts are deprived of their presence. The long hours of labor, the shock of meeting glib opponents or indifferent "contacts," and the anxiety about succeeding are legendary in a Mormon society where the missionary farewell and the homecoming testimonial are key rites.

"While serving in the mission field, one night several of the Elders stopped by a Pentecostal revival, and Elder Smith was one. The doors were closed, but they gained admission anyway. For about five minutes the demonstration went on, very loudly. Then suddenly all was quiet. The man in charge tried vainly to get it going again, but to no avail. Finally, he walked down to the rear of the building where the missionaries were standing and very emphatically told them to leave. He called them 'Mormon elders' and told them they had to leave so the meeting could continue. Several days later Elder Smith called on the man and asked him how he ever knew they were Elders, and why it disrupted their meeting so when they entered. His reply was brief and definite, 'Don't you know when your Mormon priesthood is present the Spirit won't be there?' "

"While in England two of the Elders I knew went to a Spiritualist Meeting or 'Seance' at the invitation of a friend they had made through tracting. The medium tried and tried to get the voice from the other side, but couldn't get any results. She then asked if there was someone in the congregation or group who was trying to thwart her efforts. Of course the missionaries just sat there, very innocently, and the medium tried again with the same results. Finally she said there must be someone in the group who is not 'one of us.' Since these two young men were the only strangers there, they were requested to leave. The friend who took them was embarrassed about it, but asked if they would mind if he stayed. They told him it would be all right with them. The next day the friend said that as soon as they had departed the seance was held; everything went off as planned by the medium."

A variation on this theme yields what Mormons often consider one of the funniest items of Mormon humor. The initiated know that the Gadianton referred to in the story was an ancient villain of the Book of Mormon, an "expert in wickedness" whose founding of a murderous secret order led to the downfall of the Nephites.

"These two missionaries decided to go to this spiritualist meeting where a man was calling up spirits that the audience asked for. After a while of this the one Elder decided he'd have some fun, so when the spiritualist asked for another name, he called out, 'Gadianton!' That fellow was calling on this spirit Gadianton, then, when all of a sudden he's knocked off his chair onto the floor, and then across the room to the other side. He just about wrecks the place. Finally it stops, and the spiritualist drags himself onto his feet and says, 'Who the hell is Gadianton?'"

4. FOLKSONGS OF MORMONS

THE SEVEN SONGS THAT FOLLOW display the variety of Mormon themes. "The Mountain Meadows Massacre" grows out of a cruel event of 1857 in frontier history. A providential deliverance of 1848 inspired "The Seagulls and the Crickets." Humorous folklore surrounding polygamy is reflected in "Brigham, Brigham Young," "Don't You Marry the Mormon Boys," and "The Mormon Coon." A Mormon's sensitivity and pride are seen in "Down in Utah." The comic legend of Brigham Young appears in the song bearing his name and the stanza in "Sweet Betsy from Pike." An excellent collection is Lester A. Hubbard, *Ballads and Songs from Utah* (Salt Lake City, 1961), "Utah and the Mormons," pp. 392–463.

"The Mountain Meadows Massacre"

On September 10, 1857, a body of armed Mormons accompanied by Indians visited a wagon train of emigrants which had reached Mountain Meadows in southern Utah. The Mormons promised the party safe conduct to Cedar City, and then butchered all the adults. The complex history of the affair is analyzed by Juanita Brooks in The Mountain Meadows Massacre *(Stanford, 1950). Three extant ballad variants on the massacre were uncovered and collated by Austin E. Fife, along with a newspaper text of 1870, in "A Ballad of the Mountain Meadows Massacre," Western Folklore, XII (1953), 229–41.*

The present text, and the longest, from pages 232–33, was sung by a Mr. Harter of Kahlotus, Washington, in September, 1952. It reflects the anti-Mormon point of view in laying the blame on Brigham Young; other variants shift the blame to the Indians and the local Mormon leader John D. Lee. See the stanzas printed in Dorson, American Folklore, pp. 119–20.

1. Come, all you sons of liberty,
    Unto my rhyme give ear,
    'Tis of a bloody massacre,
    You presently shall hear.

2. In splendor o'er the mountains,
    Some thirty wagons came,
    They were awaited by a wicked band.
    O, Utah, where's thy shame!

3. [*Missing*]

4. In Indian colors all wrapped in shame,
    This bloody crew was seen
    To flock around this little train,
    All on the meadows green.

5. They were attacked in the morning
    As they were on their way.
    They forthwith corralled their wagons,
    And fought in blood array.

6. Till came the captain of the band,
    He surely did deceive,
    Saying, "If you will give up your arms,
    We'll surely let you live."

7. When once they had give up their arms,
    Thinking their lives to save,
    The words were broken among the rest
    Which sent them to their graves.

8. [*Missing*]

9. When once they had give up their arms,
    They started for Cedar City.
    They rushed on them in Indian style.
    O, what a human pity!

10. They melted down with one accord
    Like wax before the flame,
    Both men and women, old and young.
    O, Utah, where's thy shame!

11. Both men and women, old and young,
    A-rolling in their gore,
    And such an awful sight and scene,
    Was ne'er beheld before!

12. Their property was divided
    Among this bloody crew,
    And Uncle Sam is bound to see
    This bloody matter through.

13. The soldiers will be stationed
    Throughout this Utah land,
    All for to find those murderers out,
    And bring them to his hand.

14. By order from their president
    This bloody deed was done.
    He was the leader of the Mormon Church,
    His name was Brigham Young.

"Brigham, Brigham Young"

A verse of this song is printed in Dorson, American Folklore, p. 120. Text from Austin E. and Alta S. Fife, "Folk Songs of Mormon Inspiration," Western Folklore, VI (1947), 49–51. Original in the Fife Mormon Collection I, 539 (Recording 8B1). Fragmentary oral

version *FMC I, 535;* ms version *FMC II, 196. The Fifes
note a variant, lacking the next to last stanza, reprinted
from Put's* Golden West Songster *(1857) in John A.
and Alan Lomax,* Cowboy Songs and Other Frontier
Ballads *(New York, 1959), pp. 400–401.*

Old Brigham Young was a Mormon bold,
And a leader of the roaring rams,
And a shepherd of a heap of pretty little sheep,
And a nice fold of pretty little lambs.
And he lived with five-and-forty wives
In the city of Great Salt Lake.
Where they woo and coo as pretty doves do
And cackle like ducks to a drake.

CHORUS:
Brigham, Brigham Young;
'Tis a miracle he survives,
With his roaring rams, his pretty little lambs,
And five-and-forty wives.

Number forty-five was about sixteen,
Number one was sixty-three,
And among such a riot how he ever keeps them quiet
Is a right-down mystery to me.
For they clatter and they claw, and they jaw, jaw, jaw,
Each one has a different desire;
It would aid the renown of the best shop in town
To supply them with half what they require.

Old Brigham Young was a stout man once,
But now he is thin and old,
And I love to state, there's no hair on his pate
Which once wore a covering of gold.
For his youngest wives won't have white wool,
And his old ones won't take red,
So in tearing it out they have taken turn about,
'Till they've pulled all the wool from his head.

Now his boys they all sing songs all day,
    And his girls they all sing psalms;
And among such a crowd he has it pretty loud
    For they're as musical as Chinese gongs.
And when they advance for a Mormon dance
    He is filled with the greatest surprise,
For they're sure to end the night with a Tabernacle
        fight,
    And scratch out one another's eyes.

There never was a home like Brigham Young's,
    So curious and so queer,
For if his joys are double he has a terrible lot of trouble
    For it gains on him year by year.
He sets in his state and bears his fate
    In a sanctified sort of way;
He has one wife to bury and one wife to marry
    And a new kid born every day.

Now if anybody envies Brigham Young
    Let them go to Great Salt Lake,
And if they have leisure to examine at their pleasure
    They'll find it's a great mistake.
One wife at a time, so says my rhyme,
    Is enough for the proudest don,
So e'er you strive to live lord of forty-five
    Live happy if you can with one.

"The Seagulls and the Crickets"

> *This best known of all Mormon providences includes
> Motif F989.16, "Extraordinary swarms of birds." The
> Church account is here summarized by Thomas E.
> Cheney, and the ballad text is from his manuscript col-
> lection, "Songs of the Wasatch and Tetons, A Compila-
> tion of Mormon Folksong." It was sung by L. M. Hilton
> in 1959. Another ballad text from Hilton, with only*

> *minor verbal differences, is in Austin and Alta Fife,*
> *Saints of Sage and Saddle, pp. 321–24, and the same*
> *authors print an oral narrative text, pp. 75–76. A*
> *recording of the song is in the album "Mormon Folk*
> *songs" sung by L. M. Hilton, recorded with notes by*
> *Willard Rhodes, Folkways Records and Service Cor-*
> *poration, FP 36 (New York, copyright 1952).*

The never-to-be-forgotten incident related in this song and in that which follows occurred in the summer of 1848. Two thousand people had gathered in Salt Lake Valley by the fall of 1847. There had been no harvest. Before winter was over vegetables and fruits were completely exhausted, flour brought from winter quarters had nearly all been consumed, and meat was scarce.

In the fall the colonizers planted nearly 2,000 acres of winter wheat, in the spring about 3,000 acres more. Excellent germination and growth cheered the people to hope for a bounteous harvest.

But they had not thought of the menace of crickets. They had only been amused when they watched Indians gather the insects for winter food. Now the loathsome, black, inch-and-a-half-long pests by hundreds and thousands swept down from the hillsides like a sea, turning the green fields to gray.

A battle was waged with men, women, and children against crickets. They beat and flayed them into ditches, buried them in trenches, drove them into fires. Then when their puny hands could no longer withstand the relentless push of the insects, in sweaty exhaustion and despairing defeat they resorted to the only alternative—prayer.

Then exploring seagulls discovered a food supply. Soon the gray-white birds descended on the grain fields, not to eat the grain but to devour the devourers. They came in thousands to eat and gorge, to gorge and disgorge and eat again. Thus the famine was averted, the pioneers were saved.

Now in Temple Square in Salt Lake City there is a memorial monument to the seagulls, the birds that saved the settlers' first grain crop.

The winter of forty-nine had passed.[1]
The winter of haunting fears,
For famine had knocked at the city gates
And threatened the pioneers.
But spring with its smiling skies lent grace
And cheer to the hosts within,
And they tilled their fields with a newborn trust
And the courage to fight and win.

With a thrill of life the tender shoots
Burst forth from the virgin plain,
And each day added its ray of hope
For a blessing of ripened grain.
But lo, in the east strange clouds appeared
And dark became the sun,
And down from the mountainsides there swept
A scourge that the boldest shun.

Black crickets by tens of millions came
Like fog on the British coast,
And the finger of devastation marked
Its course on the Mormon host.
With a vigor that desperation fanned
They battled and smote and slew,
But the clouds still gathered and broke afresh
Till the fields that waved were few.

With visions of famine and want and woe
They prayed from hearts sincere
When lo, from the west came other clouds
To succor the pioneers.
'Twas seagulls feathered in angel white,
And angels they were forsooth.
The seagulls there by the thousands came
To battle in very truth.

They charged down upon the cricket hordes
And gorging them day and night

---

[1] Folk inaccuracy in date.

They routed the devastating hosts,
And the crickets were put to flight.
And heads were bowed as they thanked their God,
And they reaped while the devil raved.
The harvest was garnered to songs of praise
And the pioneers were saved.

"Don't You Marry the Mormon Boys"

Text from Austin E. and Alta S. Fife, "Folk Songs of Mormon Inspiration," Western Folklore, VI (1947), 48. Original in the Fife Mormon Collection I, 584 (Recording 13A3). Recorded at a Mormon Pioneer Day Church program from an informant four and one-half years old, in whose family it was traditional.

Come, girls, come, and listen to my noise,
Don't you marry the Mormon boys,
For if you do your fortune it will be
Johnnycake and babies is all you'll see.

Build a little house and put it on a hill,
Make you work against your will;
Buy a little cow and milk it in a gourd,
Put it in a corner and cover it with a board.

Come, girls, come, and listen to my noise,
Don't you marry the Mormon boys,
For if you do your fortune it will be
Johnnycake and babies is all you'll see.

"The Mormon Coon"

Text from Levette J. Davidson, "Mormon Songs," Journal of American Folklore, LVIII (1945), 291–92. Davidson comments that the song was given to him

*from memory by Virgil V. Peterson of Denver, who had
learned it several years previously from a Mormon missionary. He cites a shorter variant in the American
Folksong Collection of the Library of Congress among
the Robert Gordon Manuscripts, with the opening line,
"A coon named Ephram [sic] left the town one day,"
and the final chorus line, "Great God, I'm the Mormon
Coon."*

*Davidson points out the Negro minstrelsy character of
this song.*

Young Abraham left home one day
Nobody knew just why he went away
Until a friend of his received a note
It was from Abe and this is what he wrote:

I'm out in Utah in the Mormon land
I'm not coming home, 'cause
I'm out in Utah in the Mormon land
I'm not coming home, 'cause I'm a-living grand
I used to rave about a single life
Now every day I get a brand new wife.

CHORUS:

I got a big brunette
I got a blonde petite
I got 'em short, fat, thin, and tall
I got a Zulu pal
I got a Cuban gal
They come in bunches when I call.

Now—that ain't all
I got a homely few
I got 'em pretty too
I got 'em black as the octoroon
I can cut a figure eight
I must ship them by freight
For I am a Mormon Coon.

There's one girl that ain't married yet, they say
I'm saving her up for a rainy day
If for every girl I had a single cent
Then the picture gallery I could rent.
I got me many of a homely lot
I keep the marriage license door bell hot
If a wife upon the street I chance to run
I have to ask her, "What's your number, Hon?"

"Down in Utah"

> *"This song, which no doubt originated in Sanpete County, Utah, was taken from a tape recording sung by Job Porter of Victor, Idaho, shortly before his recent death. It was contributed by his daughter, Helen De-wolf of Jackson, Wyoming, in 1959." Text from Thomas E. Cheney, "Songs of the Wasatch and Tetons."*

While the workmen stopped in Denver
One fellow came to me.
Said he, "Are you from Utah,
And why are you so free?"
I smiled and said, "Young fellow,
Unless you break my jaw,
I'm a Mormon man with residence in Utah."

CHORUS:

And if you are from Utah,
They'll often question you
All about the hated Mormons
And really what they do.
Some have a bad opinion
While others pick a flaw;
They think we live on carrots down in Utah.

We had it hot and heavy
'Til both were getting sick,

My eyes were getting black and blue
And my lips were getting thick,
But I stayed with my young smarty
'Til he was getting raw,
And the battle fell in favor of old Utah.

I know I was a-sweating
And looking mighty blue
When a cop comes stepping up to me,
Said he, "I'm on to you."
I smiled and looked upon him
While he held me in his claw,
And the battle fell in favor of old Utah.

We rode along together
Down to the city hall.
'Twas there I met my smarty
I scarcely knew at all.
The cop he said, "Young fellow,
To you I'll read the law."
And the battle fell in favor of old Utah.

"Sweet Betsy from Pike"

> *This variant of the celebrated comic ballad (see Laws
> B9 for references) has woven Brigham Young into the
> standard narrative of Western misadventure.*
>
> *Text from Thomas E. Cheney, "Songs of the Wasatch
> and Tetons," contributed by Ray Decker in 1959.*

Oh, don't you remember sweet Betsy from Pike
Who crossed the mountains with her lover Ike,
With two yoke of oxen, a large yellow dog,
A tall Shanghai rooster, and one spotted hog.

One evening quite early they camped on the Platte
Close by the roadside on a green, shady flat.

When Betsy, surefooted, lay down to repose
With wonder she gazed on his Pike County nose.

The Shanghai ran off and cattle all died;
The last piece of bacon that morning was fried.
Poor Ike was discouraged and Betsy was mad;
The dog wagged his tail and looked wonderfully sad.

At length the old wagon came down with a crash,
And out on the prairie rolled all kinds of trash,
A few little baby clothes, done up with great care,
Looked rather suspicious though all on the square.

They went by Salt Lake to inquire the way
Where Brigham declared Sweet Betsy should stay.
Betsy got frightened and ran like a deer
While Brigham stood pawing the ground like a steer.

They next reached the desert where Betsy gave out
And down on the ground she lay rolling about.
Poor Ike, half-discouraged, looked on with surprise,
Saying, "Betsy, get up, you'll get sand in your eyes."

At length they arrived on a very high hill,
With wonder looked down on old Placerville.
Ike sighed and he said when he cast his eyes down,
"Betsy, my darling, we've got to leave town."

This Pike County couple attended a dance,
And Ike wore a pair of his Pike County pants.
Betsy was dressed up with ribbons and rings;
Says Ike, "You are an angel, but where are your wings?"

A miner says, "Betsy, won't you dance with me?"
"I will that, old hoss, if you don't make too free,
Don't dance me too hard; if you want to know why,
Doggone you, I'm chock full of strong alkali."

This Pike County couple got married, of course,
And Ike became jealous, obtained a divorce;
Betsy, well satisfied, cried out with a shout,
"Goodbye, you big lummox, I'm glad you backed out."

BIBLIOGRAPHY OF WORKS CITED

ALFORD, VIOLET. *Sword Dance and Drama*. London, 1962.

*ALLISON, LELAH. "Children's Games," *Hoosier Folklore*, VII (1948), 84–93.

*————. "Folk Beliefs Collected in Southeastern Illinois," *Journal of American Folklore*, LXIII (1950), 309–24.

*————. "Folk Speech from Southeastern Illinois," *Hoosier Folklore*, V (1946), 93–102.

*————. "Water Witching," *Hoosier Folklore*, VI (1947), 88–90.

ANDRADE, MANUEL J. *Folk-Lore from the Dominican Republic*. Memoirs of the American Folklore Society, XXIII. Philadelphia, 1930.

ANGLE, PAUL M. *Bloody Williamson*. New York, 1952.

*BARBOUR, FRANCES M. "Some Foreign Proverbs in Southern Illinois," *Midwest Folklore*, IV (1954), 161–64.

BARGE, W. D., and CALDWELL, N. W. "Illinois Place-Names," *Journal of the Illinois State Historical Society*, XXIX (1936), 189–311.

BARRY, PHILLIPS (ed.). *The Maine Woods Songster*. Cambridge, Mass., 1939.

BASSETT, FLETCHER S. *Legends and Superstitions of the Sea and of Sailors*. Chicago and New York, 1885.

BAUGHMAN, ERNEST W. "A Comparative Study of the Folktales of England and North America," doctoral dissertation, Indiana University, 1953.

BECK, HORACE P. *The Folklore of Maine*. Philadelphia, 1957.

BELDEN, HENRY M. *Ballads and Songs Collected by the Missouri Folk-Lore Society*. Columbia, Mo., 1940.

*BOGGS, RALPH S. "North Carolina White Folktales and Riddles," *Journal of American Folklore*, XLVII (1934), 289–328.

BOTKIN, BENJAMIN A. *The American Play-Party Song*. Lincoln, Neb., 1937.

BOYD, ELIZABETH. *Saints and Saint Makers of New Mexico*. Santa Fe, 1946.

BOYER, WALTER E., BUFFINGTON, ALBERT F., and YODER, DON. *Songs Along the Mahantongo*. Lancaster, Pa., 1951.

* Indicates sources for reprinted texts.

BRANDON, ELIZABETH. "La Paroisse de Vermillon, Moeurs, Dictons, Contes et Légendes," *Bayou,* Nos. 64–69 (1955–57).

————. "Superstitions in Vermilion Parish," *The Golden Log,* ed. M. C. BOATRIGHT et al. Publications of the Texas Folklore Society, XXXI, pp. 108–18. Dallas, 1962.

BRENDLE, THOMAS R., and UNGER, CLAUDE W. *Folk Medicine of the Pennsylvania Germans: The Non-Occult Cures.* Pennsylvania German Society Proceedings, XLV (1931), 1–303.

*BRENDLE, THOMAS R., and TROXELL, WILLIAM S. "Pennsylvania German Songs," *Pennsylvania Songs and Legends,* ed. GEORGE KORSON, pp. 62–128. Philadelphia, 1949; reprinted Baltimore, 1960.

*————. *Pennsylvania German Folk Tales, Legends, Once-upon-a-Time Stories, Maxims and Sayings.* Pennsylvania German Folklore Society, Vol. L. Norristown, 1944.

BREWER, J. MASON. *Dog Ghosts and Other Texas Negro Folk Tales.* Austin, 1958.

BREWSTER, PAUL G. *American Nonsinging Games.* Norman, Okla., 1953.

————. "Rope-Skipping, Counting-Out, and Other Rhymes of Children," *Southern Folklore Quarterly,* III (1939), 173–85.

BRIGGS, HAROLD E. "Folklore of Southern Illinois," *Southern Folklore Quarterly,* XVI (1952), 207–17.

BROOKS, JUANITA. *The Mountain Meadows Massacre.* Stanford, Calif., 1950.

THE FRANK C. BROWN COLLECTION OF NORTH CAROLINA FOLKLORE, ed. NEWMAN I. WHITE. Vol. I, ed. P. G. Brewster et al.; Vol. VI, ed. W. D. Hand (Durham, N.C., 1952, 1961).

BROWNE, RAY B. *Popular Beliefs and Practices from Alabama.* Berkeley, 1958.

BRUNVAND, JAN H. "Folktales by Mail from Bond, Kentucky," *Kentucky Folklore Record,* VI (1960), 69–76.

————. "The Taming of the Shrew," doctoral dissertation, Indiana University, 1961.

BULEY, R. CARLYLE. "Water (?) Witching Can be Fun," *Indiana Magazine of History,* LVI (1960), 65–77.

BURMA, JOHN H. *Spanish-speaking Groups in the United States.* Durham, N.C., 1954.

CAMBIAIRE, CÉLESTIN P. *East Tennessee and Western Virginia Mountain Ballads.* London, 1934.

CAMPA, ARTHUR L. *Spanish Folk-Poetry in New Mexico.* Albuquerque, 1946.

CAMPBELL, J. F. *Popular Tales of the West Highlands.* 4 vols. 2d. ed.; London, 1890–93.

*CAMPBELL, MARIE. "Feuding Ballads from the Kentucky Mountains," *Southern Folklore Quarterly,* III (1939), 165–72.

*————. "Survivals of Old Folk Drama in the Kentucky Mountains," *Journal of American Folklore,* LI (1938), 10–24.

————. *Tales from the Cloud Walking Country.* Bloomington, Indiana, 1958.

BIBLIOGRAPHY

CANNON, M. HAMLIN. "Angels and Spirits in Mormon Doctrine," *California Folklore Quarterly*, IV (1945), 343–50.

CARRIÉRE, JOSEPH M. *Tales from the French Folk-Lore of Missouri*. Evanston, Ill., 1937.

*CARTER, ISABEL GORDON. "Mountain White Folk-Lore: Tales from the Southern Blue Ridge," *Journal of American Folklore*, XXXVIII (1925), 340–74.

CHAMBERS, EDMUND K. *The English Folk-Play*. Oxford, 1933.

CHASE, RICHARD. *American Folk Tales and Songs and other examples of English-American Tradition as preserved in the Appalachian Mountains and elsewhere in the United States*. New York, 1956.

————. *Grandfather Tales*. Cambridge, Mass., 1948.

————. *The Jack Tales*. Cambridge, Mass., 1943.

————. "The Origin of 'The Jack Tales'," *Southern Folklore Quarterly*, III (1939), 187–91.

*CHENEY, THOMAS S. "Songs of the Wasatch and Tetons, A Compilation of Mormon Folksongs." Manuscript.

CHILD, FRANCIS JAMES. *The English and Scottish Popular Ballads*. 10 vols. Boston, 1882–94.

*CLAUDEL, CALVIN. "Foolish John Tales from the French Folklore of Louisiana," *Southern Folklore Quarterly*, XII (1948), 151–65.

*————. "Louisiana Tales of Jean Sot and Bouqui and Lapin," *Southern Folklore Quarterly*, VIII (1944), 287–299.

CLOUSTON, WILLIAM A. *The Book of Noodles*. London, 1888.

COFFIN, TRISTRAM P. *The British Traditional Ballad in North America*. Philadelphia, 1950.

COLE, M. R. *Los Pastores, A Mexican Play of the Nativity*. Memoirs of the American Folklore Society, IX. Boston and New York, 1907.

COMBS, JOSIAH H. *Folk-Songs du Midi des États-Unis*. Paris, 1925.

————. *Folk-Songs from the Kentucky Highlands*. New York, 1939.

————. *The Kentucky Highlander*. Privately printed, 1913.

*————. "Some Kentucky Highland Stories," introduction and notes by HERBERT HALPERT, *Kentucky Folklore Record*, IV (1958), 45–61.

COX, JOHN HARRINGTON. *Folk-Songs of the South*. Cambridge, 1925.

————. *Traditional Ballads Mainly from West Virginia*. New York, 1939.

CREIGHTON, HELEN. *Bluenose Ghosts*. Toronto, 1957.

————. *Folklore of Lunenburg County, Nova Scotia*. Ottawa, 1950.

CRONISE, FLORENCE, and WARD, HENRY W. *Cunnie Rabbit, Mr. Spider and the Other Beef: West African Folk Tales*. London, 1903.

DAVENSON, HENRI. *Le Livre des Chansons*. Boudry, 1946.

*DAVIDSON, LEVETTE J. "Mormon Songs," *Journal of American Folklore*, LVIII (1945), 273–300.

DOBIE, J. FRANK. "Stories in Texas Place Names," *Straight Texas*, ed. J. F. DOBIE and MODY C. BOATRIGHT, Publications of the Texas Folklore Society, XIII, pp. 1–78. Austin, 1937.

DODSON, RUTH. "Don Pedrito Jaramillo: The Curandero of Los Olmos," *The Healer of Los Olmos and Other Mexican Lore*, ed. WILSON M. HUDSON,

Publications of the Texas Folklore Society, XXIV, pp. 9–70. Austin and Dallas, 1951.

DORSON, RICHARD M. *American Folklore.* Chicago, 1959.

————. "Aunt Jane Goudreau, *Roup-Garou* Storyteller," *Western Folklore,* VI (1957), 13–27.

————. *Bloodstoppers and Bearwalkers.* Cambridge, Mass., 1952.

————. "Collecting Folklore in Jonesport, Maine," *Proceedings of the American Philosophical Society,* CI (1957), 270–89.

————. "Collecting in County Kerry," *Journal of American Folklore,* LXVI (1953), 19–42.

————. "Dialect Stories of the Upper Peninsula," *Journal of American Folklore,* LXI (1948), 113–50.

————. "Folklore at a Milwaukee Wedding," *Hoosier Folklore,* VI (1947), 1–13.

————. *Folk Legends of Japan.* Tokyo and Rutland, Vt., 1962.

————. "The Folktale Repertoires of Two Maine Lobstermen," *Internationaler Kongress der Volkserzählungsforscher in Kiel und Kopenhagen,* ed. KURT RANKE, pp. 74–83. Berlin, 1961.

————. "Jewish-American Dialect Stories on Tape," *Studies in Biblical and Jewish Folklore,* ed. R. PATAI, F. L. UTLEY, and D. NOY, pp. 111–74. Indiana University Folklore Series, XIII. Bloomington, Ind., 1960.

————. *Jonathan Draws the Long Bow.* Cambridge, Mass., 1946.

————. "The Legend of Yoho Cove," *Western Folklore,* XVIII (October, 1959), 329–31.

————. "Mishaps of a Maine Lobsterman," *Northeast Folklore,* I (Spring, 1958), 1–7.

————. *Negro Folktales in Michigan.* Cambridge, Mass., 1956.

————. "Negro Tales from Bolivar County, Mississippi," *Southern Folklore Quarterly,* XIX (1955), 104–16.

————. *Negro Tales from Pine Bluff, Arkansas and Calvin, Michigan.* Indiana University Folklore Series, No. 12. Bloomington, Ind., 1958.

————. "Oral Styles of American Folk Narrators," *Style in Language,* ed. T. A. SEBEOK, pp. 27–51. Cambridge, Mass., 1960.

————. "Tales of a Greek-American Family on Tape," *Fabula,* I (1957), 114–43.

ECKSTORM, FANNIE HARDY, and SMYTH, MARY WINSLOW. *Minstrelsy of Maine.* Boston and New York, 1927.

ELWORTHY, FREDERICK T. *The Evil Eye: An Account of this Ancient and Widespread Superstition.* London, 1895.

ESPINOSA, AURELIO M. "New-Mexican Spanish Folk-Lore, IX, Riddles," *Journal of American Folklore,* XXVIII (1915), 319–52.

ESPINOSA, JOSÉ E. *Saints in the Valleys.* Albuquerque, 1960.

*FIFE, AUSTIN E. "A Ballad of the Mountain Meadows Massacre," *Western Folklore,* XII (1953), 229–41.

————. "Folk Belief and Mormon Cultural Autonomy," *Journal of American Folklore,* LVI (1948), 19–30.

BIBLIOGRAPHY

*————. "The Legend of the Three Nephites Among the Mormons," *Journal of American Folklore,* LIII (1940), 1–49.

*————. "Popular Legends of the Mormons," *California Folklore Quarterly,* I (1942), 105–25.

*FIFE, AUSTIN E., and FIFE, ALTA S. "Folk Songs of Mormon Inspiration," *Western Folklore,* VI (1947), 42–52.

————. *Saints of Sage and Saddle.* Bloomington, Ind., 1956.

*FOGEL, EDWIN MILLER. *Beliefs and Superstitions of the Pennsylvania Germans.* Philadelphia, 1915.

*————. *Proverbs of the Pennsylvania Germans.* Pennsylvania-German Society, 1929.

FORTIER, ALCÉE. *Louisiana Folk-Tales.* Memoirs of the American Folklore Society, II. Boston and New York, 1895.

*FOX, BEN. "Folk Medicine in Southern Illinois," *Illinois Folklore,* II, No. 1 (April, 1948), 3–7.

FUSON, HARVEY H. *Ballads of the Kentucky Highlands.* London, 1931.

GEROULD, GORDON H. *Saints' Legends.* Boston and New York, 1916.

GIFFORD, EDWARD S. *The Evil Eye: Studies in the Folklore of Vision.* New York, 1958.

GOMME, ALICE B. *The Traditional Games of England, Scotland, and Ireland.* 2 vols. London, 1894–98.

GORE, MRS. MOODY P., and SPEARE, MRS. GUY E. *New Hampshire Folk Tales.* New Hampshire Federation of Women's Clubs, 1932.

GOULD, JOHN. *Farmer Takes a Wife.* New York, 1945.

GOULD, ROBERT E. *Yankee Storekeeper.* New York and London, 1946.

GRAY, ROLAND. *Songs and Ballads of the Maine Lumberjacks.* Cambridge, Mass., 1924.

GRIMM, JAKOB LUDWIG KARL, and GRIMM, WILHELM. *The Grimms' German Folk Tales,* tr. F. P. MAGOUN, JR., and A. H. KRAPPE. Carbondale, Ill., 1960.

HAGGARD, HOWARD W. *Devils, Drugs and Doctors.* New York, 1929.

HALPERT, HERBERT. "The Cante Fable in New Jersey," *Journal of American Folklore,* LV (1942), 133–43.

*————. " 'Egypt'—A Wandering Place-Name Legend," *Midwest Folklore,* IV (1954), 165–68.

HARRIS, JESSE W. "Illinois Place-Name Lore," *Midwest Folklore,* IV (1954), 217–20.

————. "Some Southern Illinois Witch Lore," *Southern Folklore Quarterly,* X (1946), 183–90.

*————. "Substituting for the Off Ox," *Journal of American Folklore,* LX (1947), 298–99.

*HARRIS, JESSE W., and NEELY, JULIA. "Southern Illinois Phantoms and Bogies," *Midwest Folklore,* I (1951), 171–78.

HARRIS, JOEL CHANDLER. *Told by Uncle Remus.* New York, 1905.

HAZLITT, WILLIAM CAREW. *Shakespeare Jest-Books.* London, 1881.

HENRY, MELLINGER. *Folk-Songs from the Southern Highlands.* New York, 1938.

HOFFMAN, J. W. "Folk-Lore of the Pennsylvania Germans," *Journal of American Folklore*, I (1888), 125–35.

HOMER. *The Odyssey*, tr. E. V. RIEU. New York, 1945.

"How Egypt Got It's [sic] Name" (Anon.), *Egyptian Key*, II (March, 1947), 31–33.

HUNT, BEATRICE A. and WILSON, HARRY ROBERT. *Sing and Dance*. Chicago, 1945.

HYATT, HARRY M. *Folk-Lore from Adams County, Illinois*. New York: Memoirs of the Alma Egan Hyatt Foundation, 1935.

Idaho Lore. Federal Writers' Project, Caldwell, Idaho, 1939.

IVES, EDWARD D. *Larry Gorman: "The Man Who Made the Songs."* Indiana University Folklore Series, No. 20. Bloomington, Ind., 1964.

JACOBS, JOSEPH. *English Fairy Tales*. New York and London, 3rd. ed., 1908.

JACKSON, GEORGE PULLEN. *White Spirituals in the Southern Uplands*. Chapel Hill, N.C., 1933.

JANVIER, THOMAS A. *Legends of the City of Mexico*. New York, 1910.

JIMÉNEZ, BALDEMAR A. "Cuentos de Susto," *The Golden Log*, ed. M. C. BOATRIGHT *et al.*, Publications of the Texas Folklore Society, XXXI, pp. 156–64. Dallas, 1962.

JONES, LOUIS C. "The Evil Eye among European-Americans," *Western Folklore*, X (1951), 11–25.

KIRTLEY, BACIL F. " 'La Llorona' and Related Themes," *Western Folklore*, XIX (1960), 155–68.

KITTREDGE, GEORGE LYMAN. *Witchcraft in Old and New England*. Cambridge, Mass., 1929.

KORSON, GEORGE (ed.) *Pennsylvania Songs and Legends*. Philadelphia, 1949.

————. *Black Rock: Mining Folklore of the Pennsylvania Dutch*. Baltimore, 1960.

KRAPPE, ALEXANDER H. *The Science of Folk-Lore*. London, 1930.

KURATH, HANS. *Linguistic Atlas of New England*. 3 vols. Providence, 1939–43.

LAWS, GEORGE M. *American Balladry from British Broadsides*. Philadelphia, 1957.

————. *Native American Balladry*. Philadelphia, 1950.

LEA, AURERO LUCERO-WHITE. *Literary Folklore of the Hispanic Southwest*. San Antonio, Texas, 1953.

LEDDY, BETTY. "La Llorona in Southern Arizona," *Western Folklore*, VII (1948), 272–77.

LEE, FRED J. *Casey Jones, Epic of the American Railroad*. Kingsport, Tenn., 1939.

*LEE, HECTOR. *The Three Nephites: The Substance and Significance of the Legend in Folklore*. Albuquerque, 1949.

LOMAX, JOHN. *Adventures of a Ballad Hunter*. New York, 1947.

LOMAX, JOHN, and LOMAX, ALAN. *Cowboy Songs and Other Frontier Ballads*. New York, 1959.

LOOMIS, C. GRANT. *White Magic: An Introduction to the Folklore of Christian Legend*. Cambridge, Mass., 1948.

BIBLIOGRAPHY

MCINTOSH, DAVID S. "Blacksmith and Death," *Midwest Folklore*, I (1951), 51–54.

*————. "Southern Illinois Folk Songs," *Journal of the Illinois State Historical Society*, XXXI (1938), 297–322.

*————. *Southern Illinois Singing Games and Songs*. Carbondale, 1946.

*————. "You Haven't Packed the Saddle," *Illinois Folklore*, I, No. 1 (October, 1947), 17–19.

MACLELLAN, ANGUS. *Stories from South Uist*. Translated from the Gaelic by JOHN LORNE CAMPBELL. London, 1961.

MCLENDON, ALTHA L. "A Finding List of Play-Party Games," *Southern Folklore Quarterly*, VIII (1944), 201–34.

*MCNEIL, BROWNIE. "Corridos of the Mexican Border," *Mexican Border Ballads and Other Lore*, ed. MODY C. BOATRIGHT, Publications of the Texas Folklore Society, XXI, pp. 1–34. Austin, 1946.

Maine, A Guide 'Down East.' Federal Writers Project, Boston, 1937.

MANUEL, JUAN. *El Conde Lucaner*. Madrid and Buenos Aires, 1929.

MILLIEN, ACHILLE. *Chants et Chansons, Receuillis et Classés*. 3 vols. Paris, 1906–10.

Mississippi, A Guide to the Magnolia State. Federal Writers' Project, New York, 1938.

*NEELY, CHARLES. *Tales and Songs of Southern Illinois*. Menasha, Wis., 1938.

NEWELL, W. W. "Reports of Voodoo Worship in Hayti and Louisiana," *Journal of American Folklore*, II (1889), 41–47.

New Jersey, A Guide to its Present and Past. Federal Writers' Project, New York, 1939.

NILES, JOHN JACOBS. *Songs of the Hill-Folk*. New York, 1934.

OPIE, IONA, and OPIE, PETER. *The Lore and Language of School Children*. Oxford, 1959.

————. *The Oxford Dictionary of Nursery Rhymes*. Oxford, 1951.

*OSTER, HARRY. "Acculturation in Cajun Folk Music," *McNeese Review*, X (1958), 12–22.

Ó SÚILLEABHÁIN, SEÁN (SEAN O'SULLIVAN). *A Handbook of Irish Folklore*. Dublin, 1942.

OWEN, MARY A. *Voodoo Tales*. New York, 1893.

PALACIO, BICENTE RIVA, and PEZA, JUAN DE DIOS. *Tradiciones y Leyendos Mexicanos*. Mexico, n.d.

*PAREDES, AMÉRICO. *"With His Pistol in His Hand": A Border Ballad and Its Hero*. Austin, Texas, 1958.

*PÉREZ, SOLEDAD. "Mexican Folklore from Austin, Texas," *The Healer of Los Olmos and Other Mexican Lore*, ed. W. M. HUDSON, Publications of the Texas Folklore Society, XXIV, pp. 71–127. Dallas and Austin, 1951.

PERROW, E. C. "Songs and Rhymes from the South," *Journal of American Folklore*, XXV (1912), 137–55.

PUCKETT, NEWBELL N. *Folk Beliefs of the Southern Negro*. Chapel Hill, 1926.

QUIRT, ARTHUR. *Tales of the Woods and Mines*. n.p., n.d.

*RAEL, JUAN B. *Cuentos Españoles de Colorado y de Nuevo Méjico.* 2 vols. Stanford, 1957.

RAMSEY, CAROLYN. *Cajuns on the Bayous.* New York, 1957.

RANDOLPH, VANCE. *The Devil's Pretty Daughter.* New York, 1955.

————. *Ozark Folksongs.* 4 vols. Columbia, Mo., 1946–50.

————. *Ozark Superstitions.* New York, 1947.

————. *Sticks in the Knapsack.* New York, 1958.

————. *The Talking Turtle.* New York, 1957.

————. *We Always Lie to Strangers: Tall Tales from the Ozarks.* New York, 1951.

RANDOLPH, VANCE, and WILSON, GEORGE P. *Down in the Holler: A Gallery of Ozark Folk Speech.* Norman, Oklahoma, 1953.

RICHMOND, W. EDSON, and TILLSON, WILLIAM (eds.). *Leah Jackson Wolford's The Play-Party in Indiana.* Indianapolis, 1959.

RITCHIE, JEAN. *Singing Family of the Cumberlands.* New York, 1955.

*ROBB, JOHN D. *Hispanic Folk Songs of New Mexico.* Albuquerque, New Mexico, 1954.

*ROBERTS, LEONARD W. "The Cante Fable in Eastern Kentucky," *Midwest Folklore,* VI (1956), 69–88.

*————. "Floyd County Folklore," *Kentucky Folklore Record,* II (1956), 33–66.

————. *Up Cutshin and Down Greasy: Folkways of a Kentucky Mountain Family.* Lexington, Ky., 1959.

————. *South from Hell-fer-Sartin: Kentucky Mountain Folktales.* Lexington, Ky., 1955.

ROBERTS, WARREN E. "Children's Games and Game Rhymes," *Hoosier Folklore,* VIII (1949), 7–34.

————. *The Tale of the Kind and the Unkind Girls.* Berlin, 1958.

SAUCIER, CORINNE. *Folk Tales from French Louisiana.* New York, 1962.

————. *Traditions de la Paroisse des Avoyelles en Louisiane,* Memoirs of the American Folklore Society, XLVII. Philadelphia, 1956.

SCARBOROUGH, DOROTHY. *A Songcatcher in Southern Mountains.* New York, 1937.

SHARP, CECIL. *English Folk Songs from the Southern Appalachians.* Edited by MAUD KARPELES. 2 vols. London, 1932.

SIMMONS, MERLE E. *The Mexican Corrido as a Source for Interpretive Study of Modern Mexico (1870–1950).* Bloomington, Ind., 1957.

SMITH, ELMER L. *The Amish Today.* Pennsylvania German Folklore Society Publications, XXIV. Allentown, Pa., 1960.

*SMITH, GRACE PARTRIDGE. "Egyptian 'Lies,'" *Midwest Folklore,* I (1951), 93–97.

*————. "Folklore from 'Egypt'," *Journal of American Folklore,* LIV (1941), 48–59.

*————. "Folklore from 'Egypt'," *Hoosier Folklore,* V (1946), 45–70.

*————. "Four Irish Ballads from 'Egypt'," *Hoosier Folklore,* V (1946), 115–19.

————. "They Call It Egypt," *Names,* II (March, 1954), 51–54.

BIBLIOGRAPHY

SMITH, THOMAS L., and HITT, HOMER L. *The People of Louisiana.* Baton Rouge, 1952.

STEGNER, WALLACE. *Mormon Country.* New York, 1942.

STEVENSON, BURTON E. *The Home Book of Proverbs, Maxims and Familiar Phrases.* New York, 1948.

*STOUDT, JOHN BAER. *The Folklore of the Pennsylvania-German.* Publications of the Pennsylvania-German Society, XXIII. Norristown, Pa., 1910.

STOUDT, JOHN JOSEPH. "Pennsylvania German Folklore: An Interpretation," *Pennsylvania German Folklore Society Publications,* XVI (1951), 157–70.

*STURGILL, VIRGIL L. "The Murder of Lottie Yates," *Kentucky Folklore Record,* V (1959), 61–64.

TALLEY, THOMAS W. *Negro Folk Rhymes.* New York, 1922.

TAYLOR, ARCHER. *English Riddles from Oral Tradition.* Berkeley and Los Angeles, 1951.

———. "The Riddle," *California Folklore Quarterly,* II (1943), 129–47.

TAYLOR, ARCHER, and WHITING, B. J. *A Dictionary of American Proverbs and Proverbial Phrases, 1820–1880.* Cambridge, Mass., 1958.

THÉRIOT, MARIE, and LAHAY, MARIE. "The Legend of Foolish John," *Southern Folklore Quarterly,* VII (1943), 153–56.

THOMAS, JEAN. *Ballad Makin' in the Mountains of Kentucky.* New York, 1939.

THOMAS, LOWELL. *Tall Stories.* New York and London, 1931.

THOMPSON, STITH. *The Folktale.* New York, 1946.

TIDDY, REGINALD J. E. *The Mummers' Play.* Oxford, 1923.

UTLEY, FRANCIS L. "The Bible of the Folk," *California Folklore Quarterly,* IV (1945), 343–50.

VOGT, EVON Z., and HYMAN, RAY. *Water Witching U.S.A.* Chicago, 1959.

WHEELER, MARY. *Kentucky Mountain Folk-Songs.* Boston, 1937.

WHITFIELD, IRÈNE THÉRÈSE. *Louisiana French Folk Songs.* Baton Rouge, La., 1939.

WILLIAMS, CRATIS D. "Lottie Yates," *Kentucky Folklore Record,* V (1959), 65–69.

YATES, NORRIS W. *William T. Porter and the* Spirit of the Times. Baton Rouge, 1957.

YODER, DON. "The Folklife Studies Movement," *Pennsylvania Folklife,* XIII (1963), 43–56.

———. *Pennsylvania Spirituals.* Lancaster, Pa., 1961.

———. "Spirituals from the Pennsylvania Dutch Country," *Pennsylvania Dutchman,* VIII (1956–57), 22–33.

*———. "Witch Tales from Adams County," *Pennsylvania Folklife,* XII (1962), 29–37.

*ZUNSER, HELEN. "A New Mexican Village," *Journal of American Folklore,* XLVIII (1935), 125–78.

INDEX OF SUBJECTS, PLACES,
PERSONS, AND TITLES

INDEX OF TALE TYPES

(Type numbers are from Antti Aarne and Stith Thompson, *The Types of the Folktale* [Helsinki, 1961].)

INDEX OF MOTIFS

(Motif numbers are from Stith Thompson, *Motif-Index of Folk-Literature*
[6 vols.; Copenhagen and Bloomington, Ind., 1955–58].)

INDEX OF MOTIFS

INDEX OF INFORMANTS

INDEX OF INFORMANTS

INDEX OF COLLECTORS